Theorizing International Trade

Somesh K. Mathur • Rahul Arora •
Sarbjit Singh
Editors

Theorizing International Trade

An Indian Perspective

palgrave
macmillan

Editors
Somesh K. Mathur
Indian Institute of Technology Kanpur
Kanpur, India

Rahul Arora
Consumer Unity & Trust Society
(CUTS) International
Jaipur, India

Sarbjit Singh
Consumer Unity & Trust Society
(CUTS) International
Jaipur, India

ISBN 978-981-10-1758-2 ISBN 978-981-10-1759-9 (eBook)
https://doi.org/10.1007/978-981-10-1759-9

Library of Congress Control Number: 2017957537

Printed on acid-free paper

This Palgrave Macmillan imprint is published by Springer Nature
The registered company is Springer Nature Singapore Pte Ltd.
The registered company address is: 152 Beach Road, #21-01/04 Gateway East, Singapore 189721, Singapore

Contents

1 **Introduction** 1
Somesh K. Mathur, Rahul Arora, and Sarbjit Singh

Part I Developments in Trade Theory, Gravity Modeling and Its Applications 7

2 **Developments in International Trade Theory and Gravity Modelling** 9
Somesh K. Mathur, Rahul Arora, Sarbjit Singh, and Amrita Roy

3 **Revisiting Strategic Trade Theory** 37
Indrani Roy Chowdhury

4 **A Model of International Entry and Exit with Endogenous Sunk Costs in Vertical Markets** 69
Partha Gangopadhyay and Robert F. Owen

5 **Trade Growth Accounting in Goods and Services: An Empirical Exercise** 101
Somesh K. Mathur, Sarbjit Singh, Gaurav Doshi, and Abhishek Srivastava

6 **Calculation of Ad Valorem Equivalents of Non-Tariff Barriers: A Case Study of 16 RCEP Countries** 115
Sarbjit Singh and Rahul Arora

7 **Bilateral Trade Costs and Growth of Trade in Services: A Comparative Study of India and China** 141
Amrita Roy and Somesh K. Mathur

Part II Some Applications of General Equilibrium Analysis 163

8 **Theoretical Exposition of Some Ex Ante Approaches to Assess the Proposed Trade Policy** 165
Rahul Arora, Sarbjit Singh, and Somesh K. Mathur

9 **Assessment of Impact of Food-Safety Measures on Exports: A Gravity and CGE Analysis Focusing on India** 201
Pratima Pandey and Badri Narayanan

10 **Gains from the India–GCC Free Trade Agreement: A General Equilibrium Analysis** 221
Nitin Arora and Pouria Mohajeri

11 **Lebanon's Accession to the WTO: An *Ex Ante* Macroeconomic Impact Assessment** 243
Ghada Tabbah

12 **Goods Trade Liberalization Under Canada-India FTA and Its Impact: Partial and General Equilibrium Analysis** 269
Somesh K. Mathur, Rahul Arora, and Mayank Tripathi

Part III Other Related Topics 305

13 **Estimating the Impact of Technical Barriers to Trade: The Case of Perfumes and Toilet Waters in Ecuador** 307
Gonzalo E. Sánchez and Patricia A. Vargas

14 **Does Trade Openness Increase Wage Elasticity of Labour Demand in Indian Manufacturing Industries?** 325
Simontini Das, Ajitava Raychaudhuri, and Saikat Sinha Roy

15 **An Analysis of Dynamic Spillover in India's Forex Derivatives Markets** 351
Wasim Ahmad, Shirin Rais, and Ritesh Kumar Mishra

16 **Future Avenues in Trade Policy Research** 385
Somesh K. Mathur, Rahul Arora, and Sarbjit Singh

References 389

Index 409

Editors and Contributors

Notes on Editors

Rahul Arora is a policy analyst at the Centre for International Trade, Economics & Environment (CITEE), CUTS International, Jaipur, India. He received a Ph.D. in International Trade from the Department of Economic Sciences, IIT Kanpur, India. His research interests lie in analyzing international trade, with a particular focus on CGE modelling of free trade agreements, regional economic integration, trade facilitation and trade policy. He has worked with ARTNeT, UNESCAP, to study the trade facilitation measures in RCEP countries. He has published various research papers and chapters in journals and books of national and international repute. He can be communicated at: rahulphdeco@gmail.com.

Somesh K. Mathur is Professor of Economics at the Department of Economic Sciences at IIT Kanpur, India. He has taught at Department of Economics, Jamia Millia Islamia (Central University), India prior to joining the IIT Kanpur in 2008. He has worked as a fellow at the RIS, Ministry of External Affairs, Government of India for two years and P3 Economic affairs officer at the UNESCAP office in Bangkok. His main area of interest is the empirical analysis of international trade and applied econometrics. Prof. Mathur has written five books, including the present one from Palgrave Macmillan on theorizing international trade, on subjects varying from growth convergence, Trade and Climate Change, Applied Economics and Trade Issues. He has published in journals like Review of International

Economics, World Economy, Geneva Papers on Risk and Insurance, Economic and Political Weekly, Journal of Quantitative Economics, Global Economy Journal, Public Enterprise Journal, Journal of Economic Integration, Journal of Centrum Cathedra, Journal of Industrial Statistics, Korea and the World Economy, Journal of World Intellectual Property Rights, Foreign Trade Review, Trade and Development Review, World Economy, among others. He can be contacted at: skmathur@iitk.ac.in.

Sarbjit Singh is a policy analyst at the Centre for International Trade, Economics & Environment (CITEE), CUTS International, Jaipur, India. He obtained his Ph.D. in International Trade from the Department of Economic Sciences, IIT Kanpur, India. His broader area of research lies in the Quantitative Analysis of International Trade. In particular, he works on Gravity Modelling, Trade Facilitation, Regional Economic Integration and Trade Policy. He has completed a project with ARTNeT, UNESCAP, on trade facilitation measures in RCEP countries. He has published various research papers and chapters in journals and books of national and international repute. He can be contacted at: sarbjitphd@gmail.com.

Notes on Contributors

Nitin Arora is Assistant Professor in Economics, Department of Economics, Panjab University, Chandigarh, India. His area of interest is applied econometrics and economic modeling. He has supervised two PhD theses, and seven research scholars are working with him on the subsidiary area of monetary policy transmission mechanism and international trade. He has also supervised five MPhil theses in diverse areas of frontier modeling and published extensively in journals of national and international repute. He has also published one book entitled *Capacity Utilization, Technical Efficiency and TFP Growth: Theory and Applications to Indian Sugar Industry.*

Wasim Ahmad is Assistant Professor at the Department of Humanities and Social Sciences (Economics Discipline), Indian Institute of Technology, Kanpur. His research areas are macroeconomics, macroeconomics, international finance, commodity derivatives and energy economics. His detailed profile is available at: https://sites.google.com/site/wasimatiitk/home.

Indrani Roy Chowdhury is currently an associate professor at the Centre for the Study of Regional Development (CSRD), School of Social Science (SSS), Jawaharlal Nehru University (JNU). She has a MPhil (in Economics) from Jadavpur University and PhD (in Economics) from the Centre for International Trade and Development (CITD), Jawaharlal Nehru University (JNU). Her areas of interest are industrial organization, applied game theory and environmental economics. Her work has been published in some reputed international journals like *International Game Theory Review*, *Bulletin of Economic Research*, *International Journal of Industrial Organization*, *Economics Bulletin*, and *Keio Economic Studies.*

Simontini Das is an assistant professor in Economics at Rabindra Bharati University, Kolkata. She teaches Applied Econometrics, Development Economics, Resource Economics and Mathematical Economics. She completed her master's degree in Economics and PhD from Jadavpur University, Kolkata. Her areas of research interest are econometrics, empirical international trade and development economics. She has published in various international journals.

Gaurav Doshi is pursuing a Ph.D. in Applied Economics from the University of Wisconsin – Madison. He can be contacted at: gdoshi2@wisc.edu.

Partha Gangopadhyay is currently employed as an associate professor of Economics (equivalent to North American full professorship) at Western Sydney University. He is an analytical economist with expertise in the use of economic, econometric, econophysics and game-theoretic tools to understand, explain and predict the dynamics of individual and group behaviour. He is the editor-in-chief of *American Journal of Applied Sciences* – a top-quartile journal currently ranked 27th in the SJR rankings of multidisciplinary journals like *Nature and Science.* He has worked for six different universities around the world, from a leading research-focused think tank in India to one of the largest universities of Australia, and also at two top-tier universities in Australia. During 2001–2002, he held a chair professorship in economics of social research in Germany in a university that prides itself to have instituted the first chair in economics in human history. Since completing doctoral study in 1994, he has authored more than 90 refereed publications including six research books. He acted as a consultant for Asian Development Bank Institute and a senior expert for

Institute of Economics for Peace. As a senior editor of several journals, he leads global research in many sub-fields of economics.

Ritesh Kumar Mishra is an assistant professor of Economics at G.G.S. Indraprastha University. He holds a PhD from the University of Delhi. His research focuses on macroeconomics, international economics, and financial economics.

Pouria Mohajeri is an Indian Council for Cultural Relations (ICCR) fellow from Iran. He also got UGC fellowship for foreign students in India. He has recently submitted his PhD thesis with Dr. Nitin Arora on the topic "Gains from Free Trade between India and Persian Gulf Countries."

Badri Narayanan is an economist, with three affiliations currently: Research Economist at the Center for Global Trade Analysis at Purdue University in West Lafayette, Indiana; Visiting Scientist, School of Environmental and Forestry Sciences, University of Washington-Seattle; and Consultant, Global Economics Research, McKinsey Global Institute Knowledge Center. His broad research interests lie in the area of trade policy modeling in relation to industrial, labor, energy/environmental and health issues, both from economic and inter-disciplinary perspectives, employing a variety of quantitative models. He has published four books and dozens of research papers in reputed journals, books and other outlets. He has been a consultant with several organizations including the World Bank, Food and Agricultural Organization, World Health Organization, European Commission, International Trade Center, Woodrow Wilson International Center for Scholars, International Agricultural Trade Research Consortium, the Commonwealth of Nations, Price Water House Coopers, Bournemouth University, Indian Institute of Foreign Trade and the governments of India, the United States, Finland, Turkey and others. He is a board member of Young Professionals Chronic Diseases Network and the network for Governments' Integration through FTAs (GIFTA) project. He is also an advisor for the Asia-Pacific Research and Training Network – United Nations Economic and Social Commission for Asia and the Pacific (ARTNeT–UNESCAP).

Robert F. Owen held positions at Cornell University and Cambridge University. Since 1991, he has been Professor of Economics at the

University of Nantes. He earned his BA (with honors) in 1974 from Swarthmore College and his PhD from Princeton University in 1981, where his principal field of specialization was international economics and finance. His areas of research and teaching interest are European economic integration, industrial economics, macroeconomics, public finance, and the economics of technological innovations and networks. His major publications are in *American Economic Review*, *Journal of International Economics*, and *Review of International Economics*. He is on the editorial board of Review of International Economics.

Pratima Pandey is an independent economist. She has an MPhil in Development Studies from Indira Gandhi Institute of Development Research, Mumbai, India. She completed her master's degree in Agricultural Economics from Govind Ballabh Pant University of Agriculture & Technology, Pantnagar, India. Having a keen interest in environment conservation, she undertook an online certificate course in Solid Waste Management from UNESCO-IHE, Netherlands. Her professional experience includes a – two-year stint in the Agri-Business Intelligence Unit of ICICI Bank, Mumbai. Presently, she is based in Sharjah, UAE.

Shirin Rais has a PhD in Economics from Aligarh Muslim University, Aligarh. She has worked as ICSSR post-doctoral fellow at the Department of Economics, Aligarh Muslim University. Her research areas are macroeconomics, international trade and health economics with research papers published in several refereed journals.

Ajitava Raychaudhuri has a PhD from American University (USA). He is Professor and former Head and Coordinator of Centre for Advanced Studies, Department of Economics, Jadavpur University, Kolkata, India. He was a senior Fulbright Scholar at Economic Growth Center, Yale University and Reid Hall Scholar in Residence at Columbia University, Paris Campus. He had undertaken several important projects from UNESCAP, Asian Development Bank (ADB), World Bank, Global Development Network (GDN), United Nations Development Programme (UNDP), Partnership for Economic Policy (PEP), South Asia Network of Economic Research Institutes (SANEI), Planning Commission, and so on. He has also written numerous papers in international and national journals and edited books. Among his notable books are *India's Exports: An Analytical Study* (with Sugata Marjit) published by Oxford University Press and *International Trade in Services in India: Implications for Growth and Inequality in a Globalising World* (with Prabir De) also from Oxford University Press. He has also published two

List of Figures

Fig. 2.1	Diagnostic of trade costs (Source: Moise and Bris (2013))	26
Fig. 3.1	Free entry in the country 1 alone	55
Fig. 3.2	Free entry in the country 2 alone	58
Fig. 3.3	Free entry in both countries	60
Fig. 5.1	Tariff equivalents for India's trade with the entire world (Source: Authors' calculations)	109
Fig. 5.2	Accounting for services trade growth in India (Source: Authors' calculations)	110
Fig. 7.1	Trends in services exports and imports to the world (China and India) (Source: Francois and Pindyuk (2013))	142
Fig. 7.2	The decline in trade costs of India and China with respect to their major trading partners (1995–2010) (Source: Authors' calculations)	151
Fig. 7.3	Average bilateral trade costs (percent ad valorem equivalent) of India and China with their common trading partners (1995–2010) (Source: Authors' calculations)	151
Fig. 7.4	Average bilateral trade costs in services (percent ad valorem equivalent) of India and China with their common trading partners, 1999 and 2009 (Source: Authors' calculations)	152
Fig. 8.1	Pictorial representation of accounting relationships in GTAP model (Source: Fig. 6 in Brockmeier 2001)	186
Fig. 8.2	Representation of regional household behavior (Source: Authors' elaborations)	189
Fig. 8.3	Representation of production structure in GTAP model (Source: Authors' elaborations)	191

List of Tables

Table 4.1	The Cournot–Nash equilibrium of the downstream market (without entry)	82
Table 5.1	Percentage change in τ_{ij} for the APEC nations	103
Table 5.2	Decomposition of bilateral trade growth of APEC countries with India	105
Table 5.3	Novy's tariff equivalents for India's total trade in services	111
Table 5.4	Trade growth accounting for India's total trade in services	112
Table 6.1	Extent of trade barriers in RCEP countries in 2015	117
Table 6.2	Time and cost associated with each stage to import and export	118
Table 6.3	Types of documents in trade across borders	120
Table 6.4	Estimated results of the augmented gravity equation	125
Table 6.5	Sectorwide estimated results of the augmented gravity equation	127
Table 6.6	Sectorwide intra-RCEP trade share and AVEs of time to import and export for RCEP countries (in percent)	130
Table 6.7	Countrywide AVEs of time to import and time to export for RCEP members	132
Table 6.8	Sectorwide AVEs of time to import and time to export for RCEP members (in %)	133
Table 7.1	Regulatory restrictions in different services, India and China	146
Table 7.2	Average trade costs for India (percent ad valorem equivalent, 1995–2009)	152
Table 7.3	Average trade costs for China (percent ad valorem equivalent, 1995–2009)	153
Table 7.4	Bilateral trade growth accounting (India)	154
Table 7.5	Bilateral trade growth accounting (China)	155

Table 7.6	Trade costs of services, India (percent ad valorem equivalent)	158
Table 7.7	Trade costs of services, China (percent ad valorem equivalent)	159
Table 9.1	Regression results for a cross section 2004 at the world level	208
Table 9.2	Regression results for a cross-section of 2004 at the Indian level	210
Table 9.3	Regression results for a cross section of 1995 at the world level	211
Table 9.4	Regression results for a cross section of 2003 at the world level	212
Table 9.5	Regression results for panel analysis at the Indian level	214
Table 10.1	List of free trade partners of India and the GCC	223
Table 10.2	India's trade with GCC	225
Table 10.3	India's balance of trade with the GCC US$ Million	226
Table 10.4	Indicators of level of protection	227
Table 10.5	RCA index value for the year 2013	228
Table 10.6	Trade intensity index for India and the GCC for the other's market access in the year 2013	229
Table 10.7	Reduction in tariff values by India and the GCC	231
Table 10.8	Region's aggregations	232
Table 10.9	Sector description of the GTAP	234
Table 10.10	Comparison of India FTA with PGC and GCC	238
Table 10.11	Changes in the value of imports of India and the GCC after the FTA is in effect	239
Table 10.12	Changes in the value of imports of India and the GCC after an FTA is in effect	240
Table 11.1	Regional average customs in %	254
Table 11.2	Cumulative price variation (deviation from baseline scenario, in %)	255
Table 11.3	Scenario 1: Annual growth rates in % (in volume)	257
Table 11.4	Annual change in exchange rate in % (a positive sign of the exchange rate variation indicates depreciation)	258
Table 11.5	Scenario 2: Annual growth rates in % (in volume)	259
Table 11.6	Scenario 3: Annual growth rates in % (in volume)	260
Table 11.7	Scenario 4: Annual growth rates in % (in volume)	261
Table 11.8	Average rate of growth in each sector and its deviation from the baseline scenario (in %)	264
Table 12.1	Bilateral product trade Canada–India	272
Table 12.2	RCA for various aggregated product groups for India and Canada in 2014	274
Table 12.3	Trade Intensity Index (TII) for various aggregated product codes in 2014	275
Table 12.4	Impact of full reciprocal trade liberalization of India and Canada under the proposed free trade agreement using SMART	277

Table 12.5	Trade diversion for selected partners under different complete reciprocal liberalization scenarios	278
Table 12.6	Regional aggregation	279
Table 12.7	GTAP product classification	280
Table 12.8	Impact on welfare, changes in trade balance and changes in value of GDP	282
Table 12.9	Welfare decomposition (Million USD) when all products from Canada enters India	282
Table 12.10	Impact on welfare, trade balance and changes in value of GDP	283
Table 12.11	Welfare decomposition of total welfare (Million USD) in different regions when all products from India enters Canada	284
Table 12.12	Changes in trade balance (DTBAL) product wise (Million USD) under all products coming into Canada from India	285
Table 12.13	Changes in trade balance (DTBAL) product wise (Million USD) under all products coming into India from Canada	285
Table 12.14	Sectoral changes in India when all Canadian products (GTAP classification) enters India	286
Table 12.15	Sectoral changes in Canada when all Indian products enters Canada	287
Table 12.16	Welfare effect (Million USD) when Indian textiles and apparels enters Canada	288
Table 12.17	Welfare effect (Million USD) when Canadian heavy manufacturing enters India	288
Table 12.18	40 India's specialized products (with their HS product codes) in 2013 at 2 digit level of disaggregation	292
Table 12.19	29 Canada's specialized products (with their HS product codes) in 2014 at 2 digit level of disaggregation	293
Table 12.20	Tariff rates of India on Canada's exports reported in WITS	294
Table 12.21	Tariff rates of Canada on India's exports reported in WITS	299
Table 13.1	Products with the biggest import reductions after Resolution 116	311
Table 13.2	Weights for the construction of the synthetic control	316
Table 13.3	Synthetic control estimates	317
Table 14.1	Impact of trade openness index on the wage elasticity of labour demand of Indian manufacturing industries	340
Table 14.2	Effect of trade openness Index on wage elasticity of labour demand for production and non-production workers: *Capital constrained and unconstrained situations*	342

Table 14.3	Classification concordance between HS-1998, NIC 1987, NIC 1998, NIC 2004 and NIC2008	344
Table 15.1	Descriptive statistics	364
Table 15.2	Returns and volatility spillover results	365
Table 15.3	DCC estimation results	378

CHAPTER 1

Introduction

Somesh K. Mathur, Rahul Arora, and Sarbjit Singh

Proponents of free trade always prefer free trade over no trade due to the gains associated with the former, and use trade theories and trade trends to explain why two countries should engage in trade. Trade theories emphasize that gains from trade depend on both the pattern of trade and the type of trading countries (developed or developing). Traditional trade theories explain the sources of gains at the country level, but modern trade theories provide the explanation of these sources in a very advanced way by assuming real-world situations based on imperfections, firm level analysis, and market conditions.

Empirical analysis is the centerpoint of the emergence of modern-day trade theories which are based on real-world phenomena such as imperfect competition in a product market, the presence of economies of scale in production, and varying consumer preferences, among others. Advances in international trade theory and policy are emerging at a rapid pace, and the main reasons are the advancement of the empirical research methods and availability of country-wide detailed data on disaggregated sectors.

The empirical research tools used in quantitative research in international trade can be divided into two main categories: deterministic and stochastic.

S.K. Mathur (✉)
Indian Institute of Technology-Kanpur, Kanpur, India

R. Arora • S. Singh
Consumer Unity & Trust Society (CUTS) International, Jaipur, India

S.K. Mathur et al. (eds.), *Theorizing International Trade*,
https://doi.org/10.1007/978-981-10-1759-9_1

Among deterministic tools, two main methodologies exist, namely, partial and general equilibrium analysis. These methodologies also fall under the category of ex ante analysis as they deal with predicting trade flows in the scenario of variable changes in trade policy. With the help of general equilibrium analyses (including GTAP and dynamic GTAP models, among others), one can also consider the impact of changes in trade policy on economywide variables.

On the other hand, different econometric procedures are available under the stochastic category. Here, the estimation of gravity models is very important in explaining and accounting for trade flows among countries. The advanced estimation of any regression model (e.g., gravity models) using econometric tools falls under the category of ex post analysis, where in one studies the impact of past events on bilateral trade flows or any other dependent variable of interest. Hence, knowledge of these research tools have become necessary for researchers working in the field of quantitative analysis of international trade.

This book presents an empirical foundation of international trade theory and policy and also of international monetary theory and policy, keeping in mind new developments in both trade and international monetary theories. Broadly, this book discusses developments in trade theories including "new" new trade models accounting for firm-level trade flows; trade growth accounting using inverse gravity models (including distortions in gravity models); the impact of trade liberalization under the aegis of regional and multilateral liberalization efforts of economies using partial and general equilibrium analysis; methodologies of constructing ad valorem equivalents of nontariff barriers; determination of countries' trade and exchange rate flows; and volatility spillover effects of financial and exchange rate markets among others.

The focus of this book is to test various trade theory and international finance hypotheses and other changes in trade and international monetary policy using frontier methodologies in econometrics and simulations using partial and general equilibrium analysis. The main objective behind writing this book is to develop expertise among researchers, docents, policymakers and academicians alike, so that they can engage themselves in analyzing the impact of various trade policy instruments, and research international finance issues empirically, as per their own country's/research requirements. The discussion is focused on theoretical and empirical work related to the following issues.

- developments in trade theory including NewNew trade theories;
- advances in gravity model;
- trade growth accounting using inverse gravity model;
- calculation of tariff equivalent of non-tariff barriers;
- measurement of trade costs between the trading Partners;
- methods to analyze country's trade and tariff profile;
- partial equilibrium effects of tariff liberalization through SMART and gravity modelling;
- the impact of food safety measures on exports using gravity modelling and CGE analysis, specifically focusing on India;
- the economywide impact of tariff liberalization between trading partners using GTAP and dynamic GTAP models, and estimating the relative benefits of countries aligning with regional groups;
- trade openness and wage inequality;
- the impact of technical barriers to trade; and
- dynamic spillover effects in financial markets.

While discussing the above issues, many other research problems will also be discussed providing future avenues of research in this area.

1.1 Overview of the Book

To present the above issues in a structured pattern, the discussion is divided into three main parts which consists of 16 chapters in total. Chapter 1 provides a brief introductory overview of the contents included in each chapter. It also highlights the role of empirical methods in testing the existing theories of international trade and finance while keeping in mind new developments in trade theory.

Part 1 of the book contains six chapters that are focused mainly on advancements in trade theories and trade growth accounting using the gravity model. Part 2 also contains five chapters with the prime motive of showing the usage and procedures of both the partial and general equilibrium approaches. Part 3 contains four chapters, three of which deal with the applied parts of the topics of international trade theory and international monetary theory. The last chapter concludes the discussion and provides future avenues for trade policy research.

CHAPTER 2

Developments in International Trade Theory and Gravity Modelling

Somesh K. Mathur, Rahul Arora, Sarbjit Singh, and Amrita Roy

2.1 Traditional Trade Theories

Traditional trade theories—for example, Ricardo (1817) and Heckscher-Ohlin—have explained the pattern of trade in terms of comparative advantage, which means the low relative cost of a good in comparison to other countries in autarky. In these theories, gains from trade arise because of differences among countries. In the Ricardian theory of comparative advantage, these differences among countries have been due to differences in the technologies used in production processes, and these differences have served as a push factor toward trade. Ricardo assumed only one factor of production in terms of labor, so differences in technology represent differences in the usage of labor hours. A country that uses a fewer number of labor hours to produce a certain commodity—in relation to another country—will have a comparative advantage in production of that particular commodity. If the product with comparative advantage is then exported to another country, then the exporting country will obtain gains from trade through the specialization in production.

S.K. Mathur (✉) • A. Roy
Indian Institute of Technology Kanpur, Kanpur, India

R. Arora • S. Singh
Consumer Unity & Trust Society (CUTS) International, Jaipur, India

S.K. Mathur et al. (eds.), *Theorizing International Trade*,
https://doi.org/10.1007/978-981-10-1759-9_2

With the advent of the Heckscher–Ohlin (HO) model, the explanation of trade specialization has shifted away from technological differences to differences in endowments. One country, endowed with a particular type of factor of production, should exploit that factor more and reap gains associated with trade in that commodity which uses more of the available abundant factor. Although, the main focus has remained on the comparative advantage, the source of comparative advantage has been shifted to the difference in factor endowments.

On the basis of standard assumptions of the HO model—two goods, two countries, two factors of production, constancy of tastes and technologies across the trading partners and difference in the endowment of factors of production owned by the trading partners—four famous theorems of trade have been emerged: the HO theorem[1]; the Stolper–Samuelson theorem[2]; the Rybczynski theorem[3]; and the factor–price equalization theorem.[4] All these theorems have proven that the existence of differences in factor endowments between countries have served as reasons for trade, and that trade in return feeds back to factors of production differently. These theorems collectively form the fundamentals of trade theory.

Since the 1940s, these simple two-country, two-factor models have come under close scrutiny. Studies have focused on checking the validity of these trade theorems in a generalized framework and have found that these theorems do not hold when generalizations (*K*-goods and *N*-factors) are applied to the models. Leontief's (1953) study is considered to be the first significant attempt to test the empirical validity of the HO theory while looking at the exports and imports in the United States. Comparing the number of factors of production used in the same value of exports and imports, Leontief found that US exports were less capital intensive compared to imports even though their capital/labor ratio was relatively high and hence contradicted the basic HO theory. Later, a number of studies (Vanek 1968; Leamer 1980; Bowen et al. 1987; Davis and Weinstein 2001, among others) attempted to improve on the methodology adopted by Leontief (1953) to capture the actual scenario.

Many empirical trade economists have also noted the difficulties in applying these trade theories in complex multicountry, multifactor, multicommodity real-world situations. Over the years, with the changing pattern of trade between countries, Deardorff (1979) in his study showed that the imposition of high trade restrictions on an input will raise the price of a final commodity attached with this input and hence make the production of a final good difficult to survive even if the country is a low-cost producer of the same commodity. While testing the theory of comparative advantage for trade in services, Deardorff (1985) addressed three different characteristics of trade in services—trade in services arise as a by-product of trade in goods; trade in services are accompanied by international direct investment; and services cannot be produced somewhere and consumed somewhere else like goods. Based on his study's results, he was of the view that under certain assumptions, the weak version of the theory of comparative advantage may apply.

Many empirical studies have also touched upon the issue of whether traditional trade theories still hold in the presence of fragmentation of the production process. Deardorff (2005) has done a detailed analysis in this respect and has found that if the fragmented production process is based on the level of resources that countries have, then this process will add some value to the existing level of world welfare. Improvements in transportation and communication facilities have also helped in the splitting of production process.

2.2 New Trade Theories

Traditional trade theories are based on key assumptions: perfect competition; constant returns to scale; no externalities; and the fully flexible market of factors of production (such as capital and labor) that ensure full employment. Subsequent developments in trade theories have relaxed these assumptions to take into account the real picture. In new trade theories, a new term called "intra-industry trade" has been coined, which represents the trade of products of similar industry between two countries with similar factors of production or same endowments. Final products are differentiated but are very close substitutes of each other. This pattern of trade can even exist without differences in the technology of production.

These theories explain three main reasons behind the trade between countries: (i) economies of scale; (ii) product differentiation; and (iii) the existence of imperfect competition in the markets. These theories predict scale and selection effects as the result of international trade taking place in goods with similar factor intensities. Instead of producing all sets of varieties, countries would concentrate on a few varieties (some firms would exit, leading to a selection effect), reap economies of scale (existing firms would expand business, leading to a scale effect), and export the same at competitive costs to others, while importing other sets of varieties of the same good from other countries at lower prices.

Krugman with his ingenuity modeled the consumption side of his model with a "love for variety" utility function as a variant of the Dixit–Stiglitz utility function,[5] but never gave the exact form the same. This led him to show that scale and selection effects are present in the model. In fact, if one takes a particular function form like CES or the Dixit–Stiglitz utility function in addition to Krugman's existing model, one would not see any scale and selection effects. Consumers would gain by exchanging varieties because each variety enters the utility function ("love for variety" utility function) of each consumer present in both trading countries.

The new trade models of Krugman and others help us to understand the impact of trade liberalization on countries, wherein with liberalization one may see the exit of some firms in the short run, while in the long run the remaining firms would take up the business, reap economies of scale, and produce more goods at a lower average cost. It was Melitz (2003), however, who developed the model of heterogeneous firms to explain which firms would exit and which would take up the rest of the business. New trade models, however, could not explain the pattern of trade, as was the case with the earlier trade models.

Balassa (1966) took the initiative in this respect, but the development of trade theories to explain intra-industry trade happened in the 1980s. Krugman (1979) in his monopolistic model of trade has explained the reasons of gains from intra-industry trade between two similar (in terms of technology and factor endowments) countries. Its reciprocal dumping model has also explained the benefits associated with trade in identical products. By taking the assumptions of the presence of economies of scale in the production and love for variety in the consumption, Krugman explained the reasons behind intra-industry trade and gains from trade. As per his theory, if the scale of production is enlarged, then the producer will gain in terms of economies of scale and the consumer will gain in terms of the availability of more consumable varieties. There will be a large number of producers producing the differentiated products, but each variety should be a close substitute for each other variety. Further, Helpman and Krugman (1985) gave another explanation of the new pattern of trade by assuming the propositions of the HO model with some assumptions of the Krugman model. By assuming the absence of economies of scale in the production of goods from capital-intensive industries, they explained that a capital-rich country will produce and export capital-intensive products and import labor products produced by the labor-abundant country. The latter country can also export manufactured goods as it produces a different variety, which can be liked by the consumers in the capital-abundant nation. Therefore, new trade theories have identified new sources of gains from trade: a rise in efficiency, resulting from economies of scale in the production front, and a welfare gain for consumers resulting from the availability of new varieties in the market and lower costs of imports.

2.3 "New" New Trade Theories

Further advancements in trade theory to explain gains from trade have been elucidated by "new" new trade theories modeled on assuming differences in firms (i.e., firm heterogeneity) producing the same product. Until the 1970s, trade theories ignored the issue of firm heterogeneity and assumed that all firms in a given industry were homogeneous. In the 1980s, with the advent of wide microdata on production and trade at the firm level, it was noted that considerable differences existed among firms in terms of their size, productivity, choice of technology, quality of products, and opting to access the international market.

This empirical evidence initiated the search for new sources of gains from trade and factor allocation resulting from international trade. It was noted that only a small fraction of total firms within an industry indulged in trading, and this phenomenon cannot be explained with the help of either the traditional or new trade theories.

In the 2000s, another major development in trade theories, the "new" new trade theories, has begun to account for the dynamic industrial models of firm entry, innovation, growth, and death. "New" new trade theories have focused on the issue that it is not the countries or industries that indulge in trade but the firms that trade, and they are heterogeneous in nature. Extensive margins, firm heterogeneity, and market conditions are important components of any "new" new trade models.

By focusing on the fact that all firms in an exporting sector do not export, this theory differentiated the firms engaging in the production of similar products in the same industry. The firm heterogeneity can be best explained by differences in productivity of different firms. Melitz (2003) in his model introduced differences in firms in the Krugman model of new trade theory and explained that only more productive firms would become the exporters. He believed more trade opportunities would lead to more welfare gains through incentives associated with the enhancement of the productivity of existing firms, as well as these gains working as an incentive for the new entrant to enter with high productivity. His model was considered the most successful way to analyze firm heterogeneity and trade. The model explicates that firms need to bear several costs to enter the international market.

This finding raised the question of causality: whether the high productivity induced firms to self-select for exports, or productivity of the exporting firms increased with learning by exporting.

Though the direction of causality is not very clear, extensive studies have found the evidence that high productivity precedes entry into exporting markets, which gave rise to the concept of sunk cost. Initially, each firm invested in research and development to invent a new variety that is considered as the sunk cost or invention cost. The invention cost ultimately determines the firm's productivity level because of the uncertainty associated with the average cost of production of a new variety. Along with the sunk cost, firms need to bear the entry cost to enter a domestic market and an additional entry cost to enter an international market.

In addition to prices, demand conditions, and trade costs, threshold marginal costs determine whether firms will choose to sell their product in the domestic market or in the international market also. So, firm heterogeneity and sunk cost imply that the lowest productivity firms will exit and that overall productivity of the industry will increase. Therefore, the "new" new trade theories have identified another source of gains from trade: a rise in productivity level resulting from the exit of the least efficient firms and the reallocation of resources in favor of the most efficient firms. Most of the recent theoretical literature in this respect has tried to generalize or to elaborate the Melitz (2003) model of selection.

Bernard et al. (2007) have studied the interaction between comparative advantage and firm heterogeneity. Melitz and Ottaviano (2008) have explored the interaction between variable mark-ups and market size. Multiproduct firms have been studied by a large number of researchers (e.g., Bernard et al. 2011; Eckel and Neary 2010; Mayer et al. 2014; among others) and labor market frictions have been considered in Amiti and Davis (2011) and Helpman et al. (2011).

Helpman et al. (2004) extended the Melitz (2003) model (highlighting the role of fixed costs) to explain the decisions of firms to choose to serve international market with exports or in terms of FDI. They noted that multinationals are more productive compared to the domestically owned firms. In their framework, firms compare the costs of establishing a production unit in a foreign land to the costs of exporting to that particular country. Along with the fixed costs, firms that wish to serve the international market with exports need to bear some transportation costs. Similarly, firms that want to run their production unit in a foreign land need to bear some institutional processing costs and other costs associated with duplicating production capacity. If the transportation costs outweigh the fixed costs of setting up a foreign affiliate, firms will opt for FDI rather than exporting while producing domestically. Antras and Helpman (2004, 2007) explained the organization decision of a firm's production: whether internally, FDI, or outsourcing. In their model, trade, investment, and organizational forms of the firm were determined jointly. Firm level differences, fixed costs associated with enforcing contracts, and differences in wage rates play together to decide the organizational structure of the firm.

The Melitz (2003) model assumed a constant elasticity of substitution preferences which ensured constant firm mark-ups of price over marginal costs. Bernard et al. (2003) and Melitz and Ottaviano (2008) extended the Melitz (2003) model, allowing to endogenously determine mark-ups. In this scenario, trade liberalization might induce competition, initiating a reduction in mark-ups of price over the marginal cost. This reduction in average prices generates another source of welfare gain.

Further modifications in these models have been done by Chaney (2008), Arkolakis and Muendler (2010, 2011), and Mayer et al. (2014) where they accounted for multiproduct firms exporting to multiple destinations. Firms face fixed entry costs for each product for each market. Accordingly, firms decide on the destinations, number of products by destinations, and amount of sales by products and destinations. Their models have tried to explain why a small number of firms export many products and to a larger number of countries. Bernard et al. (2003) and Melitz (2003) have noted that firms are heterogeneous in nature and all firms do not trade in the international market because of the higher entry cost there. Only the most productive firms will be able to cover these costs. For more literature on empirical studies on testing trade theories, the reader can download the World Trade Report 2008, provided online[6] by the WTO.

2.4 Gravity Modeling

Initially, by looking at the trends in trade data, it has been established that trade between larger countries is more than the smaller countries and this trade is inversely affected by the distance between two trading partners due to the larger transportation costs related herewith. Based on this intuition, Tinbergen (1962) developed the concept of the gravity equation in trade, which he based on Newton's gravity equation, and which described that international trade between two trading nations is directly linked with their economic sizes and inversely related with the distance between them. His gravity model is given by Eq. (2.1).

$$M_{ij} = \frac{Y_i Y_j}{D_{ij}} \tag{2.1}$$

where, M_{ij} is the flow of trade (exports or imports) from origin i to destination j, Y_i and Y_j are the economic masses (GDPs) of these two nations, and D_{ij} is the distance between these countries.

Despite its empirical popularity, the gravity model was criticized in the 1970s and 1980s for not having a convincing microeconomic foundation. Tinbergen (1962) explained the determination of trade by supply potential (exporter GDP), demand potential (importer GDP), and transportation costs (distance). Linnemann (1966) used quasi-Walrasian model to justify the formulation of the trade gravity equation. Neither he nor Pöyhönen (1963) and Pulliainen (1963) were able to provide a microfoundation to the gravity equation.

As per Leamer and Levinsohn (1995), "The gravity models are strictly descriptive. They lack a theoretical underpinning so that once the facts are out, it is not clear what to make of them." Deardorff (1984) stated that the gravity equations are empirically successful but their "theoretical heritage" is "dubious." So, after Tinbergen, an urge has begun to convert this intuitive model into a theoretically acceptable model. In the literature, many theoretical explanations have become available since then, which provide various forms of the gravity equation for empirical analysis. Some of these are explained as follows:

Anderson (1979) gave one of the demand-side models and became the first to provide a theoretical basis for the gravity equation. To derive this equation, he assumed Armington preferences, and these preferences are identical over all the partners represented by a Cob–Douglas utility function. Thereafter, he derived the simplistic form of the gravity equation:

$$X_{ij} = \frac{Y_i Y_j}{\sum Y_j} \tag{2.2}$$

where X_{ij} are the imports of country j from country i (or exports of country i to country j), Y_i and Y_j are the GDPs of both the trading partners, and $\sum Y_j$ is the sum of GDPs of all the importing countries (world GDP). To make the model more operational, later, he added nontradable goods, trade costs, and many varieties of goods by using the preferences given by constant elasticity of substitution (CES).

Eaton and Kortum (2002) derived the gravity model from the Ricardian trade model with a continuum of goods. In their model, the distribution of trade between countries depended upon differences in technology, as was also assumed by Ricardo, and the country with the lowest comparative costs (production plus trade costs) will export to all other trading countries. Ricardo assumed that country *i*'s efficiency in production of good *j* is derived from probabilistic distribution (the Frechet distribution).

$$F_i(z) = e^{-T_i z^{-\theta}} \tag{2.3}$$

where *z* is the random variable depicting country *i*'s efficiency in the production of good *j*; and T_i and θ are the distribution parameters. T_i is the location parameter (country-specific) of the distribution; a high value linked with this parameter shows the high efficiency of country *i* in the production of any good *j*. Parameter θ (common to all countries) describes the level of variation within the distribution; the high value of θ depicts the low variation, and vice versa. They linked T_i and θ with the Ricardian type of trade by referring to the former as country *i*'s of technology and to the latter as heterogeneity across goods by country (given by the relative efficiencies of each country). In this sense, the parameter T_i governs country *i*'s absolute advantage, and parameter θ governs the comparative advantage. The effect of trade costs on trade is explained by the degree of comparative advantage. If it is low then the trade will be highly sensitive to trade costs, but if it is high then it will diminish the effect of trade costs on trade.

Anderson and Wincoop (2003) used the framework of Anderson (1979) and derived an equation of gravity in which the level of trade between two nations depended upon the height of resistance they both were facing from the other trading partners except each other in addition to the level of trade costs between them. They labelled these multilateral resistances. Their final equation was:

$$X_{ij} = \frac{y_i y_j}{y^w}\left(\frac{t_{ij}}{\pi_i p_j}\right)^{1-\sigma} \tag{2.4}$$

and

$$\pi_i^{1-\sigma} = \sum_j p_j^{\sigma-1} \theta_j t_{ij}^{1-\sigma} \forall_i \tag{2.4a}$$

$$p_j^{1-\sigma} = \sum_i \pi_i^{\sigma-1} \theta_i t_{ij}^{1-\sigma} \forall_j \tag{2.4b}$$

where X_{ij} is the level of trade of country i from country j; y_i,y_j, and y^w are the GDPs of country i, j, and world, respectively; t_{ij} is the level of trade costs; π_i is the outward multilateral resistance and p_j is the inward multilateral resistance; and $\sigma > 1$ is the elasticity of substitution across the goods. In the fourth and fifth equations, θ_j and θ_i represent the income shares of country i and j in the world income, i.e., $\theta_j = \frac{y_j}{y^w}$ and $\theta_i = \frac{y_i}{y^w}$. So, these two equations provide solutions to the inward and outward multilateral resistance terms. They assume trade costs to be symmetric ($t_{ij}=t_{ji}$), and these are given an observable trade cost equation in which trade costs (t_{ij}) depend on the distance and border between two trading partners, i and j. This is given by:

$$t_{ij} = b_{ij} d_{ij}^{\rho} \tag{2.5}$$

where b_{ij} is positive if there is a border between trading nations and zero otherwise; and d_{ij} measures the level of distance between the two nations.

Chaney (2008) used the Krugman (1980) model of gravity as a departure point for his own study. By assuming only one factor of production—labor; identical costs for each firm; each firm produces a differentiated good; full employment; free entry and exit of firms; transportation is the only variable cost; and consumers have preferences for variety—Krugman (1980) derived the flow of exports (X_{ij}) from country i to j given by the following equation:

$$X_{ij} = \text{Constant} * \frac{\text{GDP}_i * \text{GDP}_j}{(\text{TradeCosts}_{ij})^{\sigma}} \tag{2.6}$$

where σ represents the elasticity of substitution between varieties, so the high value of σ will lead to the very high level of competition in the market and also will lead to the high impact of trade barriers on trade flows. But when the varieties are less substitutable (low σ), the consumers will still be ready to buy that commodity even at the higher cost, dampening the impact trade barriers on the trade flows. Chaney (2008) added two new assumptions—heterogeneity of firms in productivity and fixed costs of exporting—to the Krugman (1980) model, and found that when trade costs vary, then not only the size of exports changes (intensive margin) but also the number of exporters changes (extensive margin). When elasticity of substitution is high, then it makes the intensive margin more sensitive in relation to trade costs and the extensive margin less sensitive. When the elasticity of substitution is low, then new entrants will capture the large market share and these will affect the level of trade highly. To check which one of these two effects dominates, he used Pareto distribution for modeling productivity across the firms. His model also predicts that when trade barriers decline, the exports of each firm increase, and in addition to this, new firms also start exporting. By incorporating the consumption side, production side, firm heterogeneity, market condition and trade barriers into the model, he found that the gravity model can be distorted. Chaney interacted firm heterogeneity and elasticity of substitution with traditional variables of the gravity model explaining trade flows and found that the usual sign changes (distance and bilateral trade barriers) turn out to have a positive impact on trade. Chaney gave the following gravity equation:

$$X_{ij} = \mu * \frac{Y_i Y_j}{Y} * \left(\frac{w_i \tau_{ij}}{\theta_j}\right)^{-\gamma} * f_{ij}^{-\left[\frac{\gamma}{(\sigma-1)}-1\right]} \tag{2.7}$$

Exports (X_{ij}) of country i to j depend on the weight of differentiated goods in the consumer's utility (μ), country sizes relative to the world $\left(\frac{Y_i Y_j}{Y}\right)$, workers' productivity (w_i), fixed (f_{ij}) and variable (τ_{ij}) trade costs, and importer (j)'s remoteness from the rest of world (θ_j). It is apparently clear that:

1. Exports are more elastic with respect to variable trade barriers (γ)[7] and this elasticity is larger than the elasticity for each individual firm. Any reduction in the variable costs increase the exports of each firm and, in addition to this, allows new firms to enter in the market. Hence, extensive margin will come on the top by overcoming the intensive margin, further augmenting the impact of variable trade costs.
2. The elasticity of exports with respect to variable costs does not depend on the elasticity of substitution between goods (σ), and elasticity of

exports with respect to fixed costs is inversely related to the elasticity of substitution between goods (σ).

Melitz and Ottaviano (2008) also derived the gravity equation by using the assumption of heterogeneous firms, and they replaced the constant elasticity of substitution with quasi-linear preferences. In their model, trade costs are differently related with exporter and importer countries. From the exporter's side, these are related with the comparative advantage in technology, and from importer's side these are related with the intensity of competition. Anderson (2010) noted that the distinguishing feature of gravity lies in its modularity. The distribution of goods and factors among countries is determined by the gravitational forces subject to the economic size of the countries. The model allows for disaggregation at any scale and is not restricted by any particular production and market structure.

The most recent contribution in the history of gravity modeling has been made by Baldwin and Taglioni (2011). They started with the very basic difference in the measurement of trade and GDPs, where the former is measured in gross sales basis and the latter is measured in value added basis. They pointed out that when the trade in intermediates takes place, then these proxies of supply and demand (i.e., GDPs) becomes less appropriate and hence should be corrected by an appropriate mass variable. Baldwin and Taglioni (2011) added a new correction term to the gravity model when the trade is taking place in parts and components instead of trade in final/ consumer goods. They proved that the standard gravity model 'breaks down' for the trade in intermediate goods. As the trade is measured in gross sales while the GDP is measured in terms of value added (net sales), there is something in between these two which needs some remedial measures to correctly specify the gravity model. They started with the well-known CES preferences for differentiated varieties:

$$v_{od} \equiv \left(\frac{p_{od}}{P_d}\right)^{1-\sigma} E_d; \qquad \sigma > 1 \tag{2.8}$$

The notations "o" and "d" represents the origin and destination countries, respectively; v_{od} is the expenditure in the destination country on the goods imported from the origin country; P_d is the CES price index of all varieties in destination; E_d is the consumer price in destination; σ is the elasticity of substitution among varieties; and p_{od} is the consumer price inside the destination of a variety made in the origin and is defined as:

$$p_{od} = \mu_{od} m_o \tau_{od} \tag{2.9}$$

where: μ_{od} is the optimal price mark-up; m_o is the marginal costs; and τ_{od} is the bilateral trade cost component (one plus tariff equivalent of all trade barriers). The mark-up μ_{od} is the same for all destinations by assuming the perfect competition or Dixit–Stiglitz monopolistic competition. By assuming the latter case—Dixit–Stiglitz competition—the mark-up is $\frac{\sigma}{\sigma-1}$. The price available to local consumers is $p_{oo} = \frac{\sigma}{\sigma-1} m_o \tau_{oo}$, and assuming no internal trade barrier the τ_{oo} will be equal to unity. Taking the summation over all varieties:

$$V_{od} = n_o {p_{oo}}^{1-\sigma} \left(\frac{\tau_{od}}{P_d} \right)^{1-\sigma} E_d \tag{2.10}$$

where v_{od} is the aggregated value of bilateral flow from origin (nation-o) to destination (nation-d); n_o is the number (mass) of varieties produced by nation-o.

To convert the above expenditure function into a gravitational form, Baldwin and Taglioni imposed a market clearing condition. To make supply equal to demand, the nation-o's output must be equal to above equation summed across all destinations (including the nation-o's local sales to itself). With the assumption of no trade of parts and components, the nation's output is its own GDP denoted by Y_o. Thus,

$$Y_o = n_o {p_{oo}}^{1-\sigma} \sum_d \left(\frac{\tau_{od}}{P_d} \right)^{1-\sigma} E_d \tag{2.11}$$

$$n_o {p_{oo}}^{1-\sigma} = \frac{Y_o}{\sum_d \left(\frac{\tau_{od}}{P_d} \right)^{1-\sigma} E_d} \tag{2.12}$$

$$n_o {p_{oo}}^{1-\sigma} = \frac{Y_o}{\Omega_o} \quad \text{and} \quad \Omega_o = \sum_d \left(\frac{\tau_{od}}{P_d} \right)^{1-\sigma} E_d$$

Plugging the above result into v_{od}

$$V_{od} = \tau_{od}{}^{1-\sigma} E_d Y_o \frac{1}{P_d{}^{1-\sigma}\Omega_o} \tag{2.13}$$

where P_d is the CES price index in nation-d and Ω_o is the market potential index of nation-o. The product of $P_d^{1-\sigma}$ and Ω_o is known as multilateral trade resistance. In the standard gravity equation Υ_o, E_d, and τ are proxied with nation-o's GDP, nation-d's GDP, and their bilateral distance, respectively.

Thereafter, Baldwin and Taglioni included the trade in parts and components to the gravity model. For this purpose, they used the "vertical linkages" model of Krugman and Venables (1996). After introducing intermediate goods in the utility and cost functions, they derived the following type of gravity model:

$$V_{od} = \tau_{od}{}^{1-\sigma} E_d C_o \frac{1}{P_d{}^{1-\sigma}\Omega_o} \tag{2.14}$$

$$E_d \equiv \gamma(I_d + n_d C_d) \quad \text{and} \quad C_o \equiv C[w_o P_o x_o] \tag{2.15}$$

where I_d is the income of the consumer in nation-d; C_d is the total cost of a variety in nation-d; and C is the cost function. In the above equation, the "mass" variable is different from the mass in the standard gravity equation because it includes the direct consumable as well as the intermediate goods. For the direct consumables, the demand depends upon the level of income, whereas for the intermediate goods the demand depends upon the total production cost. So, here the standard gravity breaks down, and the reason for this breakdown is that the GDPs cannot be used to represent the mass because now the intermediate goods trade is also there. So, mass should be reformulated. Baldwin and Taglioni estimated the following gravity equation for a panel of countries over the period 1967 to 2007 for 187 nations of the world:

$$\ln(V_{odt}) = G + \alpha_1 \ln \underbrace{\left(\frac{Y_{ot}}{P_d{}^{1-\sigma}}\frac{E_{dt}}{\Omega_o}\right)}_{\text{mass}} + \alpha_1 \ln(\tau_{odt}) + \varepsilon_{odt} \tag{2.16}$$

Basically, the mass term is the product of the trade partners' economic mass, which is the product of importer-d's real GDP and the exporter's nominal

GDP divided by P_d and Ω_o, and Ω_o is calculated by the method given by Baier and Bergstrand (2001) as:

$$\Omega_o = \left(\sum_d \mathrm{GDP}_{dt} (\mathrm{DIST}_{od})^{1-\sigma} \right)^{\frac{1}{1-\sigma}} \tag{2.16a}$$

To decide the value of elasticity (σ), they took help from Obstfeld and Rogoff (2001) and Carrere (2006) and took the value equal to four. Again, in Eq. (2.16) the GDPs are present in the numerator of the new mass variable. Now the question arises of how to fix the proxies of economic mass. For this, they calculated nation-*d*'s demand shifter:

$$E_d \equiv Y_d + \sum_{i \neq 0} V_{di}^{\mathrm{Interm}} \tag{2.17}$$

For the calculation of gross output, there is a simple application of the theory in terms of value added of nation-*o* in manufacturing plus its purchases of intermediate inputs from all sources except from itself, given by:

$$C_o \equiv AV_o^{\mathrm{Manu}} + \sum_{i \neq 0} V_{oi}^{\mathrm{Interm}} \tag{2.18}$$

Baldwin and Taglioni then estimated the regression by using the above two proxies for the standard GDP variables and found that the proxies worked better than the GDPs.

2.4.1 *Gravity Analysis: Estimation Issues*

Gravity analysis is another way of analyzing trade flows with the help of econometric tools. Since the introduction of the traditional model to the advanced model of gravity, econometric estimation has played a significant role in estimating the effect of country-specific effects on bilateral trade flows. The most basic cross-sectional gravity model has been estimated using the ordinary least square (OLS) method by estimating a log-linearized form of it.

McCallum (1995) estimated the traditional gravity equation for the bilateral trade between the United States and Canada with distance and border as proxies for the trade costs. He found very surprising results that the US-Canadian border led to trade between Canadian provinces that is a factor 22 (2.200 percent) times trade between US states and Canadian provinces.

Anderson and Wincoop (2003) argued that McCallum (1995) had used a misspecified model. They brought forward that not only bilateral trade barriers but also multilateral trade barriers affect the international trade, and they called these barriers the "multilateral resistance term"—the resistance from the other trading partners. Hence, Anderson and Wincoop advocated the inclusion of a multilateral resistance term in the econometric estimation of the theoretical gravity equation. The problem with adding this term is that it is not directly observable and requires advanced estimation techniques to include the impact of multilateral resistance (MR) on bilateral trade. The estimation of gravity equation in the presence of the MR term could be a good area of research for working in the area of trade policy research.

In the literature, studies are available that estimate the gravity equation by including the impact of the MR term. The easiest solution of this problem is the fixed effect estimation. The availability of countrywide data over a continuous time period led to the use of panel data estimation techniques of econometrics to estimate the gravity model. Using fixed effect estimation with panel data allowed researchers to solve the problem of heterogeneity because of different countries with the help of country-pair fixed effects. But the fixed effect estimation has an issue of dropping the collinear variable which is not time variant such as distance. Hence, in that case one should choose an appropriate panel data estimation technique to obtain the results of those time-invariant variables on trade flows. Studies have used many specifications of the gravity equation by using nation-dummies, but the matter is the correct specification of the model and the unbiased estimated results.

Baldwin and Taglioni (2011) highlighted the three main mistakes in estimating the gravity equation and gave a solution for it. These mistakes are:

- **Gold Medal Mistake**: Occurs with the inclusion of a log of GDPs in place of a log of importer- and exporter-specific factors. It generally omits the MR term from the gravity equation and creates bias in the estimation. This mistake is still very common in the literature.
- **Silver Medal Mistake**: Under this, studies have taken the average of reciprocal trade flows instead of treating bilateral trade differently. The

extent of this problem has been solved due to the availability of bilateral trade data.

- **Bronze Medal Mistake**: Under this, inappropriate usage of a deflation method to deflate the trade flows and the country's income become problematic.

Hence, one can obtain the unbiased results on the variables affecting the level of bilateral trade from the estimation of the properly specified gravity model. There exist many other issues related to the estimation of the gravity model that can be solved by taking appropriate steps using advanced econometric methods.[8] The estimation issues and the procedure to estimate the gravity equation are given in detail in Shepherd (2013). Chapter 3 of "A Practical Guide to Trade Policy Analysis" provided by United Nations and World Trade Organization (WTO) can also be helpful for the readers to study more on gravity model insights and its estimation issues.

2.4.2 Quantification of Trade Barriers

The trade policy linked to every trade agreement is the policy of reducing trade barriers that hinder the level of bilateral trade. These barriers are of two types: direct and indirect. Direct barriers include tariffs imposed by an importer on the exporter's goods; however, indirect barriers include those barriers responsible for delaying the exporting of goods from the exporter country to the destination country (importer)—also known as trade transaction costs.

In the literature, these trade barriers are termed broadly under the category of trade costs. These costs are the difference between the production cost of a traded commodity and the price paid by the ultimate consumers.

Figure 2.1 shows that trade costs are paid at three stages: (1) Getting to the border: this includes the costs of moving a good from the production site to the international border; (2) at the border: this incorporates the costs that a good encounters while crossing an international border; and (3) behind the border: this captures the costs to move a good from an international border to the final consumer.

The simplest way of calculating trade costs is to report the data on the tariff rate as a percentage of the price of the imported commodity at a given level of product classification. The extent of restriction to trade by these direct trade costs can be measured by calculating the level of protection

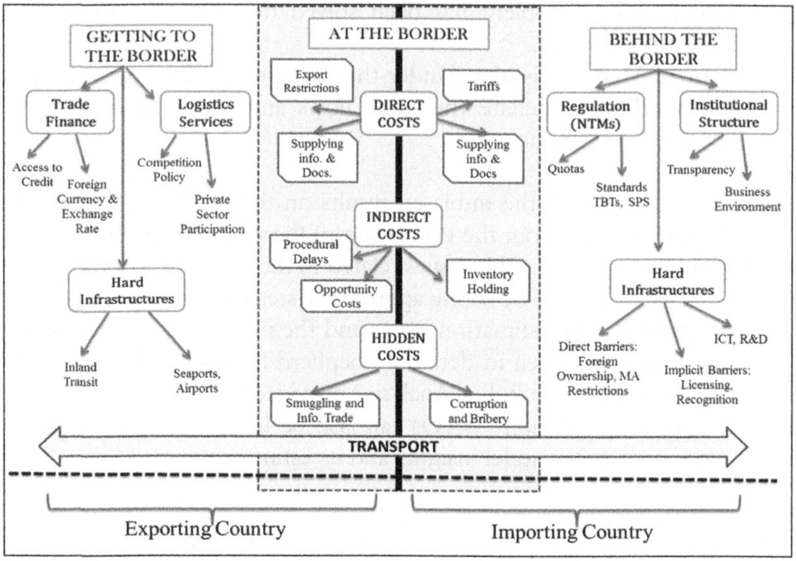

Fig. 2.1 Diagnostic of trade costs (Source: Moise and Bris (2013))

index. Other protection measures can also be used for the same purpose and require data on productwide tariff rates by country as a given level of product classification. But the use of this method underestimates the level of restrictiveness as one is totally ignoring the hurdles imposed by the indirect trade barriers.

Because we have already defined that these costs are the difference between the production cost of a traded commodity and the price paid by the ultimate consumer, this price gap not only includes the price raised by the imposition of tariffs but also raised by other factors as well which are qualitative in nature and difficult to account. To calculate these price gaps properly, data on each variable that accumulates the price of a traded commodity from source to ultimate destination is required, which is not available.

The literature provides various indirect measures to calculate the extent of restrictiveness to trade between two partners. One among these is derived by Novy (2008) by using the gravity model of international trade given by Anderson and Wincoop (2003) using the data on actual trade flows. After applying some manipulations, he derived a micro-founded measure for international trade costs. His measure overcomes the problem of assuming the symmetric and particular kind of trade cost function of Anderson and Wincoop (2003), and directly calculates the international trade costs from the observable data. This bilateral measure of trade costs is comprehensive in the sense that it includes all additional costs involved in trading goods bilaterally relative to those involved in trading goods intranationally (Duval and Utoktham 2011).

We assumed Anderson and Wincoop (2003)'s final gravity model[9] as the starting point for the derivation of the measure of trade costs, but ended up with totally different and more realistic findings. Novy (2008)'s measure of trade costs poses some merits over the Anderson and Wincoop (2003)'s trade cost function, as it does not assume bilateral trade costs to be symmetric, trade costs do not depend only on the two variables distance and border, and also these vary over time. Using the Anderson and Wincoop (2003) framework given by Eq. (2.4) to find the expression for country *i*'s intranational trade, we arrive at

$$x_{ii} = \frac{y_i y_i}{y^w} \left(\frac{t_{ii}}{\pi_i p_i} \right)^{1-\sigma} \tag{2.19}$$

where t_{ii} represents intranational trade costs, e.g., domestic transportation costs. Equation (2.19) can be solved for the product of outward and inward multilateral resistance as:

$$\pi_i p_i = \left(\frac{x_{ii}/y_i}{y_i/y^w} \right)^{\frac{1}{(\sigma-1)}} t_{ii} \tag{2.20}$$

The explicit solution for the multilateral resistance variables can be exploited to solve the general equilibrium model of bilateral trade costs. Gravity Eq. (2.4) contains the product of outward multilateral resistance of one country and inward multilateral resistance of another country, $\pi_i p_j$, whereas Eq. (2.20) provides a solution for $\pi_i p_i$. It is therefore useful to multiply gravity Eq. (2.4) by the corresponding gravity equation for trade flows in the opposite direction, x_{ji}, to obtain a bidirectional gravity equation that contains both countries' outward and inward multilateral resistance variables:

$$x_{ij}x_{ji} = \left(\frac{y_i y_j}{y^w}\right)^2 \left(\frac{t_{ij}t_{ji}}{\pi_i p_i \pi_j p_j}\right)^{1-\sigma} \tag{2.21}$$

Substituting the solution from Eq. (2.20) yields,

$$x_{ij}x_{ji} = \left(\frac{y_i y_j}{y^w}\right)^2 \left(\frac{t_{ij}t_{ji}}{\left(\frac{x_{ii}/y_i}{y_i/y^w}\right)^{\frac{1}{(\sigma-1)}} t_{ii} \left(\frac{x_{jj}/y_j}{y_j/y^w}\right)^{\frac{1}{(\sigma-1)}} t_{jj}}\right)^{1-\sigma}$$

$$x_{ij}x_{ji} = \left(\frac{y_i y_j}{y^w}\right)^2 \left(\frac{t_{ij}t_{ji}}{t_{ii}t_{jj}} \left(\frac{x_{ii}/y_i}{y_i/y^w}\right)^{\frac{1}{(1-\sigma)}} \left(\frac{x_{jj}/y_j}{y_j/y^w}\right)^{\frac{1}{(1-\sigma)}}\right)^{1-\sigma}$$

$$x_{ij}x_{ji} = \left(\frac{y_i y_j}{y^w}\right)^2 \left(\frac{x_{ii}/y_i}{y_i/y^w}\right)^{\frac{1-\sigma}{(1-\sigma)}} \left(\frac{x_{jj}/y_j}{y_j/y^w}\right)^{\frac{1-\sigma}{(1-\sigma)}} \left(\frac{t_{ij}t_{ji}}{t_{ii}t_{jj}}\right)^{1-\sigma}$$

$$x_{ij}x_{ji} = \left(\frac{y_i y_j}{y^w}\right)^2 \left(\frac{x_{ii}}{y_i}\frac{y^w}{y_i}\right) \left(\frac{x_{jj}}{y_j}\frac{y^w}{y_j}\right) \left(\frac{t_{ij}t_{ji}}{t_{ii}t_{jj}}\right)^{1-\sigma}$$

$$x_{ij}x_{ji} = \left(\frac{y_i y_j}{y^w}\right)^2 \left(\frac{y^w}{y_i^2}\right) \left(\frac{y^w}{y_j^2}\right) (x_{ii}x_{jj}) \left(\frac{t_{ij}t_{ji}}{t_{ii}t_{jj}}\right)^{1-\sigma}$$

$$x_{ij}x_{ji} = \left(\frac{y_i y_j}{y^w}\right)^2 \left(\frac{y^w}{y_i y_j}\right)^2 (x_{ii}x_{jj}) \left(\frac{t_{ij}t_{ji}}{t_{ii}t_{jj}}\right)^{1-\sigma}$$

$$x_{ij}x_{ji} = (x_{ii}x_{jj}) \left(\frac{t_{ij}t_{ji}}{t_{ii}t_{jj}}\right)^{1-\sigma}$$

$$x_{ij}x_{ji} = (x_{ii}x_{jj}) \left(\frac{t_{ii}t_{jj}}{t_{ij}t_{ji}}\right)^{\sigma-1} \tag{2.22}$$

The size variables in the gravity Eq. (2.22) are not total income $y_i y_j$ as in traditional gravity equations, but intranational trade $x_{ii}x_{jj}$. Intranational trade not only controls for the countries' economic size, but according to Eq. (2.4b) it is also directly linked to multilateral resistance. Equation (2.22) can be rearranged as:

$$\frac{t_{ij}t_{ji}}{t_{ii}t_{jj}} = \left(\frac{x_{ii}x_{jj}}{x_{ij}x_{ji}}\right)^{\frac{1}{\sigma-1}} \tag{2.23}$$

Because shipping costs between i and j can be asymmetric ($t_{ij} \neq t_{ji}$) and because domestic trade costs can differ across countries ($t_{ii} \neq t_{jj}$), it is useful to take the geometric mean of the barriers in both directions. It is also useful to deduct one to get an expression for the tariff equivalent. The resulting micro-founded trade cost measure is denoted as τ_{ij}:

$$\tau_{ij} = \left(\frac{t_{ij}t_{ji}}{t_{ii}t_{jj}}\right)^{\frac{1}{2}} - 1 = \left(\frac{x_{ii}x_{jj}}{x_{ij}x_{ji}}\right)^{\frac{1}{2(\sigma-1)}} - 1 \tag{2.24}$$

where τ_{ij} measures bilateral trade costs $t_{ij}t_{ji}$ relative to domestic trade costs $t_{ii}t_{jj}$. It therefore does not impose frictionless domestic trade and captures what makes international trade more costly than domestic trade.

2.4.3 *Ad Valorem Equivalents (AVEs) of Nontariff Barriers (NTBs)*

Another method of accounting for the impact of trade costs is to calculate the overall trade restrictiveness index. In the literature, this is calculated by using the weighted sum of tariffs and AVEs of all NTBs at the tariff line level. Here the NTBs refer to those barriers that increase the transaction costs to the trade between two countries. Doing business report, 2015 grouped all direct and indirect trade transaction costs into three main categories:

- documents required to import and export in numbers;
- time required to import and export in days; and
- cost required to import and export in USD per container.

where the number of documents required to import and export includes bank documents, customs clearance documents, port and terminal handling documents, and transport documents; the time required to import and export includes time of obtaining, filling out, and submitting all documents, inland transport and handling, customs clearance and inspections, and port and terminal handling; and the costs of all documentation, inland transport and handling, customs clearance and inspections, and port and terminal handling. All countries are compared on the same scale using the same assumptions and level of trade barriers. Using data from the above three aggregated categories of TTCs, provided by *Doing Business* reports, one can easily calculate the AVEs of these NTBs using the methodology given by Kee et al. (2009). For references purpose, one can also read Zaki (2010) for calculation of the AVEs of administrative barriers.

2.5 Concluding Remarks

Different theories of international trade have provided different reasons for international trade among nations. Each of these different trade theories has highlighted different sources of gains from trade. Each new theory has pointed out even larger gains from trade than previous theories with an indication that policy suggestions are different in each case.

Many empirical studies have been done to test these trade theories and the final results have been mixed. Some of the hypotheses obtained from different trade theories have validated results for some countries and invalidated results for others. Despite their differing results, these trade theories each have helped toward formulating the microfoundation for a famous workhorse model of trade—the gravity model. But again the quantification of trade barriers and an appropriate estimation method for the gravity model still demands extra care and concentration.

Appendix

We have the utility function:

$$\left[\sum_{i=1}^{N} c_i^{\rho}\right]^{(1/\rho)}$$

This utility should be maximized subject to the income constraint:

$$I = \sum_{i=1}^{N} p_i c_i$$

Now, we have Langragian ($\mathcal{L}$) with multiplier (λ):

$$\mathcal{L} = \left[\sum_{i=1}^{N} c_i^{\rho}\right]^{(1/\rho)} + \lambda\left[I - \sum_{i=1}^{N} p_i c_i\right]$$

Differentiating $\mathcal{L}$ with respect to c_j and equating it to zero gives us

$$\left[\sum_{i=1}^{N} c_i^{r}\right]^{(1/r)-1} c_j^{r-1} = \lambda p_j \qquad \text{for } j = 1, 2, \ldots, N$$

Take the ratio of these first-order conditions with respect to variety 1, and define $\varepsilon = 1/(1-\rho)$ as discussed in the main text. Then:

$$\frac{\left[\sum_{i=1}^{N} c_i^{\rho}\right]^{(1/\rho)-1} c_j^{\rho-1}}{\left[\sum_{i=1}^{N} c_i^{\rho}\right]^{(1/\rho)-1} c_1^{\rho-1}} = \frac{\lambda p_j}{\lambda p_1}$$

$$\frac{c_j^{\rho-1}}{c_1^{\rho-1}} = \frac{p_j}{p_1}$$

$$c_j^{\rho-1} = p_j (p_1)^{-1} c_1^{1-\rho}$$

$$c_j = p_j^{(\rho-1)} (p_1)^{-1(\rho-1)} c_1^{\frac{\rho-1}{(\rho-1)}}$$

$$c_j = p_j^{-(1-\rho)} (p_1)^{(1-\rho)} c_1^{1} \quad or \quad c_j = p_j^{-\varepsilon} p_1^{\varepsilon} c_1$$

Substituting these relations in the budget equation gives:

$$I = \sum_{i=1}^{N} p_j c_j \Rightarrow I = \sum_{i=1}^{N} p_j p_j^{-\varepsilon} p_1^{\varepsilon} c_1 \Rightarrow I = p_1^{\varepsilon} c_1 \sum_{i=1}^{N} p_j^{1-\varepsilon}$$

$$I = p_1^{\varepsilon} c_1 P^{1-\varepsilon} \quad or \quad c_1 = I p_1^{-\varepsilon} P^{\varepsilon-1}$$

$$P \equiv \left[\sum_{i=1}^{N} p_j^{1-\varepsilon}\right]^{\frac{1}{(1-\varepsilon)}}$$

In the above equation, c_1 represents the demand for variety 1. Similarly, we can derive the demand for other varieties. To answer the question of why we defined a P type of price index in the above equation, we need to substitute the derived demand for all the varieties in the utility function along with: $\varepsilon = 1/(1-\rho) \;\Rightarrow\; 1-\varepsilon = -\varepsilon\rho \;\Rightarrow\; \frac{1-\varepsilon}{\varepsilon} - = \rho \;\Rightarrow\; \frac{1}{\rho} = -\frac{\varepsilon}{1-\varepsilon}$

$$U = \left(\sum_{i=1}^{N} c_i^{\rho}\right)^{1/\rho} = \left(\sum_{i=1}^{N} \left(Ip_i{}^{-\varepsilon} P^{\varepsilon-1}\right)^{\rho}\right)^{1/\rho}$$

$$= IP^{\varepsilon-1}\left(\sum_{i=1}^{N} p_i{}^{-\varepsilon\rho}\right)^{1/\rho} = IP^{\varepsilon-1}\left(\sum_{i=1}^{N} p_i{}^{1-\varepsilon}\right)^{-\frac{\varepsilon}{1-\varepsilon}}$$

Using the price index again[10];

$$U = IP^{\varepsilon-1}\left(P^{1-\varepsilon}\right)^{-\frac{\varepsilon}{1-\varepsilon}} = IP^{\varepsilon-1}P^{-\varepsilon} = IP^{-1}$$

$$U = \frac{I}{P}$$

Notes

1. The HO theorem states that a country will produce and export that commodity that intensively uses the relatively abundant factor.
2. According to the Stolper–Samuelson theorem, an increase in the relative price of one of the two goods will increase the real return to the factor that is used intensively for the production of the good that experiences a price increase.
3. The Rybczynski theorem states that keeping the prices of goods constant, an increase in the endowment of one factor of production will increase the production of that commodity proportionately more than the one that uses the factor intensively.
4. According to the factor price equalization theorem, under certain conditions the free trade of commodities will result in complete international equalization of the prices of the factors of production.
5. See the Appendix.
6. https://www.wto.org/english/res_e/booksp_e/anrep_e/world_trade_report08_e.pdf
7. γ firm heterogeneity of firms in a particular sector, where high γ means firms are more homogeneous (less heterogeneous) and vice versa.
8. Shepherd, B. (2013). "The Gravity Model of International Trade: A User Guide." ARTNeT. New York: United Nations Publication. Available

at: http://www.unescap.org/sites/default/files/full-report-gravity-model-2013.pdf
9. See Eq. (2.13) of Anderson and Wincoop (2003).
10. For Details, refer to the Dixit Stiglitz (1977) model.

References

Amiti, M., & Davis, D. R. (2011). Trade, firms, and wages: Theory and evidence. *Review of Economic Studies, 79*, 1–36. [Accepted in 2011].

Anderson, J. E. (1979). A theoretical foundation for the gravity equation. *The American Economic Review, 69*(1), 106–116.

Anderson, E. J., & Wincoop, V. E. (2003). Gravity with gravitas: A solution to the border puzzle. *The American Economic Review, 93*, 170–192.

Anderson, J. E. (2010). *The gravity model, National Bureau of Economic Research* (Working paper no. 16576). Cambridge, MA.

Antras, P., & Helpman, E. (2004). Global sourcing. *Journal of Political Economy, 112*(3), 552–580.

Antras, P., & Helpman, E. (2007). *Contractual frictions and global sourcing*. CEPR discussion paper no. 6033. London: CEPR.

Arkolakis, C., & Muendler, M. A. (2010/2011). *The extensive margin of exporting products*. NBER working paper no. 16641. Cambridge, MA: National Bureau of Economic Research.

Arkolakis, C., & Muendler, M. A. (2011). *The extensive margin of exporting products: The continuum case* (Working paper). Retrieved from http://www.econ.yale.edu/~ka265/research/MultiProduct/ArkolakisMuendler-cont.pdf

Baier, S., & Bergstrand, J. (2001). The growth of world trade: Tariffs, transport costs, and income similarity. *Journal of International Economics, 53*(1), 1–27.

Balassa, B. (1966). Tariff reductions and trade in manufacturers among the industrial countries. *The American Economic Review, 56*(3), 466–473.

Baldwin, R., & Taglioni, D. (2011). *Gravity for dummies and dummies for gravity equations*. National Bureau of Economic Research working paper series (No. 12516). NBER.

Bernard, A. B., Eaton, J., Jensen, J. B., & Kortum, S. (2003). Plants and productivity in international trade. *The American Economic Review, 93*, 1268–1290.

Bernard, A. B., Redding, S. J., & Schott, P. K. (2007). Comparative advantage and heterogeneous firms. *Review of Economic Studies, 74*(1), 31–66.

Bernard, A. B., Redding, S. J., & Schott, P. K. (2011). Multiproduct firms and trade liberalization. *The Quarterly Journal of Economics, 126*(3), 1271–1318.

Bowen, H. P., Leamer, E. E., & Sveikauskas, L. (1987). Multi-country, multi-factor tests of the factor abundance theory. *The American Economic Review, 77*(5), 791–809.

Carrere, C. (2006). Revisiting the effects of regional trade agreements on trade flows with proper specification of the gravity model. *European Economic Review, 50*(2), 223–247.

Chaney, T. (2008). Distorted gravity: The intensive and extensive margins of international trade. *The American Economic Review, 98*(4), 1707–1721.

Davis, D. R., & Weinstein, D. E. (2001). An account of global factor trade. *The American Economic Review, 91*(5), 1423–1453.

Deardorff, A. V. (1979). Weak links in the chain of comparative advantage. *Journal of International Economics, 9*, 197–209.

Deardorff, A. V. (1984). Testing trade theories and predicting trade flows. In R. W. Jones & P. B. Kenen (Eds.), *Handbook of international economics* (Vol. I). Amsterdam: North.

Deardorff, A. V. (1985). Comparative advantage and international trade and investment in services. In R. M. Stern (Ed.), *Trade and investment in services: Canada/US perspectives.* Toronto: Ontario Economic Council.

Deardorff, A. V. (2005). *Gains from trade and fragmentation.* Research seminar in international economics discussion paper no. 543. Ann Arbor: University of Michigan.

Doing Business Report. (2015). *Going beyond efficiency* (12th ed.), provided by World Bank Group. http://www.doingbusiness.org/reports/global-reports/doing-business-2015

Duval, Y., & Utoktham, C. (2011). Intraregional trade costs in Asia: A primer. *Asia-Pacific Development Journal, 18*(2), 1–23.

Eaton, J., & Kortum, S. (2002). Technology, geography, and trade. *Econometrica, 70*(5), 1741–1779.

Eckel, C., & Neary, J. P. (2010). Multi-product firms and flexible manufacturing in the global economy. *The Review of Economic Studies., 77*(1), 188–217.

Helpman, E., & Krugman, P. (1985). *Market structure and foreign trade: Increasing returns, imperfect competition and the international economy.* Cambridge: MIT Press.

Helpman, E., Melitz, M. J., & Yeaple, S. R. (2004). Exports versus FDI with heterogeneous firms. *The American Economic Review, 94*(1), 300–316.

Helpman, E., Itskhoki, O., & Redding, S. (2011). *Trade and labor market outcomes.* NBER working paper no. 16662, National Bureau of Economic Research.

Kee, H. L., Nicita, A., & Olarreaga, M. (2009). Estimating trade restrictiveness indices. *The Economic Journal., 119*, 172–199.

Krugman, P. (1979). Increasing returns, monopolistic competition, and international trade. *Journal of International Economics, 9*(4), 469–479.

Krugman, P. (1980). Scale economies, product differentiation, and the pattern of trade. *The American Economic Review, 70*(5), 950–959.

Krugman, P., & Venables, T. (1996). Integration, specialization, and adjustment. *European Economic Review, 40*, 959–968.

Leamer, E. E. (1980). The Leontief paradox, reconsidered. *The Journal of Political Economy, 88*(3), 495–503.

Leamer, E. E., & Levinsohn, J. (1995). International trade theory: The evidence. In G. M. Grossman & K. Rogoff (Eds.), *Handbook of international economics* (pp. 1339–1396). Amsterdam: Elsevier Science.

Leontief, W. W. (1953). Domestic production and foreign trade: The American capital position re-examined. *Proceedings of the American Philosophical Society, 97* (4), 332–349. Reprinted in Richard, C., & Harry, G. J. (Eds.) (1968). *Readings in international economics.* Homewood: Irwin.

Linnemann, H. (1966). *An econometric study of international trade flows.* Amsterdam: North Holland.

Mayer, T., Melitz, M. J., & Ottaviano, G. I. P. (2014). Market size, competition, and the product mix of exporters. *The American Economic Review, 104*(2), 495–536.

McCallum, J. (1995). National borders matter: Canada-U.S. regional trade patterns. *The American Economic Review, 85*(3), 615–623.

Melitz, M. J. (2003). The impact of trade on intra-industry reallocations and aggregate industry productivity. *Econometrica, 71*(6), 1695–1725.

Melitz, M. J., & Ottaviano, G. I. (2008). Market size, trade, and productivity. *Review of Economic Studies, 75*, 295–316.

Moise, E., & Bris, L. F. (2013). *Trade costs-what have we learned?* OECD trade policy paper no. 150. Retrieved from http://www.oecd-ilibrary.org/trade/trade-costs_5k47x2hjfn48-en

Novy, D. (2008). *Gravity redux: Measuring international trade costs with panel data*, University of Warwick. Retrieved from http://economics.uwo.ca/conference/thechangingglobal_apr08/novy.pdf

Obstfeld, M., & Rogoff, K. (2001). The six major puzzles in international macroeconomics: Is there a common cause? In B. S. Bernanke & K. Rogoff (Eds.), *NBER macroeconomics annual 2000* (Vol. 15, pp. 339–412). Cambridge, MA: MIT Press.

Pöyhönen, P. (1963). A tentative model for the volume of trade between countries. *Weltwirtschaftliches Archiv, 90*(1), 93–100.

Pulliainen, K. (1963). A world trade study: An econometric model of the pattern of the commodity flows of international trade in 1948-60. *Ekonomiska Samfundets Tidskrift, 16*, 78–91.

Ricardo, D. (1817). *On the principles of political economy and taxation.* London: John Murray.

Shepherd, B. (2013). *The gravity model of international trade: A user guide.* ARTNeT Books and Research Reports.

Tinbergen, J. (1962). *Shaping the world economy: Suggestions for an international economic policy.* Books (Jan Tinbergen). New York: Twentieth Century Fund. Retrieved from http://hdl.handle.net/1765/16826

Vanek, J. (1968). The factor proportions theory: The N – Factor case. *Kyklos, 21*(4), 749–756.

World Trade Report. (2008). *Trade in globalising world.* Geneva: WTO.

Zaki, C. (2010). *Does trade facilitation matters in bilateral trade?* GTAP resources no. 4537.

CHAPTER 3

Revisiting Strategic Trade Theory

Indrani Roy Chowdhury

3.1 Introduction to Strategic Trade Theory

Traditional theories of international trade explain trade in terms of the differences in endowments of factors such as resources, technology, or even tastes. This orthodoxy has been challenged from the 1970s onward by a group of trade theorists who have tried to explain the pattern of specialization between countries, the effects of protectionism, and so on, in terms of increasing returns and imperfect competition. This departure from tradition has drawn on various concepts from industrial organization theory, in particular the concept of imperfectly competitive markets. This deviation from the standard assumption of perfect competition in the trade models naturally leads one towards a theory of strategic trade. This approach has succeeded in providing explanations for the high volume of intraindustry trade, the existence of multinational corporations, and the emergence of an international technology gap. Furthermore, the literature in this area has deepened our understanding of the issues involved in trade policy analysis.[1]

What is strategic trade theory? Let us present the argument in a stylized manner so as to highlight the central issue. Suppose there are only two trade partners, represented by one domestic firm and one foreign firm, competing

I.R. Chowdhury (✉)
Centre for the Study of Regional Development (CSRD), Jawaharlal Nehru University (JNU), New Delhi, India

S.K. Mathur et al. (eds.), *Theorizing International Trade*,
https://doi.org/10.1007/978-981-10-1759-9_3

in the world market. Since there are only two firms, they are unlikely to act as price takers under perfect competition. Strategic interaction among the trade partners arises naturally in such a scenario with the profits of each of the firm being contingent on the actions of other rival firm. Such interdependence may arise through price, output, investments, R&Ds, and so on. This generates a strategic game between the two firms, in particular a duopolistic one.

The problem is to predict how the two firms will behave optimally in such a situation. Consider a situation where the two firms are engaged in quantity competition, and one of the firms becomes cost efficient and is thus able to reduce its marginal cost. Thus, given the output of a rival firm, it is optimal for the incumbent firm to expand. The new Cournot equilibrium indicates a higher market share and profit for the cost-efficient firm and a lower market share and profit for the rival foreign firm. Therefore, the cost-efficient firm not only directly gains due to the reduction in costs, but also because the cost reduction indirectly improves its strategic position in the market, which thereby induces the rival to contract. The efficient firm therefore benefits more than the amount of the costs savings.

If we extend this idea to the intraindustry trade framework, where firms indulge in trade in a duopolistic market structure with homogenous or differentiated products, some critical insights can be drawn. Note that an export or a production subsidy, which are some policy instruments vested with the government, have the same effect as a cost reduction for the domestic firm. Now the question is, while the policy clearly benefits the domestic firm, does it serve the national interest? There are two effects of a subsidy. One effect is the direct costs saving, which is just a transfer. In addition, because of the subsidized costs, it allows the domestic firm to expand, and hence the foreign rival's best response is to contract.

Formally, given that output levels are strategic substitutes, the best response function of the domestic firm will shift out, inducing an increase in the domestic firm's market share and hence profit by an additional amount. This is the 'strategic effect' of subsidy. It implies that the profit of the domestic firm rises by more than the amount of subsidy. Thus, the benefit of the firm exceeds the cost of the taxpayers (which is used to finance the cost reduction subsidy). This idea can be traced, among others, to Brander and Spencer (1983). The basic point is quite general and helps to focus on the strategic role of government policies in diverting profits from foreign to domestic firms. Helpman concludes his theoretical survey with the statement that "international theory has taken the advantage of a new framework that has brought it closer to reality than before."

Traditional trade theory suggests that trade protection measures such as tariff or import quotas would increase the price of a good for both domestic producers and consumers and reduce imports, which is welfare-reducing except in some well understood cases. In contrast, the new trade theory shows that government protection measures may boost the welfare of the country in relation to free trade in the presence of a small number of firms. If, however, all countries try to protect their domestic industries, then there would be losses due to a fragmented world market, arising not only from the failure to specialize (according to comparative advantage), but also from the inefficient scale of production. But an individual firm can conceivably increase the scale of production in a protected industry sufficiently to reap a net benefit, possibly even to lower prices to domestic consumers. Thus, while traditional theory advocates trade protection only as a second-best measure to correct for market failure, the new trade theory identifies other possible gains from trade protection.

Trade policy is traditionally more concerned with the protection of domestic import—competing industries, rather than export promotion. Tariffs are imposed not as strategic policy, but simply as a way of raising revenue. There is, however, a very old argument for protection that does have a strategic interpretation, that is, the infant industry argument. Temporary protection of an industry that is too inefficient to compete with foreign rivals, might be justified on the grounds that this might allow the industry to become efficient enough to compete with foreign firms. One weakness of this argument is that it must rely on either the idea that firms in an industry generate positive externalities among themselves, or the claim is that the firms are unable to make efficient long-term investment through the capital markets.

The principal obstacle to the formal modelling of increasing returns to scale in the 1970s was the problem of market structure. The fact that increasing returns and perfect competition are incompatible, and therefore it was usual for the trade theorists to stick to the assumption of perfect competition, as shown by the equality $p = MC$, cannot be extended in a framework of increasing returns with marginal costs pricing (because it will lead to losses).

The rest of this chapter is organized as follows. In the next section we discuss some relevant literature. In Sect. 3.3 we seek to extend Krugman's (1984) seminal work on "import protection as export promotion." While we discuss the model in Sect. 3.4, the analysis for the three different cases of free-entry of firms is taken up in Sect. 3.5. Finally, Sect. 3.6 concludes the discussion.

3.2 Brief Literature Survey on Strategic Trade

Strategic trade theory can be broadly classified into three categories as: (i) the Marshallian external economy approach, (ii) the Chamberlinian large-group analysis of competition, and (iii) the oligopolistic approach.

3.2.1 Marshallian External Economy Approach

There is a small body of literature that allows for increasing returns of scale, but assumes that it is wholly external to the firms, so that costs fall only with an increase in the size of the industry, but not with the size of the firms. Under this framework the assumption of perfect competition is naturally preserved. However, such external economies are hard to model both theoretically, as well as empirically. Further, such a framework cannot address issues related to market structure. Explicit general equilibrium analysis of trade in the presence of external economies began with Mattews and was continued in a number of papers, including Kemp and Negeshi (1970), Melvin (1969), Chacoliades (1978), and Panagariya (1981).

However, most of the literature about this approach fails to generate useful insights. The notable contributions in this category are by Ethier. He demonstrated that the analysis of trade in the presence of Marshallian external economies is greatly clarified if we work from allocation of resources to production and trade, and not the other way around. Marshallian increasing returns and comparative advantage can be synthesized in a tractable manner through factor prices and factor content, rather than through commodity trade. To integrate Marshallian increasing returns with comparative advantage, we assume that the trading world reproduces the aggregate outcomes of a hypothetical perfectively integrated economy. Using this framework we find that both factor proportions and scale economies are sources of gains from trade. In particular, one can show that:

1. Factor proportion theory continues to hold, although there is indeterminacy in the precise pattern of trade. Consequently, a country will

be the net exporter of services of factors with which it is abundantly endowed.
2. There will be geographical concentration of each industry subject to the country-specific increasing returns. This concentration will be the compelling force for trade even in a situation of equal factor endowments in the two countries.
3. Gains from trade arises because the pretrade autarkic prices are different.
4. Additional gains arise if there are increasing returns for the traded industries (irrespective of their location).

3.2.2 Chamberlinian Approach

Chamberlin (1933) argued that in some industries firms practice product differentiation and therefore acquire some monopoly power. Thus, they face downward-sloping demand curves. However, along with the presence of economies of scale, free entry implies that firms only earn normal profits. The revival of Chamberlin's "large group" analysis in the industrial organization literature in the 1970s has motivated trade theorists to discard the assumption of perfect competition and formalize product differentiation and monopolistic competition (Dixit and Stiglitz 1977). Thus, it has become possible to build trade models involving scale of scale and imperfect competition.

In this framework, it is not the difference between the countries but economies of scale that induces trade in similar products, that is, intraindustry trade. The gains from trade (Dixit and Stiglitz 1977) comes from the increase in the number of available varieties, as well as from the scale of production of each variety. The scale effect, however, depends on the elasticity of demand of individual varieties. Under the Dixit and Stiglitz (1977) approach, this elasticity is assumed to be constant, thus leading to greater varieties through trade but not greater scale.

This framework has been widely used in the international trade. Krugman (1979, 1980, 1981), for example, proves that the international exchange of goods can, in addition to improving allocation of resources, bring about greater variety. Under the Lancaster (1979, 1980) approach, trade is likely to lead to more elastic demand, thus leading to greater diversity, as well as to lower average costs. Helpman and Krugman (1985a, b) argue that both scale and diversity will move monotonically with gross industry output. Thus, trade is beneficial if the world output is larger than what the national output would have been in the absence of trade. So, gains from scale will be translated into gains from trade. Therefore, unlike Heckscher Ohlin, here trade is motivated mainly by economies of scale, and we may expect that even the scarce factors gain.

Thus, gains for all factors are more likely the more similar is the country's endowment to that of the world as a whole (Krugman 1984). Several authors such as Kemp and Negishi (1970), Eaton and Panagariya (1979), and Markusen and Melvin (1981) have shown that gains from trade can be guaranteed if the output of all goods produced under the IRS is greater under free trade than under an autarky.

An alternative approach to product differentiation was developed by Lancaster (1979). He assumed that each product represents a bundle of characteristics, and consumers have preferences over these attributes. This again leads to a demand for varieties at the aggregate level. This extended framework has been further developed by Lancaster (1980) and Helpman (1981). Helpman generalizes the Heckscher and Ohlin model by introducing product differentiation and monopolistic competition, and demonstrates that his findings are capable of explaining North–South trade. Here intraindustry trade takes place because each country produces a unique variety of differentiated products.

In contrast to Lancaster's model, Avner and Sutton (1984) extended their analysis to vertical product differentiation where consumers of different income levels choose different varieties. In this model, the interaction of taste and technology decides the number of firms in the equilibrium, independent of market structure. Trade drives away the low-quality producers from the market and enhances consumers' welfare in the long run.

Ethier suggested that international trade under increasing returns to scale is more likely to be important in intermediate goods, than in final goods, and the gains from trade comes from the increasing specialization of their production process. Ethier also established results on the relationship between interindustry and intraindustry trade, as well as on the distributional implications of trade that reinforce the findings of the earlier works by Helpman, Dixit, Norman, Lancaster, and Krugman.

If there is factor mobility, there is an incentive for movement in large economies, a process that reinforces the size advantage of these economies (Helpman and Razin 1984; Krugman and Helpman 1985). If transport costs are important but not prohibitive, then Krugman (1980) and Venables (1985) demonstrated that, other things being equal, countries will tend to be net exporters of goods for which they have a large domestic market.

The Chamberlinian framework has been useful in analyzing the role of trade in technology and the role of multinational firms—issues which cannot be analyzed under perfect competition. Feenstra and Judd (1982) showed that fixed costs plays a significant role in trade in technology. Dixit (1984) raises the old debate on North–South trade and shows that the failure of the underdeveloped South is often due to the monopoly power of the North. Dixit also addresses the issues of technological progress and tariffs. On the empirical side, Grubel and Lloyd (1975) examine the significant role of intraindustry trade between developed countries with similar factor endowments and technological know-how. Stewart focuses on the implications of the new trade theories for the South.

3.2.3 *Oligopolistic Approach*

This approach takes place in an imperfectly competitive world where issues such as interactions and interdependence among the firms take center stage. This approach has yielded some important findings that were not captured in the earlier two approaches. The first finding is the role of trade in reducing monopoly power and increasing competition. The second finding is the possibility that market segmentation and price discrimination can lead to seemingly pointless intraindustry trade. Suppose that there is some industry in the two countries such that few firms compete over quantity. Also assume that under autarky the prices of the goods are the same in both countries. When trade is opened up, each firm will become part of the larger, more competitive market. It will find itself facing a higher elasticity of demand, leading to an expansion of output. Thus, industry output will expand and prices will fall. Moreover, if countries are symmetric, welfare will rise due to the reduction of monopoly distortion.

The possibility of gains from trade in this framework was earlier discussed by Caves (1974) and more recently by Dixit and Norman (1980). They showed that the effect of opening trade in a Cournot market is that it leads to a world industry that has fewer larger firms, but where competition is nonetheless increased. Thus, the opening of trade not only leads to a reduction in monopoly distortion, but also to an increase in productive efficiency. Moreover, Cournot quantity competition can led to a third possible explanation of trade.

Brander (1981) shows that trade may arise purely because imperfectly competitive firms have an incentive to gain incremental sales by dumping in each other's home markets. Consider an industry consisting of two firms, each in a different country, engaged in Cournot competition through trade. In the autarkic situation, each of the firms was a monopolist in their respective country. As trade opens up, each firm has an incentive to sell a little bit in the other's home market, as long as the price exceeds the marginal costs.

Brander and Krugman (1983) extended the original Brander model by establishing that trade equilibrium with cross-hauling exists for arbitrary forms of market demand and in the presence of transport costs. This approach, however, relies on the assumption that the market is segmented so that the firms make independent decisions regarding their supplies in geographically separated markets.

Ben-zvi and Helpman (1992) and Venables (1990a, b) examined a model with positive transport costs, but by dropping the assumption of a segmented market they found that cross-hauling of identical goods never takes place.

Markusen (1981) treats the world as a single integrated market where producers choose an aggregate output level and then arbitraging determine the cross-country allocation of sales. In this model, there are gains from trade even though no trade actually takes place in equilibrium. Competition between producers in the imperfectly competitive sectors of each economy leads to an expansion of sectoral output relative to that under autarky.

Itoh and Ono (1982), Harris (1984), and Krishna (1992) have studied quantitative restrictions, such as import quotas and voluntary export restraints, in the context of oligopolistic trade models. While the first two authors have assumed a domestic firm as a Stackelberg leader, Krishna (1992) assumes that both the domestic and foreign firms compete with prices simultaneously. Under an assumption of efficient rationing, she then studies the mixed strategy equilibrium of this game.

Quantitative restrictions (QR) under Stackelberg and Nash settings have different implications, compared to tariffs on the outcome of oligopolistic competition—as Bhagwati (1965) first noted for the case of a domestic monopolist facing a competitive foreign fringe. QRs limit the response of foreign rivals to noncompetitive actions by the local producers. Krishna and Itoh (1988) show that it is possible that when trade is restricted by domestic content requirements, policy intervention may cause the foreign firm to react more aggressively to price increases by the home firm, and so the equilibrium may support less collusion and yield lower profits for both firms than under free trade.

There has been substantial work carried out on the normative implications of trade policy in an oligopolistic market structure. Katrak and Svedberg argue that tariffs can be used to extract rents from foreign monopolists. Brander and Spencer (1981) extend the result to the case of general demand functions. Under Cournot duopoly, a domestic producer will always benefit from tariff protection, and a small tariff levied against a good supplied by foreign monopolists improves domestic welfare, provided the marginal revenue curve is steeper than the demand curve in the equilibrium.

However, both Corden (1974) and Brander and Spencer (1981) argue that a subsidy, rather than a tariff, may be the optimum policy. They also explain why tariff liberalization has tended to be multilateral and how tariffs can be used to extract rents, when a foreign monopolist facing potential competition from domestic firms charges an entry-deterring price. They also argue that a positive tariff may be required to maximize global welfare, but such a tariff would be generally lower than a noncooperatively selected tariff.

Brander and Spencer (1985) consider a simple framework involving two firms (domestic and foreign) engaged in Cournot competition in a segmented third world market. They show that if the home government is the only one actively using policy, then an export subsidy raises home welfare whenever the reaction functions are strategic substitutes. The subsidy lends credibility to aggressive output expansion by the home firm, and so foreign firms responds by surrendering market share and profits. Tariffs can play a similar strategic role when the firms behave as quantity competitors in the home market.

Spencer and Brander (1983) examine a two-stage competition, where R&D subsidies serve to shift profits from foreign to domestic firms. Later works have refined the Brander and Spencer argument for export subsidies and import tariffs in support of domestic competitors. Dixit (1984) and Eaton and Grossman (1986) demonstrate that export subsidy, when competition takes place in a third world country market, weakens as the number of domestic participants increases in the industry. Hence the optimal subsidy becomes zero at some critical number of domestic firms in the industry, and the orthodox terms of the trade argument lead to an optimal export tax. Eaton and Grossman (1986) also try to link the various market structures under oligopolistic competition and the nature of optimal trade policy.

Related literature examines the role of policy in regulating entry and exit by firms. Dixit and Kyle (1985) show that policies can be used strategically to deter or promote entry. Consider an industry in which a foreign firm has already borne the sunk costs of entry. Suppose a domestic firm contemplates entry but cannot cover its fixed costs in the case of duopolistic competition with the foreign incumbent. As long as the domestic firm earns positive profits as monopolists and its marginal costs are not too much higher than its foreign counterpart, then the home country will benefit from an import prohibition. This protectionist policy will generate a welfare effect as seen from the fact that consumer surplus is not affected by the switch from one monopolist to another, but the producer's surplus increases from zero is the policy induces entry by a domestic.

Horstmann and Markusen (1986) and Venables (1985) explore a case in which free entry drives the profit of the marginal entrants to zero in an oligopolistic framework. Horstmann and Markusen assume a framework where the domestic and foreign firms are engaged in quantity competition, allowing the goods to command the same price in the world market. The domestic firm will derive an advantage in the global competition through export subsidies and import tariffs. Any profit that are shifted strategically to the domestic firms are dissipated because of the costs of en-try, and national welfare falls. Venables (1985) finds a contrasting result in the case where national markets are segmented and inter market transport costs are positive, showing that import tariffs are welfare enhancing. Domestic consumers benefit from the expansion in the number of foreign firms because transport costs are reduced. These results, along with others, are synthesized in Markusen and Venables (1988).

This review establishes that certain types of trade interventions are beneficial in some circumstances, but not in others. Most of the literature cited is theoretical, however, since empirical work is lagging behind. Recent work uses calibrated equilibrium to study some of these questions. The procedures involve trying on a particular model of industry by specifying the mode of conduct, the extent of market integration, the possibilities of entry and exit, and so on. The researchers then insert into the model the data and parameters that are readily available. Finally, unavailable data and parameters are generated by the researchers, so that the equilibrium solution of the model matches the observed outcome for some base year.

Turning to specific studies, in their work on the semiconductor market, Baldwin and Krugman (1988) found that there is a great scope for government policy to alter the structure of production, but less scope to generate national welfare gains. Dixit (1989) similarly concludes that welfare gains from strategic trade policy are modest in the automobile industry, except when the social values of the government revenue generated by tariffs is large, or when much of the payment to automobile workers is viewed as rent, rather than as opportunity costs. Baldwin and Krugman (1988) find that strategic trade subsidies to Airbus in support of their wide-bodied jet aircraft may have raised aggregate European welfare, although the gains are more from consumers' surplus resulting from earlier product introduction, rather than from shifting of excess profit. Baldwin and Flam's (1989) analysis of the world market of 30–40-seat commuter aircraft reveals that strategic trade intervention will yield a potential benefit. In contrast, Smith and Venables (1991) find substantial gains to Europe from further liberalization of its external trade in a variety of oligopolistic industries, particularly in the car market.

3.3 Import Protection as Export Promotion

One of the most important insights to come out of the recent literature on international trade is that of import protection as export promotion. Krugman (1984) demonstrates that in the presence of economies of scale, a model with oligopolistic and segmented markets can be used to formalize the intuitive notion. He considers several different scenarios with static and dynamic economies of scale (e.g., cost reduction based on R&D investment, learning by doing, etc.) and shows that the argument goes through for all these scenarios. He shows that with tariffs the local producer will expand its output for the home market. With increasing returns, this would lower the local firm's marginal costs of production, so that the firm would become an effective competitor in the foreign market as well, and hence exports would *increase*.

The basic argument is quite intuitive. Suppose that there is import protection. The effect is to make the home market more profitable. Thus, domestic production will expand. If there are economies of scale (either static or dynamic), then marginal costs will decline, so that firms in country 1 become more competitive in the foreign market. Hence exports will increase. With static economies of scale the formalization, however, appears to require, as Krugman (1984) himself points out, a heterodox assumption in the form of decreasing marginal costs. Moreover, Krugman (1984) does not provide any welfare analysis.

The objective of the present chapter is thus twofold. First, we want to extend the analysis by suggesting an alternative foundation for the import protection argument that does not require marginal costs to be decreasing.

In fact, we use a model with constant marginal costs of production. Secondly, we use our framework to derive some interesting welfare implications.

We consider a model with two countries, country 1 and country 2. The markets are segregated and trade takes the form of reciprocal dumping. For simplicity, we assume that the demand functions in the two countries are identical and that the demand and the cost functions are linear in the level of output. There is free entry in the product market. We consider three versions of the model in this discussion, first when there is free entry in country 1 alone, second when there is free entry in country 2 alone, and third when there is free entry in both countries.

We show that in all three cases import protection leads to export pro motion. This demonstrates that even in the absence of dynamic scale economies, the assumption that marginal costs are decreasing is not required to formalize the idea that import protection leads to export promotion.

The intuitions are somewhat different in the three cases. The effect of import protection by, say, country 1 is to make production in country 1 more profitable. With free entry in country 1 alone, this attracts a larger number of firms into the country 1 market, making country 1 as a whole more competitive. While this leads to a fall in exports by individual firms, aggregate exports increase as the increase in the number of firms is more than enough to make up for the decline in individual exports. With free entry in both countries, there is the additional effect that the number of firms in country 2 declines. In this case the relative increase in the number of firms in country 1 is even larger.

Notice that in the above two versions of our model it is country 1 that becomes more competitive as a whole, leading to increased exports. The export levels of individual firms are, in fact, adversely affected. This is in contrast to the result in Krugman (1984) where it was individual firms that became more competitive.

If there is free entry in country 2 alone, then with an increase in import protection the number of firms in country 2 decreases. In this case the export level of each firm in country 1increases, and hence so do the aggregate exports.

Finally, turning to the welfare analysis we find that the results are model specific. If there is free entry in country 1 alone, then import protection by country 1 reduces the welfare level in country 1, whereas if there is free entry in both countries, then import protection turns out to be welfare improving.

Given the free entry assumption, in both these cases it is sufficient to focus on consumers' surplus. There are two effects in operation here. Import protection leads to a decline in imports from country 2. This tends to reduce consumption in country 1. On the other hand, production in country 1 will increase. This will tend to increase consumption, and hence welfare. With free entry in country 1 alone, the first effect dominates, while with free entry in both countries the second effect dominates. In the case when there is free entry in country 2 alone, there is the additional effect that with an increase in import protection, aggregate profits in country 1 will go up. Hence, welfare may either increase or decrease.

We now briefly relate our basic contention with the existing literature. The framework is a simplified version of the work by Roy Chowdhury and Ray Chaudhuri (2003). The basic model adopted in this book is very similar to those developed by Brander (1981), Brander and Krugman (1983), Brander and Spencer (1983), and Venables (1985), all of whom consider trade models with Cournot competition in identical commodities. While Brander (1981) and Brander and Spencer (1983) all consider models where the number of firms is given exogenously given, Dixit and Norman (1980) and Brander and Krugman (1983) consider models where the number of firms is determined endogenously.

Our model is closest to Venables (1985) who considers a model of Cournot competition with free entry in both countries. In contrast, we consider three different cases, with free entry in country 1 alone, with free entry in country 2 alone, and with free entry in both countries. Moreover, Venables (1985) does not address the central concern of this discussion, that is, whether import protection leads to export promotion. The focus in Venables (1985) is on the welfare effect of various parameter changes such as technical progress, export subsidy, and so on. Of course, he also studies the welfare implications of an increase in import protection. One important contribution of our paper is to extend the analysis in Venables (1985) by examining the sensitivity of the welfare results to the nature of product market competition.

3.4 The Basic Model

There are two countries, country 1 and country 2 with n and n^* firms, respectively, all producing a single homogeneous product that they sell in both the countries. The inverse demand functions in the two countries are identical and linear. Let y_i and x_i denote the domestic sale and export of the

ith firm in country 1, an let y_j and x_j denote the domestic sale and export of the jth firm in country 2. The demand function in country 1 is given by

$$p^1 = a - b\left(\sum_{i=1}^{n} y_i + \sum_{j=1}^{n^*} x_j\right). \tag{3.1}$$

Similarly, the demand function in country 2 is given by

$$p^2 = a - b\left(\sum_{j=1}^{n^*} y_j + \sum_{i=1}^{n} x_i\right). \tag{3.2}$$

The cost function of all firms has two components—production costs and transport costs (in the case of exports). We assume that the production costs of all firms are identical and linear in the level of output, that is, marginal costs are constant. Furthermore, there is a fixed cost as well, so that the production cost displays increasing returns to scale. Thus, the production cost of the ith firm in country 1 is given by

$$C_i(q_i) = \begin{cases} F + cq_i, & \text{if } q_i > 0, \\ 0, & \text{otherwise,} \end{cases} \tag{3.3}$$

where $q_i = y_i + x_i$. We assume that for each unit of export, firms in country 1 bear a transport cost of t per unit. Thus, the total cost of the ith firm producing q_i and exporting x_i is given by $C_i(y_i + x_i) + tx_i$. Similarly, the production cost of the jth firm in country 2 is given by

$$C_j(q_j) = \begin{cases} F + cq_j, & \text{if } q_j > 0, \\ 0, & \text{otherwise,} \end{cases} \tag{3.4}$$

where $q_j = x_j + y_j$. Moreover, for each unit of export, a firm in country 2 bears a transport cost of t^* per unit. Thus, the total cost of the jth firm in country 2 producing q_j and exporting x_j is given by $C_j(x_j + y_j) + t^*x_j$.

We solve for the Cournot equilibrium of this model. Let π_i and π_j denote, respectively, the profit function of the ith firm in country 1 and the jth firm in country 2. Then

$$\pi_i = \left(a - b\left(\sum_{i=1}^{n} y_i + \sum_{j=1}^{n^*} x_j\right)\right) y_i + \left(a - b\left(\sum_{j=1}^{n^*} y_j + \sum_{i=1}^{n} x_i\right)\right)$$
$$\times x_i - F - cy_i - cx_i - tx_i. \tag{3.5}$$

Similarly,

$$\pi_j = \left(a - b\left(\sum_{j=1}^{n^*} y_j + \sum_{i=1}^{n} x_i\right)\right) y_j + \left(a - b\left(\sum_{i=1}^{n} y_i + \sum_{j=1}^{n^*} x_j\right)\right)$$
$$\times x_j - F - cy_j - cx_j - t^* x_j. \tag{3.6}$$

Thus, the first-order conditions of the ith firm in country 1 are:

$$\frac{\partial \pi_i}{\partial y_i} = a - b\left(\sum_{i=1}^{n} y_i + \sum_{j=1}^{n^*} x_j\right) - by_i - c = 0, \tag{3.7}$$

$$\text{and } \frac{\partial \pi_i}{\partial x_i} = a - b\left(\sum_{j=1}^{n^*} y_j + \sum_{i=1}^{n} x_i\right) - bx_i - c - t = 0. \tag{3.8}$$

Similarly, the first order conditions for the jth firm in country 2 are given by:

$$\frac{\partial \pi_j}{\partial y_j} = a - b\left(\sum_{j=1}^{n^*} y_j + \sum_{i=1}^{n} x_i\right) - by_j - c = 0, \tag{3.9}$$

$$\text{and } \frac{\partial \pi_j}{\partial x_j} = a - b\left(\sum_{i=1}^{n} y_i + \sum_{j=1}^{n^*} x_j\right) - bx_j - c - t^* = 0. \tag{3.10}$$

We then simultaneously solve Eqs. (3.7), (3.8), (3.9), and (3.10) for the variables y_i, x_i, x_j and y_j. Restricting attention to symmetric solutions we can write $y_i = y^1$ and $x_i = x^1$ for all i, and $y_j = y^2$ and $x_j = x^2$ for all j.[2] Using the symmetry assumption, Eqs. (3.7), (3.8), (3.9), and (3.10) can be rewritten as follows:

$$y^1 = \frac{a - c - n^* b x^2}{b(n+1)}, \tag{3.11}$$

$$x^1 = \frac{a - c - t - n^* b y^2}{b(n+1)}, \tag{3.12}$$

$$y^2 = \frac{a - c - nbx^1}{b(n^*+1)}, \tag{3.13}$$

$$\text{and } x^2 = \frac{a - c - t^* - nby^1}{b(n^*+1)}. \tag{3.14}$$

Notice that Eqs. (3.11) and (3.14) form a subsystem of two equations in the two variables y^1 and x^2. Solving Eqs. (3.11) and (3.14) simultaneously we find

$$y^1 = \frac{a - c + n^* t^*}{b(n + n^* + 1)}, \tag{3.15}$$

$$\text{and } x^2 = \frac{a - c - t^*(1+n)}{b(n + n^* + 1)}. \tag{3.16}$$

Similarly, solving Eqs. (3.12) and (3.13) simultaneously we obtain

$$x^1 = \frac{a - c - t(n^* + 1)}{b(n + n^* + 1)}, \tag{3.17}$$

$$\text{and } y^2 = \frac{a - c + nt}{b(n + n^* + 1)}. \tag{3.18}$$

Thus, Eqs. (3.15), (3.16), (3.17), and (3.18) solve for the production levels of the firms as functions of n and n^*. Letting X^1 denote the level of aggregate export by country 1 we have

$$X^1 = nx^1 = \frac{n[a - c - t(n^* + 1)]}{b(n + n^* + 1)}. \tag{3.19}$$

Clearly,

$$\frac{\partial X^1}{\partial n} = \frac{(1+n^*)[a-c-t(n^*+1)]}{b(n+n^*+1)^2} = \frac{(1+n^*)x^1}{n^*+n+1}, \tag{3.20}$$

$$\text{and } \frac{\partial X^1}{\partial n^*} = -\frac{n[a-c-nt]}{b(n+n^*+1)^2} = -\frac{ny^2}{n^*+n+1}. \tag{3.21}$$

Thus, X^1 is increasing inn and decreasing in n^*.

We then describe the free entry conditions in country 1 and country 2. Under the symmetry assumption, the free entry condition in country 1 can be captured by the zero profit condition for country 1 firms[3]

$$\left(a-b\left(ny^1+n^*x^2\right)\right)y^1+\left(a-b\left(nx^1+n^*y^2\right)\right)x^1-F-cy^1-cx^1-tx^1=0, \tag{3.22}$$

that is,

$$b\left(y^1\right)^2+b\left(x^1\right)^2-F=0. \tag{3.23}$$

Using Eqs. (3.15) and (3.17) to substitute the values of y^1 and x^1, respectively, in the above equation, we obtain

$$2(a-c)^2+2(a-c)n^*(t^*-t)-2(a-c)t+n^{*2}\left(t^{*2}+t^2\right)+t^2+2t^2n^* = Fb(n+n^*+1). \tag{3.24}$$

We then consider the free entry condition in country 2. Under the symmetry assumption this can be written as:

$$\left(a-b\left(nx^1+n^*y^2\right)\right)y^2+\left(a-b\left(ny^1+n^*x^2\right)\right)x^2-F-cy^2-cx^2-t^*x^2=0. \tag{3.25}$$

Using Eqs. (3.15), (3.16), (3.17), and (3.18) we can simplify the above equation

$$2(a-c)^2 + 2(a-c)n(t-t^*) - 2(a-c)t^* + n^2(t^2+t^{*2}) + 2nt^{*2} + t^{*2} = Fb(n+n^*+1)^2. \tag{3.26}$$

We are now in a position to begin our analysis.

3.5 The Analysis

In this section, we analyze the impact of an increase in import protection on export and welfare.

3.5.1 Free Entry in Country 1 Alone

We first examine the case where there is free entry in country 1 alone, the number of firms in country 2 being exogenously given. The equilibrium conditions in this case are given by Eqs. (3.15), (3.16), (3.17), (3.18), and (3.22) and the condition that

$$n^* = \bar{n}^*. \tag{3.27}$$

For our purpose, it is more convenient to consider the reduced form representation consisting of Eqs. (3.24) and (3.27). Suppose that there is an increase in import protection by country 1, formalized as an increase in t^*. We can think of these protective measures as nontariff barriers. Let us now examine the effects of an increase in t^* on aggregate exports X^1. Totally differentiating Eq. (3.24) with respect to n and t^*, and collecting terms, we can write

$$\left.\frac{dn}{dt^*}\right|_{n^*=\bar{n}^*} = \frac{\bar{n}^*\left[a-c-\bar{n}^*t^*\right]}{Fb\left(n+\bar{n}^*+1\right)} = \frac{\bar{n}^*y^1}{F} > 0. \tag{3.28}$$

Notice that the above equation together with the result that X^1 is increasing in Eq. (3.24) implies that X^1 is increasing in t^*.

With an increase in t^*, exporting becomes more costly for firms in country 2, making the firms in country 1 more profitable. This attracts entry into the country 1 market, so that in equilibrium the number of firms in country 1 increases. While this leads to a decline in the export

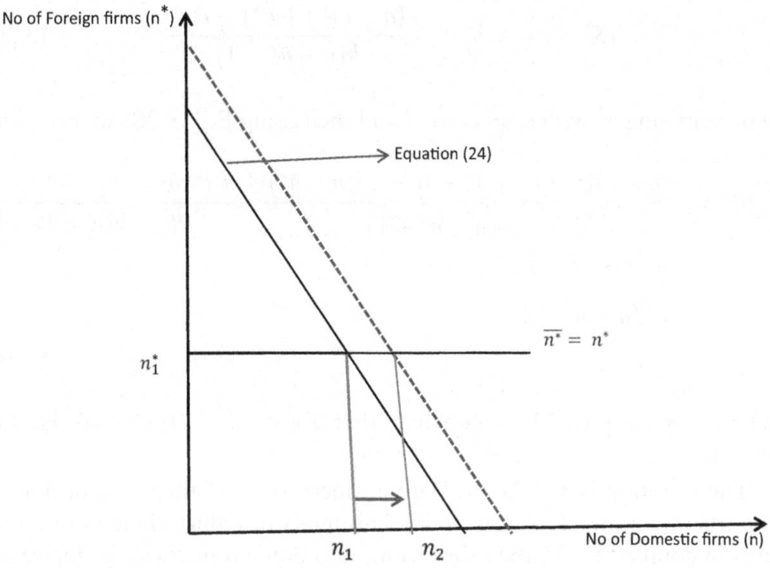

Fig. 3.1 Free entry in the country 1 alone

level of individual firms in country 1, aggregate exports increase as the increase in the number of firms more than makes up for the fall in individual exports. See Fig. 3.1 for the diagrammatic representation where the number of firms for country 2 is exogenously given and the justification is provided later in Sect. 3.6.

Summarizing the above discussion we obtain our first proposition.

Proposition 1 Suppose that there is free entry in country 1 alone. An increase in t^* leads to an increase in aggregate exports from country 1.

We now examine the effect of an increase in t^* on the welfare level in country 1. Notice that because of the free entry condition, producers' surplus in country 1 is zero. It is thus sufficient to examine the changes in consumers' surplus, that is, in the total quantity sold in country 1. From Eqs. (3.15) and (3.16) we find that total consumption in country 1 is given by

$$S^1 = ny^1 + \bar{n}^* x^2 = \frac{(a-c)(n+\bar{n}^*) - t^*\bar{n}^*}{b(n+\bar{n}^*+1)}. \tag{3.29}$$

Differentiating S^1 with respect to t^* and then using Eq. (3.28) we can write

$$\begin{aligned}\frac{dS^1}{dt^*} &= \frac{(a-c)(n+\bar{n}^*+1) - (a-c)(n+\bar{n}^*) + \bar{n}^* t^*}{b(n+\bar{n}^*+1)^2}\frac{dn}{dt^*} - \frac{\bar{n}^*}{b(n+\bar{n}^*+1)} \\ &= \frac{\bar{n}^*\left[b(y^1)^2 - F\right]}{Fb(n+\bar{n}^*+1)}.\end{aligned} \tag{3.30}$$

We then use Eq. (3.23) to conclude that $b(y^1)^2 - F = -b(x^1)^2 < 0$. Hence, $\frac{dS^1}{dt^*} < 0$.

The intuition is as follows. With an increase in t^* there is a decline in imports of country 1, that is, $\bar{n}^* x^2$. This tends to reduce the consumption level in country 1. On the other hand, domestic production ny^1 increases. This tends to increase domestic consumption, and hence welfare. With free entry in country 1 alone the first effect dominates. Hence the result.

The welfare impact on country 2, however, is ambiguous. Note that the producers' surplus in country 2 is given by

$$\begin{aligned}\Pi^2 = \bar{n}^*\big[&(a - b(nx^1 + \bar{n}^* y^2))y^2 \\ &+ (a - b(ny^1 + \bar{n}^* x^2))x^2 - F - cx^2 - cy^2 - t^* x^2\big].\end{aligned} \tag{3.31}$$

Differentiating with respect to t^* and using the envelope theorem we obtain

$$\begin{aligned}\frac{d\Pi^2}{dt^*} &= \frac{\partial \Pi^2}{\partial n}\frac{dn}{dt^*} + \frac{\partial \Pi^2}{\partial t^*} \\ &= -\frac{by^1\bar{n}^{*2}[x^1y^2 + y^1x^2]}{F} - x^2\bar{n}^* < 0.\end{aligned} \tag{3.32}$$

Thus, with an increase in t^*, the producers' surplus in country 2 declines.

As the number of firms in country 1 increases, however, this has a beneficial effect on the consumers' surplus in country 2.[4] This is because with an increase in $n + \bar{n}^*$ there is greater competition in the market in country 2 so that the total quantity sold in country 2 increases.

These two effects, however, operate in opposite directions, making the final effect ambiguous.

Proposition 2 Suppose that there is free entry in country 1 alone. An increase in t^* leads to a decline in the welfare level in country 1. The welfare effect on country 2, however, is ambiguous.

3.5.2 Free Entry in Country 2 Alone

We now examine the case where there is free entry in country 2, but the number of firms in country 1 is exogenously given. The equilibrium conditions are given by Eqs. (3.15), (3.16), (3.17), (3.18), and (3.25), and the condition that

$$n = \bar{n}. \tag{3.33}$$

Again, it is more convenient to consider the reduced form representation consisting of Eqs. (3.26) and (3.33). We begin by examining the effect of a change in the level of import protection, that is, t^*, on the level of exports. Totally differentiating Eq. (3.26) with respect to n^* and t^* we obtain that

$$\begin{aligned} \left.\frac{dn^*}{dt^*}\right|_{n=\bar{n}} &= -\frac{(1+\bar{n})\left[a-c-t^*(1+\bar{n})\right]}{Fb(n^*+\bar{n}+1)} \\ &= -\frac{(1+\bar{n})x^2}{F} < 0. \end{aligned} \tag{3.34}$$

Putting Eqs. (3.21) and (3.34) together we obtain our next proposition.

Proposition 3 Suppose that there is free entry in country 2 alone. An increase in t^* leads to an increase in aggregate exports by country 1.

In this case, with an increase in t^*, the profit level of firms in country 2 gets squeezed. Thus, in equilibrium the number of firms in country 2 declines, making country 1 more competitive vis-a-vis country 2. Hence, the export level of each firm in country 1 increases and the aggregate export increases as well. See Fig. 3.2 for a diagrammatic representation where the number of

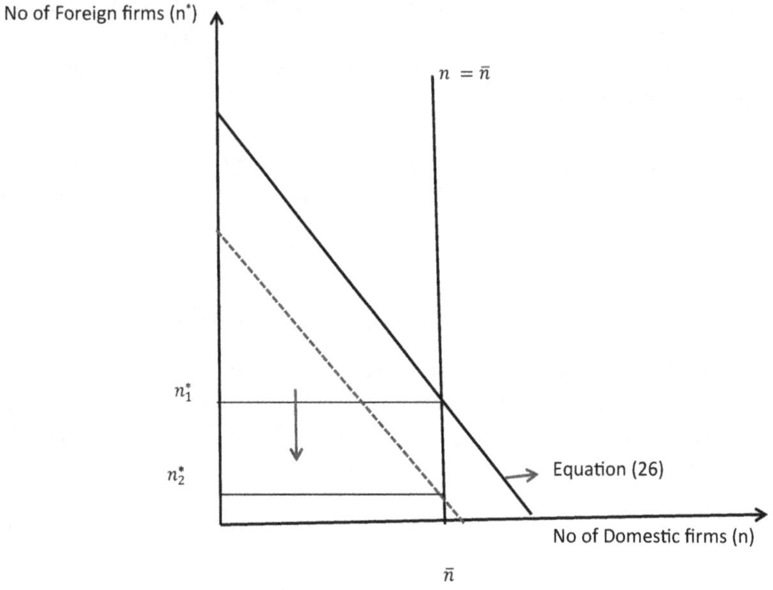

Fig. 3.2 Free entry in the country 2 alone

firms for country 1 is exogenously given and the justification is provided later in Sect. 3.6.

We now examine the impact of a change in t^* on the welfare level in country 1. First, consider the impact on consumers' surplus, that is, on aggregate consumption in country 1. Differentiating S^1 with respect to t^* we obtain

$$\frac{dS^1}{dt^*} = bx^2\frac{dn^*}{dt^*} - \frac{n^*}{b(\bar{n} + n^* + 1)}. \tag{3.35}$$

Given Eq. (3.34), $\frac{dS^1}{dt^*} < 0$. Thus, an increase in t^* leads to a decline in consumers' surplus.

However, the impact on Π^1, the producers' surplus in country 1, is positive. Note that

$$\Pi^1 = \bar{n}\left[\left(a - b\left(\bar{n}y^1 + n^*x^2\right)\right)y^1 + \left(a - b\left(\bar{n}x^1 + n^*y^2\right)\right)x^1 - F - cx^1 - cy^1 - tx^1\right]. \tag{3.36}$$

Differentiating Π^1 with respect to t^* using the envelope theorem, and then simplifying, we obtain

$$\frac{d\Pi^1}{dt^*} = \frac{\partial\Pi^1}{\partial n^*}\frac{dn^*}{dt^*} = \frac{b(1+\bar{n})\bar{n}x^2[y^1x^2 + x^1y^2]}{F} > 0. \tag{3.37}$$

This is because of two reasons: first, the number of firms in country 2 becomes less, and second, these firms become less efficient in the export market. Hence, all firms in country 1 becomes more profitable. Thus, there are two opposing effects on the welfare level in country 1 and the net effect is ambiguous.

Finally, consider the impact of a change in t^* on the welfare level in country 2. Clearly, producers' surplus in country 2 is zero. With an increase in t^* the total number of firms in country 2, $\bar{n} + n^*$, declines (Eq. (3.34)). Thus, the aggregate output in country 2 declines. Hence, the welfare level in country 2 decreases in t^*.[5]

Proposition 4 Suppose that there is free entry in country 2 alone. The effect of an increase in t^* on the welfare level in country 1 is ambiguous. The welfare level in country 2, however, is decreasing in t^*.

3.5.3 *Free Entry in Both Countries*

We examine the cage where there is free entry in both countries. Note that the equilibrium conditions in this cage are given by Eqs. (3.15), (3.16), (3.17), (3.18), (3.22), and (3.25). The reduced form representation is given by Eqs. (3.24) and (3.26).

Consider the effect of a change in t^* on the level of export in country 1. We proceed diagrammatically. Let us plot Eqs. (3.24) and (3.26) in the $n - n^*$ space (see Fig. 3.1). We say that an equilibrium $(\bar{n}, \bar{n}^*)$ is *regular* if at this equilibrium the slope of Eq. (3.24) is steeper than that of Eq. (3.26), that is,

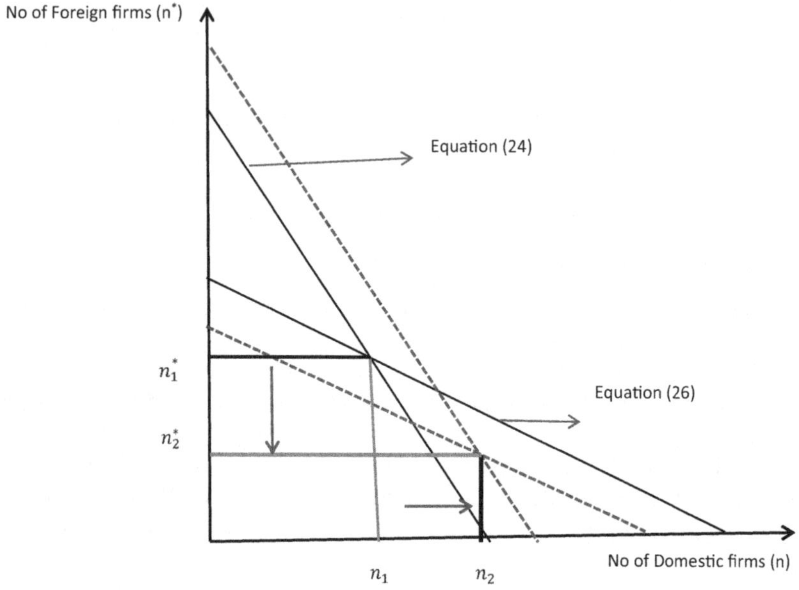

Fig. 3.3 Free entry in both countries

$$\left.\frac{dn^*}{dn}\right|_{24,\bar{n},\bar{n}^*} < \left.\frac{dn^*}{dn}\right|_{26,\bar{n},\bar{n}^*} \tag{3.38}$$

Now suppose that t^* increases. Then, from Eqs. (3.28) and (3.24) it shifts to the right, and from Eqs. (3.34) and (3.26) it shifts to the left. Clearly, if the equilibrium is unique and regular then in equilibrium n increases and n^* decreases (see Fig. 3.3). Hence, from Eqs. (3.20) and (3.21), aggregate exports increase in t^*.

We now provide a set of sufficient conditions for the existence of a regular and unique equilibrium. Note that

$$\left.\frac{dn^*}{dn}\right|_{(24)} = -\frac{Fb(1+n+n^*)}{Fb(1+n+n^*) - (a-c)(t^*-t) - t^2 - n^*(t^2+t^{*2})}, \tag{3.39}$$

$$\left.\frac{dn^*}{dn}\right|_{(26)} = -\frac{Fb(1+n+n^*) - (a-c)(t-t^*) - t^{*2} - n(t^2+t^{*2})}{Fb(1+n+n^*)}. \quad (3.40)$$

Note that if t and t^* are both small, then Eqs. (3.24) and (3.26) are both negatively sloped. Moreover, the slope of Eq. (3.24) is strictly less than -1 and that of Eq. (3.26) is strictly greater than -1.[6] This implies that Eqs. (3.24) and (3.26) have a unique and regular intersection. In fact, if t and t^* are both small then existence is also ensured.[7]

Summarizing the above discussion we obtain Proposition 5.

Proposition 5 Suppose that there is free entry in both countries.

(i) *If the equilibrium is unique and regular, then an increase in t^* leads to an increase in aggregate exports.*
(ii) *There exists some $\varepsilon > 0$ such that whenever $t, t^* < \varepsilon$, there is a unique and regular equilibrium.*

We now examine the impact of a change in t^* on the welfare levels of the two countries. Note that for the case where there is free entry in both countries our model is a simplified version of that in Venables (1985). In particular, the demand function is weakly convex. Moreover, there is a home market bias in the sense that $y^1 > x^2$ and $y^2 > x^1$; see Eqs. (3.15), (3.16), (3.17) and (3.18)).[8] Thus, proposition 5 in Venables (1985) applies. Hence, we obtain our last proposition.

Proposition 6 Suppose that there is free entry in both countries. Then the welfare level in country 1 is increasing and that in country 2 is decreasing in t^*.

Propositions 2, 4, and 6 together demonstrate that the welfare implications of an increase in t^* depends on the nature of the product market competition, that is, whether there is free entry in only one of the countries or both of them. Thus, Propositions 2, 4, and 6 together provide an extension of Proposition 7 in Venables (1985).

3.6 Discussion

Finally, in this subsection we discuss some robustness issues. The assumption that the demand functions and production costs are identical across countries is essentially simplifying in nature. All the results should go through even if we allow these functions to vary across the two countries. The assumption that the demand function is linear is *also* mainly technical in nature.[9]

The assumption that production costs are linear is, however, much more basic. Recall that with static economies of scale, the result in Krugman (1984) is driven by the assumption that marginal costs are decreasing. Suppose instead that marginal costs are strictly increasing. Then with an increase in t^*, exports would decline if the number of firms were exogenously given. If one now allows for free entry, then there will be two opposing effects. The free-entry effect will tend to increase exports, while the marginal cost effect will tend to decrease them. In general, the results will be ambiguous.

Finally, note that we interpret the import restrictions as nontariff export barriers. Alternatively, one can consider tariff restrictions. Clearly, this alternative interpretation does not affect the result that import protection leads to export promotion. An increase in the level of tariffs essentially makes the firms in country 2 less competitive in the country 1 market. Because it is this feature that drives Propositions 1, 3, and 5, all three propositions should go through in case of tariff restrictions as well. The welfare analysis, however, may be sensitive to this alternative interpretation. In this case there would be an additional component of welfare in country 1, arising out of the tariff revenue accruing to the government. Recall that with free entry in country 1 alone, an increase in t^* leads to a decline in the welfare level in country 1 (Proposition 2). Under the alternative interpretation this result need not go through. The other welfare results are, however, qualitatively unaffected.

3.7 Conclusion

In this chapter we revisited Krugman's (1984) thesis that import protection leads to export promotion. Krugman (1984) argues that in the absence of dynamic scale economies, the formalization of this idea appears to require the "heterodox" assumption that marginal costs are decreasing. We seek to extend Krugman (1984) by providing an alternative foundation of the idea based on free entry and linear marginal costs. We also derive some interesting welfare conclusions.

The welfare results suggest that the fact that exports may be increasing in the level of import protection is not enough to justify a policy of import protection. Such a policy is necessarily welfare-improving provided there is free entry in both countries, and not otherwise. In fact, with free entry in country 1 alone, the welfare level in country 1 is decreasing in the level of import protection. Thus, care is required before resorting to this idea to justify a policy of import protection.

Acknowledgements We are deeply indebted to an anonymous referee for very helpful and incisive comments that led to substantial improvements in the paper. We would like to thank Tarun Kabiraj, Sugata Marjit, Ajitava Ray Chaudhuri, and Soumyen Sikdar for their comments on earlier versions of this paper.

Notes

1. The theoretical framework developed in Sects. 3.3 and 3.4 is a simplified version of Roy Chowdhury and Ray Chaudhuri (Import Protection as Export Promotion, *Keio Economic Studies* 15, 2003, 17–35 (International Academic Printing Co., Japan).
2. It is simple to use Eqs. (3.7), (3.8), (3.9), and (3.10) to argue that the solution is, in fact, symmetric and unique.
3. As usual we ignore the integer problem.
4. Note that consumers surplus in country 2 is given by

$$S^2 = \frac{(a-c)(n+\overline{n}^*) - nt}{b(n+\overline{n}^*+1)}.$$

Differentiating the above equation with respect to t^* and using Eq. (3.28) we obtain

$$\frac{dS^2}{dt^*} = \frac{\overline{n}^* y^1 x^1}{F(n+\overline{n}^*+1)} > 0.$$

5. Note that the consumers' surplus in country 2 is

$$S^2 = \overline{n}x^1 + n^* y^2 = \frac{(a-c)(n^*+\overline{n}) - \overline{n}t}{b(\overline{n}+n^*+1)}.$$

Differentiating the above equation with respect to t^* and using Eq. (3.34) we obtain

$$\frac{dS^2}{dt^*} = -\frac{x^2 y^2 (1+\overline{n})}{F(\overline{n}+n^*+1)} < 0.$$

6. The existence of the fixed coat F implies that the equilibrium n and n^* are bounded above even if t *and* t^* *are* small. Hence, if t and t^* become very small, then in Eqs. (3.39) and (3.40) all the terms associated with t and t^* go to zero.
7. This follows from the fact that if $t = t^* = 0$, then compared to Eqs. (3.26) and (3.24) has a strictly greater intercept on the n^* axis and a strictly smaller intercept on the n axis (see Fig. 3.3).
8. See Venables (1985), Sect. 3.5, p. 9.
9. For a general demand function we shall have to impose conditions that ensure unique ness and stability, for example, the Hahn (1962) condition. Venables (1985) demonstrates that for the case where there is free entry in both the countries the comparative statics analysis also requires that the demand function be convex.

References

Avner, S., & Sutton, J. (1984). Involuntary unemployment as a perfect equilibrium in a bargaining model. *Econometrica, 52*(6), 1351–1364.

Baldwin, R. E., & Flam, H. (1989). Strategic trade policy in the market for the 30–40 seat commuter aircraft. *Weltwirtschaftliches Archive, 125*, 484–500.

Baldwin, R. E., & Krugman, P. R. (1988). Industrial policy and international competition in wide-bodied jet aircraft. In R. Baldwin (Ed.), *Trade policy issues and empirical analysis*. Chicago: University of Chicago Press for the NBER.

Ben-zvi, S., & Helpman, E. (1992). Oligopoly in segmented market. In G. Grossman (Ed.), *Imperfect competition and international trade* (pp. 31–54). Cambridge, MA: MIT Press.

Bhagwati, J. N. (1965). On the equivalence of tariff and quotas. In R. E. Baldwin (Ed.), *Trade growth and balance of payment*. Amsterdam: North Holland.

Brander, J. A. (1981). Intra-industry trade in identical commodities. *Journal of International Economics, 11*, 1–14.

Brander, J. A., & Krugman, P. R. (1983). A reciprocal dumping model of international trade. *Journal of International Economics, 15*, 313–321.

Brander, J. A., & Spencer, B. J. (1981). Tariff and the extraction of foreign monopoly rents under potential entry. *Canadian Journal of Economics, 14*, 371–389.

Brander, J. A., & Spencer, B. J. (1983). International R&D rivalry and industrial strategy. *Review of Economic Studies, 50*, 707–722.

Brander, J. A., & Spencer, B. J. (1985). Export subsidies and international market share rivalry. *Journal of International Economics, 18*, 83–100.

Caves, R. E. (1974). *International trade, international investment and imperfect markets*. Special paper in international economics no. 10, International finance section, Princeton University.

Chacoliades, M. (1978). *The theory of monopolistic competition*. Cambridge, MA: Harvard University Press.
Chamberlin, E. (1933). *The theory of monopolistic competition*. Cambridge MA: Harvard University Press.
Chowdhury, I. R., & Chaudhuri, P. R. (2003). Import protection as export promotion. *Keio Economic Studies, 15*, 17–35.
Corden, W. M. (1974). *Trade policy and economic welfare*. Oxford: Oxford University Press.
Dixit, A. K. (1984). International trade policy for oligopolistic industries. *Economic Journal, 94*, 1–16.
Dixit, A. K. (1989). Entry and exit decisions under uncertainty. *Journal of Political Economy, 97*(3), 620–638. University of Chicago Press.
Dixit, A. K., & Kyle, A. S. (1985). The use of protection and subsidies for entry promotion and deterrence. *The American Economic Review, 75*, 139–152.
Dixit, A. K., & Norman, V. (1980). *Theory of international trade*. Cambridge: Cambridge University Press.
Dixit, A. K., & Stiglitz, J. E. (1977). Monopolistic competition and optimum product diversity. *The American Economic Review, 67*, 297–308.
Eaton, J., & Grossman, G. M. (1986). Optimal trade and industrial policy under oligopoly. *Quarterly Journal of Economics, 101*(2), 383–406.
Eaton, J., & Panagariya, A. (1979). Gains from trade under variable returns to scale, commodity taxation, tariff and factor market distortions. *Journal of International Economics, 9*, 481–501.
Feenstra, R., & Judd, K. (1982). Tariff technology transfer and welfare. *Journal of Public Economics, 90*, 1142–1165.
Grubel, H. G., & Lloyd, P. J. (1975). *The international economy, MIT Press, Intra-industry trade: The theory and measurement of international trade in differentiated products*. London: Macmillan.
Hahn, F. H. (1962). The stability of the Cournot oligopoly solution. *Review of Economic Studies, 32*, 329–331.
Harris Richard, G. (1984). Applied general equilibrium of small open economies and imperfect competition. *American Economic Review, 74*(5), 1016–1032.
Helpman, E. (1981). International trade in the presence of product differentiation, economies of scale, and monopolistic competition: A Chamberlin- Heckscher-Ohlin approach. *Journal of International Economics, 11*, 305–340.
Helpman, E., & Krugman, P. (1985a). *Market structure and foreign trade: Increasing returns, imperfect competition and the international economy*. Brighton: Wheatsheaf Books.
Helpman, E., & Krugman, P. (1985b). *Market structure and foreign trade: Increasing returns, imperfect competition and the international economy*. Cambridge: MIT Press.

Helpman, E., & Razin, A. (1984). Increasing return, monopolistic competition and factor movements: A welfare analysis. In H. Kierzkowski (Ed.), *Monopolistic competition and international trade*. Oxford: Clarendon Press.
Horstmann, I. J., & Markusen, J. R. (1986). Up the average cost curve: Inefficient entry and the new protectionism. *Journal of International Economics, 20*(3–4), 225–247. Elsevier.
Kemp, M. C., & Negishi, T. (1970). Variable returns to scale, commodity taxes and their implications for trade gains, Swedish. *Journal of Economics, 72*, 1–11.
Krishna, K. (1992). On protection and the product line: A reply. *International Economic Review, 33*(4), 977–979. Department of Economics, University of Pennsylvania and Osaka University Institute of Social and Economic Research Association.
Krishna, K., & Itoh, M. (1988). Content protection and oligopolistic interactions. *Review of Economic Studies, 55*(1), 107–125. Oxford University Press.
Krugman, P. (1979). Increasing returns, monopolistic competition, and international trade. *Journal of International Economics, 9*(4), 469–479.
Krugman, P. (1980). Scale economies, product differentiation, and the pattern of trade. *The American Economic Review, 70*(5), 950–959.
Krugman, P. (1981). Intra-industry specialization and the gains from trade. *Journal of Public economies, 89*, 959–973.
Krugman, P. (1984). Import protection as export promotion: International competition in the presence of oligopoly and economies of scale. In H. Kierzkowski (Ed.), *Monopolistic competition and international trade*. Oxford: Oxford University Press.
Krugman, P., & Helpman, E. (1985). *Market structure & foreign trade*. Cambridge, MA: MIT Press.
Lancaster, K. (1979). *Variety, equity and efficiency*. New York: Columbia University Press.
Lancaster, K. (1980). Intra-industry trade under perfect monopolistic competition. *Journal of International Economics, 10*, 151–175.
Markusen, J. R. (1981). Trade and gains from trade with imperfect competition. *Journal of International Economics, 11*, 531–551.
Markusen, J. R., & Melvin, J. (1981). Trade factor prices and gains from trade with increasing returns to scale. *Canadian Journal of Economics, 14*, 450–469.
Markusen, J. R., & Venables, A. J. (1988). Trade policy with increasing returns and imperfect competition: Contradictory results from competing assumptions. *Journal of International Economics, 24*(3–4), 299–316. Elsevier.
Melvin, J. R. (1969). Increasing returns to scale as a determinant of trade. *Canadian Journal of Economics, 11*, 389–402.
Itoh, M., & Ono, Y. (1982). Tariffs, quotas, and market structure. *The Quarterly Journal of Economics, 97*(2), 295–305. Oxford University Press.

Panagariya, A. (1981). Variable returns to scale in production and patterns of specialization. *American Economic Review, 71*, 221–230.
Smith, A., & Venebles, A. (1991). Economic integration and market access. *European Economic Review, 35*, 385–395.
Spencer, B. J., & Brander, J. A. (1983). International R & D Rivalry and industrial strategy. *Review of Economic Studies, 50*(4), 707–722. Oxford University Press.
Venables, A. (1985). Trade and trade policy with imperfect competition: The case of identical products and free-entry. *Journal of International Economics, 19*, 1–19.
Venables, A. (1990a). The economic integration of oligopolistic markets. *European Economic Integration, 34*, 753–769.
Venables, A. (1990b). International capacity choice and the national market games. *Journal of International Economics, 29*, 23–42.

CHAPTER 4

A Model of International Entry and Exit with Endogenous Sunk Costs in Vertical Markets

Partha Gangopadhyay and Robert F. Owen

4.1 Introduction

Modern economics often seeks to explain the enigma of market concentration in an ever-changing world: as most markets steadily grow why some markets show remarkable stability in their levels of concentrated, while many others fragment. In an earlier work, Sutton (1991) develops a theoretical framework based on Shaked and Sutton (1983, 1982, 1987) to discriminate among markets by exploring the interactions between exogenous and endogenous elements of sunk costs to determine the equilibrium market structure in an industry. If the endogenous sunk costs like advertisement, R&D and product quality are (relatively) more significant than the setup costs, the theory of endogenous sunk costs predicts that the market will be dominated by a few firms as the market size grows over time since large endogenous sunk costs can deter entry and limit competition. The empirical work hence highlights how the market structure is

P. Gangopadhyay (✉)
Western Sydney University, Sydney, NSW, Australia

University of the South Pacific, Suva, Fiji

R.F. Owen
University of Nantes, Nantes, France

S.K. Mathur et al. (eds.), *Theorizing International Trade*,
https://doi.org/10.1007/978-981-10-1759-9_4

sustained by increasing competitive investments in advertising, R&D, product quality, wage discrimination, network formation and geographic diversification, and so on (see Elickson 2013; Berry and Waldfogel 2014). In other words, the size of sunk costs and their endogeneity are important factors in forecasting the dynamics of market shares and concentration over time. In a parallel development in the international trade theory, Melitz (2003), by adapting Hopenhayn's (1992) model of monopolistic competition, examines the dynamics of competition by exploring entry and exit behaviours of heterogeneous firms for understanding the time profile of inter-firm relocation within an industry. Ghironi and Melitz (2005) explore the macroeconomic consequences of sunk costs in entry when the product market is monopolistically competitive and conclude that only relatively more efficient firms access the international market. As a natural corollary, Bilbiie et al. (2012) consider endogenous entry in a market with a diversity of product variety to develop a framework for modelling the macroeconomic consequences of endogenous entry and product quality with a special focus on business cycles.

In our work we offer an alternative model of oligopoly, similar in spirit to Shaked and Sutton (1983), to consider entry, exit and endogenous sunk costs in determining the market structure by introducing market access costs as endogenous sunk costs as highlighted by Owen and Ulph (2002). We develop a baseline model of vertical markets to examine the *strategic* role of access costs, as endogenous sunk costs chosen by the incumbent and integrated firm in a home market, for forestalling future foreign entry into the downstream market. We establish that the incumbents can effectively collude to deter entry if the integrated home firm is free to commit to an access cost before foreign entry. We highlight that the *regulation* of the access cost can often control such anti-competitive price distortion in vertical markets in international trade, but not always.

The plan of the chapter is as follows: in Sect. 4.2 we provide a review of extant and related literature. In Sect. 4.3 we present the static model in which a given number of incumbents compete for shares in the downstream market. In Sect. 4.4 we examine the issues related to entry in the retail market. We analyse strategic entry-deterrence by upward price distortion by an upward escalation of access costs/price. In Sect. 4.5 we establish that the strategy of upward price distortion is an optimal collusive device to deter entry. We also establish that the control of the input price can effectively forestall such anti-competitive behaviour of the incumbents. We conclude in Sect. 4.6.

4.2 Related Literature

The related literature has several important interfaces with the trade theory and theories of industrial organisation, which we examine under four different headings in what follows.

4.2.1 Sunk Costs and Barriers to Entry and Exit

Barriers to entry are of fundamental importance in the determinant of market structure, and play a central role in industrial economics and trade theory. Both trade models and industrial economics have serious concerns about the likely impact of trade and industrial policies on the market structure and market outcomes, mainly market prices, and the extent to which that impact would be conditioned on the potential entry of new firms. The possible exits of some of the existing firms from the relevant industry can also impact on the market structure and the consequent market outcomes and their desirability. Barriers to entry can originate from a variety of sources, but if entry into a market calls forth large *sunk* costs, the risks of entry into a market can be magnified as the ex-ante and ex-post post-entry profits will turn out to be particularly important for entry and exit decisions. Since the advent of the new millennium—with the revolution in modern technologies along with the increased pace of globalisation—the size and evolution of sunk costs have especially become critical for rapidly evolving industries and markets for new products in the rapidly expanding global markets. But there is little consensus as to the mechanisms through which sunk costs affect entry and industry equilibrium. When the profession is far from being comfortable with sunk costs, it is a bit too much to expect the final word of endogenous sunk costs. In other words, the role of *endogenous* sunk costs in determining the market outcome is still in its infancy (see Owen and Ulph 2002) and our current work will be a minor step towards incorporating endogenous sunk costs as a determinant of firm-level decisions that are now increasingly emphasised, not only for industrial economics, but also to be the causes and consequences of aggregate trade (see Bilbiie et al. 2012; Melitz and Redding 2012).

The role of sunk costs in shaping "entry barrier" is well articulated in economics since an entry barrier is usually taken to imply any additional cost that an entrant must pay that an incumbent does not need to pay just after entry, which is sufficient to allow the incumbent to raise price without inducing entry. Sunk costs and entry barrier can thus be defined in terms of its effects—it limits the number of profitable firms in the industry and increases price-cost margins. Large sunk costs are thus an entry barrier as they create scale economies. In other words, sunk costs cause an industry equilibrium with relatively few firms. This is always the case whether or not incumbent firms or potential entrants face any uncertainty with respect to future cash flows (see Cabral and Ross 2008; Carlton 2004 among many). From Cabral and Ross (2008), Carlton (2004), McAfee et al. (2004), Murti (2004), Pindyck (2008), Schmalensee (2004), we now know how and to what extent different types of uncertainty with respect to cash flows can magnify the effects of sunk costs. Underlying risks of entry can magnify sunk costs of entry simply because the act of entry wipes out the potential benefit of waiting before entry for new information about the post-entry profits. This is so since firms exercise their options to enter a market they burn down the associated option value from waiting. This destruction of the option value is a form of endogenous sunk costs. However, the option value from waiting and not entering a market does not always arise. It arises only if a particular type of uncertainty leads to a possibility of an asymmetric distribution of post-entry profits specifically against the interests of the potential entrants. In what follows we consider the endogenous sunk cost in the sense that the sunk cost is chosen by the incumbent, as opposed to the endogenous sunk costs due to uncertain changes in the post-entry profit distribution.

4.2.2 *Endogenous Sunk Costs as a Choice Variable of the Incumbent to Influence the Sunk Costs of the Potential Entrants*

The work of Sutton (1991) offers a theoretical framework to highlight the role of sunk costs in explaining the structure of a market. In other words, the goal of endogenous sunk costs in industrial economics is to explain why some markets remain concentrated as they expand in size, while others fragment. The theory of endogenous sunk costs according to Sutton (1991) introduces a crucial distinction between exogenous sunk costs vis-a-vis endogenous sunk costs. The exogenous sunk costs are a part of the datum that do not evolve over time while the endogenous sunk costs change over time as a consequence of a rational decision-making by incumbents. The endogenous sunk costs are usually conceived as advertisement outlays and quality investments undertaken by incumbents and are fixed to the market shares of incumbent firms. They are endogenous in the sense that they are irreversibly chosen by incumbents and they change over time as the market size changes. Once such endogenous sunk costs assume a critical importance relative to the setup costs of incumbents, the structure of the market becomes and remains concentrated with rising endogenous sunk costs with the increasing size of the market. On the other hand, if the exogenous setup costs are more important, or significantly larger, than the endogenous sunk costs, then the market should experience a declining concentration due to increased entry activities. It is important to note that Sutton's work makes robust theoretical predictions about the relationship between market concentration and market size, while the empirical confirmation of these predictions has not come thick and fast. In his work, Sutton (1991) offers a cross-country analysis of various industries in trying to find empirical counterparts to the theory, however, he faced many of the measurement problems in the context of cross sections. Elickson (2013) applies the Sutton framework to the empirical study of US supermarkets. His work is the first to test the tenability of the prediction of the theory on a large data set of markets within a single industry. Subsequently, Berry and Waldfogel (2003) examine the relationships between market size and product quality in the newspaper and restaurant industries, where the quality production processes are believed to differ from the prediction of Sutton (1991).

As opposed to the endogenous sunk cost theory of Sutton (1991), we propose that the incumbents can choose a set of strategic variables, like access price, that can influence the sunk costs of the potential entrants. It is endogenous in the sense that the sunk cost is *strategically* chosen by the incumbents. This is something new in the literature on entry and exit and it has a close resemblance with what is known as endogenous switching costs for network industries.

Network industries differ in many respects from other industries. There are two important distinguishing features of network industries. First, producers must enter a network industry with potential switching costs. Second, consumer also face switching costs if they want to move from one network to another network of products. The literature has adequately addressed the switching costs of consumers: if consumers decide not to purchase from their previous network any longer, but to switch to a different network instead, they are expected to incur some additional cost—even if the products across networks are functionally identical (see Klemperer 1987). These so-called switching costs for consumers may be exogenous or endogenous. Exogenous switching costs are not deliberately created by the relevant networks and their members, but can be taken as a datum of some sort of immobility factors between networks. A common example is the consumer's cost of giving up a telephone number if there is no number portability. In contrast, endogenous switching costs are strategically created by networks, for example, through contract termination fees or through customer loyalty schemes such as frequent flyer programmes, such that mobility from one network to another is costly for consumers. While exogenous switching costs have received considerable attention in the economics literature (see Klemperer 1995, for a survey), there is less literature on the strategic creation of endogenous switching costs.

In a paper, Mariñoso (2001) examined the issue in the context of product systems and the strategic choice of product compatibility.[1] If the different product systems are compatible, then there is no switching cost while system incompatibility will create switching costs from one system/ network to another. In this pioneering paper, Mariñoso (2001) investigates whether "incompatibility can be used by firms as a *strategic* tool to lock-in consumers and thereby limit competition in networks." The controversial result is that, while the preceding is a possibility, networks have strong incentives to voluntarily make their platforms compatible if the sunk/fixed cost of achieving compatibility/non-exclusivity is sufficiently low. Furthermore, compatibility is efficient if the fixed costs of achieving and maintaining compatibility are not prohibitively high. If these costs are sufficiently high, there can be even excess compatibility. The driving force behind this theoretical result, which sharply contrasts with the stark reality of exclusivity in network industries, is the intuition that compatibility improves inflows of consumers, if access to their preferred complement without incurring switching costs, which in turn increases the willingness of consumers to pay a higher price and, thereby, the profits of the producers in the specific network. However, the main weakness of this model is that little attention is given to the switching costs of producers if they want to enter a new network or exit from an old network, which can create significant sunk costs to influence the overall market outcome.

The goal of our study is to set up the simplest possible model in terms of linear demand and cost functions in a duopolistic framework with an emerging triopoly with entry to establish how access costs of mobility into a network, or out of a network, can create endogenous sunk costs with a significant consequence on entry, exit and competition within a network. It is important to stress that the endogenous sunk cost in our model is a strategic choice of incumbents.

4.2.3 Vertical Markets of International Trade

It has been widely held that globalisation delivers a positive (net) welfare effect if it is accompanied with an increased market integration that usually calls forth a reduction in variable costs of trade like tariffs. (see Venables 1990a, b). In an important contribution, Owen and Ulph (2002) introduced a dichotomy between sunk costs and fixed costs to establish that the net welfare effect of economic integration can turn out to be negative due to the reduction of incumbency rents of existing producers. Their primary intuition is founded on the early work of Smith and Venables (1991) that assumes the existence of access costs that are *independent* of the volume of trade but necessary to get access to markets. Owen and Ulph (2002) highlighted the possibility that the market access costs have a sunk component that cannot be recouped if a firm decides to exit the market, which in turn engenders the hysteresis effect such that the characteristics of the post-integration equilibrium are critically predicated upon the pre-integration equilibrium. In the current chapter, we develop an important baseline model by making two modifications to Owen and Ulph (2002): first, we assume away the sunk costs. Second, we introduce a case in which the market access cost is not only a component of the variable cost but gets *strategically* chosen by one of the incumbent firms.

Vertical markets have assumed significance in the modern theory of international trade. The research, in this context, has focussed on two related issues: first, a large number of papers explore the incentive of the integrated firm to foreclose the downstream market to limit actual competition (e.g., Jones 1996; Bernhofen 1996; Spencer and Jones 1991, 1992). Vertical foreclosure therefore involves some kind of a market conflict in which a powerful player, in order to increase its market share, forces out its rivals from a market. The vertical arrangement in such markets is hardly a level-playing field. One typically wonders how to control the vertical foreclosure. Second, several papers also examine the discriminating tariff policy that can prevent such anti-competitive behaviour (e.g., Spencer and Jones 1991, 1992; Chang and Kim 1991; Chang and Chen 1994). In their paper, Ishikawa and Lee (1997) introduce entry/exit of foreign firms and demonstrate that the discriminatory tariffs may turn out to be counterproductive since they may have adverse effects on the profits of the domestic firms. However, relatively little attention has been paid to the collusive behaviour among the incumbent firms in vertical markets, which can seriously warp competition and may cause significant deadweight losses. Our primary objective is to analyse the collusive behaviour in vertical world markets in the presence of variable access costs as introduced by Smith and Venables (1991) and Owen and Ulph (2002).

An important issue in this context is *potential competition*, which is driven by the entry of new firms in the downstream market in the presence of access costs. A gap in the existing literature is the neglect of the impact of non-integrated foreign firm's entry into the retail market on potential competition and the role of access costs as a strategic variable chosen by an incumbent and integrated firm. Our purpose is to fill this gap. We fill the gap in the existing literature by analysing the possible entry of a non-integrated foreign firm in the domestic downstream market.[2] The focus of Ishikawa and Lee (1997) in recent paper is the impact of tariffs on the entry/exit decision of a foreign firm, which is shown to lead to adverse effects of tariff on domestic firms. On the contrary, our focus is on the impact of collusive activities of the incumbents on the entry decision of the non-integrated foreign firm under sketchy information. Hence, we examine the *dynamic* analysis of the vertical market in international trade in the context of strategically chosen access costs. We posit the global/international market as a formation whose privileges are constantly threatened by entry. We follow Bain (1956), Sylos (1956), Milgrom and Roberts (1982), Harrington (1986, 1987) and Bagwell and Ramey (1991) among others to adopt the theory of limit pricing to examine the dynamics of entry and extend the analysis to vertical markets in international trade.

4.2.4 *Information Linkage of the Industrial Organisation Literature*

In order to model the access cost we consider a stylised market where an integrated home firm has monopolistic control over the supply of a key input in the upstream market and competes with non-integrated foreign firms in the downstream market. The downstream retail market is characterised by Cournot competition while the integrated home firm enjoys monopolistic power in the upstream input market. In our model, the price of input determines the variable access costs. The key question for the incumbents, both home and foreign firms, is how to ward off entry in order to maintain the status quo. This is a time-honoured problem in the theory of oligopoly (see Bagwell and Ramey 1991): Bain (1956), Modigliani (1956) and Sylos (1969) advanced the notion of limit pricing, which involves incumbents choosing a low price to convince a potential entrant that entry will be unprofitable. The limit price signals a lower post-entry profit to the entrant. Thus, the main intuition of limit pricing is that the current price may signal the probable nature of the incumbent's policy if entry occurs. The incumbent firm indicates its *commitment/threat* to maintain output consistent with low limit price. If the threat is credible then the potential foreign entrant is deterred by a low price and high output.[3]

The seminal paper of Milgrom and Roberts (1982) highlighted the likelihood that incumbent firms may control the entry decision, through prices, by influencing a potential entrant's "*perceptions of the profitability*" when prices convey critical information about the exogenous determinants of post-entry profitability. The fundamental notion turns on an *informational asymmetry* between incumbents and potential entrants: the incumbents have a relevant piece of information that potential entrants do not possess. Matthews and Mirman (1983) examined the case where a potential entrant does not have critical information about the *demand conditions.* Milgrom and Roberts (1982) and Salop (1979) developed *signalling models* where prices convey information about the *cost conditions.* These works demonstrate the rationale behind an incumbent's decision to set prices below the short-run profit-maximising level in order to forestall entry.

These models firmly establish an *interdependence* between pre-entry price and the expected post-entry profit of the potential entrant and spell out the rationale behind *downward distortion* of price to prevent entry. The only exception is the *pioneering and "provocative"* works of Harrington (1986, 1987) who postulates positively correlated cost functions of the incumbent and of the entrant in order to reverse the limit pricing result. In his works the incumbent firm prices above the simple monopoly price, or Nash-Cournot price, to signal high-cost and, hence, low post-entry profitability. Our basic premise is similar to that of Harrington (1986, 1987) since the foreign entrant relies on the price signals to learn about the cost conditions.

We extend the IO literature by applying the model of informational linkage to vertical international markets with multiple incumbents. We adopt a particular form of information asymmetry in this context: we assume that a foreign entrant does not know the local cost of production and access costs and expects the cost to be positively correlated with the cost of production of the incumbents. The potential foreign entrant observes the price statistic to infer about the cost of production. As a result, the incumbents have an incentive to distort price upward in the retail market to signal high cost and, hence, low post-entry profit to the potential foreign entrant.[4] We develop a model to examine the effects of this informational asymmetry in vertical markets in international trade. We establish that an equilibrium exists in which the incumbents can strategically deter entry by conveying to the potential foreign entrant that this industry is a high cost one with limited/zero post-entry profit.

Our primary contribution to the IO literature is twofold: first, we extend the information-based model of limit pricing to the important case of vertically related markets in international trade. Assuming a particular type of informational asymmetry, we establish that the access cost/input price plays a critical role in deterring entry into vertical markets. A pre-commitment to an input price and hence access costs by the integrated firm acts as a *commitment linkage* in such markets that can effectively deter entry and, thereby, limit potential competition. We are thus able to identify the bounds on access costs/input price for which an upward price distortion will act as a collusive device to deter entry and would, thereby, limit potential competition. Second, we show that the control of access costs by regulating the input price can sometimes, but not always, thwart collusion among the incumbents and, hence, will promote potential competition in such markets.

4.3 Static Model of Vertical Markets

4.3.1 An Outline

To keep the model tractable we postulate an industry that supplies a single final product. Each unit of it is produced by combining a necessary input from the upstream industry with labour and other inputs from the competitive markets. The upstream home firm is an integrated firm that has a monopolistic control over the supply of a key input and competes with the downstream foreign firm in the market for the final product.[5] In other words, the upstream firm has the gatekeeping power and can charge and access price for entrants into the network that serves the downstream market. The relevance of a key input in our model is to allow for the endogenous determination of the access costs, which is strategically chosen by the integrated domestic firm and borne by any foreign entrants/firms. The precise market structure in the downstream sector entails a simple duopoly. We thus postulate a Cournot type of quantity competition in the downstream market while the integrated home firm has naturally monopolistic power in the upstream market.

As in his pioneering paper, Mariñoso (2001) investigates whether "incompatibility can be used by firms as a *strategic* tool to lock in consumers and thereby limit competition in networks". We investigate if the domestic firm can use the access price to lock in competitors to the advantage of the domestic firm to retain the market concentration. Our goal is to learn if networks have strong incentives to voluntarily choose partners by setting the access price as sunk costs to make their networks more difficult to access for outsiders. In this chapter, we only look at the possible role of access price as an entry deterrence and in another chapter we will examine how the entry price can be used to choose the composition of a network to block further and undesired entry.

The downstream foreign firm is competitive in the input market as it takes the access cost/price as a datum. The implicit assumption is that there are infinitely many foreign firms who buy the inputs from the integrated domestic firm, but not all compete with this domestic monopolist in the same downstream market. Only a few foreign firms engage in quantity competition in the downstream market. Thus, one may assume that there is also a third market as in Brander and Spencer (1985). Alternatively, there is a unified world market for the final goods and at least part of the market is in the domestic economy (see Brander and Spencer 1985; pp. 228–29). We thus make the assumption that a foreign firm takes the access cost, or input price, as given. Production takes place in two discrete stages: in the first stage, the key input is produced and priced by the integrated home firm by using natural monopoly technology. The second stage is potentially competitive as the integrated firm engages in Cournot type quantity competition with the vertically separated foreign firms. Hence, all the foreign firms rely on the integrated home firm for the supply of the essential input.

4.3.2 *The Static Framework*

We assume a highly stylised framework, which is the bedrock of the modern analysis of the vertical markets and latent in pioneering models of Jones (1996) and Spencer and Jones (1992, 1991). The integrated home firm faces a duopolist in the downstream (final product) market while it wields naturally monopolistic power in the upstream (input) market. During the first stage, or **Stage I**, the integrated home firm sells the essential input, or access, to the non-integrated foreign firm. During **Stage II**, both integrated home and non-integrated foreign firms will compete as Cournot-type duopolists in the downstream market to sell the final product. If the information is complete in the static market, in the relevant rational expectations equilibrium both the firms correctly predict the Cournot–Nash equilibrium of the second stage, or Stage II, competition and both the firms will seek to maximise their profits in Stage II given the input price of Stage I. We need the following preliminary to characterise the market equilibrium:

Definition 1 The profit accruing to the integrated home firm (Π^m) is given as:

$$\Pi^m = (A - w)\,q_n + (P(Q) - c - w)q_m \tag{4.1}$$

where Q $(=q_m+q_n)$ is the market output of the final product, q_m is the output of the integrated firm and q_n is the output of the non-integrated firm, A is the access/input price, w is the cost of producing the essential input (access), c is the cost of producing the final good for both firms, and P (Q) is the inverse market demand. Note that we assume there is neither fixed cost nor sunk cost for the integrated and non-integrated firms.

Definition 2 The profit accruing to the non-integrated foreign firm from the downstream market:

$$\Pi^n = (P(Q) - c - A)q_n \tag{4.2}$$

Assumption 1 We assume the inverse demand function to be linear:

$$P(Q) = a - bQ \tag{4.3}$$

Based on the preceding, we derive the Cournot–Nash equilibrium of the duopoly at Stage II.

4.3.3 Cournot–Nash Equilibrium of the Duopoly in the Static Market

In Stage II, the integrated home firm earns Π^{m1} from the sales of final product:

$$\Pi^{m1} = (P(Q) - c - w)q_m \tag{4.1a}$$

Substituting (4.3) in (4.1a) and simplification would yield:

$$\Pi^{m1} = (a - c - w)q_m - bq_nq_m - bq_{m^2} \tag{4.1b}$$

Similarly, the profit function of the non-integrated foreign firm reduces to:

$$\Pi^{n} = (a - c - A)q_n - bq_mq_n - bq_{n^2} \tag{4.2a}$$

Maximising the profit function (4.1b) yields the reaction function of the integrated home firm, which is essentially the first-order condition to maximise (4.1b) with respect to q_m taking q_n as datum. This would yield:

$$q_m = [(a - c - w)/(2b) - (q_n/2)] \tag{4.4a}$$

Similarly, from the maximisation of (4.2a) with respect to q_m we obtain the reaction function of the non-integrated foreign firm as:

$$q_n = [(a - c - A)/(2b) - (q_m/2)] \tag{4.4b}$$

The Cournot–Nash equilibrium of the downstream duopoly is determined by the solution to the simultaneous equation system (4.4a) and (4.4b). Table 4.1 presents the Cournot–Nash equilibrium:

(4.5a) and (4.5b) are derived from the solution to the simultaneous equation system (4.4a) and (4.4b). And q_{i^*} labels the Cournot–Nash equilibrium output dfof firm *i* and we derive Eq. (4.5c) by adding (4.5a) and (4.5b). By substituting (4.5c) into Eq. (4.3) we obtain the Cournot-Nash price of the final product as given by Eq. (4.5d).

We substitute Eq. (4.5a), (4.5b), (4.5c), and (4.5d) into Eq. (4.1) to yield the maximised profit of the integrated home firm as the following:

$$\Pi^{m**} = \left[\frac{(a - c - 2w + A)^2}{9b} + A\frac{(a - c + 3w)}{3b} - \frac{2}{3b}A^2 - \frac{w(a - c + w)}{3b}\right] \tag{4.6a}$$

Table 4.1 The Cournot–Nash equilibrium of the downstream market (without entry)

$q_{n^*} = [(a - c - 2A + w)/(3b)]$	(4.5a)
$q_{m^*} = [(a - c + A - 2w)/(3b)]$	(4.5b)
$Q^* = [(2(a - c) - (A + w)]/(3b)]$	(4.5c)
$P^* = [(a + 2c + A + w)/(3)]$	(4.5d)

The profit accruing to the non-integrated foreign firm, Π^{n*}, from the downstream duopoly is:

$$\Pi^{n*} = (P^* - c - A)q^{n*} \tag{4.6b}$$

Substituting q^{n*} by (4.5a) and P^* by (4.5d) into (4.6b) yields:

$$\Pi^{n*} = \frac{(a - c + w - 2A)^2}{9b} \tag{4.6c}$$

Equations (4.6a) and (4.6c) represent the profits of the incumbent firms in a static market characterised by fixed number of competitors, stable demand and cost conditions. The excess profits of these incumbents attract new firms from overseas into the retail market, which opens up the dynamic issues that we now turn to in Sect. 4.4.

4.4 The Threat of Foreign Entry and Strategic Entry Deterrence

4.4.1 *Post-Entry Competition in the Downstream Market*

We considered a stylised market in which there are two incumbent firms who engage in quantity competition in the retail market. Suppose there is a single potential foreign entrant who decides whether to enter this retail market, or not. We assume that the market is characterised by information asymmetry: the incumbent firms have full information about the cost and demand conditions while the potential foreign entrant has sketchy information about the access cost and the cost of production. The potential foreign entrant infers about the costs from the price statistic. The game unwinds in a market in which the demand and cost conditions remain invariant through time. Suppose the potential foreign entrant decides to enter the retail market: then there are three competitors in the downstream retail market who engage in quantity competition that leads to the following post-entry market configuration.

Proposition 1 The post-entry Cournot–Nash outputs and price are given by:

$$q_m^{**} = (a - c + 2A - 3w)/(4b) \tag{4.7a}$$

$$q_n^{**} = (a - c - 2A + w)/(4b) \tag{4.7b}$$

$$q_e^{**} = (a - c - 2A + w)/(4b) \tag{4.7c}$$

$$P^{**} = (a + 3c + 2A + w)/4 \tag{4.7d}$$

$$Q^{**} = (3a - 3c - 2A - w)/(4b) \tag{4.7e}$$

where q_e is the output of the foreign entrant.

Proof The derivation is exactly similar to that of Sect. 4.3.3. Instead of having two firms and two reaction functions, we now have three firms and three reaction functions that form the simultaneous equation system. The solution to the system gives the optimal outputs of the firms as represented by (4.7a), (4.7b), and (4.7c). The price follows from the demand function. Q.E.D.

Proposition 2 The post-entry profits of the three Cournot competitors are as follows:

$$\Pi^{m**} = n_1 + n_2A + n_3A^2 \tag{4.8a}$$

where

$$n_1 = \left[\frac{(a-c-2A+w)^2}{16b} - \frac{3w(a-c+w)}{4b}\right], ..n_2 = \frac{(3a-3c+5w)}{4b}, ..n_3 = -\frac{3}{4b}$$

$$\Pi^{n**} = s_1 + s_2A + s_3A^2 \tag{4.8b}$$

where

$$s_1 = \frac{(a-c-2A+w)^2}{16b}, ..s_2 = -\frac{a-c+w}{4b}, ..s_3 = \frac{1}{4b}$$

$$\Pi^{e**} = \frac{(a-c-2A+w)^2}{16b} \tag{4.8c}$$

Proof We get (4.8a) by substituting (4.7a), (4.7b), (4.7c), and (4.7d) into (4.1). We get (4.8b) by substituting (4.7b) and (4.7d) into (4.6b). (4.8c) is arrived at in the same fashion as (4.8b). Q.E.D.

4.4.2 *Entry Prevention by Upward Price Distortion*

If entry occurs, then the post-entry outcome is a three-firm Cournot–Nash equilibrium and under complete information Propositions 1 and 2 hold. We assume that all information before entry is a common knowledge except the cost of production in the retail market, which remains private information to the incumbent firms.[6]

Since the incumbents have asymmetric information on the cost of production, their pre-entry outputs and the resultant market price contain information about the cost parameters. As a result, the entry decision is critically hinged on the pre-entry price, which derives from the Cournot-type competition between the incumbents (see Milgrom and Roberts 1982). Thus, the post-entry profit of the potential foreign entrant is decreasing in the pre-entry price of the retail market. The rationale is that a high pre-entry price brings a signal to the potential foreign entrant that this is a high-cost industry that will, in turn, signal low post-entry profit. The fallout is that the incumbent firms may have an incentive to strategically distort the price upward in the retail market to signal high costs and low post-entry profits (see Harrington 1986, 1987). The rest of the section is devoted to the analysis of the rationale and feasibility of such price distortion in vertical markets.

Theorem 1 The distorted price signal, P^D, that conveys a message of high cost and low, or, zero profitability to the potential foreign entrant, which will, thereby, forestall entry is given by:

$$P^D = \frac{a-A+w}{b} \tag{4.9a}$$

Proof Since the potential foreign entrant does not know the unit cost of production c, hence the incumbents set a price P such that the profit accruing to the entrant, Π^e, is reduced to zero and, hence, the foreign entrant will stay away from the market. Thus, the foreign entrant does not enter if:

$$\Pi^e = 0 \tag{4.9b}$$

We substitute (4.8c) into (4.9b) to yield:

$$\frac{(a - 2A + w - c^*)^2}{16b} = 0 \tag{4.9c}$$

where c^* is the distorted cost that will signal zero profitability in the concerned market. From (4.9c) we derive:

$$c^* = a - 2A + w \tag{4.9d}$$

Substituting (4.9d) into (4.7d) yields the distorted price signal P^D:

$$P^D = (a - A + w)/b \tag{4.9a}$$

The distorted price signal P^D is determined by Eq. (4.9a) that signals a high cost c^*, given by Eq. (4.9d), that will convey low (zero) post-entry profits to the potential foreign entrant. Hence, the foreign entrant will be deterred by this price statistic P^D. Q.E.D.

4.5 Is the Upward Price Distortion an Optimal Strategy?

4.5.1 *Integrated Home Incumbent and Upward Price Distortion*

In this section, we turn to the important question of whether the incumbent firms have an incentive to adopt the strategy of upward price distortion as laid out in Theorem 1. In order to find that, we need to compare their profits from such distortion with their profits from the no-distortion market equilibrium. The strategy of upward price distortion is optimal only when it yields higher profits to the incumbents vis-a-vis their profits from the no-distortion equilibrium. We set the stage with the following:

Theorem 2 The profit, Π^{m***}, accruing to the integrated home incumbent from the strategy of upward price distortion is given by the following:

$$\Pi^{m***} = m_1 + m_2 A + m_3 A^2 \tag{4.10a}$$

where

$$m_1 = \frac{(ab - a - w)(a - bc - (b-1)w)}{2b^3} \tag{4.10b}$$

$$m_2 = \frac{(ab - a + w)(b-1) + (a - bc - (b-1)w)}{2b^3} \tag{4.10c}$$

$$m_3 = (b-1)/\left(2b^3\right) \tag{4.10d}$$

Proof At price P^D the quantity demanded, Q^D, in the retail market is:

$$Q^D = \left(a - P^D\right)/b = (ab - a + A - w)/b^2 \tag{4.11a}$$

Assuming the incumbents have tacit agreement about market shares, we simplify the analysis by an equal output share. Hence their outputs and profit of the integrated home incumbent from the retail market respectively are:

$$Q^{m***} = Q^{n***} = (ab - a + A - w)/b^2 \tag{4.11a'}$$

$$\Pi^{m***} = \left[\frac{(ab - a + A - w)}{2b^2}\right]\left[\frac{a - (A - w) + b(A - w) - bc}{b}\right] \tag{4.11b}$$

(4.11b) is expanded to yield (4.10a). Q.E.D.

Definition 3 We define G_M as the gains, or increase, in profit from the price distortion strategy to the integrated home incumbent, which is given by:

$$G_M = \Pi^{m***} - \Pi^{m**} \tag{4.11c}$$

where Π^{m***} is the profit accruing to the integrated home incumbent from price distortion strategy while Π^{m**} is his profit from no-distortion strategy which allows entry.

Observation 1 The gains from price distortion, G_M, can be reduced to the following:

$$G_M = h_1 + h_2 A + h_3 A^2 \tag{4.11d}$$

where $h_1 = (m_1 - n_1)$, $h_2 = (m_2 - n_2)$, $h_3 = (m_3 - n_3)$.

We define A^C:

$$A^C = (n_2 - m_2)/[2(m_3 - n_3)] \tag{4.11e}$$

and for $A > A^C$ G_M is an increasing function of A and for $A < A^C$ G_M is decreasing in A.

We substitute Eqs. (4.8a) and (4.11b) into (4.11c) to yield (4.11d) and find:

$$\frac{\delta G_M}{\delta A} > 01 \tag{4.12a}$$

If

$$2h_3 A + h_2 > 0 \tag{4.12b}$$

or,[7]

$$A > A^C = (n_2 - m_2)/[2(m_3 - n_3)] \tag{4.12c}$$

Theorem 3 The integrated home incumbent will adopt an upward distortion of the price of the final good if the access cost/input price A is such that:

$$A < A_1{}^* \tag{4.13a}$$

or,

$$A > A_2{}^* \tag{4.13b}$$

where

$$A_1{}^* = \frac{-h_2 - \sqrt{h_2^2 - 4h_1h_3}}{2h_3} \tag{4.13c}$$

and

$$A_2{}^* = \frac{-h_2 + \sqrt{h_2^2 - 4h_1h_3}}{2h_3} \tag{4.13d}$$

Proof We set G_M equal to zero and from the resultant quadratic equation we derive two roots $A_1{}^*$ and $A_2{}^*$. For any A, such that $A_1{}^* < A < A_2{}^*$, $G_M < 0$ and hence the integrated home incumbent has no incentive to distort price since the no-distortion equilibrium yields larger profits than what the upward price distortion does. On the other hand, if the input price lies outside this range, the integrated home incumbent gains from an upward distortion of the price of the final good. Q.E.D.

Thus, we establish that the integrated home incumbent will adopt an upward distortion of price as an optimal strategy to deter entry if the proposed conditions (4.13a) and/or (4.13b) are satisfied and if the non-integrated foreign incumbent also adopts the price distortion strategy. We now turn to the question of whether the non-integrated foreign incumbent has an incentive to distort the price upward.

4.5.2 *The Non-integrated Foreign Incumbent and Upward Price Distortion*

The non-integrated foreign incumbent sells $Q^D/2$ at a price of P^D if it colludes to distort the price upward. From the quantity sold and the price we are to determine its profit Π^{n***} from the strategy of price distortion.

Proposition 3 The non-integrated foreign incumbent sells $Q^D/2$ at a price of P^D and, hence, its profit, Π^{n***}, from the price distortion strategy is given by:

$$\Pi^{n***} = t_1 + t_2 A + t_3 A^2 \tag{4.14a}$$

where

$$t_1 = \frac{(a - bc + w)(ab - a - w)}{2b^3} \tag{4.14b}$$

$$t_2 = \frac{a - bc + w - (b+1)ab + a(b+1) + w(b-1)}{2b^3} \tag{4.14c}$$

$$t_3 = -1/\left(2b^2\right) \tag{4.14d}$$

Proof We know that the profit accruing to the non-integrated foreign incumbent from price distortion is:

$$\Pi^{n***} = \left(P^D - c - A\right)Q^D/2 \tag{4.14e}$$

Substituting P^D by Eq. (4.9a) and Q^D by Eq. (4.11a) we arrive at (4.14a).

Q.E.D.

Definition 4 The gains from the price distortion strategy to the non-integrated foreign incumbent, G_N, are defined as:

$$G_N = \Pi^{n***} - \Pi^{n**} \tag{4.15a}$$

Observation 2 Substituting Π^{n***} by (4.14a) and Π^{n**} by (4.8b) yields the following:

$$G_N = H_1 + H_2 A + H_3 A^2 \tag{4.15b}$$

where $H_1 = (t_1 - s_1), H_2 = (t_2 - s_2), H_3 = (t_3 - s_3)$.

Theorem 4 The non-integrated foreign incumbent will adopt an upward distortion of the retail price to forestall entry if the following conditions are satisfied:

$$A > A_1^{**} \tag{4.16a}$$

or,

$$A < A_2^{**} \tag{4.16b}$$

where

$$A_1^{**} = \frac{-H_2 - \sqrt{H_2^2 - 4H_1H_3}}{4H_3} \tag{4.16c}$$

and

$$A_2^{**} = \frac{-H_2 + \sqrt{H_2^2 - 4H_1H_2}}{4H_3} \tag{4.16d}$$

Proof The non-integrated foreign incumbent is indifferent between price distortion and non-price distortion strategy if G_N is zero. That is:

$$H_1 + H_2A + H_3A^2 = 0 \tag{4.16e}$$

Thus, there are two roots of the quadratic Eq. (4.16e) for which the non-integrated foreign incumbent is indifferent between two alternative strategies. The roots are given by (4.16c) and (4.16d). Since $H_3 < 0$ and $H_2 > 0$, hence $G^N > 0$ for (4.16a) and (4.16b) since the first derivative of G_N is positive until a critical value of A, A^{CC}, such that $A^{CC}=[-H_2/(H_3)]$. Q.E.D.

We combine G_N and G_M in the above diagram to consider the possibility whether both the incumbents will collude to deter entry by strategic distortion of the price of the final good. From the above, it is evident that the crucial determinant of such collusion is the value of the input price. If the access cost/input price lies $\{A_2^{**}, A_1^{*}\}$ and/or $\{A_2^{*}, A_1^{**}\}$, then the upward distortion of price yields larger profit for each incumbent than its profit from no-distortion strategy. Thus, we come to the following:

Statement 1 The upward price distortion strategy is chosen by the colluding incumbents to deter foreign entry and the potential foreign entrant decides not to enter the retail market if one of the following conditions holds:

$$A_1^* - A_2^{**} > 0 \tag{4.17a}$$

$$A_1^{**} - A_2^* > 0 \tag{4.17b}$$

and the actual access cost/input price lies within the bounds $\{A_2^{**}, A_1^*\}$, or $\{A_2^*, A_1^{**}\}$.

Statement 2 The collusion to strategically deter entry fails if one of the condition holds:

$$A_1^* - A_2^{**} < 0 \tag{4.17c}$$

$$A_1^{**} - A_2^* < 0 \tag{4.17d}$$

Statement 3 It is important to note that the upward price strategy inflicts a cost on the consumers as they pay a high price for the final product. They not only pay a high price due to limited actual competition, but also due to upward price distortion, which does not conform with the cost of production.

Statement 4 Can the regulatory authority control the anti-competitive behaviour to limit potential competition?[8] From the finding, one can see that the regulatory authority can break such collusion by simple price capping. If the maximum input price is set below A_2^{**}, then the collusion collapses since the non-integrated foreign firm has no incentive to adopt the price distortion strategy. Thus, by strictly regulating the input price the regulatory authority can forestall such entry-deterring and anti-competitive price distortion.

4.5.3 Trigger Strategy Equilibrium

From Sub-sect. 4.5.2, we have learned that incumbents have an incentive to collude by adopting the upward price distortion strategy to deter foreign entry. Under a set of conditions, such a collusive strategy is also shown to be successful in deterring entry. However, collusion gives rise to the familiar problem that each incumbent has an incentive to defect, when its rival abides by the collusive agreement. As is usual in supergame theory, we assume that incumbents deter defection from the collusive agreement by employing the trigger strategy to punish defection: incumbents abide by the collusive agreement unless one firm cheats. If an incumbent cheats, they revert to the non-cooperative Cournot–Nash equilibrium for once. We now explore the possibility that an infinite repetition of a profile of P^D, q_m***, q_n*** which makes the incumbents better off than defection in terms of their respective profit functions, can be sustained as a subgame perfect equilibrium by means of a trigger strategy with one-shot Nash reversion (see Tirole 1988).

As long as both incumbents stay in equilibrium, profits are Π^m***, Π^n***. The integrated home incumbent chooses to stay on the equilibrium path if and only if the following incentive compatibility no-defection constraint is satisfied:

$$\Pi^m(DF) - \Pi^{m***} < \sum_{u=1}^{\infty} \delta^u G_M \tag{4.18a}$$

where Π^m (DF) is the one-shot profit of the integrated home incumbent from defection if the non-integrated foreign incumbent sticks to the collusive arrangement. δ is the common discount rate of the incumbents while G_M labels the gains from price distortion to the integrated home incumbent and given by Eq. (4.11d). Similarly, we define the incentive compatibility no-defection constraint for the non-integrated foreign incumbent as:

$$\Pi^n(DF) - \Pi^{n***} < \sum_{u=1}^{\infty} \delta^u G_N \tag{4.18b}$$

where Π^n (DF) is the one-shot profit of the non-integrated firm from defection if the other incumbent sticks to the collusive agreement. The following lemma delineates the trigger strategy equilibrium.

Lemma 1 The repetition of the profile P^D, Q^{m***}, Q^{n***} is sustainable by means of trigger strategies with one-shot Nash reversion if

$$\delta > \text{maximum}\{\delta^{m*}, \delta^{n*}\}$$

where

$$\delta^{m*} = \frac{\left(a - \frac{a-c-w}{2} + \frac{ab-a+A-w}{4b} - \frac{ab-a+A-w}{2b} - c\right)\left(\frac{a-c-w}{2b} - \frac{ab-a+A-w}{4b^2}\right) + (A-w)\left(\frac{ab-a+A-w}{2b^2}\right)}{h_1 + h_2A + h_3A^2} - \frac{\left(\frac{ab-a+A-w}{2b^2}\right)\left(\frac{a-(A-w)+b(A-w)-bc}{b}\right)}{h_1 + h_2A + h_3A^2} \tag{4.18c}$$

$$\delta^{n*} = \frac{\left[\left(a - \frac{ab-2bc-2Ab-a+A-w}{4b} - \frac{ab-a+A-w}{2b} - c - A\right]\left[\frac{ab-2bc-2Ab-a+A-w}{4b^2}\right]}{H_1 + H_2 + H_3A^2} - \frac{t_1 + t_2A + t_3A_2}{H_1 + H_2A + H_3A^2} \tag{4.18d}$$

Proof is given in Appendix.

4.6 Concluding Comments

As in his pioneering paper, Mariñoso (2001) investigates whether "incompatibility can be used by firms as a *strategic* tool to lock-in consumers and thereby limit competition in networks." We investigate if an integrated domestic firm can *strategically* use the access price to lock in foreign competitors to the advantage of the domestic firm to perpetuate the market concentration by discouraging future entry. Our goal is to learn if networks have strong incentives to voluntarily choose partners by setting the access price as endogenous sunk costs to make their networks more difficult to access for outside firms. In this chapter, we only looked at the possible role of access price as a collusive device for entry deterrence and in the subsequent chapter we will examine how the entry price can also be used to choose the composition of a network to block further, future and undesired entry. In other words, by using the access price appropriately, incumbents can create a market structure in which the integrated firm does not need to limit current competition by vertically foreclosing the downstream market to other incumbents, but can use the access price to prevent potential/future competition in the downstream market.

To achieve this task, we have examined an extension of the information-based approach to entry deterrence to the important case of vertical markets in international trade with endogenous access costs. We considered a market in which two incumbent firms face the danger of entry by a foreign firm. One of the incumbents can choose the cost of accessing the market by potential entrants and the other incumbent. Being a foreign firm the potential entrant has sketchy information about the local cost condition. This sketchy information unravels the possibility of collusion between incumbents to block the foreign firm by suitably choosing the access price. Assuming an information asymmetry about the cost of production, we find that the incumbents, namely the integrated home and non-integrated foreign firms, can effectively deter entry in the retail market by an upward distortion of the price of the final good. We note, under a set of conditions, that an effective collusion among the incumbents is feasible if the integrated home firm can freely commit to an access cost/input price before foreign entry takes place. We thus establish a new *commitment linkage* whereby the integrated home firm is able to pre-commit to an access cost/price, which enables incumbents to effectively block entry in the downstream retail market. We also find that the regulation of the access cost/price can sometimes, but not always, thwart such anti-competitive price distortions and, hence, would promote potential competition in vertical markets in international trade. In our future research, we will introduce sunk and fixed costs to enhance our collective understanding of the role of access costs in shaping the actual composition of networks relevant for vertical markets.

Appendix

Proof of Lemma 1

The no-defection incentive compatibility constraints state that defection will be unprofitable if and only if the one-period gain from defection is less than the present value of collusive profits foregone due to one-shot Nash reversion. The left-hand sides of (4.18a) and (4.18b), respectively, represent the one-shot gain from cheating for the integrated and non-integrated incumbents. In contrast, the right-hand sides label the net-present value of collusive profits sacrificed by ditching the price distortion strategy. The constraints thus summarise the opportunity cost of defecting from the collusive agreement. In Eq. (4.18a), the only unknown is $\Pi^m\,(DF)$ while Π^{m***}, G_M are respectively given by Eq. (4.11b) and (4.11d). Similarly, in Eq. (4.18b) the only unknown is $\Pi^n\,(DF)$ while Π^{n***} and G_N are captured by Eqs. (4.14e) and (4.15b). Also note that (4.18a) is satisfied so long as:

$$\delta > [\Pi^m(DF) - \Pi^{m***}]/G_M \tag{4.18e}$$

Inequality (4.18b) is satisfied so long as

$$\delta > [\Pi^n(DF) - \Pi^{n****}]/G_N \tag{4.18f}$$

We define δ^{m*} and δ^{n*} as the following:

$$\delta^{m*} = [\Pi^m(DF) - \Pi^{m***}]/G_M \tag{4.19a}$$
$$\delta^{n*} = [\Pi^n(DF) - \Pi^{n***}]/G_N \tag{4.19b}$$

It is important to note that (4.18a) and (4.18b) will hold so long as $\delta > \delta^{m*}$ and $\delta > \delta^{n*}$. We complete the proof by deriving $\Pi^m\,(DF)$ and $\Pi^n\,(DF)$ and substituting the relevant values in (4.19a) and (4.19b).

Derivation of π^{m} (DF)

The non-integrated incumbent sticks to the collusive agreement and produces output given by Eq. (4.11a′). Substituting (4.11a′) in the reaction function of integrated incumbent, (3.4a), we get the optimal defection output of the integrated firm, $Q^m\,(DF)$,

$$Q^m(DF) = (a - c - w)/(2b) - (ab - a + A - w)/\left(4b^2\right) \tag{4.19c}$$

The resultant price, $P^m\,(DF)$, when the integrated firm defects is

$$P^m(DF) = a - \left(\frac{a-c-w}{2} - \frac{ab-a+A-w}{4b} + \frac{ab-a+A-w}{2b}\right) \quad (4.19d)$$

We substitute (4.11a′), (4.19c) and (4.19d) into Eq. (4.1) to get Π^m (DF) as:

$$\begin{aligned}\Pi^m(DF) = {} & [a-(a-c-w)/2+(ab-a+A-w)/(4b) \\ & +(ab-a+A-w)/(2b)-c-A] \\ & [(a-c-w)/(2b)](ab-a+A-w)/\left(4b^2\right) \end{aligned} \quad (4.20a)$$

Substituting (4.20a) into (4.19a) yields (4.18c). Following similar steps we derive (4.18d). Q.E.D.

Notes

1. Product systems consist of various components or interrelated services that can only be used together—though they may be bought separately. An example is video game systems such as Nintendo's GameCube, Sony's PlayStation or Microsoft's Xbox consisting of a console and system-specific games. Similarly, for mobile telecommunications services one needs a mobile handset/equipment and various complementing services. Since consumers often purchase them sequentially in these markets, intra-brand incompatibility generates consumer switching costs.
2. There is only one paper that has examined the impact of entry/exit in vertical markets: Ishikawa and Lee (1997) examined the impact of entry/exit of an integrated foreign firm while we analyse the entry of a non-integrated foreign firm. Our focus is also different as we solely concentrate on the collusive behaviour in such markets.
3. These early works highlighted a **commitment linkage** whereby the incumbents are able to pre-commit to a higher output if entry occurs (see Bagwell and Ramey 1991). However, such a threat by the incumbents may not be credible since the incumbents may have an incentive to deviate from the committed output once entry occurs. Friedman (1979) forcefully argued that such a commitment cannot be sustained in a perfect Nash equilibrium. However, most of the earlier studies ignored the credibility problem (see Kamien and Schwartz 1971, 1975; Gaskins 1971; Pyatt 1971). Subsequently, the commitment to maintain low price is justified in terms of irreversible decision such as plant investment, advertising (see Flaherty 1980; Friedman

1979, 1983; Salop 1979). Dixit (1980), Fudenberg and Tirole (1983) introduced strategic capacity choices to ensure credibility of commitment. Gilbert and Vives (1986) examined output commitment in multiple-incumbent model. Bonanno (1987) theorised the entry-deterring power of product differentiation. Another plausible way out is to introduce imperfect information to beat the *chain store paradox* which has initiated a fresh lease of research (see Milgrom and Roberts 1982).

4. Harrington (1987) writes, "By virtue of having been a supplier in past periods an incumbent firm generally possesses some advantages over a potential entrant. One obvious source of advantage is that an incumbent firm has first hand experience with the production process; while a potential entrant does not. . .it is then reasonable to assume that an incumbent firm will hold private information on cost function. (p. 211)".
5. In order to simplify the analysis we assume that there is a single non-integrated foreign firm in the downstream market and, hence, this market is postulated to be a duopoly. The conclusions will extend to the case with a finite number of firms. We also assume that the non-integrated firm is a foreign firm. It is perfectly possible that this firm is a home firm. We maintain this assumption for stylistic reasons. What is crucial is that the potential entrant is from foreign market and, hence, confronts asymmetric information about the local conditions that determine the cost of production.
6. Note that while considering the entry-issues we call the integrated (home) incumbent firm and the non-integrated (foreign) incumbent firm as the integrated home incumbent and the non-integrated foreign incumbent respectively.
7. See that the denominator of (4.12c) is always positive if $b > 1$ and we assume $n_2 > m_2$ to get a positive critical value of A, A^C. Also note that the second derivative of G_M with respect to A is positive for $b > 1$. These restrictions give us a bell-shaped function for G_M as depicted.
8. We shelve the question of why the regulatory (domestic) authority will intend to enhance domestic competition by allowing foreign firms. Instead we suppose that the regulatory authority seeks to foster competition. If so, our question is what should they do to control such anti-competitive activities of the incumbents.

References

Bagwell, K., & Ramey, G. (1991). Oligopoly limit pricing. *RAND Journal of Economics, 22*(2), 155–170.

Bain, J. S. (1956). *Barriers to competition*. Cambridge: Harvard University Press.

Bernhofen, D. M. (1996). Vertical integration and international predation. *Review of International Economics, 4*, 90–98.

Berry, S., & Waldfogel, J. (2003). Product quality and market size. *Journal of Industrial Economics, 51*(1), 1–31.

Berry, S., & Waldfogel, J. (2014). *Fixed costs and product market treatment of minorities.* NBER working paper, 20488. NBER Inc.

Bilbiie, F. O., Ghironi, F., & Melitz, M. J. (2012). Endogenous entry, product variety, and business cycles. *Journal of Political Economy, 120*(2), 304–345.

Bonanno, G. (1987). Location choice, product proliferation and entry deterrence. *Review of Economic Studies, 54*, 37–45.

Brander, J. A., & Spencer, B. J. (1985). Export subsidies and international market share rivalry. *Journal of International Economics, 18*, 83–100.

Cabral, L., & Ross, T. W. (2008). Are sunk costs a barrier to entry. *Journal of Economics and Management Strategy, 17*(1), 97–112.

Carlton, D. W. (2004). Why barriers to entry are barriers to understanding. *The American Economic Review, 94*(2), 466.

Chang, W., & Chen, F. Y. (1994). Vertically related markets: Export rivalry between DC and LDC firms. *Review of International Economics, 2*, 131–142.

Chang, W., & Kim, J. C. (1991). Strategic tariff policy in a model of trade in intermediate and final products. In A. Takayama, M. Ohyama, & H. Ohta (Eds.), *Trade policy, international adjustments* (pp. 36–59). New York: Academic Press.

Dixit, A. K. (1980). The role of investment in entry deterrence. *Economic Journal, 90*, 95–106.

Elickson, P. B. (2013). Supermarket as a natural oligopoly. *Economic Inquiry, 51*(2), 1142–1154.

Flaherty, M. T. (1980). Dynamic limit pricing, barriers to entry, and rational firms. *Journal of Economic Theory, 23*, 160–182.

Friedman, J. W. (1979). On entry preventing behaviour. In S. J. Brams (Ed.), *Applied game theory* (pp. 236–253). Vienna: Verlag.

Friedman, J. W. (1983). Limit price entry prevention when information is lacking. *Journal of Economic Dynamics and Control, 5*, 187–199.

Fudenberg, D., & Tirole, J. (1983). Capital as a commitment: Strategic investment to deter mobility. *Journal of Economic Theory, 31*, 227–250.

Gaskins, D. W. (1971). Dynamic limit pricing: Optimal pricing under threat of entry. *Journal of Economic Theory, 3*, 306–322.

Ghironi, F., & Melitz, M. J. (2005). International trade and macroeconomic dynamics with heterogeneous firms. *Quarterly Journal of Economics, 120*(3), 864–915.

Gilbert, R., & Vives, X. (1986). Entry deterrence and free rider problem. *Review of Economic Studies, 53*, 71–83.

Harrington, J. E. (1986). Limit pricing when the potential entrant is uncertain about its cost functions. *Econometrica, 54*, 429–437.

Harrington, J. E. (1987). Oligopolistic entry deterrence under incomplete information. *RAND Journal of Economics, 18*, 211–229.
Hopenhayn, H. A. (1992). Entry, exit and firm dynamics long-run equilibrium. *Econometrica, 60*, 1127–1150.
Ishikawa, J., & Lee, K.-D. (1997). Backfiring tariffs in vertically related markets. *Journal of International Economics, 42*, 395–423.
Jones, R. W. (1996). *Vertical markets in international trade*. Working paper no. 432, Rochester Center for Economic Research.
Kamien, M. I., & Schwartz, N. L. (1971). Limit pricing and uncertain entry. *Econometrica, 39*, 441–454.
Kamien, M., & Schwarz, N. L. (1975). Self-financing of an R&D project. *American Economic Review, 68*(3), 252–261.
Klemperer, P. (1987). Markets with consumer switching costs. *Quarterly Journal of Economics, 102*, 375–394.
Klemperer, P. (1995). Competition when consumers have switching costs: An overview with applications to industrial organization, macroeconomics, and international trade. *Review of Economic Studies, 62*, 515–539.
Mariñoso, G. B. (2001). Technological incompatibility, endogenous switching costs and lock-in. *Journal of Industrial Economics, 49*, 281–298.
Matthews, S. A., & Mirman, L. J. (1983). Equilibrium limit pricing: The effects of private information and stochastic demand. *Econometrica, 51*, 981–996.
McAfee, R. P., Mialon, H. M., & Williams, M. A. (2004). What is a Barrier to entry? *The American Economic Review, 94*(3), 94–127.
Melitz, M. J. (2003). The impact of trade on intra-industry reallocations and aggregate industry productivity. *Econometrica, 71*(6), 1695–1725.
Melitz, M. J., & Redding, S. J. (2012, December). *Heterogeneous firms and trade*. Working paper, NBER.
Milgrom, P., & Roberts, J. (1982). Equilibrium limit pricing and entry under incomplete information: An equilibrium analysis. *Econometrica, 50*, 443–460.
Modigliani, F. (1956). New developments on the oligopoly front. *Journal of Political Economy, 66*, 215–232.
Murti, P. (2004). Exit in duopoly under uncertainty. *RAND Journal of Economics, 35*, 111–127.
Owen, R. F., & Ulph, D. (2002). Sunk costs, market access, economic integration and welfare. *Review of International Economics, 1093*, 539–555.
Pindyck, R. S. (2008, November 12). *Sunk costs and risk-based barriers to entry*. Working paper, Massachusetts Institute of Technology.
Pyatt, G. (1971). Profit maximisation and threat of new entry. *Economic Journal, 81*, 242–255.
Salop, S. C. (1979). Strategic entry deterrence. *The American Economic Review, 81*, 242–255.

Schmalensee, R. (2004). Sunk costs and antitrust barriers to entry. *American Economic Review, 94*(3), 471–475.

Shaked, A., & Sutton, J. (1982). Relaxing price competition through product differentiation. *Review of Economic Studies, 49*, 1–13.

Shaked, A., & Sutton, J. (1983). Natural oligopolies. *Econometrica, 51*, 1469–1484.

Shaked, A., & Sutton, J. (1987). Product differentiation and industrial structure. *Journal of Industrial Economics, 36*, 131–146.

Smith, A., & Venables, A. (1991). Economic integration and market access. *European Economic Review, 35*, 385–395.

Spencer, B., & Jones, R. W. (1991). Vertical foreclosure and international trade policy. *Review of Economic Studies, 58*(1), 153–170.

Spencer, B., & Jones, R. W. (1992). Trade and protection in vertically related markets. *Journal of International Economics, 32*, 31–35.

Sutton, J. (1991). *Sunk costs and market structure.* Cambridge, MA: MIT Press.

Sylos, L. P. (1956). *Oligopolio e Progresso Técnico.* Milano: Giuffré.

Sylos, L. P. (1969). *Oligopoly and technical progress.* Cambridge: Harvard University Press.

Tirole, J. (1988). *The theory of industrial organization.* Cambridge, MA: MIT Press.

Venables, A. (1990a). The economic integration of oligopolistic markets. *European Economic Integration, 34*, 753–769.

Venables, A. (1990b). International capacity choice and the national market games. *Journal of International Economics, 29*, 23–42.

CHAPTER 5

Trade Growth Accounting in Goods and Services: An Empirical Exercise

Somesh K. Mathur, Sarbjit Singh, Gaurav Doshi, and Abhishek Srivastava

5.1 Introduction

The second half of the twentieth century and the beginning of the twenty-first century have seen an enormous surge in trade across nations in various sectors. Almost every country in the world engages in trade with multiple other countries based on various factors, and this trade is of interest to academicians, politicians, bureaucratic officials, corporate firms, and even activists. Trade in the modern world is not just limited to fulfilling a nation's need for the resources it lacks, but it is also crucial from a strategic point of view. The types of trading partners a nation has also determines its stance in international politics.

Another major reason why trade has become so important is the lowering of trade costs through the years. Technological advancements and better trade policies have played a major role in easing trade and lowering trade barriers across nations. In this chapter, we describe the reasons behind trade growth in goods and services over the years for selected countries by using

S.K. Mathur (✉) • G. Doshi • A. Srivastava
Indian Institute of Technology Kanpur, Kanpur, India

S. Singh
Consumer Unity & Trust Society (CUTS) International, Jaipur, India

S.K. Mathur et al. (eds.), *Theorizing International Trade*,
https://doi.org/10.1007/978-981-10-1759-9_5

Novy's measure given in Chap. 2. We also calculate trade costs in terms of tariff equivalents by using the indirect trade cost measure given by Novy. The calculation of trade costs and trade growth accounting for both goods and services is shown in two separate sections as follows.

5.2 Trade Growth Accounting in Goods Trade

The present study focuses on the calculation of trade costs of APEC[1] (Asia Pacific Economic Cooperation) nations and the growth of goods trade between APEC nations and India over the period of 25 years between 1990 and 2014. The data for this study has been extracted from OECD, UN (United Nations), and IMF (International Monetary Fund) databases. Because this study focuses in particular on aggregate trade in merchandise goods between India and the 21 APEC nations, it is essential that the services part of trade be excluded.

The IMF's Direction of Trade Statistics (DOTS) provides bilateral trade data about merchandise goods. Export data is free on board (FOB) and import data is cost, insurance, and freight (CIF). We have downloaded the annual bilateral data from 1990 to 2014 for India and the APEC nations. The export data of goods is taken from the IMF's International Financial Statistics (IFS). The data on GDP and services produced (value added) of India and the APEC nations is taken from World Development Indicators from the World Bank. Because we use value added data for finding international trade, no further manipulation is performed on these datasets. Missing data from these sources is complemented with data extracted from the OECD, Unstat, and APEC databases. All data is expressed in current US dollars.

In order to construct the tariff equivalent, τ_{ij} India is considered to be country i and the APEC nations as a whole are considered to be country j. The elasticity of substitution σ is assumed to be eight as specified by Anderson and van Wincoop (2003). The tariff equivalents derived from the observable trade flow of merchandise goods following the methodology adopted by Novy (2013) are given in Table 5.1.

The results in Table 5.1 reveal that the decrease in tariff equivalents is found to be at a maximum in the case of China, at about 68.09 percent, whereas the minimum is in case of Canada, only about 14.50 percent from 1990 to 2010.[2] A fall of more than 50 percent in tariff equivalents is observed in bilateral trade with Chile (−55.19%), Republic of Korea (−54.26%), Mexico (−53.31%), and Peru (−56.1%).

Table 5.1 Percentage change in τ_{ij} for the APEC nations

Trading partner	$t_{initial}$	$\tau_{initial}$	t_{final}	τ_{final}	τ_{mean}	*Percentage change*
China	1990	2.78	2014	0.89	1.30	−68.09
Peru	1991	3.34	2012	1.47	2.24	−56.14
Chile	1990	2.48	2014	1.11	1.63	−55.19
Korea, Rep. of	1990	1.58	2014	0.72	1.08	−54.26
Mexico	1990	2.23	2014	1.04	1.80	−53.31
Papua New Guinea	1990	3.04	2004	1.53	2.70	−49.77
Philippines	1990	2.64	2014	1.38	1.55	−47.56
Indonesia	1990	1.68	2014	0.92	1.17	−45.42
Malaysia	1990	1.32	2014	0.86	1.07	−35.14
Singapore	1990	1.06	2013	0.69	0.87	−34.94
Australia	1990	1.42	2014	1.01	1.16	−29.14
Japan	1990	1.30	2013	0.98	1.23	−24.96
New Zealand	1990	1.87	2011	1.41	1.61	−24.39
United States	1997	1.11	2013	0.84	0.99	−24.29
Russian Federation	1992	1.61	2013	1.26	1.26	−21.61
Canada	1990	1.71	2010	1.46	1.54	−14.50

Source: Authors' calculations

5.2.1 *Trade Growth Accounting*

In order to better understand the question of how trade between nations has evolved over time and what factor(s) contribute the most, one needs to look over the various components of growth of trade. The gravity model provides a simple yet powerful framework for analysis. We use the similar logic of decomposition for growth of trade between three main components given by Novy (2013), as derived in the previous chapter. The study further decompose the first component, income growth, into two parts using the work by Baier and Bergstrand (2001). Using the formula of income shares (s), $s_i = y_i/(y_i + y_j)$, $\Delta\ln(y_i y_j)$ becomes: $\Delta\ln(s_i s_j) + 2\Delta\ln(y_i + y_j)$. Hence, the final equation becomes:

$$\Delta\ln\left(x_{ij}x_{ji}\right) = 2\Delta\ln\left(s_i s_j\right) + 2\Delta\ln\left(\frac{\left(y_i + y_j\right)^2}{y^W}\right) + 2(1-\sigma)\Delta\ln\left(1+\tau_{ij}\right) - 2(1-\sigma)\Delta\ln\left(\Phi_i\Phi_j\right)$$

where $\Delta\ln(s_i s_j)$ can be interpreted as income convergence or the change in income inequality between countries i and j. The second term,

$\Delta\ln\left(\frac{(y_i+y_j)^2}{y^W}\right)$ can be interpreted as growth in the incomes of countries *i* and *j* relative to world income.[3] Dividing the final equation throughout by the left-hand term, we obtain:

$$100\% = \underbrace{\frac{2\Delta\ln(s_i s_j)}{\Delta\ln(x_{ij}x_{ji})}}_{(a)} + \underbrace{\frac{2\Delta\ln\left(\frac{(y_i+y_j)^2}{y^W}\right)}{\Delta\ln(x_{ij}x_{ji})}}_{(b)} + \underbrace{\frac{2(1-\sigma)\Delta\ln(1+\tau_{ij})}{\Delta\ln(x_{ij}x_{ji})}}_{(c)}$$

$$- \underbrace{\frac{2(1-\sigma)\Delta\ln(\Phi_i\Phi_j)}{\Delta\ln(x_{ij}x_{ji})}}_{(d)}$$

As per the above equation, the growth of bilateral trade decomposed into four components which are the focus of the current study. The contributions are: (a) income inequality or income convergence; (b) growth of incomes (in an additive sense) relative to world income; (c) a change in relative bilateral trade costs measured using the tariff equivalent τ_{ij}; and (d) a change in relative multilateral resistance. The contributions of (c) and (d) can be positive or negative depending on various factors which will not be analyzed in this study.[4] Novy (2013) refers to the negative contribution of (d) as the trade diversion effect, that is, if multilateral resistance of a country falls, its trade with other countries rises, but bilateral trade with country *j* falls. The decomposition equation takes a similar form if other gravity model formulations such as the Ricardian model by Eaton and Kortum (2002) or the heterogeneous firms model by Chaney (2008) or Melitz and Ottaviano (2008) are used.[5] Table 5.2 presents results of the decomposition of sampled APEC countries' trade growth with India into four components over the given study period.

Results in Table 5.2 reveal that on average income convergence is found to have the lowest contribution followed by a decrease in the multilateral trade barrier. The negative sign on a value for the multilateral trade barrier (third component) indicates that a decrease in the multilateral trade barriers of country *j* with nations other than India led to a decline in its bilateral trade with India. Income growth and a decline in the bilateral trade barrier

Table 5.2 Decomposition of bilateral trade growth of APEC countries with India

Trading partner	$t_{initial}$	t_{final}	*Growth of trade*	*Income convergence*	*Growth of income*	*Decline in bilateral trade costs*	*Decline in multilateral resistance*	*Total*
Australia	1990	2014	528.51	−1.03	84.51	49.35	−32.83	100.00
Canada	1990	2010	400.81	4.11	75.63	33.12	−12.86	100.00
Chile	1990	2014	1004.16	3.90	50.36	69.53	−23.79	100.00
China	1990	2014	1411.65	−7.84	63.86	68.86	−24.88	100.00
Indonesia	1990	2014	837.01	2.60	62.40	55.83	−20.82	100.00
Japan	1990	2013	319.64	52.54	10.86	66.88	−30.27	100.00
Korea, Rep. of	1990	2014	712.79	−1.03	62.86	79.44	−41.27	100.00
Mexico	1990	2014	857.76	−1.00	53.20	75.10	−27.31	100.00
Malaysia	1990	2014	656.20	3.74	76.85	47.60	−28.20	100.00
New Zealand	1990	2011	490.70	−11.91	88.15	49.11	−25.36	100.00
Peru	1991	2012	1105.48	−2.53	47.61	71.88	−16.96	100.00
Philippines	1990	2014	875.61	0.61	56.84	67.72	−25.17	100.00
Papua New Guinea	1990	2004	648.68	−17.69	28.55	101.29	−12.16	100.00
Russian Federation	1992	2013	450.94	2.23	99.17	43.76	−45.16	100.00
Singapore	1990	2013	612.72	7.18	77.54	45.38	−30.10	100.00
United States	1997	2013	363.12	39.18	32.09	51.87	−23.14	100.00
Mean			**704.74**	**4.57**	**60.66**	**61.04**	**−26.27**	**100.00**
Mean (excluding JPN, USA)			**753.18**	**−0.94**	**65.88**	**61.27**	**−26.21**	–

Source: Authors' calculations

have different contributions across different nations, but on average both have almost the same contribution, that is, approximately 61percent.

Further, by looking at the countrywide results, the study observed unusually high values of income convergence in the case of Japan (52.54%) and the United States (39.18%). Excluding these two nations, the mean contributions of the four components were −0.94, 65.88, 61.27, and −26.21 percent, respectively, and income convergence/inequality was found to have the least contribution towards the growth of bilateral trade.

The income convergence term measures the contribution of change in incomes of nation *i* and *j* with respect to the income shares on bilateral trade. Hence, a fall in incomes of either *i* or *j* in some particular period would lead to a negative contribution towards bilateral trade. In other words, a substantive fall in either trading nation in some period could impact bilateral trade in that period. This is what is observed in the cases of nations like Australia, China, Republic of Korea, Mexico, New Zealand, Peru, and Papua New Guinea. The overall trade growth and income convergence is constructed from individual changes between two periods. A fall in income of nation *i* or *j* or both, which is enough to lower the value of the income convergence term with respect to the previous period leads to a negative contribution to total bilateral trade. Such a pattern is observed in the above-mentioned nations across a few periods, leading to an overall negative contribution of income convergence.

Moreover, for most nations, the growth of income is the primary factor behind the rise of bilateral trade. Growth in income is the dominant factor in the case of Australia, Canada, Indonesia, Malaysia, New Zealand, the Russia Federation, and Singapore with a contribution of over 75 percent towards bilateral trade (with the exception of Indonesia, where the growth of income contributes 62.40 percent but is still the dominant factor). The other dominant factor is the decline in bilateral trade costs, which is the case of Chile, China, Republic of Korea, Mexico, Peru, and the Philippines. The United States is the largest contributor to the growth of bilateral trade with India. The effect of the decline in bilateral trade costs is offset by the decline in multilateral trade barriers or multilateral resistance, which has a negative impact on the growth of bilateral trade. This is at a maximum in the case of the Russian Federation, where a decline in multilateral resistance has led to a decline in bilateral trade by about 45 percent.

5.2.2 *Concluding Remarks*

The results obtained from income convergence or income inequality in trade growth decomposition raise additional questions that need to be consiered, such as why do we observe a positive contribution of income inequality for some nations and a negative contribution in the case of others? What factors come into play that lead to different scales of contributions of income growth and decline in bilateral trade cost terms across different countries? All these questions, and others, require a thorough analysis of the economies in context.

5.3 Trade Growth Accounting in Trade in Services

The WTO's General Agreement on Trade in Services (GATS) became effective in January 1995 with the objective of increasing bilateral as well as multilateral trade in services. It defines four mode of supply of services. These are (i) cross-border supply; (ii) consumption abroad; (iii) commercial presence; and (iv) the presence of a natural person. In mode 3 and 4, the exporter remains in the territory of the importer country, and it is very difficult to account the information. The data is available mainly in mode 1 and 2, which reflect directly on a country's balance of payment.

In our study, we look at the trade costs associated with India's bilateral trade in services with the 61 countries for which data is available. Very few studies have been done on trade in services due to an unavailability of data. Miroudot et al. (2010) have looked into data on trade in services from 1995 to 2007 and have found that trade costs in services have remained steady or have increased during this period (with the exception of China), whereas the trade costs in goods have fallen substantially. They also found out that Regional Trade Agreements (RTAs) have much less effect on trade costs in services as compared to trade costs in goods.

PrabirDe has applied the three-stage gravity model to panel data for India's bilateral trade in services from 2000 to 2006 with 31 countries for 10 major components of service trade including the following: transportation, travel, communication services, financial services, insurance services, computer services, and information services. He found a coefficient with a similar sign to that in the gravity model of trade by Anderson and Wincoop. He also calculated a services trade facilitation index for these countries' bilateral trade in services with India for the same time period.

5.3.1 Database

There are five major databases for trade in services: (i) Eurostat, covering 32 countries; (ii) the IMF and OECD, covering 35 countries; (iii) the UN, covering 46 countries; and (iv) the WTO, covering 49 countries. Services trade data for many countries is not available. The present study utilizes consolidated data based on these databases by Francois and Pindyuk (2013). The data set contains a large number of missing entries because of the unavailability of data. This is also because many countries started accounting and publishing services trade data after 1995. In the context of India, the data set contains bilateral trade data from 60 countries as well as some country groups. The data is highly unbalanced. Data on the GDP in trade in services is taken from the World Bank. The data on total exports and imports in services have been taken from Francois and Pindyuk (2013).

5.3.2 Empirical Findings

Figure 5.1 shows the tariff equivalents calculated for India's trade with the entire world. The value of x_{ii} has been derived by subtracting net exports to India from the value of services GDP of the rest of the world (excluding India, of course). The tariff equivalents declined until 2005, and there have been some fluctuations thereafter.

Contrary to the conclusions of Miroudot et al. (2010), the tariff equivalents of trade in services have fallen in India during the period 1995–2005. They went back up in 2006–2007, but then fell again in 2008, and then rose again in 2009–2010. The tariff equivalents of India's trade in services has followed a different trend for different countries, but it went up for many countries in the period 2008–2010. This may have been because of the 2008 recession because India's services export was mainly concentrated in richer, developed countries whose economies were affected by those economic troubles.

Figure 5.2 shows the contribution of three components, derived using Novy's method, in India's trade in services from 1995 to 2010. The trend shows that the contribution of growth in income was 61.49 percent, the contribution of a decline in bilateral trade costs (i.e., tariff equivalents) was 48.50 percent, and the contribution of the decline in MTR was –9.99 percent. Here, the value of x_{ii} (world) has been derived by subtracting net

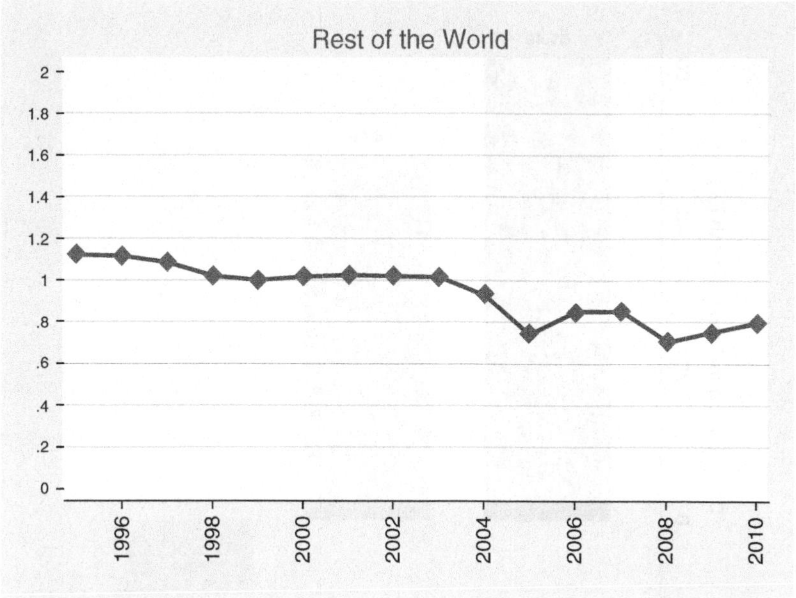

Fig. 5.1 Tariff equivalents for India's trade with the entire world (Source: Authors' calculations)

exports to India from the value of services GDP with the rest of the world (excluding India).

Tables 5.3 and 5.4 show the countrywide results of tariff equivalents and decomposition of trade growth in services of India with sampled countries in detail.

5.3.3 Concluding Remarks

Overall, India's tariff equivalents have gone down since 1995 with some fluctuations over the years. On the trade growth accounting front, our study found that income growth and decline in tariff equivalents contributed to trade growth while the contribution due to the decline in MTR was much less. Hence, from the point of view of policy, there is a need to focus on income growth and a reduction in tariffs. Governments should promote exports, FDI, and use other monitoring tools to improve GDP, which will

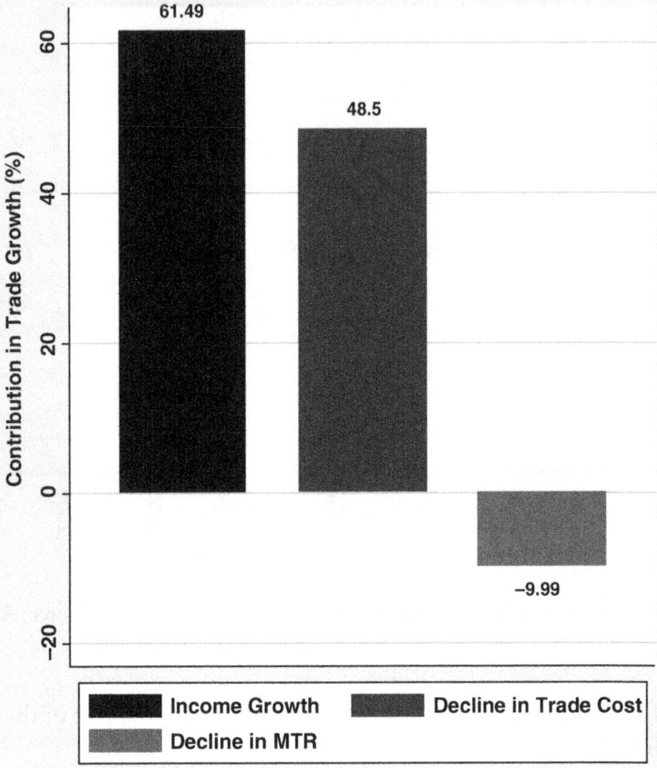

Fig. 5.2 Accounting for services trade growth in India (Source: Authors' calculations)

result in increased welfare of the people as well as an increase in the trade in services. As the decline in trade costs reaches a 48.5 percent contribution in services trade growth, tools such as a free trade agreement for trade in services will result in more trade taking place. So, a free trade agreement for trade in services with the European Union, Hong Kong, the United States, Singapore, and the United Kingdom will result in more trade with these countries.

Table 5.3 Novy's tariff equivalents for India's total trade in services

Year	*AUT*	*DEU*	*FIN*	*FRA*	*GBR*	*ITA*	*NLD*	*JPN*	*PRT*	*GRC*	*DNK*	*ESP*	*SWE*	*CZE*	*HUN*	*USA*
1995	2.49	1.58	2.89	1.97	1.45	2.17	1.92	–	–	3.41	–	–	–	–	–	–
1996	2.26	1.59	3.00	1.74	1.51	1.96	1.85	1.90	3.36	3.05	–	–	–	–	–	–
1997	2.30	1.68	3.28	1.74	1.44	1.91	1.85	1.89	3.21	–	–	–	–	–	–	–
1998	2.26	1.66	3.20	1.61	1.46	1.85	1.80	1.89	3.19	–	–	–	–	–	–	–
1999	2.23	1.75	3.79	1.76	1.43	1.83	1.80	1.96	3.26	3.25	1.79	3.69	2.39	–	3.93	1.54
2000	2.09	1.72	3.47	1.76	1.40	1.90	1.87	1.95	3.09	3.36	1.69	3.49	2.42	3.15	–	1.48
2001	2.14	1.80	3.86	1.94	1.40	2.00	1.77	2.03	3.19	3.38	1.69	3.40	2.50	2.88	4.14	1.48
2002	2.25	1.72	3.52	2.11	1.46	2.19	2.00	2.09	3.21	2.95	1.75	3.32	2.47	2.95	4.22	1.49
2003	2.13	1.66	1.77	1.77	1.30	2.00	1.64	1.98	3.21	2.63	1.68	3.28	1.93	3.08	3.05	1.40
2004	2.20	1.67	1.86	1.83	1.36	2.07	1.70	1.97	3.30	2.60	1.74	3.38	2.00	3.18	3.02	1.43
2005	1.26	1.35	1.37	1.40	1.10	1.49	1.28	1.69	2.68	2.04	1.31	1.64	1.37	2.31	1.62	1.19
2006	2.03	1.53	1.59	1.63	1.28	1.92	1.70	2.00	3.22	2.38	1.47	2.24	1.92	2.93	2.46	1.28
2007	2.03	1.54	1.47	1.67	1.30	1.94	1.62	1.92	2.73	–	1.49	2.22	1.95	2.79	2.63	1.25
2008	1.27	1.23	1.17	1.36	1.46	1.50	1.44	1.52	1.87	1.79	1.46	1.64	1.27	2.15	1.60	1.08
2009	1.36	1.32	1.18	1.43	1.29	1.70	1.47	1.72	2.05	1.88	1.56	1.77	1.33	2.09	2.17	1.12
2010	2.23	1.49	1.30	1.68	1.32	2.00	1.66	1.86	3.09	3.04	1.59	2.28	1.89	2.45	2.52	1.23

Year	*AUS*	*HKG*	*SGP*	*SVK*	*BEL*	*CYP*	*IRL*	*LUX*	*BGR*	*EST*	*HRV*	*POL*	*RUS*	*SVN*	*LTU*	*MLT*
1999	1.83	–	–	3.77	–	–	–	–	–	–	–	–	–	–	–	–
2000	1.80	1.73	1.32	–	–	–	–	–	–	–	–	–	–	–	–	–
2001	1.82	1.71	1.27	3.93	–	–	–	–	–	–	–	–	–	–	–	–
2002	1.84	1.74	1.24	–	2.33	3.11	2.58	2.53	–	–	–	–	–	–	–	–
2003	1.77	1.70	1.16	5.41	2.20	2.96	2.05	2.18	3.37	3.60	3.35	2.96	1.79	3.42	–	3.35
2004	1.71	1.54	1.12	5.34	2.27	3.06	2.31	2.25	3.49	3.68	3.40	3.04	1.99	3.52	4.06	3.47
2005	1.39	1.08	0.83	2.64	1.06	2.36	1.41	1.04	1.90	2.63	3.96	1.55	1.74	3.35	3.24	2.20
2006	1.58	1.49	1.08	3.93	2.10	2.88	1.74	2.11	3.52	3.32	3.26	2.68	2.11	3.64	2.70	3.36
2007	1.56	1.49	1.07	3.66	1.91	2.84	1.60	1.85	3.35	3.44	3.24	2.68	2.11	3.65	3.46	3.26
2008	1.61	1.17	0.89	2.45	1.36	2.18	1.11	1.00	2.60	2.48	3.01	1.95	2.24	2.87	2.76	1.92
2009	1.67	1.15	0.87	2.83	1.34	2.20	1.02	1.04	2.52	2.52	3.10	2.23	1.75	3.03	3.27	2.00
2010		1.42	1.04	4.12	1.70	2.96	1.62	2.39	3.59	3.40	2.71	2.63	2.24	3.22	4.18	3.02

Source: Authors' calculations

Table 5.4 Trade growth accounting for India's total trade in services

Country	*ISO code*	*Start year*	*End year*	*Contribution of*		
				Income growth (%)	*Decline in trade cost (%)*	*Decline in MTR (%)*
Austria	AUT	1995	2010	73.05	31.34	−4.39
Germany	DEU	1995	2010	80.66	18.59	0.74
Finland	FIN	1995	2010	28.25	74.39	−2.64
France	FRA	1995	2010	67.11	37.74	−4.85
United Kingdom	GBR	1995	2010	85.31	22.78	−8.08
Italy	ITA	1995	2010	85.58	23.65	−9.23
Netherlands	NLD	1995	2010	73.89	34.14	−8.03
Japan	JPN	1996	2010	81.46	7.70	10.84
Portugal	PRT	1996	2010	80.28	26.02	−6.30
Greece	GRC	1995	2010	79.92	31.06	−10.98
Denmark	DNK	1999	2010	73.61	33.39	−7.01
Spain	ESP	1999	2010	38.19	67.94	−6.13
Sweden	SWE	1999	2010	54.10	50.97	−5.07
Czech Republic	CZE	2000	2010	69.66	49.58	−19.24
Hungary	HUN	1999	2010	43.36	65.32	−8.69
United States	USA	1999	2010	55.21	47.89	−3.10
Australia	AUS	1999	2009	92.29	28.95	−21.25
Hong Kong	HKG	2000	2010	49.50	46.93	3.57
Singapore	SGP	2000	2010	73.70	43.10	−16.80
Slovak Republic	SVK	1999	2010	215.30	−65.16	−50.15
Belgium	BEL	2002	2010	47.89	60.31	−8.20
Cyprus	CYP	2002	2010	101.82	20.38	−22.20
Ireland	IRL	2002	2010	32.92	66.59	0.49
Luxembourg	LUX	2002	2010	92.79	20.43	−13.22
Bulgaria	BGR	2003	2010	202.08	−52.28	−49.80
Estonia	EST	2003	2010	100.09	25.69	−25.79
Croatia	HRV	2003	2010	54.02	57.71	−11.73
Poland	POL	2003	2010	83.12	39.73	−22.85
Russian Federation	RUS	2003	2010	1411.08	−841.58	−469.50
Slovenia	SVN	2003	2010	85.51	28.02	−13.53
Lithuania	LTU	2004	2010	171.50	−31.65	−39.85
Malta	MLT	2003	2010	66.09	38.49	−4.59

Source: Authors' calculations

Notes

1. Its member nations include the 21 Pacific Rim nations: Australia, Brunei Darussalam, Canada, Chile, People's Republic of China, Hong Kong, Indonesia, Japan, Republic of Korea, Malaysia, Mexico, New Zealand, Papua New Guinea, Peru, the Philippines, Russia, Singapore, Chinese Taipei (Taiwan), Thailand, the United States, and Vietnam. Due to data limitations and errors we have excluded Brunei Darussalam, Hong Kong, Taiwan, Thailand, and Vietnam from the sample.
2. Data for Canada was available only until 2010.
3. Novy (2013) interprets $\Delta \ln\left(\frac{y_i y_j}{y^W}\right)$ as the growth in incomes of country i and j relative to world income. The equation $\Delta \ln\left(\frac{(y_i+y_j)^2}{y^W}\right)$ has been derived from the same term by a small mathematical manipulation, hence it is plausible to assume this as income growth as well. The only difference is that the present study assumed income growth in an additive sense, whereas Novy assumed it in a multiplicative sense.
4. If $\Delta \ln(1+\tau_{ij})<0$, then the contribution of (c) becomes positive and if $\Delta \ln(\Phi_i\Phi_j)<0$, then the contribution of (d) becomes negative.
5. See Novy (2013) for the decompositions of other models.

References

Anderson, E. J., & Wincoop, V. E. (2003). Gravity with gravitas: A solution to the border puzzle. *The American Economic Review, 93*, 170–192.

Baier, S. L., & Bergstrand, J. H. (2001). The growth of world trade: Tariffs, transport costs, and income similarity. *Journal of International Economics, 53*(1), 1–27.

Chaney, T. (2008). Distorted gravity: The intensive and extensive margins of international trade. *The American Economic Review, 98*(4), 1707–1721.

Eaton, J., & Kortum, S. (2002). Technology, geography, and trade. *Econometrica, 70*(5), 1741–1779.

Francois J., & Pindyuk O. (2013). *Consolidated data on international trade in services v8.7.* IIDE discussion paper no. 20130101. Retrieved from www. I4ide. org/content/wpaper/dp20130101.

Melitz, M. J., & Ottaviano, G. I. (2008). Market size, trade, and productivity. *Review of Economic Studies, 75*, 295–316.

Miroudot, S., Sauvage, J., & Shepherd, B. (2010). *Measuring the cost of international trade in services* (MPRA paper 27655). University Library of Munich, Germany.

Novy, D. (2013). Gravity redux: Measuring international trade costs with panel data. *Economic Enquiry, 51*(1), 101–121.

CHAPTER 6

Calculation of Ad Valorem Equivalents of Non-Tariff Barriers: A Case Study of 16 RCEP Countries

Sarbjit Singh and Rahul Arora

6.1 Introduction

Apart from tariff barriers, administrative and geographical barriers to trade also have a negative impact on trade. All these barriers restrict trade by increasing the number of days to exchange goods from one country to another. These barriers include: number of documents required to trade, online availability of information related to trade procedures, number of procedures requested to start a business, and existing levels of corruption and infrastructure, among others. Reduction in all these hurdles to trade is called trade facilitation (TF). Regional trade agreements (RTAs) include commitments aimed at reducing all the existing and potential barriers to trade, some of which are administrative barriers. Under the proposed Regional Comprehensive Economic Partnership (RCEP) agreement, the guiding principles of negotiation include provisions to facilitate trade and investment among member countries. Under this provision, member countries shall try "*to enhance transparency in trade and investment relations between the participating countries, as well as to facilitate the participating countries' engagement in global and regional supply chains.*"

S. Singh (✉) • R. Arora
Consumer Unity & Trust Society (CUTS) International, Jaipur, India

S.K. Mathur et al. (eds.), *Theorizing International Trade*,
https://doi.org/10.1007/978-981-10-1759-9_6

In recent literature, studies have focused on the calculation of ad valorem equivalents (AVEs) of these barriers (sectorwide as well as countrywide) and have attempted to look into the impact of these barriers on trade and other macroeconomic variables using partial and general equilibrium approaches. Both approaches have their own merits over the other, and sometimes one approach complements the other by providing the extent of the restriction of the barriers on trade.

Results from these studies have raised the need for a countrywide detailed analysis that can provide the sectorwide extent of the restrictiveness of these trade barriers. Information on sectorwide restrictiveness would further help to form an appropriate policy framework to remove the barriers that hinder trade.

The study in the present chapter attempts to enrich the literature by calculating the restrictiveness of administrative barriers to trade in tariff-equivalent terms for 42 merchandise sectors in order to quantify the effects of these barriers on bilateral trade among the 16 RCEP member countries. To the best of our knowledge, not even a single study exists in the literature assuming such a detailed level of disaggregation at the product level for countrywide analysis.

Using an econometric approach, following Zaki (2010), sectorwide AVEs of time to import and time to export have been calculated, and the results of the estimated augmented gravity model have been presented to show the impact of time to import and time to export on bilateral trade flows. To pursue the study's objective, this chapter is divided into five sections. Section 6.2 explains the extent of trade barriers in the 16 member countries of the proposed RCEP. In Sect. 6.3, econometric methodology is discussed with the help of the AVEs that have been calculated. In Sect. 6.4, detailed empirical results are discussed. The final section concludes the study with some policy implications.

6.2 Trade Barriers in RCEP Economies

Tables 6.1 and 6.2 present existing levels of trade barriers related to trade transaction costs (TTCs) in RCEP member countries and their ranking regarding the ease of trade across borders as provided in the Doing Business Report 2015. Table 6.1 also shows the average level of the ad valorem most favored nation (MFN) tariff rate in addition to the trade barriers related to the TTCs. On the basis of data given in both tables, the major highlights of

Table 6.1 Extent of trade barriers in RCEP countries in 2015

S. no.	*Country*	*AVE MFN applied tariff*	*Time to import (in days)*	*Time to export (in days)*	*Documents to import (in umber)*	*Documents to export (in umber)*	*Costs to import (in SD)*	*Costs to export (in USD)*	*Ease of trading across borders (ranking)*
1.	Australia	2.7	8	9	7	5	1220	1200	49
2.	China	9.6	24	21	5	8	800	823	98
3.	India	13.5	21	17	10	7	1462	1332	126
4.	Japan	4.2	11	11	5	3	1021.3	829.3	20
5.	New Zealand	2.0	9	10	6	4	825	870	27
6.	South Korea	13.3	7	8	3	3	695	670	03
7.	Brunei	1.2	15	19	5	5	770	705	46
8.	Burma	5.6[a]	22	20	8	8	610	620	103
9.	Cambodia	11.2	24	22	9	8	930	795	124
10.	Indonesia	6.9	26	17	8	4	646.8	571.8	62
11.	Laos PDR	10	26	23	10	10	1910	1950	156
12.	Malaysia	6.1	8	11	4	4	560	525	11
13.	Philippines	6.3	15	15	7	6	915	755	65
14.	Singapore	0.2	4	6	3	3	440	460	1
15.	Thailand	11.6	13	14	5	5	760	595	36
16.	Vietnam	9.5	21	21	8	5	600	610	75

Notes: [a]Represents data for year 2013; Rank 1 shows the best and 189 shows the worst in the ease of trading across borders
Source: Authors' elaboration using data from *Doing Business* and World Tariff Profile, 2015

Table 6.2 Time and cost associated with each stage to import and export

Stages →	*Customs clearance and inspections*	*Documents preparation*	*Inland transportation and handling*	*Ports and terminal handling*
Australia				
Days (cost) to import	1 (170)	3 (200)	2 (450)	2 (400)
Days (cost) to export	1 (65)	5 (285)	2 (450)	1 (400)
China (Shanghai)				
Days (cost) to import	4 (80)	15 (260)	2 (135)	3 (140)
Days (cost) to export	2 (80)	14 (305)	2 (95)	3 (140)
India				
Days (cost) to import	4 (200)	8 (400)	3 (400)	5 (250)
Days (cost) to export	2 (130)	8 (365)	3 (400)	3 (225)
Japan				
Days (cost) to import	2 (135)	5 (277)	2 (200)	2 (250)
Days (cost) to export	2 (75)	5 (145)	2 (200)	2 (250)
New Zealand				
Days (cost) to import	1 (50)	5 (175)	2 (300)	1 (300)
Days (cost) to export	1 (50)	5 (220)	2 (300)	2 (300)
South Korea				
Days (cost) to import	1 (30)	2 (65)	2 (500)	2 (100)
Days (cost) to export	1 (15)	3 (55)	2 (500)	2 (100)
Brunei				
Days (cost) to import	1 (80)	11 (150)	1 (225)	2 (315)
Days (cost) to export	2 (50)	11 (190)	3 (225)	3 (240)
Burma (Myanmar)				
Days (cost) to import	4 (80)	10 (165)	2 (200)	6 (165)
Days (cost) to export	3 (80)	12 (175)	2 (200)	3 (165)
Cambodia				
Days (cost) to import	3 (280)	15 (225)	2 (200)	4 (225)
Days (cost) to export	3 (275)	14 (220)	2 (200)	3 (100)
Indonesia				
Days (cost) to import	4 (125)	13 (210)	2 (160)	7 (165)
Days (cost) to export	1 (125)	11 (135)	3 (160)	2 (165)
Laos PDR				
Days (cost) to import	7 (195)	13 (205)	4 (1350)	2 (160)
Days (cost) to export	2 (150)	15 (290)	3 (1350)	3 (160)
Malaysia				
Days (cost) to import	1 (60)	3 (120)	2 (260)	2 (120)
Days (cost) to export	1 (60)	5 (85)	3 (260)	2 (120)
Philippines				
Days (cost) to import	2 (185)	8 (90)	2 (340)	3 (300)
Days (cost) to export	2 (85)	8 (105)	2 (340)	3 (225)

(*continued*)

Table 6.2 (continued)

Stages →	*Customs clearance and inspections*	*Documents preparation*	*Inland transportation and handling*	*Ports and terminal handling*
Singapore				
Days (cost) to import	1 (50)	1 (100)	1 (140)	1 (150)
Days (cost) to export	1 (50)	2 (120)	2 (140)	1 (150)
Thailand				
Days (cost) to import	2 (255)	8 (135)	1 (210)	2 (160)
Days (cost) to export	1 (50)	8 (175)	2 (210)	3 (160)
Vietnam				
Days (cost) to import	4 (95)	12 (130)	1 (200)	4 (175)
Days (cost) to export	4 (100)	12 (160)	2 (200)	3 (150)

Note: Cost is in USD
Source: Doing Business Database (2015)

country-level obstacles and recent reforms in trading across borders by RCEP countries are given as follows:

- In all RCEP countries, document preparation takes the maximum number of days, which can be reduced further to facilitate trade. Table 6.3 shows the types of documents used in trading across borders.
- Singapore, South Korea, and Malaysia are in the top 15 ranked countries for ease of trade across borders, requiring a fewer number of documents.
- Countries ranked high for ease of trading across borders include: Laos, India, Cambodia, Burma, China, and Vietnam. However, the time taken to import and export for these countries is very high.
- China relaxed trade credit restrictions to ease trading across borders (DB, 2010).
- Indonesia launched a single window service to reduce the time to export (DB, 2010).
- Vietnam reduced the time to trade by implementing rules for customs administration and increasing competition in the logistics industry (DB, 2010), but It still takes more time in document preparation.
- Brunei introduced an electronic customs system that made trade easier (DB, 2011).

Table 6.3 Types of documents in trade across borders

Documents to import	*Documents to export*
Bill of lading	Bill of lading
Commercial invoice	Commercial invoice
Customs import declaration	Customs export declaration
Packing declaration	Packing list
Packing list	Technical standard/health certificate
Release order	Contract between exporter and importer
Technical standard/health certificate	Foreign exchange form
Contract between exporter and importer	Station receipts
Cargo release order	Terminal handling receipts
Insurance documentation	Export declaration form
Proof of payments of customs, excise, and taxation	Export permit
Certified engineer's report (NOC)	Inspection report
Foreign currency exchange form	Insurance certificate
Inspection report	Certificate of origin
Product manual	Customs transit document
Terminal handling receipts	Bank certificate
Tax certificate	Sales contract
Certificate of origin	Shipping instruction
Preshipment inspection clean report of findings	
Customs delivery order for imports	
Quarantine certificate (container packing declaration)	
Gate pass	
Delivery order	
Import permit	

Note: The list of documents is exhaustive and includes all types of documents required to trade across borders
Source: Doing Business Report (2015)

- Cambodia eliminated preshipment inspections which reduced the time and number of documents required in trade (DB, 2011).
- The Philippines improved its electronic customs system by adding electronic payments and online submission of declarations (DB, 2011).
- Laos implemented an electronic data interchange system at the Thanaleng-Friendship bridge border crossing (DB, 2013).
- Myanmar reduced the number of documents required for exports and imports (DB, 2015).

- In the Philippines, new city ordinances in Manila restricted truck traffic, which made trading across the border more difficult (DB, 2015).
- In Indonesia, due to insufficient infrastructure at Tanjung Priok port in Jakarta, trading across borders became more difficult (DB, 2015).

6.3 Methodology and Data

Following Zaki (2010), our present study utilizes the augmented gravity model to discover the impact of trade facilitation on bilateral trade flows (TFs). Estimation of the augmented gravity model provides the effect of TF on bilateral import flows. Here, the term TF relates to a reduction in the number of days in time to import and time to export due to better implementation of TFMs, due to which the TTCs decline, thus improving the level of bilateral trade. The effect is shown by the coefficients of estimated time to export and time to import variables. The study also calculates the AVEs of administrative barriers using the methodology given by Kee et al. (2009). The stepwise procedure of the econometric approach is given as follows:

Step 1 In step 1, two regression Eqs. (6.1) and (6.2), *Time to Import* ($Time^{imp}$), *Time to Export* ($Time^{exp}$) have been estimated with a host of independent variables as control variables. As already shown in the previous section, time to import and time to export are positively related with the number of documents required for imports (*ImDoc*) and exports (*ExDoc*), the number of procedures (*ImProc* and *ExProc*) to start a business in the home country, and the level of corruption[1] (*Corr*) in the country, and they are inversely related to the internet intensity (*InterInt*) representing the technological advancement in relation to computerization of all trading processes. In addition, both equations include the *Island* dummy to represent the geographical nature of a country, that is, 1 if a country is an island country, 0 otherwise.

$$\ln(Time_i^{imp}) = k + \beta_0 \ln(InterInt_i) + \beta_1 \ln(\mathrm{Im}Doc_i) + \beta_2 \ln(Corr_i) + \beta_3 \ln(ImProc_i) + \beta_4 Island_i + e_i \quad (6.1)$$

$$\ln\left(Time_j^{\exp}\right) = k + \beta_0 \ln\left(InterInt_j\right) + \beta_1 \ln\left(ExDoc_j\right) + \beta_2 \ln\left(Corr_j\right) + \beta_3 \ln\left(ExProc_j\right) + \beta_4\, Island_j + e_j \tag{6.2}$$

where i and j are importer and exporter, respectively. Estimation of these two regression equations provides the estimated values of time to import and time to export variables.

Step 2 In step 2, an augmented gravity equation has been estimated with a host of independent variables including the estimated time to import and time to export variables calculated in step 1. Equation (6.3) shows the augmented gravity model which has been estimated to provide the effect of TFMs—such as reducing the time to import and export—on bilateral trade flows between RCEP economies.

$$\ln\left(\frac{m_{ij}}{m_{ii}}\right) = A + \beta_1 \ln\left(\frac{v_j}{v_i}\right) + \beta_2 \ln\left(\frac{p_j}{p_i}\right) + \beta_3 \ln\left(\frac{d_{ij}}{d_{ii}}\right) + \beta_4 \ln\left(1 + t_{ij}\right) + \beta_5 Conti_{ij} + \beta_6 ComLang_{ij} + \beta_7 Comcol + \beta_8 \ln\left(\widehat{Time}_i^{\text{imp}}\right) + \beta_9 \ln\left(\widehat{Time}_j^{\text{exp}}\right) + e_j \tag{6.3}$$

where m_{ij} is the value of imports of country i from country j; m_{ii} is the intranational flow of goods in country i; v_j and v_i are the values of domestic production in country i and j, respectively; p_i and p_j are the consumer price indices in country i and j, respectively; t_{ij} is the bilateral tariff rates imposed by country i on country j's exports; *Conti*, *ComLang*, and *Comcol* are the dummy variables for common border, common language, and common colony, respectively; and the last two variables are the estimated values of time to import and time to export from Eqs. (6.1) and (6.2), respectively. The coefficients of these two variables provide the effect of time to import and time to export on bilateral imports.

Step 3 In the final step, following Eq. (6.4), we have estimated sectorwide to calculate the AVEs for each member country of RCEP:

$$\ln\left(\frac{m_{ij}^k}{m_{ii}^k}\right) = A + \beta_1 \ln\left(\frac{v_j^k}{v_i^k}\right) + \beta_2 \ln(p_i) + \beta_3 \ln(p_j)$$

$$+ \beta_4 \ln\left(\frac{d_{ij}}{d_{ii}}\right) + \beta_5 \ln\left(1 + t_{ij}^k\right) + \beta_6 Conti_{ij}$$

$$+ \beta_7 ComLang_{ij} + \beta_8 Comcol + \beta_9 \ln\left(\overset{\wedge}{Time_i^{\text{imp}}}\right)$$

$$+ \beta_{10} \ln\left(\overset{\wedge}{Time_j^{\text{exp}}}\right) + e_{ij}^k \qquad (6.4)$$

Using the coefficients of Eq. (6.4), the sectorwide AVE of time to import (AVE_{TI}) and time to export (AVE_{TE}) can be calculated as:

$$AVE_{\text{TI}} = \frac{\beta_9}{\beta_2} \quad \text{and} \quad AVE_{\text{TE}} = \frac{\beta_{10}}{\beta_3}$$

where AVE_{TI} and AVE_{TE} are the AVEs of time to import and time to export, respectively. Where the numerator is the proportionate change in relative imports due to the proportionate change in time to import (export) and the denominator is the proportionate change in bilateral imports to proportionate change in domestic prices. Hence, the ratio becomes the proportionate change in prices of imports (exports) due to the proportionate change in time to import (export) and thus represent AVEs. We report productwide AVEs for the 16 member countries of RCEP in the next section.

Source of Data and Variable Construction

For the empirical analysis, data from various sources have been utilized. Aggregated data on Time to import, Time to export, Documents to import, Documents to export, and Number of procedures to start a business are culled from *Doing Business* report provided by the World Bank Group. The data for the Corruption Perceptions Index (CPI) was developed by Transparency International and we used the same information for our analysis. Further, to represent the widespread use of the internet in the country, data on the number of internet users per thousand people in the population was taken from World Development Indicators (WDI). WDI was also used to obtain data for countrywide consumer price indices to represent the level of prices in both the importing and exporting countries. The CEPII database was used to get data on various gravity equation variables such as Island, International distance, Domestic distance, Contiguity, Common language, and Common colony.

In addition, to estimate the augmented gravity equation for GTAP sectors, the GTAP-9 database is used with the latest available data from the year 2011. The study utilizes the GTAP sectors and regions breakdown for the detailed analysis. The recent available GTAP database—version 9—provides the economywide data aggregated over 57 sectors for a total of 140 regions of the world. For the purposes of analysis, the entire economy of 57 sectors is further aggregated into 43 sectors wherein 42 sectors cover all the goods produced in the economy and one sector covers the services production. Further, to show the effect of TFMs on RCEP economies, the 140 regions of the world are finally aggregated into 17 countries/regions wherein 16 are the member nations of RCEP and one includes all other remaining regions under the classification "Rest of the World (ROW)."

GTAP-9 is the source of bilateral information on sectorwide import flows valued at world prices (*VIWS*), internal flow proxies ranked by the value of domestic sales of tradable commodities at agent prices (*VDA*), the value of production of all tradable sector proxies by the ranked by the productwide value of the output at agent's prices (*VOA*), and the bilateral tariff rate proxies ranked by level of import taxes (*tms*). Because we use GTAP data for 2011 as the reference year, data for all other variables are also taken from the same year. However, countrywide AVEs are calculated for the year 2015 by using data on time to import and time to export for that year.

6.4 Empirical Results

Table 6.4 shows the estimated results of the augmented gravity equation given under step 2 in Sect. 6.3. Three different models of the gravity equation have been estimated and presented in three separate columns. The first column represents the results analogous to the gravity model results, and the next two columns represent the results of trade facilitation focusing on the estimated variables of time to import and time to export estimated using Eqs. (6.1) and (6.2) as given in step 1 of Sect. 6.3. The results show that the relative production has affected the trade positively and significantly in all three models. Relative prices have a negative and significant impact on the bilateral trade of RCEP nations in the first two models, and their effect becomes positive in the third specification but is insignificant. The distance variable has a positive impact on trade in the first two

Table 6.4 Estimated results of the augmented gravity equation

Variables	*Model 1*	*Model 2*	*Model 3*
	ln (Rel. Imp)	*ln* (Rel. Imp)	*ln* (Rel. Imp)
Log (v_j/v_i)	0.459***	0.468***	0.628***
	(0.0143)	(0.0147)	(0.0192)
Log (p_j/p_i)	−2.354*	−2.721**	0.109
	(1.204)	(1.175)	(1.090)
Log (d_{ij}/d_{ii})	0.184***	0.0873	−0.436***
	(0.0635)	(0.0689)	(0.0758)
Log ($1+t_{ij}$)	−0.137***	−0.106***	0.0843
	(0.0400)	(0.0402)	(0.0705)
Conti	0.740***	0.716***	0.500**
	(0.240)	(0.230)	(0.217)
Comlang	0.0295	−0.0160	−0.0265
	(0.190)	(0.170)	(0.168)
Comcol	0.843***	0.892***	0.434*
	(0.242)	(0.228)	(0.239)
Log ($Time_i^{Imp}$)	−0.377**	–	–
	(0.149)		
Log ($Time_i^{Exp}$)	−0.260	–	–
	(0.169)		
Log ($Time_i^{Imp}$)_*Hat*	–	−1.617***	−2.127***
		(0.406)	(0.394)
Log ($Time_i^{Exp}$)_*Hat*	–	−1.128**	−1.850***
		(0.435)	(0.419)
Log ($Time_i^{Imp} * t_{ij}$)	–	–	−0.0694**
			(0.0278)
Constant (A)	−3.799***	−2.606***	0.113
	(0.786)	(0.774)	(0.854)
Observations	**10,080**	**10,080**	**4883**
R-squared	**0.634**	**0.638**	**0.686**
Sector dummies	*YES*	*YES*	*YES*

Notes: Figures in parentheses of type ( ) are the standard error of respective coefficient; *, **, and *** show the level of significance at 10, 5, and 1 percent levels, respectively
Source: Authors' calculations

models, but it has a negative and significant impact on trade in the third model. Imposition of tariffs has an inverse and significant relation with trade in the first two models, and a positive but insignificant relation in the last model. Contiguity and common colony have a positive and significant impact on trade in all of the models, but the insignificant coefficient of common language does not provide evidence of any type of relationship.

Further, the remaining five independent variables in Table 6.4 represent the TF variables. In model 1, the TF aspects have been directly inferred from the observed time to import and export variables. In model 2 and model 3, the TF aspect has been observed via the estimated time to import and export variables using Eqs. (6.1) and (6.2). In all three models, variables pertaining to the impact of TF on trade show the inverse relationship between administrative delays and bilateral trade, which directly points out that trade facilitation will lead to more trade between RCEP member countries. Further, the negative and significant coefficient of interaction variable in model 3 depicts that the advantages from tariff reductions can only be availed through the enhanced TF levels.

6.4.1 Calculation of AVEs

To calculate the sectorwide AVEs of each member country, Eq. (6.4) has been estimated for each individual sector (42 GTAP sectors) to get the coefficients of price indices and estimated time to import and export. Table 6.5 shows the results of sectorwide estimation of the augmented gravity equation specified using Eq. (6.4) (see Sect. 6.3). Further, Table 6.6 presents the sectorwide value of tariff equivalent (AVEs) of time to import and time to export for one day calculated using the required coefficients of estimated sectorwide regressions given in Table 6.5. As per the results, the average AVEs of a one day delay in import and export of one container of goods for RCEP member countries are approximately 84 and 82 percent, respectively. So a one day delay leads to more than an 80 percent increment in the price of the tradable good among the RCEP countries.

Further, sectors having a value of AVE of more than 100 percent are, from the importer side, products such as chemical, rubber, and plastic products; nonmetallic mineral products; dairy products; paddy rice; petroleum and coal products; fishing; sugar; food products; and nonferrous metals. From the exporter side, these include products such as chemical, rubber, an plastic products; animal products; gas; textiles; beverages and tobacco products; paper and publishing products; machinery and equipment; electronic equipment; and nonmetallic mineral products.

In total, the high value of the AVEs of these 16 sectors from both sides shows that the price of the tradable good coming under these sectors would rise to more than 100 percent in the case of a delay of one extra day. These 16 sectors cover 72.51 percent of intra-RCEP trade, which shows the

Table 6.5 Sectorwide estimated results of the augmented gravity equation

Variables	*Sector 1*	*Sector 2*	*Sector 3*	*Sector 4*	*Sector 5*	*Sector 6*	*Sector 7*
Log (v_j/v_i)	0.373***	0.429***	0.347***	0.554***	0.286***	0.248***	0.315***
Log (p_j)	−3.237	−2.820	−5.993*	4.903	1.813	−3.194	−3.616
Log (p_i)	1.421	7.016	4.978	4.832	13.51***	3.420	2.989
Log (d_{ij}/d_{ii})	0.553***	−0.144	0.221	−0.0590	0.821***	0.907***	0.451***
Log ($1+t_{ij}$)	−0.220**	0.236	0.0557	−0.139**	−0.162*	0.421	−0.405*
Conti	−0.153	0.0973	0.296	0.844**	0.753*	0.386	0.640
Comlang	0.522	−0.716	−0.389	0.513*	−0.236	−0.134	−0.448
Comcol	1.564***	0.990*	1.812***	1.212***	0.599	0.946**	0.502
Log ($Time_i^{Imp}$)_*Hat*	−2.727***	−2.089*	−3.116***	−3.928***	−2.451***	−1.808**	−1.465**
Log ($Time_i^{Exp}$)_*Hat*	−1.133	1.477	−0.630	−1.286	0.637	−0.490	−0.848
Constant (A)	3.692	−21.37	2.611	−46.53**	−76.86***	−6.187	0.326
Observations	**240**	**240**	**240**	**240**	**240**	**240**	**240**
R-squared	0.712	0.564	0.631	0.714	0.680	0.651	0.610

Variables	*Sector 8*	*Sector 9*	*Sector 10*	*Sector 11*	*Sector 12*	*Sector 13*	*Sector 14*
Log (v_j/v_i)	0.449***	0.454***	0.436***	0.386***	0.288***	0.292***	0.437***
Log (p_j)	6.369**	−4.812	−0.755	4.040	−8.265**	−1.146	−5.150**
Log (p_i)	25.33***	−1.935	4.933*	12.19***	2.598	5.340*	−2.560
Log (d_{ij}/d_{ii})	0.178	0.299**	0.461***	0.377*	0.444**	1.024***	0.266**
Log ($1+t_{ij}$)	−0.204**	−0.458***	−0.127		−0.828***	−0.185	−0.328***
Conti	1.091***	0.536	0.810***	0.583	0.502	1.229***	0.607**
Comlang	0.0212	0.139	0.105	−0.719*	−0.130	0.291	−0.206
Comcol	0.754**	1.546***	0.763**	1.716***	1.487***	1.614***	1.138***
Log ($Time_i^{Imp}$)_*Hat*	−5.779***	−0.704	−2.503***	1.911*	1.348	−1.149*	−3.220***
Log ($Time_i^{Exp}$)_*Hat*	−0.260	−2.328***	−2.314***	3.848***	3.331***	−0.194	−2.413***
Constant (A)	−147.1***	26.79	−22.93	−87.15***	17.22	−26.93	34.11*
Observations	**240**	**240**	**240**	**240**	**240**	**240**	**240**
R-squared	0.741	0.636	0.704	0.631	0.617	0.715	0.734

(continued)

Table 6.5 (continued)

Variables	*Sector 15*	*Sector 16*	*Sector 17*	*Sector 18*	*Sector 19*	*Sector 20*	*Sector 21*
Log (v_j/v_i)	0.293***	0.368***	0.286***	0.645***	0.502***	0.481***	0.420***
Log (p_j)	4.006	0.808	0.925	8.329**	2.226	−0.658	−5.280
Log (p_i)	−14.91***	−7.298	−6.798	13.14***	3.386	2.226	10.36***
Log (d_{ij}/d_{ii})	0.606***	0.359**	0.152	−0.0639	0.178	0.248**	0.0724
Log ($1+t_{ij}$)	−0.381	−0.0716	1.806***	−0.00780	−0.00743	−0.227***	−0.288***
Conti	0.611	0.572	0.666	1.676***	−0.146	0.237	0.275
Comlang	−0.469	−0.806*	−0.927*	−0.0752	0.324	0.345	0.106
Comcol	1.334***	0.442	0.0118	0.755*	1.742***	1.253***	1.005**
Log ($Time_i^{Imp}$)_*Hat*	1.194	−2.325**	−2.123*	−3.031***	0.550	0.111	−1.799**
Log ($Time_i^{Exp}$)_*Hat*	−1.905*	0.399	−2.614*	−2.696***	−0.145	−0.227	−0.185
Constant (A)	45.59	25.61	27.67	−99.35***	−33.17	−14.36	−26.80
Observations	**240**	**240**	**240**	**240**	**240**	**240**	**240**
R-squared	0.622	0.521	0.470	0.602	0.597	0.626	0.683

Variables	*Sector 22*	*Sector 23*	*Sector 24*	*Sector 25*	*Sector 26*	*Sector 27*	*Sector 28*
Log (v_j/v_i)	0.330***	0.511***	0.400***	0.670***	0.623***	0.712***	0.648***
Log (p_j)	−3.034	5.374	−15.34***	7.788***	1.288	0.714	−0.817
Log (p_i)	0.767	−8.654**	0.556	5.560*	1.748	8.823***	3.816
Log (d_{ij}/d_{ii})	0.951***	0.236*	0.150	−0.565***	−0.124	−0.183*	−0.174*
Log ($1+t_{ij}$)	−0.470***	−0.147*	−0.465***	0.0298	−0.213***	0.0647	−0.148**
Conti	1.592***	−0.127	1.147**	0.478	0.869**	0.452	0.391
Comlang	0.233	0.00980	−0.265	0.191	0.492*	0.135	0.0688
Comcol	0.993**	0.936**	0.895*	0.532	0.933***	0.443	0.537*
Log ($Time_i^{Imp}$)_*Hat*	3.415***	−1.449*	−0.678	−6.069***	−1.296*	−3.997***	−2.188***
Log ($Time_i^{Exp}$)_*Hat*	−2.733***	−1.074	0.852	−4.001***	−3.110***	−1.796***	0.291
Constant (A)	2.130	10.29	63.74**	−57.24***	−16.18	−43.37**	−17.29
Observations	**240**	**240**	**240**	**240**	**240**	**240**	**240**
R-squared	0.699	0.629	0.615	0.688	0.640	0.774	0.683

Variables	*Sector 29*	*Sector 30*	*Sector 31*	*Sector 32*	*Sector 33*	*Sector 34*	*Sector 35*
Log (v_j/v_i)	0.635***	0.711***	0.611***	0.685***	0.762***	0.765***	0.687***
Log (p_j)	1.049	−2.236	−0.793	−7.346**	−0.323	−0.859	5.015*
Log (p_i)	3.613*	14.54***	5.240**	2.743	−0.216	0.768	32.07***
Log (d_{ij}/d_{ii})	−0.277***	−0.533***	−0.296***	−0.629***	−0.455***	−0.646***	−0.284**
Log ($1+t_{ij}$)	−0.162**	−0.249**	−0.181*	0.116	−0.313***	−0.234***	−0.373***
Conti	0.144	1.232***	0.882***	1.050***	1.243***	0.705***	1.031***
Comlang	0.0565	−0.481**	0.206	0.539*	−0.0688	−0.0319	−0.245
Comcol	0.451*	0.758**	0.455*	0.484	0.812***	0.153	0.803**
Log ($Time_i^{Imp}$)_*Hat*	−3.100***	−3.208***	−1.227**	−4.809***	−1.217**	−3.659***	−4.036***
Log ($Time_i^{Exp}$)_*Hat*	−0.513	−1.352**	−1.733***	−1.623*	−1.738***	−1.078*	−2.042***
Constant (A)	−22.11	−56.38***	−22.68	22.62	2.114	0.414	−170.6***
Observations	**240**	**240**	**240**	**240**	**240**	**240**	**240**
R-squared	0.811	0.706	0.821	0.729	0.881	0.812	0.852

Variables	*Sector 36*	*Sector 37*	*Sector 38*	*Sector 39*	*Sector 40*	*Sector 41*	*Sector 42*
Log (v_j/v_i)	0.631***	0.729***	0.684***	0.647***	0.665***	0.774***	0.740***
Log (p_j)	−5.693*	3.178	−7.812***	−7.884***	0.976	−1.137	−4.442*
Log (p_i)	5.019	11.51***	3.261	−5.413*	8.654***	8.316***	−4.315
Log (d_{ij}/d_{ii})	−0.339**	−0.672***	−0.209*	−0.148	−0.553***	−0.487***	−0.135
Log ($1+t_{ij}$)	0.0173	−0.0575	−0.170*	−0.0347	−0.450***	−0.0763	−0.337***
Conti	1.412***	0.699**	0.570	1.051***	0.762**	0.697**	0.565*
Comlang	−0.0513	−0.300	0.193	0.213	0.102	0.145	0.155
Comcol	0.709*	0.509*	0.739**	0.498	0.0739	0.663**	0.955***
Log ($Time_i^{Imp}$)_*Hat*	−4.948***	−3.369***	−2.360***	−1.581**	−3.568***	−4.050***	−1.525**
Log ($Time_i^{Exp}$)_*Hat*	−2.768***	0.178	−1.221	0.393	−1.868**	−2.311***	−1.014
Constant (A)	7.287	−69.38***	19.99	58.23***	−42.87**	−30.46*	38.06**
Observations	**240**	**240**	**240**	**240**	**240**	**240**	**240**
R-squared	0.662	0.843	0.832	0.793	0.782	0.867	0.783

Notes: *, **, and *** show the level of significance at 10, 5, and 1 percent level, respectively
Source: Authors' calculations

Table 6.6 Sectorwide intra-RCEP trade share and AVEs of time to import and export for RCEP countries (in percent)

S. No.	*Sector*	*Intra-RCEP trade*	*One day ad valorem equivalent of*	
		Imports share in total goods imports	*Time to import* (AVE_{TI})	*Time to export* (AVE_{TE})
1	Paddy rice	0.01	191.90	34.99
2	Wheat	0.15	29.78	52.38
3	Cereal grains	0.10	62.60	10.51
4	Vegetables, fruit, nuts	0.60	81.28	26.23
5	Oil seeds	0.06	18.15	35.14
6	Sugar cane and beets	0.00	52.85	15.36
7	Plant-based fibers	0.17	49.01	23.44
8	Crops	0.25	22.82	4.08
9	Bovine cattle, sheep and goats, horses	0.08	36.41	48.38
10	Animal products	0.13	50.73	306.69
11	Raw milk	–	15.68	95.25
12	Wool, silk-worm cocoons	0.08	51.87	40.30
13	Forestry	0.28	21.51	16.97
14	Fishing	0.13	125.78	46.85
15	Coal	2.40	8.01	47.55
16	Oil	1.86	31.85	49.35
17	Gas	2.49	31.23	282.63
18	Minerals	4.18	23.07	32.37
19	Bovine meat products	0.29	16.24	6.52
20	Meat products	0.14	5.00	34.48
21	Vegetable oils and fats	0.85	17.36	3.50
22	Dairy products	0.39	444.93	90.09
23	Processed rice	0.11	16.74	19.99
24	Sugar	0.15	121.90	5.55
25	Food products	1.70	109.16	51.37
26	Beverages and tobacco products	0.23	74.12	241.48
27	Textiles	2.61	45.30	251.59
28	Wearing apparel	1.52	57.33	35.65
29	Leather products	0.94	85.81	48.92
30	Wood products (lumber)	1.25	22.06	60.45
31	Paper products, publishing	0.94	23.42	218.66
32	Petroleum, coal products	6.34	175.30	22.09

(*continued*)

Table 6.6 (continued)

S. No.	*Sector*	*Intra-RCEP trade*	*One day ad valorem equivalent of*	
		Imports share in total goods imports	*Time to import* (AVE_{TI})	*Time to export* (AVE_{TE})
33	Chemical, rubber, plastic products	12.11	563.54	537.35
34	Mineral products (nonmetallic)	1.12	476.26	125.46
35	Ferrous metals (iron and steel)	3.62	12.58	40.71
36	Metals (nonferrous)	3.15	98.58	48.61
37	Metal products (fabricated)	2.08	29.27	5.61
38	Motor vehicles and parts	3.37	72.38	15.63
39	Transport equipment	0.83	29.21	4.98
40	Electronic equipment	19.67	41.22	191.27
41	Machinery and equipment	21.34	48.69	203.33
42	Manufactures	2.25	35.34	22.82
Average		–	**83.96**	**82.25**

Source: Authors' calculations

importance of adopting trade facilitation measures (TFMs) by RCEP countries to get more benefits from bilateral trade.

In addition, the multiplication of total number of days required to import or export a good from one country to another with the value of a one day tariff equivalent provides the countrywide AVEs. Table 6.7 shows the countrywide average AVEs of time to import and time to export for the year 2015. Results reveal that the AVE is lowest for Singapore because it takes the least time to import, followed by South Korea, Australia, Malaysia, New Zealand, Japan, Thailand, Brunei, the Philippines, India, Vietnam, Burma, China, Cambodia, Indonesia, and Laos. On the exporting side, Singapore is again in the top rank because it takes the least number of days to export, followed by South Korea, Australia, New Zealand, Japan, Malaysia, Thailand, the Philippines, India, Indonesia, Brunei, Burma, China, Vietnam, Cambodia, and Laos. Further, Table 6.8 shows the countrywide differences of AVEs over a total of 42 GTAP sectors taken for the purposes of analysis.

Table 6.7 Countrywide AVEs of time to import and time to export for RCEP members

S. No.	*Region*	*AVE MFN applied tariff*	*Time to import (In days)*	AVE_{TI} *(in %)*	*Time to export (in days)*	AVE_{TE} *(in %)*
1.	Australia	2.7	8	671.68	9	740.25
2.	China	9.6	24	2015.04	21	1727.25
3.	India	13.5	21	1763.16	17	1398.25
4.	Japan	4.2	11	923.56	11	904.75
5.	New Zealand	2.0	9	755.64	10	822.5
6.	South Korea	13.3	7	587.72	8	658
7.	Brunei	1.2	15	1259.4	19	1562.75
8.	Burma	5.6#	22*	1847.12	20	1645
9.	Cambodia	11.2	24	2015.04	22	1809.5
10.	Indonesia	6.9	26	2182.96	17	1398.25
11.	Laos PDR	10	26	2182.96	23	1891.75
12.	Malaysia	6.1	8	671.68	11	904.75
13.	Philippines	6.3	15	1259.4	15	1233.75
14.	Singapore	0.2	4	335.84	6	493.5
15.	Thailand	11.6	13	1091.48	14	1151.5
16.	Vietnam	9.5	21	1763.16	21	1727.25

Notes: Entries marked with * represent data from the year 2014 and # represents data for the year 2013. The least time taken for a country to import and export is 4 and 6 days, respectively. The one day tariff equivalent of time to import and time to export are 83.96 and 82.25 percent, respectively

Source: Authors' calculations using data from *Doing Business* indicators, World Tariff Profile, 2015, and estimated results

6.5 Conclusion

In the present chapter, an attempt has been made to evaluate the impact of TFs in RCEP member countries on their bilateral trade flows. Using an econometric approach, the study concluded that TF in RCEP member countries has a positive impact on their bilateral trade. The results also reveal that the policy of trade liberalization should be a mixture of the reduction of TTCs as well as the reduction of tariff barriers. If both e policies can be adopted together, then RCEP member economies can gain more than changes in an individual policy set-up. Hence, trade liberalization between RCEP countries would become more successful if all types of barriers to trade could be focused simultaneously.

Table 6.8 Sectorwide AVEs of time to import and time to export for RCEP members (in %)

Region sector	*Australia*		*China*		*India*		*Japan*		*New Zealand*		*South Korea*	
	AVE_{TI}	AVE_{TE}	AVE_{TI}	AVE_{TE}	AVE_{TI}	AVE_{TE}	AVE_{TI}	AVE_{TE}	AVE_{TI}	AVE_{TE}	AVE_{TI}	AVE_{TE}
1	1535.19	314.90	4605.56	734.77	4029.87	594.81	2110.88	384.88	1727.09	349.89	1343.29	279.91
2	238.26	471.46	714.79	1100.07	625.44	890.53	327.61	576.22	268.05	523.84	208.48	419.07
3	500.80	94.55	1502.40	220.63	1314.60	178.60	688.60	115.57	563.40	105.06	438.20	84.05
4	650.26	236.07	1950.77	550.83	1706.93	445.91	894.10	288.53	731.54	262.30	568.98	209.84
5	145.17	316.26	435.51	737.95	381.07	597.39	199.61	386.54	163.32	351.40	127.02	281.12
6	422.81	138.22	1268.44	322.51	1109.88	261.08	581.37	168.93	475.66	153.57	369.96	122.86
7	392.10	210.96	1176.29	492.23	1029.26	398.47	539.13	257.83	441.11	234.39	343.09	187.52
8	182.54	36.74	547.61	85.73	479.16	69.40	250.99	44.91	205.35	40.82	159.72	32.66
9	291.29	435.39	873.87	1015.90	764.64	822.40	400.53	532.14	327.70	483.76	254.88	387.01
10	405.81	2760.17	1217.44	6440.40	1065.26	5213.66	558.00	3373.54	456.54	3066.86	355.09	2453.49
11	125.46	857.22	376.39	2000.19	329.35	1619.20	172.51	1047.72	141.15	952.47	109.78	761.98
12	415.00	362.69	1245.00	846.28	1089.37	685.09	570.62	443.29	466.87	402.99	363.12	322.39
13	172.09	152.69	516.27	356.27	451.74	288.41	236.62	186.62	193.60	169.65	150.58	135.72
14	1006.24	421.65	3018.73	983.85	2641.39	796.45	1383.58	515.35	1132.02	468.50	880.46	374.80
15	64.06	427.98	192.19	998.63	168.17	808.41	88.09	523.09	72.07	475.54	56.06	380.43
16	254.84	444.13	764.51	1036.31	668.95	838.92	350.40	542.83	286.69	493.48	222.98	394.78
17	249.80	2543.68	749.41	5935.25	655.74	4804.72	343.48	3108.94	281.03	2826.31	218.58	2261.05
18	184.52	291.31	553.56	679.72	484.37	550.25	253.72	356.04	207.59	323.67	161.46	258.94
19	129.94	58.67	389.81	136.89	341.08	110.82	178.66	71.71	146.18	65.19	113.69	52.15
20	40.02	310.33	120.07	724.09	105.06	586.17	55.03	379.29	45.03	344.81	35.02	275.84
21	138.87	31.50	416.61	73.49	364.53	59.50	190.94	38.50	156.23	35.00	121.51	28.00

(*continued*)

Table 6.8 (continued)

Region sector	*Australia*		*China*		*India*		*Japan*		*New Zealand*		*South Korea*	
	AVE_{TI}	AVE_{TE}	AVE_{TI}	AVE_{TE}	AVE_{TI}	AVE_{TE}	AVE_{TI}	AVE_{TE}	AVE_{TI}	AVE_{TE}	AVE_{TI}	AVE_{TE}
22	3559.46	810.79	10678.37	1891.84	9343.57	1531.49	4894.25	990.96	4004.39	900.88	3114.52	720.70
23	133.94	179.91	401.82	419.80	351.59	339.84	184.17	219.89	150.68	199.90	117.20	159.92
24	975.18	49.98	2925.54	116.62	2559.85	94.41	1340.87	61.09	1097.08	55.53	853.28	44.43
25	873.25	462.35	2619.76	1078.81	2292.29	873.32	1200.73	565.09	982.41	513.72	764.10	410.97
26	593.00	2173.33	1778.99	5071.09	1556.62	4105.17	815.37	2656.29	667.12	2414.81	518.87	1931.84
27	362.43	2264.35	1087.30	5283.49	951.39	4277.11	498.35	2767.54	407.74	2515.95	317.13	2012.76
28	458.67	320.86	1376.00	748.68	1204.00	606.07	630.67	392.17	516.00	356.51	401.33	285.21
29	686.50	440.26	2059.50	1027.27	1802.06	831.60	943.94	538.09	772.31	489.18	600.69	391.34
30	176.49	544.05	529.46	1269.46	463.28	1027.66	242.67	664.96	198.55	604.51	154.43	483.60
31	187.38	1967.90	562.14	4591.77	491.87	3717.15	257.65	2405.22	210.80	2186.56	163.96	1749.25
32	1402.38	198.80	4207.15	463.86	3681.25	375.51	1928.28	242.97	1577.68	220.89	1227.08	176.71
33	4508.28	4836.14	13524.85	11284.34	11834.24	9134.94	6198.89	5910.84	5071.82	5373.49	3944.75	4298.79
34	3810.10	1129.11	11430.29	2634.60	10001.50	2132.77	5238.88	1380.03	4286.36	1254.57	3333.83	1003.66
35	100.66	366.37	301.99	854.86	264.24	692.03	138.41	447.79	113.25	407.08	88.08	325.66
36	788.62	437.52	2365.87	1020.88	2070.13	826.43	1084.36	534.75	887.20	486.13	690.04	388.91
37	234.14	50.52	702.41	117.89	614.61	95.43	321.94	61.75	263.40	56.14	204.87	44.91
38	579.01	140.66	1737.02	328.21	1519.89	265.69	796.13	171.92	651.38	156.29	506.63	125.03
39	233.68	44.84	701.05	104.62	613.42	84.69	321.31	54.80	262.89	49.82	204.47	39.85
40	329.78	1721.46	989.34	4016.75	865.67	3251.65	453.45	2104.01	371.00	1912.74	288.56	1530.19
41	389.55	1829.98	1168.66	4269.96	1022.58	3456.64	535.64	2236.65	438.25	2033.32	340.86	1626.65
42	282.71	205.37	848.14	479.19	742.13	387.92	388.73	251.00	318.05	228.19	247.38	182.55

Region sector	*Brunei*		*Burma*		*Cambodia*		*Indonesia*		*Laos*	
	AVE_{TI}	AVE_{TE}	AVE_{TI}	AVE_{TE}	AVE_{TI}	AVE_{TE}	AVE_{TI}	AVE_{TE}	AVE_{TI}	AVE_{TE}
1	2878.48	664.79	4221.77	699.78	4605.56	769.76	4989.36	594.81	4989.36	804.74
2	446.75	995.30	655.23	1047.68	714.79	1152.45	774.36	890.53	774.36	1204.83
3	939.00	199.61	1377.20	210.12	1502.40	231.13	1627.60	178.60	1627.60	241.64
4	1219.23	498.37	1788.21	524.60	1950.77	577.06	2113.34	445.91	2113.34	603.29
5	272.19	667.67	399.22	702.81	435.51	773.09	471.80	597.39	471.80	808.23
6	792.77	291.79	1162.73	307.15	1268.44	337.86	1374.14	261.08	1374.14	353.22
7	735.18	445.35	1078.27	468.79	1176.29	515.67	1274.32	398.47	1274.32	539.11
8	342.25	77.57	501.97	81.65	547.61	89.81	593.24	69.40	593.24	93.90
9	546.17	919.15	801.05	967.53	873.87	1064.28	946.70	822.40	946.70	1112.65
10	760.90	5827.03	1115.99	6133.72	1217.44	6747.09	1318.90	5213.66	1318.90	7053.78
11	235.25	1809.70	345.03	1904.94	376.39	2095.44	407.76	1619.20	407.76	2190.68
12	778.12	765.68	1141.25	805.98	1245.00	886.58	1348.75	685.09	1348.75	926.88
13	322.67	322.34	473.25	339.30	516.27	373.23	559.29	288.41	559.29	390.20
14	1886.70	890.15	2767.17	937.00	3018.73	1030.70	3270.29	796.45	3270.29	1077.55
15	120.12	903.52	176.17	951.07	192.19	1046.18	208.21	808.41	208.21	1093.73
16	477.82	937.61	700.80	986.96	764.51	1085.65	828.22	838.92	828.22	1135.00
17	468.38	5369.99	686.96	5652.62	749.41	6217.88	811.86	4804.72	811.86	6500.51
18	345.98	614.98	507.43	647.35	553.56	712.08	599.69	550.25	599.69	744.45
19	243.63	123.86	357.32	130.38	389.81	143.41	422.29	110.82	422.29	149.93
20	75.05	655.13	110.07	689.61	120.07	758.57	130.08	586.17	130.08	793.05
21	260.38	66.49	381.89	69.99	416.61	76.99	451.32	59.50	451.32	80.49
22	6673.98	1711.67	9788.50	1801.75	10678.37	1981.93	11568.23	1531.49	11568.23	2072.02

(*continued*)

Table 6.8 (continued)

Region sector	*Brunei*		*Burma*		*Cambodia*		*Indonesia*		*Laos*	
	AVE_{TI}	AVE_{TE}	AVE_{TI}	AVE_{TE}	AVE_{TI}	AVE_{TE}	AVE_{TI}	AVE_{TE}	AVE_{TI}	AVE_{TE}
23	251.14	379.82	368.33	399.81	401.82	439.79	435.30	339.84	435.30	459.78
24	1828.46	105.51	2681.74	111.07	2925.54	122.17	3169.33	94.41	3169.33	127.73
25	1637.35	976.07	2401.45	1027.44	2619.76	1130.18	2838.08	873.32	2838.08	1181.55
26	1111.87	4588.13	1630.74	4829.61	1778.99	5312.57	1927.24	4105.17	1927.24	5554.05
27	679.56	4780.30	996.69	5031.90	1087.30	5535.09	1177.91	4277.11	1177.91	5786.68
28	860.00	677.38	1261.33	713.03	1376.00	784.33	1490.67	606.07	1490.67	819.98
29	1287.19	929.43	1887.88	978.35	2059.50	1076.19	2231.13	831.60	2231.13	1125.10
30	330.91	1148.56	485.34	1209.01	529.46	1329.91	573.58	1027.66	573.58	1390.36
31	351.34	4154.46	515.30	4373.12	562.14	4810.43	608.99	3717.15	608.99	5029.09
32	2629.47	419.68	3856.55	441.77	4207.15	485.95	4557.74	375.51	4557.74	508.04
33	8453.03	10209.64	12397.78	10746.99	13524.85	11821.69	14651.92	9134.94	14651.92	12359.03
34	7143.93	2383.69	10477.77	2509.14	11430.29	2760.06	12382.82	2132.77	12382.82	2885.51
35	188.74	773.45	276.83	814.15	301.99	895.57	327.16	692.03	327.16	936.28
36	1478.67	923.65	2168.71	972.26	2365.87	1069.49	2563.02	826.43	2563.02	1118.10
37	439.00	106.66	643.87	112.27	702.41	123.50	760.94	95.43	760.94	129.11
38	1085.63	296.95	1592.26	312.58	1737.02	343.84	1881.77	265.69	1881.77	359.47
39	438.15	94.65	642.63	99.63	701.05	109.60	759.47	84.69	759.47	114.58
40	618.34	3634.20	906.89	3825.47	989.34	4208.02	1071.78	3251.65	1071.78	4399.29
41	730.41	3863.30	1071.27	4066.63	1168.66	4473.29	1266.05	3456.64	1266.05	4676.62
42	530.09	433.55	777.47	456.37	848.14	502.01	918.82	387.92	918.82	524.83

Region sector	*Malaysia*		*Philippines*		*Singapore*		*Thailand*		*Vietnam*	
	AVE_{TI}	AVE_{TE}	AVE_{TI}	AVE_{TE}	AVE_{TI}	AVE_{TE}	AVE_{TI}	AVE_{TE}	AVE_{TI}	AVE_{TE}
1	1535.19	384.88	2878.48	524.83	767.59	209.93	2494.68	489.84	4029.87	734.77
2	238.26	576.22	446.75	785.76	119.13	314.30	387.18	733.38	625.44	1100.07
3	500.80	115.57	939.00	157.59	250.40	63.04	813.80	147.08	1314.60	220.63
4	650.26	288.53	1219.23	393.45	325.13	157.38	1056.67	367.22	1706.93	550.83
5	145.17	386.54	272.19	527.10	72.59	210.84	235.90	491.96	381.07	737.95
6	422.81	168.93	792.77	230.36	211.41	92.14	687.07	215.00	1109.88	322.51
7	392.10	257.83	735.18	351.59	196.05	140.64	637.16	328.15	1029.26	492.23
8	182.54	44.91	342.25	61.24	91.27	24.49	296.62	57.15	479.16	85.73
9	291.29	532.14	546.17	725.64	145.65	290.26	473.35	677.27	764.64	1015.90
10	405.81	3373.54	760.90	4600.29	202.91	1840.12	659.45	4293.60	1065.26	6440.40
11	125.46	1047.72	235.25	1428.71	62.73	571.48	203.88	1333.46	329.35	2000.19
12	415.00	443.29	778.12	604.49	207.50	241.80	674.37	564.19	1089.37	846.28
13	172.09	186.62	322.67	254.48	86.05	101.79	279.65	237.51	451.74	356.27
14	1006.24	515.35	1886.70	702.75	503.12	281.10	1635.14	655.90	2641.39	983.85
15	64.06	523.09	120.12	713.31	32.03	285.32	104.10	665.75	168.17	998.63
16	254.84	542.83	477.82	740.22	127.42	296.09	414.11	690.87	668.95	1036.31
17	249.80	3108.94	468.38	4239.46	124.90	1695.78	405.93	3956.83	655.74	5935.25
18	184.52	356.04	345.98	485.51	92.26	194.20	299.85	453.14	484.37	679.72
19	129.94	71.71	243.63	97.78	64.97	39.11	211.15	91.26	341.08	136.89
20	40.02	379.29	75.05	517.21	20.01	206.88	65.04	482.73	105.06	724.09
21	138.87	38.50	260.38	52.50	69.43	21.00	225.66	49.00	364.53	73.49
22	3559.46	990.96	6673.98	1351.32	1779.73	540.53	5784.12	1261.23	9343.57	1891.84

(*continued*)

Table 6.8 (continued)

Region sector	*Malaysia*		*Philippines*		*Singapore*		*Thailand*		*Vietnam*	
	AVE_{TI}	AVE_{TE}	AVE_{TI}	AVE_{TE}	AVE_{TI}	AVE_{TE}	AVE_{TI}	AVE_{TE}	AVE_{TI}	AVE_{TE}
23	133.94	219.89	251.14	299.86	66.97	119.94	217.65	279.86	351.59	419.80
24	975.18	61.09	1828.46	83.30	487.59	33.32	1584.67	77.75	2559.85	116.62
25	873.25	565.09	1637.35	770.58	436.63	308.23	1419.04	719.21	2292.29	1078.81
26	593.00	2656.29	1111.87	3622.21	296.50	1448.88	963.62	3380.73	1556.62	5071.09
27	362.43	2767.54	679.56	3773.92	181.22	1509.57	588.96	3522.33	951.39	5283.49
28	458.67	392.17	860.00	534.77	229.33	213.91	745.33	499.12	1204.00	748.68
29	686.50	538.09	1287.19	733.76	343.25	293.51	1115.56	684.85	1802.06	1027.27
30	176.49	664.96	330.91	906.76	88.24	362.70	286.79	846.31	463.28	1269.46
31	187.38	2405.22	351.34	3279.84	93.69	1311.94	304.49	3061.18	491.87	4591.77
32	1402.38	242.97	2629.47	331.33	701.19	132.53	2278.87	309.24	3681.25	463.86
33	4508.28	5910.84	8453.03	8060.24	2254.14	3224.10	7325.96	7522.89	11834.24	11284.34
34	3810.10	1380.03	7143.93	1881.86	1905.05	752.74	6191.41	1756.40	10001.50	2634.60
35	100.66	447.79	188.74	610.62	50.33	244.25	163.58	569.91	264.24	854.86
36	788.62	534.75	1478.67	729.20	394.31	291.68	1281.51	680.59	2070.13	1020.88
37	234.14	61.75	439.00	84.21	117.07	33.68	380.47	78.59	614.61	117.89
38	579.01	171.92	1085.63	234.44	289.50	93.77	940.88	218.81	1519.89	328.21
39	233.68	54.80	438.15	74.73	116.84	29.89	379.73	69.74	613.42	104.62
40	329.78	2104.01	618.34	2869.10	164.89	1147.64	535.89	2677.83	865.67	4016.75
41	389.55	2236.65	730.41	3049.97	194.78	1219.99	633.02	2846.64	1022.58	4269.96
42	282.71	251.00	530.09	342.28	141.36	136.91	459.41	319.46	742.13	479.19

Notes: See Table 6.6 for sector description
Source: Authors' calculations

Note

1. The study used a level of corruption index ranging from 1 to 10, where 1 represents most corrupted and 10 represents least corrupted.

References

DBR (2015). Going beyond efficiency: Complete report. Washington DC, USA: The World Bank.

Kee, H. L., Nicita, A., & Olarreaga, M. (2009). Estimating trade restrictiveness indices. *The Economic Journal., 119*, 172–199.

Zaki, C. (2010). *Does trade facilitation matters in bilateral trade?* GTAP resources no. 4537.

CHAPTER 7

Bilateral Trade Costs and Growth of Trade in Services: A Comparative Study of India and China

Amrita Roy and Somesh K. Mathur

7.1 Introduction

The story of the growth of the world economy since the late twentieth century is broadly driven by the emergence of two Asian countries, China and India. Since 1980, both countries have been able to sustain a significantly rapid growth, and yet their growth experiences are quite different from each other. China's growth has been mostly dominated by expansion of the industrial sector and relatively broad-based expansion across the agriculture, industry, and services sectors compared to India. On the other hand, India's growth has been primarily dominated by expansion of the services sector.

Similar to the contribution of different sectors to GDP, the contributions of different sectors in total exports differ substantially across these two countries. In the case of China, manufacturing exports account for the maximum share in total exports. According to the OECD (2015), services contributed 9 percent of total exports in China in 2014. By way of contrast, India's exports have a larger services share even though in terms of total value of exports of services, it is significantly less compared to China. For

A. Roy (✉) • S.K. Mathur
Indian Institute of Technology Kanpur, Kanpur, India

S.K. Mathur et al. (eds.), *Theorizing International Trade*,
https://doi.org/10.1007/978-981-10-1759-9_7

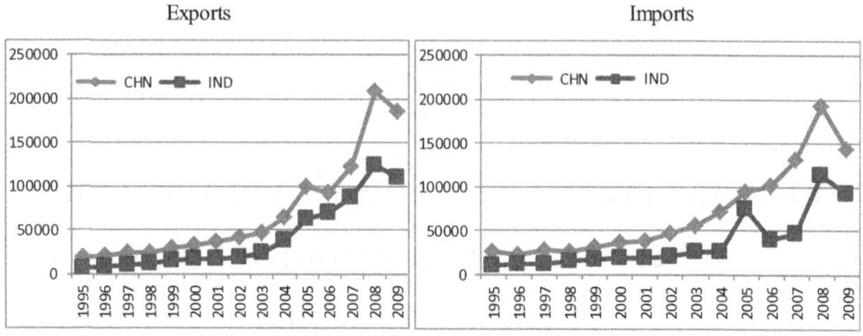

Fig. 7.1 Trends in services exports and imports to the world (China and India) (Source: Francois and Pindyuk (2013))

example, in 2014, India exported USD 156 billion and imported USD 147 billion worth of services, and India is the largest exporter of computer services in the world. Compared to India, in 2014, China exported USD 232 billion and imported USD 382 billion worth of services (OECD 2015), and "Other business services" contributed the maximum share of China's total services exports.

Even if the values of both exports and imports of services are larger in China compared to India, because of the relative importance of the manufacturing sector in total exports, less of an attempt has been made to study the trade pattern of services in China compared to the much-discussed expansion of trade in services in India.

We can see in Fig. 7.1 that both India (IND) and China (CHN) have experienced a steady growth in their exports and imports of services to the rest of the world. over the period 1995–2009.

Panagariya (2006) and Dimaranan et al. (2007) noted that even though India and China have started greater liberalization since the early 1990s, their performances in terms of trade are very different from each other. First of all, their patterns of trade are significantly different. In the 1980s, China specialized in and experienced a massive growth in the exports of light manufacturing (e.g., apparel, toys sporting goods, etc.). In the 1990s, China then made a shift towards relatively more sophisticated products (e.g., office machines, electronic equipment, electrical machinery, etc.) still employing large volumes of labor.

Contrary to the export pattern of China, the major portion of India's exports are skilled labor-intensive or capital-intensive services and products (e.g., IT, ITES, textiles, petroleum products, iron and steel). According to Panagariya (2006), differences in the trade pattern and performance between these two countries lies in their domestic policies related to constraints in the labor market and infrastructure (particularly specific to power) rather than their foreign trade and investment policies. Because of the differences in their domestic policies, investment in India concentrated on capital-intensive or skilled-labor-intensive sectors and in the case of China, investment concentrated on unskilled-labor-intensive manufacturing.

Over the last three decades, China's economic policies have focused on investment activities and export-led manufacturing. Two major changes have been experienced by the economy in recent years. First, the emergence of high-value manufacturing (e.g., high-end equipment manufacturing, the chip industry) and the increasing importance of the service sector as a driver of the economy. Over time, the costs of China's labor and other factors of production have risen significantly and China has been reorganizing its industrial growth by also shifting its focus from the (low-cost) labor-intensive manufacturing sectors towards the technology- and innovation-oriented high value added manufacturing and services. For example, in recent times, increased demand for services from the middle class and the government's encouragement for a consumption-led economy is tending a new dimensional shift in the services sector. This is reflected particularly in the growth of the services sector FDI. In 2014, the services sector accounted for more than 55 percent of FDI compared to 46 percent in 2010 (KPMG 2015). The new economic reform guidelines encouraged foreign companies to invest in financial services, tourism, entertainment and healthcare, and other similar services. The WTO (2015) notes that there is a significant correlation between investment and the services trade, and thus increasing FDI in services will further increase the services trade in developing countries.

Over the last few decades, technological innovations (e.g., the internet) have played an important role behind the decline in trade costs and the recent increase in world trade in services. According to the WTO (2015), contributions of developing countries in world services exports have increased from 11percent in 1990 to 20 percent in 2011. But despite recent technological advances, trade costs in services are significantly higher because of the existence of numerous domestic laws and regulations that mainly impair trade and investment in this sector (WTO 2015).

It is generally noted that unlike the manufacturing sector, high levels of public ownership and regulatory barriers still continue to prevail in the services sector in China. Based on the information on regulations related to restriction on foreign entry, movement of people, barriers to competition, other discriminatory measures, regulatory transparency, and so on, the OECD Services Trade Restrictiveness Index (STRI indices, 2015) have been calculated for 42 countries (including China and India) for 18 different services sectors.

The STRIs are composite indices that take values between zero and one, where zero represents a complete open market and one represents a market completely closed to foreign services providers. According to the indices, both China and India score above average on STRI for all the sectors (except road freight in India). Again, if the regulatory barriers are considered, services trade policies overall are more restrictive in India compared to China (OECD STRI).

Therefore, it is important to look at the factors behind the relative importance of services exports (relative to the manufacturing sector) in India compared to China. Is it mostly associated with the expansion of output in the services sectors (relative to the manufacturing sector) or related to trade costs of services that are mostly considered to be associated with strict domestic regulations?

In this chapter, we estimate the bilateral trade costs of services both in India and China and check whether trade costs are significantly different for these two countries with respect to their major trading partners. We also assess how much the decline in trade costs account for the growth of trade in services in these two countries over the period 1995–2010. Our study has found that over this period, both countries have witnessed a significant decline in trade costs with respect to many of their major trading partners, but compared to India the decline in trade costs are larger in China.

The study has also found that even though bilateral trade costs declined with many of their major trade partners over our sample period, an increase in the economic size of these countries relative to the world played the most important role behind the growth of bilateral services trade both for India and China. This study adds to the very scanty literature on the analysis of trade costs in services comparing the case of India and China. Existing estimates largely use total trade or the goods sector without any focus on the services trade. Although, it would obviously be desirable to extend the study to the disaggregated level, our problem lies in obtaining sufficient disaggregated production data that our approach requires.

The rest of the chapter is structured as follows. Section 7.2 reviews the studies that have looked at the issues related to the estimation of trade costs in services. Section 7.3 briefly describes the method and data that have been used in this paper to estimated trade costs in services. Section 7.4 reports and discusses the results, and Sect. 7.5 concludes.

7.2 Costs Associated with the Services Trade

Trade costs play an important role in determining the trade patterns among nations. In international trade theories, trade costa are considered to be the sum of factors resulting in a wedge between the export price and the import price. Trade costs in general can be considered to include transport costs, border-related trade barriers, wholesale and retail distribution costs, traditional trade policies such as tariffs and RTA membership, language barriers, currency barriers (due to the use of different currencies), information cost barriers, and security barriers. Over time, whether or not the significant reduction in tariff rates has been able to reduce trade costs among countries, it is a matter of empirical question. Arvis et al. (2013) notes that trade costs of a representative rich country might be as high as 170% ad valorem—far in excess of the 5% or so accounted for by tariffs (Anderson and Wincoop 2004).

Nordås and Rouzet (2015) note that compared to goods for which trade restrictions are largely associated with tariffs and other costs on goods imports at the border, most restrictions associated with trade and investment of services are "behind the border in nature," They cite the examples of "impediments to the entry and operation of foreign service providers" in support of their arguments. For example, discrimination in providing licenses to foreign investors and recognition of educational degrees earned abroad, and these are very much specific to each country's laws. Miroudot et al. (2013) notes that "in services sectors, trade costs are largely related to regulatory measures," and trade costs can explain a large part of the huge difference between the total value of trade in goods and services.

According to the OECD STRI index (2015), road transport, engineering, and construction are the least restricted sectors in India. These sectors are subject to a general regulatory framework and no sector-specific restrictions apply at the national level. The most restricted sectors include rail freight transport, legal services, and air transport. Compared to India, in China the least restricted sectors include architecture, engineering, and computer services, whereas the most restricted sectors include courier services, broadcasting, and air transport (Table 7.1).

Table 7.1 Regulatory restrictions in different services, India and China

Services	*China*	*India*
Logistics storage and warehouse	0.2990477	0.2692013
Logistics freight forwarding	0.2529791	0.2492181
Logistics customs brokerage	0.3007415	0.2541592
Accounting	0.3903609	0.8867621
Architecture	0.2489108	0.6096109
Engineering	0.2453022	0.2855195
Legal	0.4603289	0.9457697
Broadcasting	0.7781873	0.4930616
Telecom	0.4143245	0.4569809
Air transport	0.5997208	0.649116
Maritime transport	0.3942059	0.319193
Road freight transport	0.3862816	0.1480144
Rail freight transport	0.4214754	1
Courier	0.8609087	0.518616
Distribution	0.3305613	0.3578947
Commercial banking	0.4709847	0.4908043
Insurance	0.4911061	0.6314303
Computer	0.2430103	0.3573338
Construction	0.3235059	0.3177442

Source: OECD (STRI 2015)
Note: The STRI database is based on regulations currently in force. The STRI indices take the value from 0 to 1, where 0 is completely open and 1 is completely closed. They are calculated on the basis of information provided in the STRI database

We note that empirical studies that have estimated trade costs have mostly concentrated on the goods sectors, especially because of the limitations in data availability in the services sector. Arvis et al. (2013) estimate trade costs in agriculture and manufactured goods for the period 1995–2010 considering 178 countries. They found that trade costs are strongly declining in per capita income. Moreover, trade costs are falling noticeably faster in developed countries than in developing ones.

Due to constraints on the availability of widescale data for the services trade, studies looking at trade costs in services, especially in developing countries, are difficult to find. Using Novy's (2013) methodology, Miroudot et al. (2013) measure trade costs in services for 61 countries and 12 services sectors for the period 1995–2007. They found that trade costs in services are much higher than in goods sectors (two to three times higher in many cases) and remained relatively steady for over a decade. They used OECD input–output (IO) tables for major Asian economies such as China, India, Indonesia, and Taiwan. But the main problem with this dataset is that IO tables are available only for every five years. Therefore, they had to interpolate the missing values for these four countries which inevitably entailed some smoothing.

7.3 Novy's (2013) Indirect Approach to Estimate Trade Costs

Studies that have concentrated on empirically estimating trade costs among countries have used the direct approach (i.e., the traditional gravity model) mostly focusing on geographical distance as a source of trade costs. The literature has also considered other observable factors that are considered responsible for overall trade costs. Two of the major problems of the direct approach to estimating trade costs are: (1) to estimate the effect of trade costs on trade, one needs to specify a trade cost function by relating the unobservable bilateral trade cost variable to observable trade cost proxies (such as distance between countries, a range of cultural, historical, or political variables, standards, and technical regulations); (2) many trade cost elements are unobservable.

Chen and Novy (2012) note that one problem with specifying the trade cost function is its inherent arbitrariness, and the theory generally gives no guidance as to the appropriate functional form. Since these studies consider a subset of the total factors influencing trade costs, the main problem with these approaches is that they capture a part of the total trade cost. Therefore, in these approaches, we cannot control for the problem of omitted variable bias in calculating trade costs among countries. Again, because many of the trade cost variables do not change over time (e.g., distance), it is difficult to track the changes in trade costs.

Anderson and Wincoop (2004) have done a pioneering work to unify the literature on the various determinants of trade costs. Later, Novy (2013), following Head and Ries (2001), took a different approach to come to an all-inclusive measure of trade costs based on the observed pattern of production and trade. These indirect approaches infer trade costs from trade data without specifying a trade cost function. Chen and Novy (2012) note that the direct approach uses measures for standards and regulations that are used to estimate the sensitivity of trade flows to standards and regulations, whereas the indirect approach allows for decomposition of the variance of total trade costs into the contribution that is attributable to standards and regulations.

Novy's model is based on the Anderson and Wincoop (2003) "gravity with gravitas" model. This model is consistent with all the other gravity models and does not depend on an assumption of CES preferences. It starts with the gravity model,

$$\mathrm{x}_{ij} = \frac{y_i y_j}{y_w} + \left(\frac{t_{ij}}{\pi_i p_j}\right)^{(1-\sigma)} \tag{7.1}$$

where x_{ij} denotes nominal exports from i to j, y_i and y_j are nominal incomes of country i and y_w is world income. The expression $\sigma > 1$ is the elasticity of substitution across goods.[1] π_i and p_j are country i's and country j's price indices. The gravity equation implies that, all else being equal, bigger countries trade more with each other. Bilateral trade costs t_{ij} decrease bilateral trade, but they have to be measured against the price indices π_i and p_j. Anderson and Wincoop (2003) call these price indices multilateral resistance variables because they include trade costs with all other partners and can be interpreted as average trade costs. The value π_i is the outward multilateral resistance variable, whereas p_j is the inward multilateral resistance variable.

It is therefore useful to multiply gravity Eq. (7.1) by the corresponding gravity equation for trade flows in the opposite direction to obtain a bidirectional gravity equation that contains both countries' outward and inward multilateral resistance variables. Substituting the solution from Eq. (7.1) and rearranging the bidirectional gravity equation yields[2]

$$\tau_{ij} = \left(\frac{t_{ij} t_{ji}}{t_{ii} t_{jj}}\right)^{\frac{1}{2}} - 1 = \left(\frac{x_{ii} x_{jj}}{x_{ij} x_{ji}}\right)^{\frac{1}{2(\sigma-1)}} \tag{7.2}$$

Equation (7.2) presents that measure in ad valorem equivalent terms. It is the geometric average of bilateral trade costs for exports from country i to country j and from country j to country i, expressed relative to domestic trade costs in each country ($\frac{t_{ij}}{t_{ii}}$ and $\frac{t_{ji}}{t_{jj}}$).

Because these trade flows vary over time, trade costs can be computed not only for cross-sectional data but also for time series and panel data. This is an advantage over the procedure adopted by Anderson and Wincoop (2003) who only use cross-sectional data.

Novy (2013) also uses the gravity framework to examine the driving forces behind the strong growth of international trade over the last decades. The growth of bilateral trade was decomposed into three distinct contributions—the growth of income, the decline of bilateral trade barriers, and the decline of multilateral barriers:

$$100\% = \frac{2\Delta \ln\left(\frac{y_i y_j}{y_w}\right)}{\Delta \ln\left(x_{ij}x_{ji}\right)} + \frac{2(1-\sigma)\Delta \ln\left(\tau_{ij}\right)}{\Delta ln\left(x_{ij}x_{ji}\right)} - \frac{2(1-\sigma)\Delta \ln\left(\varnothing_i \varnothing_j\right)}{\Delta \ln\left(x_{ij}x_{ji}\right)} \qquad (7.3)$$

where $\varnothing_i = \left(\frac{\pi_i p_i}{t_{ii}}\right)^{\frac{1}{2}}$ and $\varnothing_j = \left(\frac{\pi_j p_j}{t_{jj}}\right)^{\frac{1}{2}}$

The main advantages of this method over the gravity model are: Aggregate trade costs are inferred indirectly from observable trade data; and there is no need to assume any particular trade cost function. Many typical trade cost proxies such as distance do not vary over time. Therefore, a static trade cost function cannot capture the variation of trade costs over time. However, the measure derived in Novy (2013) is a function of time-varying observable trade data and thus allows researchers to trace changes in bilateral trade costs over time.

Data To estimate trade costs among countries using Novy's (2013) methodology, we need data on two aspects, intranational trade (i.e., transaction within the boundary) and trade among countries. Francois and Pindyuk (2013) provide a consolidated version of multiple sources (OECD, UN, Eurostat, and IMF) of bilateral trade in services. The panel spans over the period 1981–2010. The dataset contains bilateral services trade flows for 248 countries as reporters and partners, plus the rest of the world, including 20 economic activities according to the BOP classification. However, in terms of data availability, the higher is the level of disaggregation, the fewer observations are available. Therefore, we have considered the aggregate services sector for our study.

To get data on intranational trade in services, we need to deduct total services trade from the total services output. Novy (2013) notes that since trade data are available in gross value terms, to get the intranational trade data we should also consider the gross output of services (rather than value added). Because data for the gross value of services output are not available over time, we have completed the exercise taking the value added services output as a proxy for the gross output of services. The UN's National Accounts statistics provide data on the gross value added output of different services groups for most countries. Using these data, we estimate trade costs of services with the most important services trading partners of India and China.

Francois and Pindyuk (2013) data shows that in 2009, Belgium (BEL), Germany (DEU), Denmark (DNK), Finland (FIN), France (FRA), the United Kingdom (GBR), Ireland (IRL), Italy (ITA), Japan (JPN), the Netherlands (NLD), and the United States (USA) were the major trading partners of India for trade in services. On the other hand, in terms of total trade in services, China's major trading partners were: Australia (AUS), Germany (DEU), Denmark (DNK), France (FRA), the United Kingdom (GBR), Hong Kong (HKG), Ireland (IRL), Italy (ITA), Japan (JPN), India (IND), Korea (KOR), Singapore (SGP), Thailand (THA), the United States (USA), Russia (RUS), and Saudi Arabia (SAU). In this study, we have considered the time period 1995–2010 (based on the availability of data) to estimate the trade costs and trade growth accounting for this set of countries. In 1995, GATS became operational to promote trade in services. So, it is expected that over that period, trade costs of services have gone down.

7.4 Decline in Services Trade Costs

Figure 7.2 shows the decline in trade costs with respect to some their major trading partners over the period 1995–2010. For both China and India, we can see that in general trade costs of services have shown a declining trend.[3] In these figures we have considered the year 1995 as the base year (the trade cost for year 1995 = 100) and thus the trade cost lines can be considered as a proportional change in trade costs over the period 1995–2009.

Compared to the year 1995, even though bilateral trade costs of services have experienced a declining trend for both countries, the decline is not similar for all the trading partners. In the case of India, the highest decline in trade costs has happened for Finland, and in the case of China it has happened for France. For example, in the case of India, bilateral trade costs in services with Finland was nearly 60 percent lower in 2009 compared to 1995.

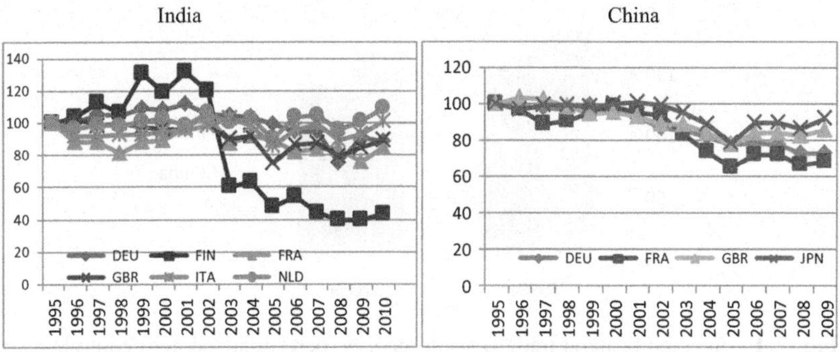

Fig. 7.2 The decline in trade costs of India and China with respect to their major trading partners (1995–2010) (Source: Authors' calculations)

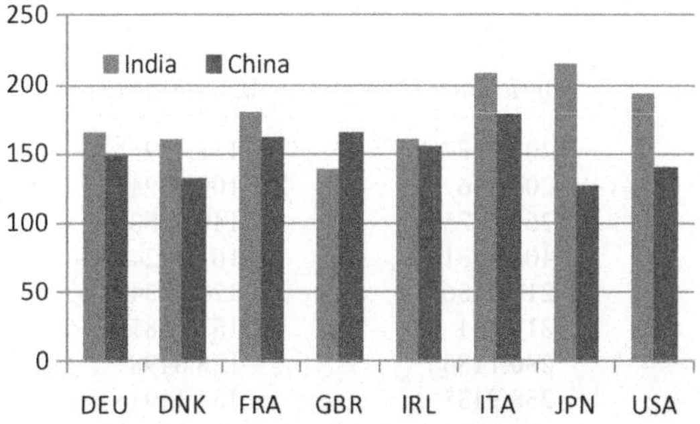

Fig. 7.3 Average bilateral trade costs (percent ad valorem equivalent) of India and China with their common trading partners (1995–2010) (Source: Authors' calculations)

Similarly, in the case of China, bilateral trade costs in services with France declined by almost 40 percent in 2009 compared to 1995. It is also interesting to note that in the case of India, bilateral trade costs in services for some countries (e.g., Finland, Germany) first increased and then declined over the sample period, but we do not find a similar trend for China with respect to its trading partners in Fig. 7.2. Tariff equivalence of trade costs of services for India and China with respect to their major trading partners have been reported in the appendix (Tables 7.6 and 7.7).

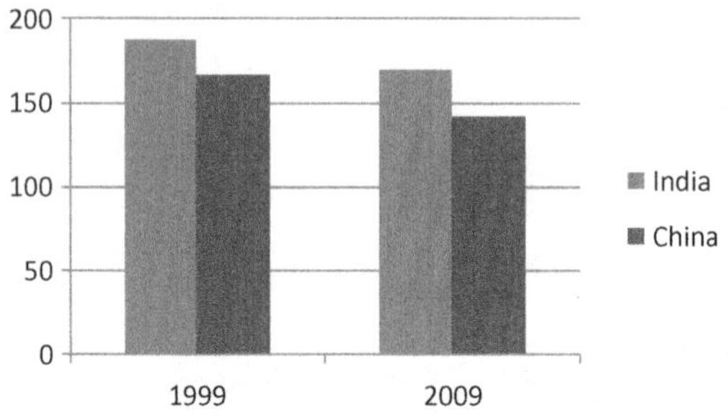

Fig. 7.4 Average bilateral trade costs in services (percent ad valorem equivalent) of India and China with their common trading partners, 1999 and 2009 (Source: Authors' calculations)

Table 7.2 Average trade costs for India (percent ad valorem equivalent, 1995–2009)

Partner code	*Agriculture*	*Manufacturing*	*Services*
BEL	202.9537	112.429	188.9985
DEU	206.886	109.6094	165.8642
DNK	264.2775	140.5253	160.0621
FIN	401.2051	161.6124	247.8062
FRA	218.0456	124.4434	180.8416
IRL	317.704	151.7381	139.219
ITA	230.1435	125.3498	159.9282
JPN	258.9435	134.1494	208.6485
NLD	175.6091	93.22162	214.726
GBR	208.955	107.3212	179.5193
USA	148.5462	105.8441	192.9042

Source: ESCAP World Bank International Trade Costs database (agriculture and manufacturing) and our own calculations (services)

In Fig. 7.3 we compare the average bilateral trade costs in services for India and China with respect to their common trading partners over the period 1995–2009. In this figure, we see that except for the UK, for all the trading partners, bilateral trade costs are higher for India compared to China. Compared to China in the case of India, the average trade costs are quite high with Italy, Japan, and the United States. In Fig. 7.4 we see that in 2009 compared to 1999 the average trade cost in services (with

Table 7.3 Average trade costs for China (percent ad valorem equivalent, 1995–2009)

Partner	*Agriculture*	*Manufacturing*	*Services*
DEU	180.1805	78.24621	149.3781
DNK	224.9661	109.8788	132.6236
FRA	208.9938	101.1459	162.462
IRL	315.8816	112.0339	154.7146
ITA	263.8574	107.1299	178.0609
JPN	168.6904	64.59309	127.057
GBR	222.3629	99.71814	164.6549
USA	130.6814	74.83359	141.3417

Source: ESCAP World Bank International Trade Costs database (agriculture and manufacturing) and our own calculations (services)

common trading partners) declined both for India and China, but the decline was larger in China compared to India over the same period.

In Tables 7.2 and 7.3, we compare trade costs in agriculture, manufacturing, and services for India and China, respectively, with regard to their major trading partners in terms of services trade. In order to compare the trade costs sectors, we use data from the ESCAP World Bank International Trade Costs database for trade costs in agriculture and manufacturing where they have also used Novy's (2013) methodology to calculate trade costs.

Arvis et al. (2013) note that trade costs are high across countries in the agricultural sector when compared with the manufacturing sector, and this is especially so when we consider countries with lower incomes. Tables 7.2 and 7.3 report the average bilateral trade costs in agriculture, manufacturing, and services with their major trading partners over the period 1995–2009.

In Table 7.2 we see that the average trade cost in agriculture for India with Finland was as high as 400% ad valorem. Similar is the case of China which is as high as 315% ad valorem with Ireland (Table 7.3). Average trade costs for services are in general lower than trade costs in agriculture, but compared to the manufacturing sector, trade costs are quite high both in India and China. If we study Tables 7.2 and 7.3, we see that the average bilateral trade costs are lower in China compared to India for agriculture, manufacturing, and even for services. Major findings that arise from the above discussions are:

- In general, the average trade cost is higher in India compared to China for agriculture, manufacturing, and also for services.
- Trade costs in services with respect to their major trading partners have declined over the period 1995–2010, both for India and China.
- Compared to India, a decline in average trade costs in services is higher in China for the period 1999–2009.

7.4.1 Bilateral Trade Growth Accounting of India and China with Their Major Trading Partners

There has been a significant growth in trade in services both for India and China with their major trading partners over the period 1995–2010. Using Novy's methodology we have decomposed the bilateral trade growth in services into three components: growth of the two country's economies relative to the world output (A), changes in bilateral trade costs (B), and changes in multilateral trade barriers (C). We have reported the results in the following Tables 7.4 and 7.5.

In Table 7.4, we see that over the period 1995–2010, the bilateral output growth of India and its trading partners (relative to the world) explains the maximum share of the total increase in trade in services between the trading partners. Income growth can explain almost the entire growth in trade with Italy and Netherlands. From Table 7.6 in the appendix we see

Table 7.4 Bilateral trade growth accounting (India)

Country	*Trade growth*	*A*	*B*	*C*	
BEL (2002–2010)	481	0.498014	0.615355	−0.113369	1
DEU (1995–2010)	291	0.715199	0.363817	−0.079017	1
DNK (1999–2010)	322	0.743888	0.407651	−0.151539	1
FIN (1995–2010)	995	0.277449	0.774136	−0.051585	1
FRA (1995–2010)	373	0.67802	0.414989	−0.093008	1
GBR (1995–2010)	327	0.875459	0.27805	−0.153509	1
IRL (2002–2010)	339	0.6543	0.598484	−0.252785	1
ITA (1995–2010)	222	1.229193	−0.04411	−0.185083	1
JPN (1996–2010)	187	0.953352	0.055743	−0.009095	1
NLD (1995–2010)	149	1.872532	−0.53272	−0.339814	1
USA (1999–2009)	209	0.825752	0.276446	−0.102198	1

Note: Growth between the time periods noted in the respective parenthesis. All numbers in percent
Source: Authors' calculations

Table 7.5 Bilateral trade growth accounting (China)

	Trade growth	*A*	*B*	*C*	
AUS (1999–2009)	358	0.995362	0.282505	−0.277868	1
DEU (1995–2009)	502	0.60422	0.527803	−0.132023	1
DNK (1995–2009)	407	0.739288	0.452295	−0.191583	1
FRA (1995–2009)	603	0.582358	0.554333	−0.136691	1
GBR (1995–2009)	422	0.884396	0.341228	−0.225624	1
HKG (2000–2009)	−61	−3.56797	3.592579	−0.9754	1
IND (2005–2009)	143	1.441005	0.035806	−0.476811	1
IRL (2002–2009)	868	0.301794	0.84293	−0.144724	1
ITA (1995–2009)	508	0.73394	0.442893	−0.176832	1
JPN (2005–2009)	275	0.858987	0.236131	−0.095118	1
KOR (1999–2009)	302	1.01563	0.257997	−0.273627	1
RUS (2002–2009)	385	1.020367	0.322255	−0.342622	1
SAU (2005–2009)	186	0.895279	0.269418	−0.164698	1
SGP (2005–2009)	178	1.103743	0.186483	−0.290226	1
THA (2005–2009)	104	1.848156	−0.24751	−0.600647	1
USA (1999–2009)	165	1.598505	−0.25966	−0.338843	1

Note: Growth between the time periods noted in the respective parenthesis. All numbers in percent
Source: Authors' calculations

that bilateral trade costs with these two countries did increase in 2010 compared to 1995.

A decline in trade costs played a significant role behind the increase in bilateral trade with Belgium and Finland for India. Netherland's trade barriers with its other trading partners declined significantly for the sample period and thus the trade diversion effect is relatively strong (34%) for Netherlands. Similar to India, China's bilateral trade in services with its major trading partners is mostly driven by their growth in output relative to the world (Table 7.5). Decline in trade cost plays a significant role behind the growth of trade in services with respect to the trading partners, Ireland, France and Germany. Trade diversion effect is relatively strong with respect to the trading partners, Thailand and India.

7.5 Conclusion

In this study, we have estimated trade costs in services both for India and China (with respect to their major trading partners in services) for the period 1995–2010. We have found that trade costs in services are quite high for both countries especially relative to the manufacturing sector. Over the sample period (1995–2010) both countries have witnessed a significant decline in trade costs with respect to many of their major trading partners, but compared to India the decline in trade costs are larger in China.

Similar to our results, Miroudot et al. (2013) also found a significant decline in trade costs in services in China over the period 2000–2005. They noted that accession to the WTO led to significant liberalization of the services sector, especially related to access to foreign markets, which has resulted in a substantial decline in trade costs over time in many countries. We have also found that the average trade costs in services vary considerably across their major trading partners for both countries, and the decline in trade costs are also not symmetric with their major trading partners in services.

Our findings are consistent with the findings of Miroudot et al. (2013) and Duval et al. (2015) that at the general level trade costs in services are relatively high compared to the manufacturing sector. This difference in trade costs between the manufacturing and the services sectors is natural since the legal and regulatory requirements are more binding in the services sector compared to the manufacturing sector.

Using Novy (2013)'s methodology to decompose growth in bilateral trade in services for India and China over the period 1995–2010, we find that growth in the output of the trading partners mostly explains the growth in trade with their major trading partners. It is important to note from the results that even though bilateral trade costs declined with many of their major trade partners over our sample period, an increase in the economic size of these countries relative to the world played the most important role behind the growth of bilateral services trade both for India and China.

Services contribute a larger share in GDP as well as in total exports in India compared to China. But from our estimates of trade costs in services we find that, like agriculture and manufacturing, the average trade costs of services are also higher in India compared to China with respect to their major trading partners. If we compare the average trade of services relative to the manufacturing sector in India and China (with respect to their common set of major trading partners), we find that the trade cost in services is 1.66 times higher in China and in the case of India this is 1.42 times higher. Hence, we can say that even if the average trade costs in services in India is higher compared to China, but relative to the manufacturing sector, trade in services are costlier in China compared to India. Therefore, in terms of trade costs of services, this gives a justification for the relative importance of services in total trade in India compared to China.

Compared to the other middle income group of countries, the contribution of the service sector in GDP is significantly low in the case of China. Services account for 48 percent of GDP in China. Citing Lardy (2014), Rutkowski (2015) notes that the underdevelopment of the service sector compared to other middle-income countries are broadly related to two major factors: one, subsidized production (e.g., controlled interest rate, subsidized energy consumption in industry) in the industrial sector, and two, significant regulation and government control in the services sectors.

China still retains substantial control over transportation, education, and health care where the share of government investment was more than 70 percent in 2013. Rutkowski (2015) notes that, recently, China's government has initiated several reform measures to accelerate growth of the services sector. Major broad reforms in this respect include: elimination of market distortions related to the cost of capital, energy and resources, and the reduction of regulatory barriers for private and foreign investors to enter the services sector.

Therefore, we can expect that in the coming years, with an increasing contribution of the services sector in China's GDP, services will contribute a larger share in total trade even if trade costs with its major trading partner do not experience a major decline.

Here we should note that if we could have studied the services sectors at the disaggregated level, we could have shed light on why these two countries specialize in different services while at the same time considering their services exports. One problem with this study is that because of the limitations of data on the gross output of services, we used the valued added output of services. Since we were interested in looking at the trend in trade costs for India and China and the major players behind the growth in trade with their major trading partners, we could have used value added output in services as a proxy for the gross output in services.

Appendix

Table 7.6 Trade costs of services, India (percent ad valorem equivalent)

YEAR	*BEL*	*DEU*	*DNK*	*FIN*	*FRA*	*GBR*	*IRL*	*ITA*	*JPN*	*NLD*	*USA*
1995		166.5		301.3	204.2	151.3		219.3		178.5	
1996		166.1		311.6	180.7	156.7		201.7	217.4	172.4	
1997		175.2		338.9	180.7	148.9		202.2	214.3	177.1	
1998		173.5		320.3	166.3	150.9		203.7	212.3	175.7	
1999		181.6	183.6	392.5	181.2	147.0		203.0	219.8	179.9	198.6
2000		180.4	173.1	358.2	181.9	146.2		206.8	220.9	182.8	196.3
2001		186.3	171.1	395.6	198.1	143.9		210.1	222.3	175.1	194.8
2002	234.7	175.6	175.5	360.6	214.2	148.4	185.8	215.4	222.3	190.5	195.6
2003	222.0	174.0	173.6	181.4	179.3	135.9	174.3	225.7	219.4	179.3	193.4
2004	229.3	172.1	176.2	191.3	187.0	139.4	184.9	216.1	220.0	183.6	198.7
2005	146.4	164.4	120.6	145.0	182.3	113.5	171.8	187.0	197.7	160.7	182.4
2006	210.7	157.3	148.4	163.6	167.7	130.7	166.7	210.4	218.7	184.5	197.3
2007	189.1	157.9	148.3	133.4	171.0	131.7	163.0	216.5	214.4	186.6	196.6
2008	158.4	124.9	140.4	119.5	171.5	120.1	125.6	195.3	199.6	170.8	181.8
2009	139.6	151.0	151.8	120.4	155.0	127.5	120.0	203.6	206.9	180.1	186.5
2010	170.8	147.0	158.2	131.3	172.3	135.4	147.2	221.6	215.0	194.8	
Average	189.0	165.9	160.1	247.8	180.8	139.2	159.9	208.6	214.7	179.5	192.9

Note: Empty cells indicate that data are not available for those specific years
Source: Authors' calculations

Table 7.7 Trade costs of services, China (percent ad valorem equivalent)

Year	*AUS*	*DEU*	*DNK*	*FRA*	*GBR*	*HKG*	*IND*	*IRL*
1995		178.2		202.5	189.7			
1996		174.3		196.0	195.1			
1997		173.8		179.4	194.1			
1998		172.2		182.5	185.8			
1999	166.8	177.0	153.9	192.5	178.2			
2000	162.0	172.7	141.9	198.8	180.3	60.9		
2001	159.0	164.4	137.4	192.6	175.1	61.1		
2002	154.5	154.2	136.8	189.6	168.4	59.4		248.0
2003	152.1	152.6	136.1	169.0	167.6	59.8		233.9
2004	144.2	145.7	137.1	149.1	158.7	58.2		173.9
2005	135.3	138.0	121.6	130.8	146.6	55.6	130.0	108.2
2006	149.4	140.1	129.7	146.3	159.8			143.5
2007	147.8	138.2	127.9	146.4	159.8			119.0
2008	134.9	130.1	113.8	133.6	155.4	70.2	120.5	104.7
2009	148.2	130.3	122.6	138.3	161.4	88.2	129.2	106.4
Average	150.4	149.4	132.6	162.5	164.7	64.2	126.5	154.7

Year	*ITA*	*JPN*	*KOR*	*RUS*	*SAU*	*SGP*	*THA*	*USA*
1995	200.8	137.5						
1996	185.1	132.7						
1997	194.8	135.8						
1998	180.9	136.2						
1999	186.4	135.5	111.8					147.2
2000	184.2	137.0	108.1					141.6
2001	192.6	138.4	107.4					141.5
2002	173.5	135.6	103.9	201.8				141.2
2003	200.3	130.3	101.1	203.6				139.9
2004	195.7	121.6	95.7	205.3				133.3
2005	145.6	108.1	93.5	149.9	164.2	106.8	131.6	130.2
2006	185.8	122.9	95.9	205.6				134.9
2007	187.1	122.5	94.1					133.4
2008	151.3	119.0	97.1	162.3	146.8	99.5	118.4	156.8
2009	156.1	126.8	100.3	176.2	154.9	101.9	135.9	154.8
Average	178.1	127.1	100.8	186.4	155.3	102.7	128.6	141.3

Note: Empty cells indicate that data are not available for those specific years
Source: Authors' calculations

Notes

1. σ is set to eight following Novy (2013).
2. For detailed derivation refer to Novy (2013).
3. Even if the numbers regarding absolute levels of trade costs in services are subject to uncertainty because of the limitations on data and assumption that the value of elasticity of substitution between goods and services are same (eight), we can be sure about the relative patterns of trade costs in our results.

References

Anderson, E. J., & Wincoop, V. E. (2003). Gravity with gravitas: A solution to the border puzzle. *The American Economic Review, 93*, 170–192.

Anderson, E. J., & Wincoop, V. E. (2004). Trade costs. *Journal of Economic Literature, 42*(3), 691–751.

Arvis, J. F., Ben, Y. D., & Utoktham, S. C. (2013). *Trade costs in the developing world 1995–2010.* Policy research working paper no. 6309, The World Bank.

Chen, N., & Novy, D. (2012). On the measurement of trade costs: Direct vs. indirect approaches to quantifying standards and technical regulations. *World Trade Review, 11*(03), 401–414.

Dimaranan, B., Ianchovichina, E., & Martinr, W. (2007). *China, India, and the future of the world economy: Fierce competition or shared growth?* Policy research working paper no. 4304, The World Bank group.

Duval, Y., Saggu, A., & Utoktham, C. (2015). *Value added trade costs in goods and services.* TID working paper no. 01/15, ESCAP Trade and Investment Division, Bangkok.

Francois J., & Pindyuk O. (2013). *Consolidated data on international trade in services v8.7.* IIDE discussion paper no. 20130101. Retrieved from www.I4ide.org/content/wpaper/dp20130101

Head, K., & Ries, J. (2001). Overseas investment and firm exports. *Review of International Economics, 9*(1), 108–122.

KPMG. (2015). China outlook 2015. *Global China Practice*, kpmg.com

Lardy, N. R. (2014). *Markets over Mao: The rise of private business in China.* Washington, DC: Peterson Institute for International Economics.

Miroudot S., Sauvage J., & Shepherd B. (2013). *Measuring the cost of international trade in services.* Developing Trade Consultants, New York. developing-trade.com/wp-content/uploads/2014/11/DTC-Article-Chapter-2013-5.pdf

Nordås, H. K., & Rouzet, D. (2015). *The impact of services trade restrictiveness on trade flows: First estimates.* OECD trade policy papers no. 178, OECD Publishing. Retrieved from https://doi.org/10.1787/5js6ds9b6kjb-en

Novy, D. (2013). Gravity redux: Measuring international trade costs with panel data. *Economic Enquiry, 51*(1), 101–121.

OECD. (2015). *Services trade restrictiveness index*. www.oecd.org/tad/services-trade/country-notes-trade-restrictiveness-index.htm. Accessed 04 Apr 2016.

OECD/WTO. (2015). *Aid for trade at a glance 2015: Reducing trade costs for inclusive, sustainable growth*. Paris: OECD Publishing.

Panagariya A. (2006). *India and China: Trade and foreign investment*. http://www.columbia.edu/~ap2231/Policy%20Papers/Stanford%20India%20China%20Revised%20October%202006.pdf

Rutkowski, R. (2015). *Service sector reform in China*. Policy brief no. 15-2, Peterson Institute for International Economics, Washington, DC. www.Piie.com/publications/pb/pb15-2.pdf

Head, K., & Ries, J. (2001). Overseas investment and firm exports. Review of International Economics, 9(1), 108-122.

KPMG (2015). China Outlook 2015. Global China Practice, kpmg.com.

PART II

Some Applications of General Equilibrium Analysis

CHAPTER 8

Theoretical Exposition of Some Ex Ante Approaches to Assess the Proposed Trade Policy

Rahul Arora, Sarbjit Singh, and Somesh K. Mathur

The application of methods under the ex ante approach might be useful to evaluate the different trade policy options for any country. The literature also highlights the importance of calculating gains/losses associated with any proposed trade policy, which further helps in policy making.

This chapter begins with an explanation of some of the important and basic trade indicators that help to assess countrywide trade growth followed by other methods through which one can gauge the impact of changes in policy variables on trade and other macroeconomic variables. Broadly, the tools in trade policy research are divided into two main categories: Ex post and ex ante approaches. Under the ex post approach, those methods are covered that provide the results of changes in trade policy in the past. The estimation of the gravity equation and the quantification of direct and indirect trade barriers using econometric tools comes under this category. On the other hand, the ex ante approach covers those methods that measure the impact of future changes in trade policy concerning bilateral trade flows and other macroeconomic variables.

R. Arora (✉) • S. Singh
Consumer Unity & Trust Society (CUTS) International, Jaipur, India

S.K. Mathur
Indian Institute of Technology Kanpur, Kanpur, India

S.K. Mathur et al. (eds.), *Theorizing International Trade*,
https://doi.org/10.1007/978-981-10-1759-9_8

A key strength of this approach is its ability to highlight which sectors may expand and which may contract in the face of given changes in policy variable(s). One of the main applications of this approach is to answer the research question pertaining to study the impact of preferential removal of tariffs against a limited set of trading partners, given the assumed model structure. Under this approach, two main tools have been explained to assess the effect of proposed changes in trade policy: (i) partial equilibrium analysis and (ii) general equilibrium analysis.

The main difference between the two methods is the sectoral coverage. Partial equilibrium analysis does not consider the linkage effect in the economy, while general equilibrium considers all linkage and feedback effects while evaluating the effects of proposed changes in trade policy. Also, data requirements in the case of partial analysis are less than in the general equilibrium analysis.[1] The present chapter explains SMART and GTAP analysis approaches in detail to evaluate the impact of assumed upcoming changes in trade policy on various macroeconomic variables.

8.1 Descriptive Statistics in Trade

As in statistics, descriptive statistics in trade are intended to study trade data in detail. It is used to evaluate the trade pattern and performance, which is helpful to assess the country's dependence on trade. In the literature, there exist many manuals that explain the formulas to calculate the descriptive statistics in trade policy research. These formulas are known as trade indices. Trade indices are very easy to calculate if someone has the required data. Many types of software are available, and with the help of these, indices can be calculated very easily. Among these, the most commonly used are STATA and Excel.

Today, there also exists the option of online calculation of most of these indices by making a query of selecting the required database and index type. Trade outcome indicators under WITS[2] is the best example of ready-to-use indicators. By creating a personal username and password, one can access this option and enjoy the benefit. For details behind the calculations, one can look into the manual of these indicators.[3] Many handbooks/ user guides are available to read about more detail concerning these indicators. Among those, two simplest user guides except WITS manual are: "A Handbook of Commonly Used Trade Indices and Indicators" by Mikic and Gilbert (2007); and "A Practical Guide to Trade Policy Analysis" provided by the UNations and the WTO.

The main purpose of these handbooks is to promote systematic trade policy research which should start in the preliminary analysis of studying the data on imports and exports of countries' concerned over the period of time. The present chapter will not go into detail on the calculation part and instead lists those indicators categorywise for explaining the purpose of the particular indicator. Readers can use the above-referred manuals for more details. Categorywide bifurcation of trade indices is as follows:

1. *Trade and Economy*: Includes indicators showing the extent of economic dependence on trade. Under this category, commonly used indicators are:
   - Trade Dependence Index;
   - Import Penetration Index;
   - Export Propensity Index; and
   - Marginal Propensity to Import Index.
2. *Trade Performance*: This category includes the ratios used to evaluate the trade performance over the period of time. It includes:
   - Growth rate of exports;
   - Normalized trade balance; and
   - Export/import coverage.
3. *Direction of Trade*: Includes those indices that indicate the direction of one country's trade. In other words, it includes those ratios which evaluate the regionwide/countrywide import and export shares. Main indices under this category are:
   - Trade shares;
   - Regional market share;
   - Trade intensity;
   - Regional Hirschman; and
   - Trade entropy index.
4. *Sectoral Structure*: Includes those indices that show the goodswide structure of trade of any country. These indices are very helpful in trade negotiations before the conclusion of any trade agreement. The indices under this category include:
   - Competitiveness;
   - Main export or import category;
   - Revealed comparative advantage;
   - Trade complementarity;
   - Export similarity index; and
   - Trade overlap index.
5. *Protection Indices*: These indices require data on tariff rates applied by the importer on products coming from the exporter country. It

includes those indices that calculate the level of protection of an importer country. It includes the calculation of:

- Average Tariff Rate (Simple and Weighted);
- Tariff Dispersion; and
- Effective Rates of Protection Index.

In addition to the above four categories given in Mikic and Gilbert (2007), many other advanced trade indices are also helpful in assessing the trade profile of any country. Calculation of these trade indices requires detailed data on many variables. Some of those advanced trade indices are: Industrywide level of intermediate goods trade; off-shoring; vertical specialization; Grubel–Lloyd (GL) index of intraindustry trade; and intensive and extensive margins; among others.[4]

8.2 Partial Equilibrium Tool to Assess the Proposed Trade Policy

The present chapter discusses only the SMART tool that is freely available online for partial equilibrium analysis of changes in the rate of tariffs between the trading countries. Other available options are: GSIM, TRIST, and ATPSM. One can read the available manuals/user guides to read more on the theories behind these measures. Some of the important references are the ATPSM manual (2004)[5]; Plummer et al. (2010)[6]; the WITS manual (2011)[7]; the TRIST manual[8]; and Mathur (2012).

8.2.1 *Single Market Partial Equilibrium Simulation Tool (SMART)*

This tool can be used to anticipate the likely economic effects of various trade policy alternatives. It allows us to investigate the impact of preferential trade reforms at home or abroad on the following variables:

Trade creation	Trade diversion
Imports and exports	Tariff revenue
World prices	Welfare effect

This tool is included in the WITS (World Integrated Trade Solutions) software developed by the World Bank to produce aggregate statistics and to simulate the impact of tariff changes on all of the above-mentioned variables. The rationale for using this tool for market analysis is that it permits an analysis at a fairly disaggregated level, which resolves the number of aggregation biases. This tool considers only one reporter market/country at a time and assumes the rate of its tariff reductions on goods imports from the partner country or group of partner countries as per the specification in the simulation scenario.

The Model

Jammes and Olarreaga (2005) have explained the analytical setup behind this tool on the basis of certain assumptions. The assumptions of the SMART model are:

- Products imported from different countries are imperfect substitutes. This assumption is also known as the Armington assumption.
- World prices of each variety are given, which makes export supplies perfectly elastic. The model assumes that the reporter country is small on order to affect prices of the tradable commodity.
- No other restriction on growth of imports in order to permit the expansion of trade due to the tariff reduction.
- The model uses the given information on the behavioral parameters such as import demand elasticity, among others.
- Changes in tariffs will directly affect the changes in prices, that is, no income effect and the benefit of the change in tariffs directly pass on to the consumer in terms of price changes.

By looking at the demand structure of the SMART model, and on the basis of the above assumptions, Jammes and Olarreaga (2005) defined an additive utility function (U), also quasi linear, which is additive of the consumption of the aggregate import good (m_k) and composite numeraire good (n). The utility function is given as:

$$U = \sum_k u_k(m_k) + n \qquad (8.1)$$

The maximization of the utility function given in (8.1) that is subject to a budget constraint yields the demand function for the imported good as:

$$m_{k,j} = f\left(p^d_{k,j}; p^d_{k,\neq j}\right), \quad \forall k, j \qquad (8.2)$$

And the demand function for the composite numeraire good[9] (n) would be obtained as:

$$n = y - \sum_j \sum_k p_{k,j}^d m_{k,j} \tag{8.3}$$

where $m_{k,j}$ are the imports of good k from country j; $p_{k,j}^d$ and $p_{k,\neq j}^d$ are the domestic prices of good k imported from country j and from all other countries other than j, respectively; and y is the national income of the country.

Further, in the importing country, the domestic price ($p_{k,j}^d$) of the imported good k from country j can be obtained by adding the effect of tariffs ($t_{k,j}$) imposed by the importer on its imports from country j in the world price of good k, and is given as:

$$p_{k,j}^d = p_{k,j}^w \left(1 + t_{k,j}\right) \tag{8.4}$$

And the preference tariff imposed on imports of good k imported from country j is defined as:

$$t_{k,j} = t_k^{MFN} \left(1 - \theta_{k,j}\right) \tag{8.5}$$

Where, t_k^{MFN} is the Most Favored Nation (MFN) tariff imposed on good k, and $\theta_{k,j}$ is the tariff preference ratio on good k when imported from country j and defined as:

$$\theta_{k,j} = 1 - \frac{t_{k,j}}{t_k^{MFN}}$$

On the basis of above specifications, the model provides the results on four main effects: Trade; Welfare; Revenue effect to the importer; and revenue effect to the exporter. Following sub-sections present these four effects in detail.

Trade Effect

Total trade effects in SMART include the quantity and price effects of trade. Quantity effect further composed of trade creation and trade diversion effect. The sum total of trade creation, trade diversion and price effect is known as trade effect in SMART.

Trade Creation Effect

After the reduction of tariffs on imported product, an increase in domestic demand for imports in the importing country due to reduction in price of imports is known as trade creation. In the SMART model, the whole benefit of reduction in tariffs is fully enjoyed by the consumer in terms of price reduction. This effect is shown by the direct increase in imports after the reduction of tariffs imposed on the imports coming from the member exporter. To obtain this effect, SMART uses the concept of price elasticity of import demand ($\varepsilon_{k,j}$) given as follows:

$$\varepsilon_{k,j} = \frac{dm_{k,j}/m_{k,j}}{dp^d_{k,j}/p^d_{k,j}} < 0 \tag{8.6}$$

By solving (8.6) for $dm_{k,j}$ will provide the trade creation effect in terms of change in imports of product k from country j. In terms of values, trade creation effect evaluated at world prices can be expressed as:

$$TC_{k,j} = p^w_{k,j} dm_{k,j} = p^w_{k,j} \varepsilon_{k,j} m_{k,j} \frac{dp^d_{k,j}}{p^d_{k,j}} \tag{8.7}$$

Further, using expression (8.4), one can also show the impact of change in tariff on imports given as:

$$dp^d_{k,j} = p^w_{k,j} dt_{k,j} \quad \text{Using (8.4).}$$

Substitute the above expression into (8.7) provides the final expression of trade creation given in (8.8).

$$TC_{k,j} = p^w_{k,j} dm_{k,j} = p^w_{k,j} \varepsilon_{k,j} m_{k,j} \frac{dt_{k,j}}{1 + t_{k,j}} = \varepsilon_{k,j} m_{k,j} \frac{dt_{k,j}}{1 + t_{k,j}} \tag{8.8}$$

Finally, to obtain the overall level of trade creation, one can simply sum the expression (8.8) across goods or countries as per the requirement of the analysis.

Trade creation across countries for a single product k would be: $TC_k = \sum_j TC_{k,j}$

Trade creation across all goods from an exporter j would be: $TC_j = \sum_k TC_{k,j}$

The Overall level of trade creation would be: $TC = \sum_k \sum_j TC_{k,j}$

Trade Diversion Effect

It occurs when an importer starts importing a product from the member importing country which it is previously importing from non-member country. The reason of this substitution is the decrease in price of imports from member country due to the preferential treatment which is not given to the non-member countries. This effect shows the amount of diverted trade from non-member country to member country after the adoption of tariff reduction policy in a preferential trading arrangement. The positive trade diversion shows the diversion of the trade from non-member to the member country. SMART model uses the concept of elasticity of substitution of imports between member country and non-member countries ($\sigma_{k,\ j,\neq j}$). As per the formula,

$$\sigma_{k,j,\neq j} = \frac{d\left(\frac{m_{k,j}}{m_{k,\neq j}}\right) \Big/ \frac{m_{k,j}}{m_{k,\neq j}}}{d\left(\frac{p^d_{k,j}}{p^d_{k,\neq j}}\right) \Big/ \frac{p^d_{k,j}}{p^d_{k,\neq j}}} < 0 \tag{8.9}$$

By using (8.4), the denominator of above expression (8.9) can be replaced with the final expression of (8.10) as: (Assuming $dp^d_{k,\neq j} = 0$)

$$d\left(\frac{p^d_{k,j}}{p^d_{k,\neq j}}\right) \Big/ \frac{p^d_{k,j}}{p^d_{k,\neq j}} = \frac{\frac{p^w_{k,j} dt_{k,j}}{p^w_{k,\neq j}(1+t_{k,\neq j})}}{\frac{p^w_{k,j}(1+t_{k,j})}{p^w_{k,\neq j}(1+t_{k,\neq j})}} = \frac{p^w_{k,j} dt_{k,j}}{p^w_{k,j}(1+t_{k,j})} = \frac{dt_{k,j}}{(1+t_{k,j})} \tag{8.10}$$

And the simplification of a part of numerator of (8.9) will provide the following:

$$d\left(\frac{m_{k,j}}{m_{k,\neq j}}\right) = \frac{m_{k,\neq j} dm_{k,j} - m_{k,j} dm_{k,\neq j}}{m^2_{k,\neq j}} = \frac{dm_{k,j}}{m_{k,\neq j}} - \frac{m_{k,j} dm_{k,\neq j}}{m^2_{k,\neq j}}$$

Further, by following the theory of trade diversion, the increment in imports must be equal to the decrease (diverted) in imports from non-member countries to which preferential access is not granted and are given as:

$$dm_{k,j} = -dm_{k,\neq j}$$

And the numerator of Eq. (8.9) becomes:

$$d\left(\frac{m_{k,j}}{m_{k,\neq j}}\right) = \frac{dm_{k,j}\left(m_{k,j} + m_{k,\neq j}\right)}{m_{k,\neq j}^2}$$

$$d\left(\frac{m_{k,j}}{m_{k,\neq j}}\right) \Big/ \frac{m_{k,j}}{m_{k,\neq j}} = \frac{dm_{k,j}\left(m_{k,j} + m_{k,\neq j}\right)}{m_{k,\neq j} m_{k,j}} \tag{8.11}$$

By substituting (8.10) and (8.11) into (8.9), we get the expression for trade diversion in terms of change in imports ($dm_{k,j}$) as:

$$TD_{k,j} = dm_{k,j} = \frac{m_{k,\neq j} m_{k,j}}{m_{k,\neq j} + m_{k,j}} \frac{dt_{k,j}}{1 + t_{k,j}} \sigma_{k,j,\neq j} \tag{8.12}$$

There is an upper limit on the value of trade diversion because as per the definition of trade diversion, the diverted trade cannot be greater than the actual trade previously existed between member and non-member countries. Jammes and Olarreaga (2005) suggested to use the simple way of introducing the constraint on the value of trade diversion given in (8.13).

$$TD_{k,j} = dm_{k,j} = -dm_{k,\neq j}$$
$$= \begin{cases} \dfrac{m_{k,\neq j} m_{k,j}}{m_{k,\neq j} + m_{k,j}} \dfrac{dt_{k,j}}{1 + t_{k,j}} \sigma_{k,j,\neq j} & \text{if } -dm_{k,\neq j} \leq m_{k,\neq j} \\ m_{k,\neq j} & \text{if } -dm_{k,\neq j} > m_{k,\neq j} \end{cases} \tag{8.13}$$

Price Effect

With the assumption of infinite export supply elasticity, price effect would be zero because the exporter is ready to supply as much as the importer demands at the world price existing in the economy for that particular product. In other words, increased demand for exports in the importing country can be easily met by the exporter and there will be no effect on prices.

However, in case when export supply elasticity is inelastic then it will have a positive impact on prices received by the exporter to compensate the increased demand from the importer(s) which arises due to decrease in importing price because of tariff reduction. In this case, price effect arises and adds to the total trade effect. Mathematically, price effect can be obtained by calculating the change in world prices ($p^w_{k,j}$) of import of good k coming from country j through the expression of export supply elasticity given as:

$$\mu_{k,j} = \frac{\frac{dx_{k,j}}{x_{k,j}}}{\frac{dp^w_{k,j}}{p^w_{k,j}}} > 0 \tag{8.14}$$

Solving the above expression of export supply elasticity for change in world prices of commodity k coming from country j will provide the price effect for the SMART model.

$$dp^w_{k,j} = \frac{\frac{dx_{k,j}}{x_{k,j}}}{\frac{\mu_{k,j}}{p^w_{k,j}}}$$

With the assumption of normalization of initial world prices at one ($p^w_{k,j} = 1$), the above expression can be written as:

$$dp^w_{k,j} = \frac{\frac{dx_{k,j}}{x_{k,j}}}{\mu_{k,j}} \tag{8.15}$$

By using (8.4), domestic prices become:

$$dp^d_{k,j} = p^w_{k,j} dt_{k,j} + dp^w_{k,j}(1 + t_{k,j}) \tag{8.16}$$

And the price effect can be written as (use expression (8.4)):

$$\frac{dp^d_{k,j}}{p^d_{k,j}} = \frac{dt_{k,j}}{(1 + t_{k,j})} + dp^w_{k,j}$$

Substituting the value of $dp^w_{k,j}$ from (8.15), the final expression of price effect becomes (use $dx_{k,j}=dm_{k,j}$)[10]:

$$\frac{dp^d_{k,j}}{p^d_{k,j}} = \frac{dt_{k,j}}{(1+t_{k,j})} + \frac{dm_{k,j}}{m_{k,j}}\frac{1}{\mu_{k,j}} \tag{8.17}$$

Where, $dm_{k,j}$ is the value of trade creation arrived under the assumption of inelastic export supply elasticity which is derived using the results given in (8.15) and (8.16). The formula for trade diversion, given in (8.8), will also alter and derived in following sub-sections.

Trade Creation with Inelastic Export Supply Elasticity As per the definition of trade creation given in (8.7):

$$dm_{k,j} = \varepsilon_{k,j} m_{k,j} \frac{dp^d_{k,j}}{p^d_{k,j}}$$

$$dm_{k,j} = \varepsilon_{k,j} m_{k,j} \frac{p^w_{k,j} dt_{k,j} + dp^w_{k,j}(1+t_{k,j})}{p^w_{k,j}(1+t_{k,j})}$$

$$dm_{k,j} = \varepsilon_{k,j} m_{k,j} \left(\frac{dt_{k,j}}{(1+t_{k,j})} + \frac{dp^w_{k,j}}{p^w_{k,j}} \right)$$

From (8.15)

$$dm_{k,j} = \varepsilon_{k,j} m_{k,j} \left(\frac{dt_{k,j}}{(1+t_{k,j})} + \frac{\frac{dx_{k,j}}{x_{k,j}}}{\mu_{k,j}} \right)$$

As per the partial equilibrium condition, $m_{k,j}=x_{k,j}$ and $dm_{k,j}=dx_{k,j}$

$$\frac{dm_{k,j}}{m_{k,j}} = \varepsilon_{k,j} \frac{dt_{k,j}}{(1+t_{k,j})} + \frac{\varepsilon_{k,j}}{\mu_{k,j}} \frac{dm_{k,j}}{m_{k,j}}$$

$$\frac{dm_{k,j}}{m_{k,j}} \left(1 - \frac{\varepsilon_{k,j}}{\mu_{k,j}} \right) = \varepsilon_{k,j} \frac{dt_{k,j}}{(1+t_{k,j})}$$

$$TC_{k,j} = dm_{k,j} == \varepsilon_{k,j} m_{k,j} \frac{dt_{k,j}}{1 + t_{k,j}} \left(\frac{1}{1 - \frac{\varepsilon_{k,j}}{\mu_{k,j}}} \right) \tag{8.18}$$

The expression in (8.18) above shows that if export supply elasticity is perfectly elastic (i.e., infinite), then it becomes equal to the old expression of trade creation given in (8.8). On the other hand, with finite export supply elasticity, the bracketed term of (8.18) becomes less than one which reduces the change in quantity of imports due to increased world price of good *k* coming from country *j*.

Trade Diversion with Inelastic Export Supply Elasticity Recalling the definition of trade diversion from (8.9):

$$\sigma_{k,j,\neq j} = \frac{d\left(\frac{m_{k,j}}{m_{k,\neq j}}\right) \Big/ \frac{m_{k,j}}{m_{k,\neq j}}}{d\left(\frac{p^d_{k,j}}{p^d_{k,\neq j}}\right) \Big/ \frac{p^d_{k,j}}{p^d_{k,\neq j}}} < 0$$

Using (8.11) for the numerator:

$$d\left(\frac{m_{k,j}}{m_{k,\neq j}}\right) = \frac{dm_{k,j}\left(m_{k,j} + m_{k,\neq j}\right)}{m^2_{k,\neq j}} \tag{8.11}$$

And alter the (8.10) for denominator using (8.16) as:

$$d\left(\frac{p^d_{k,j}}{p^d_{k,\neq j}}\right) \Big/ \frac{p^d_{k,j}}{p^d_{k,\neq j}} = \frac{\frac{p^d_{k,\neq j} dp^d_{k,j} - p^d_{k,j} dp^d_{k,\neq j}}{\left(p^d_{k,\neq j}\right)^2}}{\frac{p^w_{k,j}\left(1+t_{k,j}\right)}{p^w_{k,\neq j}\left(1+t_{k,\neq j}\right)}}$$

Assuming initial world prices are equal to 1:

$$d\left(\frac{p^d_{k,j}}{p^d_{k,\neq j}}\right) \Big/ \frac{p^d_{k,j}}{p^d_{k,\neq j}} = \frac{\frac{dp^d_{k,j}}{p^d_{k,\neq j}} - \frac{p^d_{k,j} dp^d_{k,\neq j}}{\left(p^d_{k,\neq j}\right)^2}}{\frac{\left(1+t_{k,j}\right)}{\left(1+t_{k,\neq j}\right)}}$$

Before trade policy change, it is assumed that all countries face same level of tariffs which implies $t_{k,j} = t_{k,\neq j}$ due to which denominator becomes 1.

$$d\left(\frac{p^d_{k,j}}{p^d_{k,\neq j}}\right) \Big/ \frac{p^d_{k,j}}{p^d_{k,\neq j}} = \frac{dp^d_{k,j}}{p^d_{k,\neq j}} - \frac{p^d_{k,j} dp^d_{k,\neq j}}{\left(p^d_{k,\neq j}\right)^2}$$

Using (8.16), we get

$$d\left(\frac{p^d_{k,j}}{p^d_{k,\neq j}}\right) \Big/ \frac{p^d_{k,j}}{p^d_{k,\neq j}} = \frac{p^w_{k,j} dt_{k,j} + dp^w_{k,j}(1 + t_{k,j})}{p^w_{k,\neq j}(1 + t_{k,\neq j})} - p^w_{k,j}(1 + t_{k,j}) \frac{p^w_{k,\neq j} dt_{k,\neq j} + dp^w_{k,\neq j}(1 + t_{k,\neq j})}{\left(p^w_{k,\neq j}(1 + t_{k,\neq j})\right)^2}$$

With $dt_{k,\neq j} = 0$ and $p^w_{k,\neq j} = p^w_{k,j} = 1$

$$d\left(\frac{p^d_{k,j}}{p^d_{k,\neq j}}\right) \Big/ \frac{p^d_{k,j}}{p^d_{k,\neq j}} = \frac{dt_{k,j} + dp^w_{k,j}(1 + t_{k,j})}{(1 + t_{k,\neq j})} - dp^w_{k,\neq j} \tag{8.19}$$

$$d\left(\frac{p^d_{k,j}}{p^d_{k,\neq j}}\right) \Big/ \frac{p^d_{k,j}}{p^d_{k,\neq j}} = \frac{dt_{k,j}}{(1 + t_{k,\neq j})} + dp^w_{k,j} - dp^w_{k,\neq j}$$

Using (8.15)

$$d\left(\frac{p^d_{k,j}}{p^d_{k,\neq j}}\right) \Big/ \frac{p^d_{k,j}}{p^d_{k,\neq j}} = \frac{dt_{k,j}}{(1 + t_{k,\neq j})} + \frac{\frac{dx_{k,j}}{x_{k,j}}}{\mu_{k,j}} - \frac{\frac{dx_{k,\neq j}}{x_{k,\neq j}}}{\mu_{k,\neq j}}$$

Since $dx_{k,j} = -dx_{k,\neq j}$ and $dm_{k,j} = -dm_{k,\neq j}$, therefore

$$d\left(\frac{p^d_{k,j}}{p^d_{k,\neq j}}\right) \Big/ \frac{p^d_{k,j}}{p^d_{k,\neq j}} = \frac{dt_{k,j}}{(1 + t_{k,\neq j})} + dx_{k,j}\left(\frac{1}{x_{k,j}\mu_{k,j}} + \frac{1}{x_{k,\neq j}\mu_{k,\neq j}}\right) \tag{8.20}$$

By substituting (8.20) and (8.11) and solving for change in imports ($dm_{k,j}$) will provide us the trade diversion effect as follows:

$$\frac{dm_{k,j}\left(m_{k,j}+m_{k,\neq j}\right)}{m_{k,\neq j}m_{k,j}}=\sigma_{k,j,\neq j}\left[\frac{dt_{k,j}}{\left(1+t_{k,\neq j}\right)}+dx_{k,j}\left(\frac{1}{x_{k,j}\mu_{k,j}}+\frac{1}{x_{k,\neq j}\mu_{k,\neq j}}\right)\right]$$

Using $dx_{k,j}=dm_{k,j}$ and $x_{k,j}=m_{k,j}$

$$\frac{dm_{k,j}\left(m_{k,j}+m_{k,\neq j}\right)}{m_{k,\neq j}m_{k,j}}=\sigma_{k,j,\neq j}\left[\frac{dt_{k,j}}{\left(1+t_{k,\neq j}\right)}+dm_{k,j}\left(\frac{1}{x_{k,j}\mu_{k,j}}+\frac{1}{x_{k,\neq j}\mu_{k,\neq j}}\right)\right]$$

$$dm_{k,j}\left[\frac{\left(m_{k,j}+m_{k,\neq j}\right)}{m_{k,\neq j}m_{k,j}}-\sigma_{k,j,\neq j}\left(\frac{1}{m_{k,j}\mu_{k,j}}+\frac{1}{m_{k,\neq j}\mu_{k,\neq j}}\right)\right]=\sigma_{k,j,\neq j}\frac{dt_{k,j}}{\left(1+t_{k,\neq j}\right)}$$

$$dm_{k,j}=\sigma_{k,j,\neq j}\frac{dt_{k,j}}{\left(1+t_{k,\neq j}\right)}\left[\frac{m_{k,\neq j}m_{k,j}\mu_{k,j}\mu_{k,\neq j}}{\left(m_{k,j}+m_{k,\neq j}\right)\mu_{k,j}\mu_{k,\neq j}-\sigma_{k,j,\neq j}\left(m_{k,\neq j}\mu_{k,\neq j}\right)-\sigma_{k,j,\neq j}\left(m_{k,j}\mu_{k,j}\right)}\right]$$

$$\begin{aligned}TD_{k,j}&=dm_{k,j}\\&=\frac{m_{k,\neq j}m_{k,j}}{m_{k,\neq j}+m_{k,j}}\frac{dt_{k,j}}{1+t_{k,j}}\sigma_{k,j,\neq j}\\&\quad\left[\frac{\left(m_{k,j}+m_{k,\neq j}\right)\mu_{k,j}\mu_{k,\neq j}}{\left(m_{k,j}+m_{k,\neq j}\right)\mu_{k,j}\mu_{k,\neq j}-\sigma_{k,j,\neq j}\left(m_{k,j}\mu_{k,j}\right)-\sigma_{k,j,\neq j}\left(m_{k,\neq j}\mu_{k,\neq j}\right)}\right]\end{aligned} \tag{8.21}$$

The above new expression for trade diversion shows that in case export supply elasticities are infinitely elastic then (8.21) becomes (8.12). In case if export supply elasticities are perfectly inelastic ($\mu_{k,j}=0$ *and* $\mu_{k,\neq j}=0$) then the extent of trade diversion will become zero. In addition, another interesting case becomes in which export supply elasticity of rest of the world is infinitely elastic but not of the partner country then (8.21) becomes (8.23) derived as follows.

To get the final expression of TD in this case, the numerator of (8.9) remain same as derived in (8.11) and the denominator will be change assuming $dp^{d}_{k,\neq j}=0$ and the existence of price effect for partner country only. In that case, the denominator of (8.9) becomes:

$$d\left(\frac{p^d_{k,j}}{p^d_{k,\neq j}}\right) \Big/ \frac{p^d_{k,j}}{p^d_{k,\neq j}} = \frac{dp^d_{k,j}}{p^d_{k,j}}$$

Using expression (8.17):

$$d\left(\frac{p^d_{k,j}}{p^d_{k,\neq j}}\right) \Big/ \frac{p^d_{k,j}}{p^d_{k,\neq j}} = \frac{dp^d_{k,j}}{p^d_{k,j}} = \frac{dt_{k,j}}{(1+t_{k,j})} + \frac{dm_{k,j}}{m_{k,j}} \frac{1}{\mu_{k,j}} \tag{8.22}$$

By substituting (8.22) and (8.11) and solving for change in imports $(dm_{k,j})$ will provide us the trade diversion effect as follows:

$$\begin{aligned} TD_{k,j} &= dm_{k,j} \\ &= \frac{m_{k,\neq j} m_{k,j}}{m_{k,\neq j} + m_{k,j}} \frac{dt_{k,j}}{1+t_{k,j}} \sigma_{k,j,\neq j} \left[\frac{(m_{k,j} + m_{k,\neq j})\mu_{k,j}}{(m_{k,j} + m_{k,\neq j})\mu_{k,j} - \sigma_{k,j,\neq j} m_{k,\neq j}} \right] \end{aligned} \tag{8.23}$$

Tariff Revenue Effect

In the SMART model, change in tariff revenue can be easily calculated using the following formula:

$$dTR_i = TR_{i\text{Post}} - TR_{i\text{Pre}} \tag{8.24}$$

$$TR^0_i = \sum_k t^0_{k,j} \left(p^w_{k,j} m^0_{k,j} \right) \tag{8.24a}$$

$$TR^1_i = \sum_k t^1_{k,j} \left(p^w_{k,j} m^1_{k,j} \right) \tag{8.24b}$$

Where, TR^0_i and TR^1_i are the total tariff revenues incurred by the importing country (i) before and after the change in trade policy; $t^0_{k,j}$ and $t^1_{k,j}$ are the tariff rates before and after trade policy shock; and $\left(p^w_{k,j} m^0_{k,j}\right)$ and $\left(p^w_{k,j} m^1_{k,j}\right)$ are the value of imports before and after the trade policy change at world prices.

Welfare Effect

The net welfare effect is estimated by multiplying the change in imports with the average between the incidence of tariff barriers before and after their change (Laird and Yeats 1986).

$$w_{k,i} = \frac{\left[dm_{k,j} \times \frac{\left(t^0_{k,j}+t^1_{k,j}\right)}{2}\right]}{100} \tag{8.25}$$

Generally, welfare effect is defined as the sum of producer and consumer surplus in the economy due to the adoption of tariff reduction policy. With the infinite export supply elasticity, the whole welfare effect is composed of consumer surplus only which arises because of decrease in price of imported product with the reduction of tariffs on that product. However, with less than infinite export supply elasticity, one can calculate the producer welfare existed in the exporting country due to increment in the world price of imports because of increase in demand for imported product.

Revenue Effect to the Exporter

In this partial equilibrium setup, change in revenue to the exporter in a post simulation environment, can also be calculated. The result on this effect is not directly reported by SMART model but one can get the answer by using the following mathematical relation given in Laird and Yeats (1986). The revenue to the exporter (ER) can be written as:

By assuming: $x_{k,j}=m_{k,j}$

$$\mathrm{ER}_{k,j} = p^w_{k,j} m_{k,j} \tag{8.26}$$

It can be changed either by change in world prices or change in imports of product k from country exporter j or both. In case of infinite export supply elasticity, there is no price effect and exporter's revenue increases with the increase in imports only. However, in case of finite export supply elasticity, the change in exporter's revenue depends upon both of the variables: changes in world prices and changes in imports from country j. Following expression (8.27) shows the change in revenue in case when export supply elasticity is finite.

$$d\mathrm{ER}_{k,j} = p^w_{k,j} dm_{k,j} + m_{k,j} dp^w_{k,j} \tag{8.27}$$

By dividing (8.27) with (8.26); we get

$$\frac{d\mathrm{ER}_{k,j}}{\mathrm{ER}_{k,j}} = \frac{dm_{k,j}}{m_{k,j}} + \frac{dp^w_{k,j}}{p^w_{k,j}}$$

Using (8.15) and (8.18), we get the final expression for revenue effect to the exporter as:

$$\frac{d\mathrm{ER}_{k,j}}{\mathrm{ER}_{k,j}} = \frac{dm_{k,j}}{m_{k,j}} + \frac{dm_{k,j}}{m_{k,j}}\frac{1}{\mu_{k,j}}$$

$$\frac{d\mathrm{ER}_{k,j}}{\mathrm{ER}_{k,j}} = \frac{dm_{k,j}}{m_{k,j}}\left[1 + \frac{1}{\mu_{k,j}}\right]$$

$$\frac{d\mathrm{ER}_{k,j}}{\mathrm{ER}_{k,j}} = \varepsilon_{k,j}\frac{dt_{k,j}}{1+t_{k,j}}\left(\frac{1}{1-\frac{\varepsilon_{k,j}}{\mu_{k,j}}}\right)\left[1 + \frac{1}{\mu_{k,j}}\right]$$

$$\frac{d\mathrm{ER}_{k,j}}{\mathrm{ER}_{k,j}} = \varepsilon_{k,j}\frac{dt_{k,j}}{1+t_{k,j}}\left(\frac{\mu_{k,j}}{\mu_{k,j}-\varepsilon_{k,j}}\right)\left[\frac{\mu_{k,j}+1}{\mu_{k,j}}\right]$$

$$\frac{d\mathrm{ER}_{k,j}}{\mathrm{ER}_{k,j}} = \varepsilon_{k,j}\frac{dt_{k,j}}{1+t_{k,j}}\left(\frac{\mu_{k,j}+1}{\mu_{k,j}-\varepsilon_{k,j}}\right) \tag{8.28}$$

Implementation of the Model
SMART model is easily implemented in WITS database available online and uses the inbuilt data on applied tariff rates and imports. One can chose between the two tariff rates available: MFN applied and Bound rates, while making the simulation scenario. The model has also assumed the given values of elasticity parameters. As explained in the above section, there are three main elasticity parameters: Import demand elasticity[11] (ε); Substitution elasticity[12] (σ); and Export supply elasticity[13] (μ). The value of these parameters varies over the products but remains same for the partner country. While doing simulations using SMART, one can update/change the value of substitution and export supply elasticity instead of using the default values: 1.5 and 99 respectively but the value of Import demand elasticity is system defined and cannot be changed. The SMART tool in WITS database provides the detailed results on above mentioned effects in the way given in the Box 8.1.

Box 8.1

Detailed Data The Detailed Data report is to check the raw data used for smart simulation just to make sure the dataset corresponds to expectations.

Exporter View Report The Export View report shows the impact of the tariff reform on partners' exports to the considered market. It displays the pre value of exports (before the tariff change), the post value of exports (after the tariff change) to the considered market as well as the net value between the two, considered as the change in exports revenue.

Market View Report The Market View report returns all three types of effects affecting the market (trade value, tariff revenue and welfare change) by individual product code and for all products as one aggregate.

Revenue Impact Report The Revenue Impact report returns individual results on the market's revenue by product code and for all products as one aggregate. The report displays the tariff revenue change between the pre and post tariff cut situation as well as the trade total effects.

Trade Creation Effect The Trade Creation Effect report returns individual results on Trade Total effect by product code/partner combination and for all products as one aggregate. This report also shows the trade diversion effect among partners and trade creation effect for both the market and its partners.

Welfare Effect Report The Welfare Effect report returns individual results on the market's welfare by product code and for all products as one aggregate. The report displays the Total Trade Effect, which is defined as the sum of Trade Diversion effect, Trade Creation Effect and Price Effect as well as the Welfare Effect defined as the benefits consumers in the importing country derive from the lower domestic prices after the removal or reduction of tariffs.

Source: WITS Results Window

8.3 General Equilibrium Tool to Assess the Proposed Trade Policy

The main disadvantage of the partial equilibrium analysis is that it ignores the interaction effect between sectors. It also misses the existing constraints that apply to the various factors of production and their movement across sectors and very sensitive to some behavioral parameters such as elasticities. However, General Equilibrium modeling captures all these feedback effect of an economy and captures all indirect impacts on other market of any change in policy variable. In any general equilibrium model, an economy is represented by many accounting relationships which are linked with each other. The common idea behind this is to divide the whole economy into different markets which are related with each other and then determine the equilibrium prices and quantities for each market simultaneously. In the words of Starr (2011), "general equilibrium for an economy consists of an array of prices for each good, while taking account of the interactions across markets. In this analysis, the equilibrium concept deals with all markets simultaneously and all their interactions, rather than a single market in isolation in a partial equilibrium analysis".

A general equilibrium model is a complete picture of an economy describing the behavior of consumers and producers and their relationships with the help of mathematical equations. Any general equilibrium model which is computable by using the appropriate data is known as Computable General Equilibrium (CGE) model. In CGE model, an economy is assumed to be in equilibrium at the initial prices and all agents are satisfied with the reward they are getting and with their economic activities. Change in trade policy, such as changes in tariff rate, acts as a shock and create disequilibrium in the model which further causes reactions into the whole economic system. All of the mathematical equations will be resolved to get new equilibrium solution which again satisfy market clearing conditions. There exists very large number of country specific general equilibrium models which differs in their economic structure, as different countries have different economic structure. They also differ from one another due to different assumptions. For detailed reading on applied general equilibrium see: Shoven and Whalley (1992), Bouet (2008), Burfisher (2011); and other handbook and user guides of trade policy analysis already mentioned above.

The change in trade policy such as reduction/elimination of tariff rates barriers has impact on both importer and exporter country. It has direct effects through the reduction in price of the imported product in the importer country and increase in exports from an exporter country. In addition to these, due to presence of linkage and feedback effects in an economy, it also affects the demand for its substitutes available in the home market and in foreign market with other supplier. Due to change in demand for substitute good, price will also be affected and hence affect the overall income of an economy through number of other linkage effects. Due to ignorance of these linkage and feedback effects in partial equilibrium analysis makes it simpler to understand because it focuses only on one market at a time. But in reality these linkages and feedback effects cannot be ignored and played a very important role in an economy. Hence, there arises a need to take all these effects together and study the effect of change in trade policy variable on all sectors of the economy rather than concentrating on one market at a time. In this chapter, the structure of one of the famous model of world trade, i.e. GTAP model of trade, has been discussed in detail.

8.3.1 GTAP Model Framework

The GTAP model (see Brockmeier 2001; Hertel 1997) is a static multi-region general equilibrium model, which divides the whole economy into various agents' dependent upon each other. It is static in nature in the sense that it provides a comparison of the state of the economy before and after changing the value of shock variable and its impact on economy-wide variables. The framework of this model is provided under the Global Trade Analysis Project (GTAP) which was started in 1992 to facilitate the researchers working in the area of quantitative analysis of international trade. Under this project, a fully documented database, GTAP database, is also provided which gives economy-wide data of all 140 defined regions of the world. The analysis of trade liberalization and its impact on economy-wide variables among countries are the main research application of this project. It also provides the software, a tool to implement the GTAP model using data from GTAP database. Under the GTAP model framework, each separate region assumes common domestic structure and linked through trade and investment flows between them. The domestic structure consists of one regional household specified over private consumption, government consumption and saving activities; production behavior of the region; and two global sectors through which all the regions of the world are linked with each other.

It is already explained that GTAP model is a general equilibrium model in the sense that it takes care of feedback and linkage effects existed in the entire economy. Therefore, to present the whole framework of this model, one should describe the accounting relationships within the region and between the regions; and behavioral equations used to represent the behavior of economic agents in the model. Following sub-sections present the whole GTAP model structure by giving details on accounting relationships and behavioral equation.

Accounting Relationships

The whole GTAP model structure can be easily explained with the help of accounting relationships which makes this model general equilibrium in nature. Accounting relationships for each region are defined in such a way that the whole economy remain in balance. These relationships remain same for each region[14] with common producer and consumer behavior. In GTAP model, each separate region assumes common domestic structure which is shown in Fig. 8.1 given in Hertel (2004) to show the structural[15] representation of this model. The pictorial representation of these relationships represents the circular flow for any GTAP region.

As shown in the Fig. 8.1, GTAP model assumes one regional household who collects all income in the economy and allocates expenditure over private consumption expenditure (*PRIVEXP*), government consumption expenditure (*GOVEXP*), and savings (*SAVE*). The private and government household further allocates the given expenditure over domestic (*VDPA*& *VDGA*) and imported goods (*VIPA*& *VIGA*). Saving is assumed as single commodity and fully exhausted by investment demand. Income to the regional household comes from the producer who pays to the regional household for using endowments (*VOA*) in production process. The regional household spent all income in such a way that it exhaust between three forms of demand.

Further, the producer in the GTAP model involves in purchasing intermediate goods and primary factors to use as inputs in the production process to produce output in the economy. The intermediate input can be either sourced from domestic region (*VDFA*) or from other country through imports (*VIFA*) or from both sources which happens most of the time. On the other hand, the purchase of primary inputs by the producer in GTAP model is known as purchase of endowment commodities.[16] Producer also sells the consumption and investment good to the regional household and intermediate good to the other producers and receives

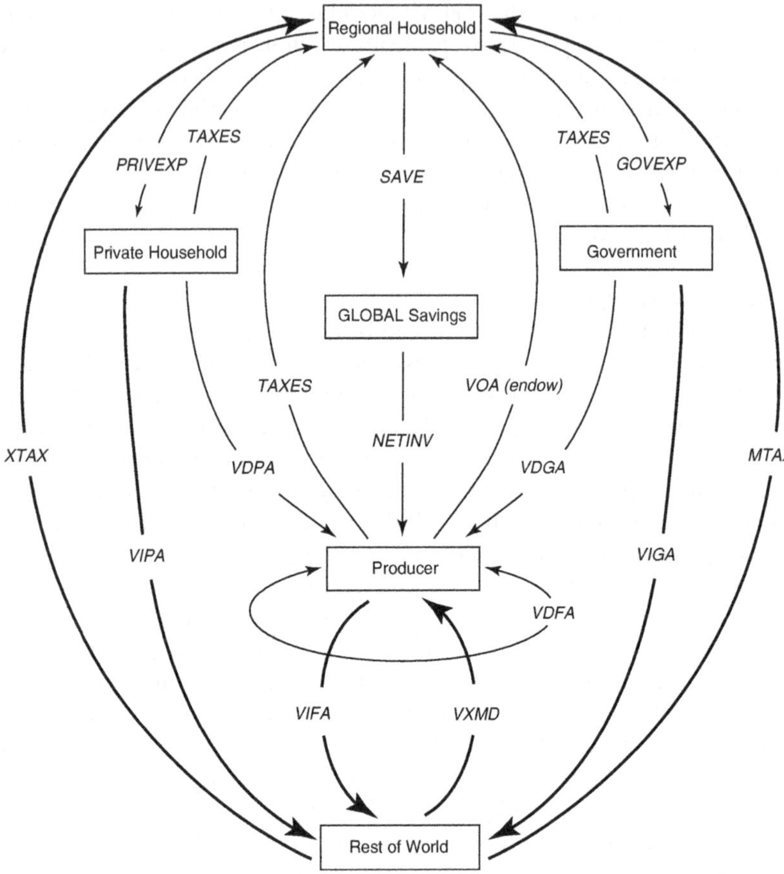

Fig. 8.1 Pictorial representation of accounting relationships in GTAP model (Source: Fig. 6 in Brockmeier 2001)

payments. The firms will get extra revenue by selling their products to the outside world.

The policy interventions in the economy refer to the imposition of taxes by the government on demand and supply activities. Due to the introduction of these transfer payments, there will be changes in the accounting relationships which are captured by difference between market prices and agent's prices. In other words, in this model taxes and subsidies drive a wedge between the market and agent's price.

The multi-region GTAP model also includes two global sectors through which regions are linked together. The first global sector is the external sector which accounts the International trade and transport activities between the regions. Under this sector, a composite good consist of exports of commodity, transport, and insurance services are produced and used to move in between regions. The value of these services exhausts the difference between global *fob* exports and global imports at *cif* prices. Demand for domestic product coming from the external sector (other regions of the world) generates additional revenue to the domestic producer and also it provides the additional source of intermediate goods from the outside by paying the import taxes which is already explained in the policy interventions. As the current GTAP-9 database divides the whole world into 140 regions so to differentiate the goods from different regions, the model employs the Armington assumption[17] in the trading sector. The model also includes the separate conditional demand equations for private and government consumption for imported commodity.

The other global sector is Global Bank which intermediates between global savings and investments of all regions at same prices. This sector satisfies the regional household's demand for savings by selling shares from regional investment good assembled for this purpose. In the GTAP model, the implication of this sector is that if all sectors in a multi-region model are in equilibrium then the global investments must be equal to global savings to satisfy Walras' law. Following points briefly explains theoretically the accounting relationships existed in this model.

- Producer pays to the regional household for using his endowments which is equal to the value of output at agent's prices (*VOA*) and regional household allocates this regional income across private expenditures (*VDPA*), government expenditure (*VDGA*) and savings activities in such a way that all regional income earned is exhausted between three forms of final demand;
- The producer also purchases intermediate goods as inputs use in the production process;
- After the production, the producer sells the consumption and investment good to the regional household and intermediate good to the other producers and receives payments. *VDFA* is the payment received by the domestic producer for selling intermediate goods to other producer in the economy;

- Under the zero profit assumption, all income earned is exhausted between the purchases of value added services and intermediate goods;
- *NETINV* is the payment received by the producer for selling investment good to the regional household for the saving activity;
- Further under the closed economy, due to government interventions, taxes have been introduced. Due to which private household and government have to pay taxes in addition to their expenditure on consumption good;
- Producer also have to pay taxes on the purchase of intermediate goods used in the process of production;
- Tax revenues are computed by comparing the value of transaction at agent's and market prices separately;
- To show the relationship with outside word, one region, say rest of the world, has been introduced. In this setup, the firms will get extra revenue (*VXMD*) by selling their products to the outside world and also spend (*VIFA*) on the purchases of intermediate inputs from the rest of the world;
- Private households and government also spend on imported commodities and flows are represented by *VIPA* and *VIGA* respectively;
- To accommodate the third source of final demand such as savings, the GTAP model computes global savings and investment which creates the equilibrium system;
- At the end, the rest of the world region also earns revenue from the exports to single domestic region and spent on exports of domestic household to rest of the world (*VXMD*) and on import (*MTAX*) and export (*XTAX*) taxes to the regional household. It completes the circular flow in the open economy.

Behavioral Equations

These equations are defined to specify the behavior of optimizing agents in the economy such as demand functions in consumer behavior, production function in producer behavior among others. Under the GTAP model framework, each separate region assumes common domestic structure and linked through trade and investment flows between them. The domestic structure consists of one regional household specified over private

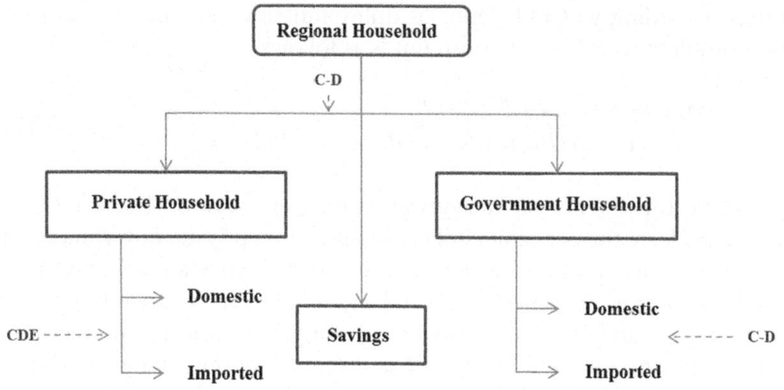

Fig. 8.2 Representation of regional household behavior (Source: Authors' elaborations)

consumption, government consumption and saving activities; and the behavior of the production in the region.

Regional Household Behavior

Regional household allocates the expenditure across private consumption expenditure, government consumption expenditure and savings activities. The private household further allocates the given expenditure over domestic and imported goods through CDE (Constant Difference Elasticity) implicit expenditure function. However, the government household allocates the given expenditure among domestic and imported goods following a Cobb-Douglas (CD) utility function. In last, saving is assumed as single commodity and fully exhausted by investment demand. The base data in this case are: *VDPA*, *VDGA*, *VIPA*, *VIGA*, & *SAVE* (Fig. 8.2).

Utility from Private Consumption

The behavior of a regional household is governed by an aggregated utility function that allocates the expenditure across private, government and savings activities (McDougall 2001). In GTAP model, in each region, household allocates regional income so as to maximize per capita aggregate utility according to Cobb-Douglas utility function. The utility maximization problem with budget constraint is as follows:

$$\begin{aligned} &\text{Maximise } U = CU_P^{B_P} U_G^{B_G} U_S^{B_S} \\ &\text{s.t.} \quad E_P(P_P, U_P) + E_G(P_G, U_G) + P_P U_S = X \end{aligned} \tag{8.29}$$

Where U is the per capita aggregate utility of a regional household; U_P, U_G, and U_S are the per capita utility obtained from private, government and real savings activities and at lower level these utilities are specified using some expenditure function[18]; E_P and E_G are per capita expenditure functions; P_P, P_G, and P_S are the price vectors for private consumption, government consumption, and savings; B_i is the distribution parameter which is assumed as variable; and X is the per capita income. Regional household receives income by selling his endowments to the producer and spend over private household expenditure, government expenditure and savings.

Production Structure and Firms Behavior

As shown in the Fig. 8.3, in the first stage, the inputs required to produce an output is divided into two categories of intermediate goods and factor inputs. Factor inputs are clubbed under the endowment category and under intermediate category, two sources have been mentioned. The source of these intermediate inputs can be the domestic industry at home and/or from the industry of other country termed as imported one. Further, these imports may come from different exporters depending upon per unit cost of production of the required good.

In GTAP model, producer tries to minimize the cost of production and his behavior is specified by the nested Constant Elasticity of Substitution (CES) function (Gohin and Hertel 2003). In case of more than two inputs, Sato (1967) proposed a nested CES function with less restrictive conditions on elasticity of substitution which is a good approximation for empirical applications. In GTAP model, the same nested structure has been used to specify the substitution possibilities between various inputs. At the upper level, CES function is defined to indicate the substitution possibility between intermediate inputs and value added and at the lower level CES function is defined to show substitution between primary factors in the value added nest. The basic idea behind nested CES structure is to accommodate the substitution possibilities within the aggregated input category which is composed from other individual inputs. The mathematical structure of nested CES production function with four inputs is given as follows. Suppose x_1 and

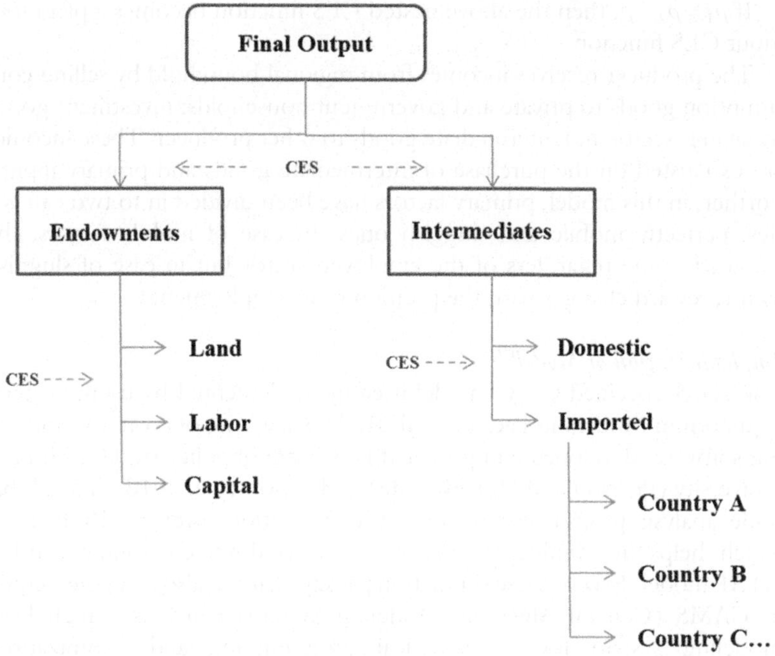

Fig. 8.3 Representation of production structure in GTAP model (Source: Authors' elaborations)

x_2 are aggregated into one single input and x_3 and x_4 are aggregated into another single input then the upper level CES function composed of two lower level CES functions with two inputs each shown as follows:

$$Q = \gamma(\delta \mathrm{CES}_1 + (1-\delta)\mathrm{CES}_2)^{\frac{-1}{\rho}} \tag{8.30}$$

Where $\mathrm{CES}_i = \gamma_i\left(\delta_i x_{2i-1}^{-\rho_i} + (1-\delta_i)x_{2i}^{-\rho_i}\right)^{\frac{-1}{\rho_i}}, i = 1,2$ are the two lower level CES functions. The final specification of the four input nested CES function becomes:

$$Q = \gamma\left[\delta\left(\delta_1 x_1^{-\rho_1} + (1-\delta_1)x_2^{-\rho_1}\right)^{\frac{\rho}{\rho_1}} + (1-\delta)\left(\delta_2 x_3^{-\rho_2} + (1-\delta_2)x_4^{-\rho_2}\right)^{\frac{\rho}{\rho_2}}\right]^{\frac{-1}{\rho}} \tag{8.31}$$

If $\rho_1 = \rho_2 = \rho$, then the above nested CES function becomes a plain four input CES function.

The producer receives incomes from regional household by selling consumption goods to private and government households; investment goods to savings sector and intermediate goods to other producer. These incomes are exhausted on the purchase of intermediate goods and primary inputs. Further, in this model, primary factors have been divided in to two categories: perfectly mobile and sluggish ones. In case of mobile factors, the reward is same regardless of the employed sector but in case of sluggish factor, reward changes with the position of its employment.

Implementation of Model[19]

The above specified GTAP model is easily implemented by using General Equilibrium Modelling Package (GEMPACK), a suite of economic modeling software, developed and provided by Centre of policy studies, Monash University (Pearson and Horridge 2005; Harrison et al. 2013). The global trade analysis project also provides the simulation software, RunGTAP, which helps in running simulations in a windows environment using GTAP model. Except these simulation packages, it can also be implemented in GAMS (General Algebraic Modeling System) which is a high level modeling system for mathematical programming and optimization. GAMS is tailored for complex, large scale modeling applications, and allows you to build large maintainable models that can be adapted quickly to new situations. The estimation of this model using GTAP database provides new equilibrium solution which contains the updated value of each variable in the model. From those results, one can meaningfully calculate the number of effects through which a comparison can be made in a pre and post simulation values. Among those effects, some of them are presented as follows:

Trade Effects

Under this effect, trade creation and trade diversion can be calculated by showing the change in imports of the concerned country from its various partners in a post simulation environment. Whenever there will be changes in the tariff liberalization policy, there will be changes in imports and exports. The net positive change in the imports or exports of a country from all regions would be termed as trade creation and from the region-wise figures one can estimate the extent of trade diversion from one region to the other. Under this effect, one can also report the changes in imports and exports[20] in a post simulation environment. The GTAP simulation results also provide the changes in imports and exports both in value and quantity terms.

Terms of Trade Effect

Moreover, one can also report the changes in terms of trade of any GTAP region to show the impact of given policy shock. The terms of trade of a region is defined as the ratio of price index received for tradable produced in the region (*PSW*) to the price index paid for tradable used in the same region (*PDW*). The percentage change in terms of trade (*tot*) can be easily calculated by subtracting the percentage change in price index paid for the tradable (*pdw*) from the percentage change in price index received from tradable (*psw*).

Trade Balance

Trade balance or balance of trade is calculated by subtracting region's imports from the total exports of same region. Positive value of trade balance indicates the surplus and the negative value indicates deficit. In a post-simulation environment, one can report the value of change in trade balance to show the changes in current account for each region.

Regional GDP

One may report the changes in gross domestic product (GDP) of any region by subtracting the value of GDP in a post-simulation environment from the value of GDP calculated in a pre- simulation environment. The value of GDP can be calculated by summing the values of Private household expenditures (*VPA*), Government consumption expenditure (*VGA*), Capital goods (*VOA*), Exports at world prices (*VXWD*), Exports of margin commodities (*VST*), and negative of values of imports at world prices (*VIWS*). In addition, one may also be interested in reporting the quantity index of GDP and in this model, the percentage change in quantity index can be easily calculated by subtracting percentage change in price index of GDP (*pgdp*) from percentage change in value index of GDP (*vgdp*). The increment in quantity index of GDP represents the shift in the economy's production possibility frontier. With the assumption of fixed endowments, the shifting will be due to the improved allocation of resource base; and with the assumption of endogenous growth, this will reflect the regional growth.

Welfare Effect

In GTAP model, measurement of economic welfare depends upon household's own consumption expenditure, government consumption expenditure (government spending on public goods and services) and net national savings which will benefit his future consumption. Any distortion in the model has an effect on these variables and thus, affects economic welfare of a region. The estimation of GTAP model provides the regional equivalent variation (*EV*) measure in monetary terms which represent the welfare effect in this model (Huff and Hertel 2000). From the household point of view, it measures the cost to the household of the same bundle of goods, before and after a given policy shock. In other words, it is the difference between the expenditure required to obtain the new level of utility at initial prices and the initial expenditure. In GTAP model, the regional household utility level depends upon per capita household consumption, per capita government expenditure, and per capita savings. Any change in this aggregate utility level provides the welfare effect in this model. In other words, welfare change in the GTAP model is measured by change in aggregate utility due to any distortion specified over per capita private household consumption, per capita government expenditure and per capita savings and calculation of EV provides the value of the same percentage change in level of utility in terms of money value. Consider two policy options, the existing one with prices p^0 and income m^0, and a policy shock with price p^1 and income m^1; then the equivalent variation can be expressed as:

$$EV = \mu(p^0; p^1; m^1) - \mu(p^0; p^0; m^0) = \mu(p^0; p^1; m^1) - m^0 \qquad (8.32)$$

Where $\mu(p^0; p; m)$ is called money metric indirect utility function, measures how much income the consumer would need at prices p^0 to be as well off he would be facing price p^1 and having income m^1. For GTAP model, McDougall (2001) obtained the EV associated with a perturbation to the GTAP model as follows:

$$\text{EV} = Y_{\text{EV}} - \bar{Y} \qquad (8.33)$$

Where Υ_{EV} is the expenditure required to obtain the new level of utility at initial prices, that is equal to $\mu(p^0; p^1, m^1)$ in (8.1), whereas $\bar{\Upsilon}$ is the initial expenditure, that is, m^0 in (8.32).

Differentiating (8.33) we get:

$$dEV = dY_{EV}$$

$$\frac{dEV}{Y_{EV}} \times 100 = \frac{dY_{EV}}{Y_{EV}} \times 100$$

$$\frac{dEV}{Y_{EV}} \times 100 = y_{EV}$$

$$dEV = \frac{Y_{EV} y_{EV}}{100}$$

Or

$$dEV = 0.01 Y_{EV} y_{EV} \tag{8.34}$$

Where Y_{EV} is the percentage change in Y_{EV} required to achieve the current actual utility level, in which the prices are fixed.

Further, change in welfare can also be decomposed into various other effects and the details are given in Huff and Hertel (2000). Any distortion which changes the level of expenditure will change the level of utility and lead to welfare change. In a multi-region general equilibrium model, there exist several sources which contribute in the total change in expenditure and also to welfare. In the GTAP model, these sources are clubbed into the following main six sources:

(I) *Allocative Efficiency Effect*: It occurs due to reallocation of resources from one use to another in a post-simulation environment in a particular region. In this model, allocative efficiency effect for a region is explained by summing all types of changes in tax revenues associated with the change in quantity demanded of non-saving commodities[21] in a post-simulation environment with initial tax rates. The different types of taxes are: Input taxes (taxes on use of domestic and imported intermediate goods); Consumption taxes (taxes on private consumption of domestic & imported good and taxes on government consumption of domestic and imported good); Endowment tax (tax on use of endowment good as an input; Export tax (tax on exports); and Import tax (tax on imports of goods). For each tax, the change in tax revenue can be calculated by multiplying percentage change in per capita demand for its associated quantity with its initial tax revenue. One can report the contribution of every type of quantity change in total change in welfare effect of a given region.

(II) *Terms of Trade Effect*: In a multi-region general equilibrium model, terms of trade effect also plays an important role in changing economic welfare of a particular region. This effect arises due to changes in *fob* prices of exports from both sides (exporter and importer) when compared with price index of world trade. Changes in prices of commodities and services provided to international transport sector are also included in the calculation of terms of trade effect. To calculate it, change in the value of imports of region *s* and services paid to international transport sector is subtracted from change in value of exports of region *r* at fob prices and changes in value of sales to international transport sector by region *r*. Positive difference shows the positive contribution of this effect.

(III) *Investment–Saving Effect*: Under this effect, change in price of saving and investment is compared. Percentage change in prices of capital goods when multiplied with the net initial investment of the region gives the value of change in net investment and the percentage change in price of savings when multiplied with regional savings gives the value of change in savings and the difference between the two provides the contribution of this effect in total welfare. As the utility level is also depends upon the net national savings so the regions with net suppliers of savings (savings > investment) to the global bank benefit from rise in price of savings relative to investment goods.

(IV) *Effect of Change in Technology*: In this model, the contribution of this effect comes from various technological changes *viz.*, output augmenting technology change, primary factor augmenting technology change, value added augmenting technology change, composite intermediate input augmenting technical change, technical change in transportation sector and contribution of bilateral import-augmenting technical change. Change in any technology would lead to change in associated demand which further affect level of utility. In a comparative static model setup in which technology is assumed fixed, the contribution of this effect is zero.

(V) *Endowment Effect*: Under this effect, percentage change in per capita quantity of endowment commodity is calculated and then multiplied with the initial value of output of the same endowment commodity at agent's prices to evaluate the contribution of changes in quantity of endowments. Value of capital depreciation is also subtracted while giving the final figure to this effect. In case of fixed endowment assumption, this effect is zero. However, the positive figure of this effect in the final results would represent the increasing productive capacity of the corresponding region.

(VI) *Effect of change in population*: The effect of change in population on change in expenditure level is known as population effect. Contribution of this effect is zero in comparative static model with the assumption of fixed population.

In addition to the above effects, the researchers' working in this field may also report other effects based on the theory and study's requirements from the simulation results obtained after giving a policy shock using the GTAP model.

8.4 Concluding Remarks

The evaluation of proposed change in trade policy is very necessary because it provides an idea how this trade policy will affect the economy if it will be implemented in the coming future. The evaluation may also help the negotiators, countries involving in proposed free trade agreements, to negotiate their country's position very strongly. For this type of evaluation, literature proposes two main methods: Partial and General Equilibrium analyses. This chapter discussed only two such existing and largely used methodologies which come in the category of ex-ante evaluation and generally used for evaluating the proposed changes in trade policy. There also exists many other such tools in the literature and many are still evolving on the basis of country specific requirements.

Notes

1. Download using http://wits.worldbank.org/WITS/docs/wto_unctad12_e.pdf and read Chap. 4 for details.
2. http://wits.worldbank.org/WITS/WITS/AdvanceQuery/TradeOutcomes/IndicatorDefinition.aspx?Page=Indicator
3. http://wits.worldbank.org/trade_outcomes.html

4. Download using http://wits.worldbank.org/WITS/docs/wto_unctad 12_e.pdf and read Chap. 1 for details.
5. http://unctad.org/en/Docs/itcdtab25_en.pdf
6. https://aric.adb.org/pdf/FTA_Impact_Assessment.pdf
7. http://wits.worldbank.org/data/public/WITS_User_Manual.pdf
8. http://siteresources.worldbank.org/INTRANETTRADE/Resources/239054-1196261607599/4442906-1253911939559/TRIST_Manual.pdf
9. The consumption of the composite and numeraire good (n) absorbs all income effects.
10. $dx_{k,j} = dm_{k,j}$ implies that changes in exports of good k by country j are equal to the imports of good k coming from country j.
11. Import demand elasticity varies from importer to importer and proportionally affects the change in imports. Doubling this elasticity will double the change in imports.
12. The substitution elasticity also varies by product and remains same for all the varieties of the considered product. It also implies that elasticity remains same irrespective of exporting partner. It also affects proportionally to the value of trade diversion but with a ceiling as explained in the previous section. The total diverted trade cannot be greater than the actual trade existed before the change in trade policy. One can use the original value of this elasticity parameter which is relevant to the concerned simulation.
13. The value of export supply elasticity varies by product but remains same for all varieties of that product. It implies that elasticity remains same irrespective of exporting partner. WITS assumed infinite export supply elasticity by default with its representing value 99 with zero price effect. As per this model structure, maximum trade creation can be achieved with infinite export supply elasticity and total trade effect (creation effect + price effect) becomes lower with any other value of this elasticity parameter. It is recommended that one should take finitely elastic export supply function in case when the importing country is sufficiently large to influence the world prices by importing very large quantity after the reduction in tariff rates from the preference receiving country.
14. Here the term region is used for the individual country or collection of countries in one region. The number of regions in any study may vary as per the study's requirement. GTAP-9 database clubbed mostly all countries of the world into 140 regions.
15. See Brockmeier (2001) for details.
16. Endowment commodities include agricultural land, labor and capital.
17. As per this assumption, products of the same industry, produced in different countries are distinct but substitute to each other. In GTAP model, elasticity of substitution between domestic and imported goods and elasticity of substitution among imports of different destinations are defined in the Armington aggregation structure for all agents in all the regions.

18. The government consumption expenditure (E_G) system is governed by Cobb-Douglas utility function with constant expenditure shares over all goods; the private consumption expenditure (E_P) system is modeled by using CDE implicit expenditure function and is non-homothetic given by Hanoch (1975); and the third component of final demand system, i.e. savings (E_S) is a single commodity and fully exhausted by the investment demand.
19. Read Burfisher (2011) for details on implementation of GTAP model.
20. Researcher should be careful while selecting the variable for calculating the changes in imports and exports. The selection of wrong variable for interpretation can lead to misleading conclusions. Please see GTAP sets and variables for the correct definitions of all GTAP variables. The list is available on GTAP website at: https://www.gtap.agecon.purdue.edu/models/setsVariables.asp
21. Set of non-saving commodities consist of endowment commodities, tradable commodities and capital goods.

References

Bouet, A. (2008). *The expected benefits of trade liberalization for world income and development: Opening the "black box" of global trade modeling.* Food policy review no. 8, International Food Policy Research Institute, Washington, DC.

Brockmeier, M. (2001). *A graphical exposition of the GTAP model* (GTAP technical paper no. 3-1-2001). IN, USA: Center for Global Trade Analysis, Purdue University.

Burfisher, M. E. (2011). *Introduction to computable general equilibrium models.* New York: Cambridge University Press.

Gohin, A., & Hertel, T. W. (2003). *A note on the CES functional form and its use in the GTAP model* (GTAP Research Memorandum No. 2). IN, USA: Center for Global Trade Analysis, Purdue University.

Harrison, J., Horridge, M., Jerie, M., & Pearson, K. (2013). *GEMPACK manual: GEMPACK software.*

Hertel, T. W. (Ed.). (1997). *Global trade analysis: Modeling and applications.* New York: Cambridge University Press.

Huff, K., & Hertel, T. (2000). *Decomposing welfare changes in the GTAP model.* GTAP technical paper no. 5, Center for Global Trade Analysis, Purdue University.

Jammes, O., & Olarreaga, M. (2005). *Explaining smart and GSIM*, The World Bank. Retrieved from http://citeseerx.ist.psu.edu/viewdoc/download?doi=10.1.1.547.8636&rep=rep1&type=pdf

Laird, S., & Yeats, A. (1986). *The UNCTAD trade policy simulation model: A note on the methodology, data and uses.* (No. 19). Geneva: UNCTAD.

Mathur, S. K. (2012). *Trade in climate smart and other specialized products of Ecuador*, E-book, bookboon.com, Denmark and UK. http://bookboon.com/en/trade-in-climate-smart-goods-ebook
McDougall, R. (2001). *A new regional household demand system for GTAP. Revised in 2003.* GTAP technical paper no. 20, Purdue University.
Mikic, M., & Gilbert, J. (2007). *Trade statistics in policymaking-A handbook of commonly used trade indices and indicators.* Bangkok: United Nations.
Pearson, K., & Horridge, M. (2005). *Hands-on computing with RunGTAP and WinGEM to introduce GTAP and GEMPACK* (GTAP Resource No. 1638). IN, USA: Center for Global Trade Analysis, Purdue University, USA. Retrieved from https://www.gtap.agecon.purdue.edu/resources/res_display.asp?RecordID=1638
Shoven, J. B., & Whalley, J. (1992). *Applying general equilibrium.* Cambridge: Cambridge University Press.
Starr, R. M. (2011). *General equilibrium theory: An introduction.* Cambridge: Cambridge University Press.

CHAPTER 9

Assessment of Impact of Food-Safety Measures on Exports: A Gravity and CGE Analysis Focusing on India

Pratima Pandey and Badri Narayanan

9.1 Introduction

The Uruguay round of negotiations of the World Trade Organization (WTO) which culminated in 1995 was historic for trade in agriculture. One significant achievement was the signing of the SPS Agreement. The focal point of the agreement was to reduce distortions in trade by means of disciplining the use of sanitary and phytosanitary measures (SPSM).[1] SPSM related to food safety have particularly been gaining prominence due to enhanced awareness among people about food safety. However, over the last few years, it has been noted that in certain trade transactions, the effect of SPSM on trade has been rather trade-restrictive. Despite their welfare motive, they can by their very nature have unintended consequences.

Unjustified requirements in importing markets, irrelevance of foreign standards on local conditions, time and cost involved in carrying out conformity tests, and uncertainty arising from rapidly changing standards'

P. Pandey (✉)
Cactus Communications, Mumbai, India

B. Narayanan
University of Washington, Seattle, WA, USA

S.K. Mathur et al. (eds.), *Theorizing International Trade*,
https://doi.org/10.1007/978-981-10-1759-9_9

requirements in overseas markets as well as differences in compliance capacity among countries can all hinder trade. Several discussions have taken place at the WTO level over the last decade focussing on the application of SPSM and the implementation of the SPS Agreement in spirit, indicating that this has been one of the critical issues of trade in agriculture[2] (WTO 2008a). SPS-related disputes among countries have been coming to the fore again and again, particularly between developed and developing countries[3] (WTO 2008b).

India has had its share of SPS-related trade concerns with respect to certain commodities and specific trade partners. For example, the US prohibition of shrimp from India (and three other countries), which later, the appellate body of the WTO (in its rulings in May 2008 and October 2008, respectively) found to be "unjustifiably" discriminatory.[4] (WTO 2008c) Another example is the European Union (EU) following the Rapid Alert System for Food and Feed (RASFF) system, about which India had expressed concerns, calling it a paranoid reaction, which could cause potential harm to exports from India (WTO 2008a, b).[5]

Though it may not be correct to say that the strictness regarding standards which is at the crux of these disputes is unjustified, such strictness may create trade-distorting effects for the reasons stated above. But this may not always be so. These standards need not always impede trade of even developing countries. Standards can be a trading advantage for countries implementing them by way of raising quality and/or generating economies of scale (Link 1983). Also, international standards are likely to increase intraindustry trade because they make specialization in trade more practical (Greenway 1987). Though the last two arguments apply to the manufacturing sector, they may also be relevant in the case of food products. A similar view is that implementing international (usually meaning higher) standards can put developing countries in a better position to exercise their comparative advantage (Jensen 2002). One example is the success story of Kenya with respect to exports of fish.[6]

Empirical studies have also been divided on this issue. Swann et al. (1996) analyzed the trade performance of UK manufacturing (where similar issues exist with respect to technical barriers to trade (TBT), and found that additional UK standards have a positive effect on net trade and exports. Similarly, Moenius (1999) studied 471 industries in 12 countries and concluded that standards have a positive effect on trade with the United States. On the contrary, some other studies have pointed out the negative effects of

SPS measures on trade (Otsuki et al. 2001; Iacovone 2003). Hence, the question of what impact standards have is an open empirical issue.

At this juncture, it must be borne in mind that SPS measures are not subject to negotiations or removal (like other nontariff measures) due to their welfare aim and hence are here to stay. Hence, it becomes important to find out the impact of SPS measures on trade flows. An empirical study dealing with the impact of food safety regulations has not been made for India so far, underlining the need to conduct such a study.

With the above discussion as a backdrop, an analysis is made here with the following specific objective: To analyze the impact of specific food safety measures on exports of select commodities at the world level and in particular for India, that is, do high import standards act as a barrier to exports, particularly in developing countries?

9.2 Methodology

9.2.1 *Methodology*

The basic framework for the model used in this analysis comes from "gravity trade mode."[7] The model explains the bilateral trade flows between two countries with two main sets of determinants—the size of trading partners, normally expressed in terms of their GDP (direct proportionality), and trade costs which are captured mainly by the geographical distance variable (inverse proportionality).[8] The typically used specification for the gravity model (in double log formulation) is as follows:

$$\ln X_{ij} = \beta_1 + \beta_2 \ln Y_i + \beta_3 \ln Y_j + \beta_4 \ln y_i + \beta_5 \ln y_j + \beta_6 \ln D_{ij} + \varepsilon_{ij} \quad (9.1)$$

Here, X_{ij} is the trade between countries *i* and j, Υ_i and Υ_j represent GNP of the two countries, D_{ij} represents the distance between them, and y_i and y_j represent the GNP per capita. Often, GNP per capita is included as an additional explanatory variable to control for the difference in the levels of development [with respect to production/consumption basket, levels of infrastructure, and so on, across countries (Rahman 2003)].

The above model is modified in three ways in this analysis. The first modification is that outputs of the commodity in the exporter and importer countries are included as additional explanatory variables. This is expected to capture the supply capacity in the exporting country and the domestic competition in the importing country.[9] This modification is feasible because the analysis is conducted at the commodity level where data on outputs are available for various countries. Here, if i represents the exporting country and j is the importing country, β_7 and β_8 are expected to be positive and negative, respectively.[10]

Secondly, commodity-based standards are included as an additional explanatory variable (Otsuki et al. 2001). Here ST_i and ST_j are some measure of the standards in country i and j, respectively. The standards variables for the ith and jth countries are not in log formulation, due to the fact that these variables can take zero values for countries with no standards.

The equation, with these modifications looks like as follows:

$$\ln X_{ij} = \beta_1 + \beta_2 \ln Y_i + \beta_3 \ln Y_j + \beta_4 \ln y_i + \beta_5 \ln y_j + \beta_6 \ln D_{ij} + \beta_7 \ln O_i + \beta_8 \ln O_j + \beta_9 ST_i + \beta_{10} ST_j + \varepsilon_{ij} \quad (9.2)$$

The final modification is the inclusion of quadratic terms of the standards variables to capture the nonlinearity in the response of trade flows to standards. The complete equation therefore is

$$\ln X_{ij} = \beta_1 + \beta_2 \ln Y_i + \beta_3 \ln Y_j + \beta_4 \ln y_i + \beta_5 \ln y_j + \beta_6 \ln D_{ij} + \beta_7 \ln O_i + \beta_8 \ln O_j + \beta_9 ST_i + \beta_{10} ST_j + \beta_{11} ST_i^2 + \beta_{12} ST_j^2 + \varepsilon_{ij} \quad (9.3)$$

Equations (9.2) and (9.3) are used for analysis for two commodities, viz. fresh grapes[11] and shelled groundnuts.[12] These commodities satisfy the four criteria that are put forth for selection, as follows:

1. The commodity should be important from an SPS point of view.
2. Standards must be quantifiable and must have variation across countries.
3. The commodity should be an important commodity in the trade basket.
4. The commodity should be free from government intervention and other distortions.

Here, exports are the dependent variable and the analysis is done at two levels—the world level and the India level. Before discussing the data used, the standards variable used in this analysis is defined.

9.2.2 *Need for a Standard Code*

In the studies conducted so far, different proxies for standards have been used. Certain studies use the count of standards (Swann et al. 1996; Moenius 1999), but the obvious shortcoming in this method is the assumption of similarity among all standards in terms of direction and magnitude, which is not the case in reality. To address this shortcoming, the actual value of standards are used as variables in the equation. (Otsuki et al. 2001; Wilson and Otsuki 2001; Iacovone 2003) However, in this approach, difficulty arises for countries that do not have standards or do not report them. Excluding those countries from the analysis restricts the scope of the analysis and may bias the results.

To overcome this problem, in this analysis the actual standards data are transformed in such a manner that (a) assigns a value to indicate the absence of standards, and (b) provides a direct measure of the severity of the standard. The transformed variable, referred to as the stringency code, is used as a proxy for standards in the analysis. The transformation involves comparing the original data on standards with a reference value. The CODEX standard is used as the reference value. For any particular standard (such as the maximum residue limit for pesticides) the formula used for this transformation is as follows:

$$\text{Stringency Code} = \text{Codex Standard}/\text{Country-specific Standard}$$

In implementing this code, the absence of data for a country is assumed to reflect the absence of standards, and for such cases a numerically very large value (e.g., infinity) is assigned for the denominator in the above transformation, so that the stringency code takes a value of zero. Where standards data are available for a country, the above transformation will result in numerically small (large) values if the standard is lax (strict). A value of 1 for the code will indicate that the country follows the CODEX standard.[13]

While for grapes, the pesticides' Maximum Residue Limits (MRLs) are taken as standards,[14] for shelled groundnuts, the aflatoxin standards are used. Aflatoxins in nuts have been an issue of overriding concern for India and many developing countries, especially after the strict norms implemented by the EU regarding the maximum permissible limit of aflatoxins.

Further to our gravity analysis, we also perform a CGE exercise using the widely used GTAP model (Hertel 1997) and database (Narayanan et al. 2015) by modifying it slightly to include the variable "standards," with its effect on trade determined by our econometrically estimated coefficient in this chapter. Using this model, we evaluate the economywide impact of the removal of all stringent standards in the vegetables and fruits exports from India.

9.3 Data

9.3.1 Trade Data

Trade data have been extracted from two sources—the Commodity Trade (COMTRADE) database of the UN Statistical Division compiled as World Integrated Trade Solution (WITS) for the world-level and India-level data for fresh grapes, and the India Trades Statistics database of the Center for Monitoring Indian Economy (CMIE) for the Indian level for groundnuts.[15] Natural logarithms of the trade flows (exports/imports) in quantity terms (kg) form the dependent variable in this analysis.

The world bilateral trade matrix for fresh grapes has been extracted for the year 2004, while for groundnuts we use data for the years 1995 and 2003. The choice of these years has been dictated by the availability of data on trade and also on standards.

Additionally, an "India-level" analysis has been carried out in which only India's exports to its trading partners have been studied. Such an analysis in the case of fresh grapes is done over 25 countries for the year 2004, while for groundnuts a panel data set of over 24 countries for the period 1995–2003 has been used.

9.3.2 Data on Gravity Variables

The basic variables of the gravity trade model include GDP, GDP per capita, and distance and production data. GDP and GDP per capita data are expressed in 2000 constant US$ to take into account the exchange rate and price fluctuations across countries and time. The data have been taken from the World Development Indicators for the years 1995–2004. Distance has been taken into account between capital cities from the website www.indo.com/distance measured in kilometers. The production data for grapes and groundnuts are taken from the Food and Agriculture Organization (FAO) database. The units are metric tonnes.

9.3.3 Standards Data

Fresh grapes The website www.mrldatabase.com reports the most recent standards on the maximum residue limits (MRL) for pesticides as applied to fresh grapes.[16] Data on the MRLs in parts per million (ppm), is available for 79 countries and 33 pesticides[17] which is used to create the stringency code. Additionally, for the India-specific analysis, a variant of the above measure of the standards is constructed by considering only 7 of the 33 chemicals, which are relevant for Indian exports as per the National Research Centre for Grapes, Pune.

Groundnuts The FAO conducted two surveys on the aflatoxin standards in about 80 countries in the years 1995 and 2003. These surveys are the source of data on maximum permissible limits, in parts per billion (ppb), of aflatoxin B1.[18] Analysis at the world level is carried out for these two years only (as separate cross sections and by pooling the two years[19]). For the India-level analysis, panel data of the aflatoxin standards have been constructed across 24 trading partners for the years 1995–2003. The choice of analysis, being cross-sectional or panel data-based and years for which it is to be made, is based on the availability of standards data.

9.4 Results and Discussion

All the regressions presented have been tested for heteroscedasticity using the Breusch Pagan test, and if heteroscedasticity is found to be present, the standard errors are appropriately corrected using the White (1980) procedure before conducting *t*-tests for the significance of coefficients and robust R^2 are reported. Also, the possibility of multicollinearity between GDP and GDP per capita was explored, but it was not found to be significant. That R^2 of regressions is not very high is also a pointer to the fact.

9.5 Fresh Grapes

9.5.1 World-Level Analysis

The regression results are presented in Table 9.1. Model A in this table is the basic linear specification (9.2). In Model B, quadratic terms for the importer and exporter standards are introduced (9.3). The results of Model A indicate that, in linear form, the variables for standards of both importer and

Table 9.1 Regression results for a cross section 2004 at the world level

Variables	*Model A*	*Model B*
Importer standards	0.0113246	0.02218
	(0.83)[a]	(0.66)
Exporter standards	0.0112243	0.0504596*
	(1.31)	(1.76)
Importer standards square	–	−0.0004321
		(−0.39)
Exporter standards square	–	−0.0012183
		(−1.50)
Importer GDP	0.5479235***	0.5467348***
	(9.26)	(9.08)
Exporter GDP	0.4400623***	0.4439508***
	(6.41)	(6.45)
Importer GDP per capita	−0.103071	−0.1081879
	(−1.35)	(−1.42)
Exporter GDP per capita	−0.4046385***	−0.4364328***
	(−4.08)	(−4.27)
Distance	−0.2394326***	−0.2292741***
	(−2.71)	(−2.57)
Importer production	−0.0012148	−0.0011641
	(−1.54)	(−1.44)
Exporter production	0.0064548***	0.0065633***
	(5.29)	(5.34)
Constant	−7.224901***	−7.127409***
	(−3.83)	(−3.71)
Robust R^2	0.2076	0.2093
F value	28.70	23.31
Probability > F	0.0000	0.0000

Notes: ***, **, and * show 1 percent, 5 percent, and 10 percent levels of significance, respectively. The results shown in the above table have been corrected for heteroscedasticity after the regression was tested for it and it showed a significant heteroscedasticity. The number of observations in both tables for model A and model B are both 866

Source: Authors' calculations

[a]The figures in bracket in this table and all regression tables are the t-values associated with the coefficients of corresponding variables

exporter are not significant. In Model B, importer standards are still not significant. *These findings hence do not support the hypothesis that importer standards have an effect on exports.*

However, in the case of exporter standards, while the linear term is significant with a positive sign, the quadratic term shows a negative sign, though with little significance. *These coefficients imply an inverted U-shape relationship between the exporter standards and exports.* This can be explained in the following plausible way: for countries that have standards up to a certain level, the higher are the exporter standards, the greater are the exports. This may be due to the fact that adherence to a reasonably high level of standards help them to increase the volume of exports. On top of it, it may even have widened their market due to the competitive advantage they have gained over their competitors (Jensen 2002). Only when the standards cross a certain threshold level does the stringency imposed start getting reflected in the costs, and hence the price.[20] The reduced price-competitiveness may result in the fall of exports as reflected in the negative sign of the quadratic term.

Turning to the other variables, almost all the variables of the gravity trade model have turned out to be significant with the expected signs.[21]

9.5.2 *India-Level Analysis*

A similar analysis of the impact of importer standards on India's exports of fresh grapes is carried out separately. For this analysis, logarithms of India's exports to different countries for the year 2004 is the dependent variable, the independent variables are the standards of the importing country, and the logarithms of GDP and GDP per capita of the importing country, and distance from India.

The results are presented in Table 9.2.[22] The importer standards do not come significant in model A. However, when the quadratic term is incorporated, the second model shows that the importer standards become significant at 5 percent level of significance with the sign changing from positive in the linear term to negative in the quadratic term. GDP of the importer and distance variables are significant in both models with expected signs.

The positive sign of the importer standards is quite unexpected, though it becomes negative after a certain high level of standards. One line of reasoning for this result may be as follows: Up to a particular level, India has the potential to meet the standards due to the infrastructural improvements that have been made. The Agricultural and Processed Food Products Exports Development Authority (APEDA) and the NRC, Pune, are actively engaged in export promotion activities.

These efforts, plausibly, help India to comply with fairly high standards, and thus the country is in a position to increase exports to markets with high standards. Indeed, India manages to export substantial quantities of grapes

Table 9.2 Regression results for a cross-section of 2004 at the Indian level

Variables	*Model A*	*Model B*
Importer standards	0.1137	1.0444**
	(1.50)	(2.41)
Importer standards square	–	−0.0608**
		(−2.18)
Importer GDP	0.8971***	0.6114***
	(4.30)	(2.97)
Importer GDP per capita	−0.3600	–
	(−0.95)	
Distance	−2.5628**	−3.1979***
	(−2.62)	(−4.69)
Constant	13.9968*	22.7256
	(1.95)	(3.61)
Adjusted R^2	0.5670	0.6562
F-value	6.89	9.59
Prob > *F*	0.0028	0.0006

Notes: ***, **, and * show 1 percent, 5 percent, and 10 percent levels of significance, respectively. The underlying regression did not show significant heteroscedasticity. The number of observations in both models *A* and *B* is 19

Source: Authors' calculations

to the EU countries that have incidentally also the highest standards.[23] That model B shows an inflection point might point to current capacity constraints acting upon India in achieving compliance of standards beyond certain levels, which works out to be 8.6 times CODEX levels that would result in a reduction of exports beyond this level.

9.6 Shelled Groundnuts

9.6.1 World-Level Studies

At the world level, cross-sectional regressions for 1995 and 2003 are reported. Equations used are similar to those that have been used for fresh grapes. For the year 1995, in general, it turns out that *the importer standards have no role to play in explaining the export flows at the world level (as was also the case for grapes)*. Only the exporter standards matter. Results are presented in Table 9.3.

The exporter standards variable is significant at 5 percent, and with a positive sign in model A. However, when the quadratic terms are also introduced (model B), then the linear term results in a negative sign and

Table 9.3 Regression results for a cross section of 1995 at the world level

Independent variables	*Model A*	*Model B*
Importer standards	0.004978	–
	(0.62)	
Exporter standards	0.01618**	−0.3356***
	(2.04)	(−3.18)
Importer standards squared	–	–
Exporter standards squared	–	0.0034***
		(3.36)
Exporter GDP	0.2270**	0.2598***
	(2.49)	(3.14)
Importer GDP	0.3399***	0.3208***
	(4.15)	(5.27)
Exporter GDP per capita	−0.3295***	−0.1906*
	(−3.02)	(−1.78)
Importer GDP per capita	−0.1384	–
	(−1.14)	
Exporter production	0.0041***	0.0039***
	(2.76)	(2.92)
Importer production	−0.000086	–
	(−0.07)	
Distance	0.06613	–
	(0.45)	
Constant	0.4408	−1.2437
	(0.17)	(0.48)
Number of observations	391	409
Adjusted R^2	0.1258	0.1688
F-value	7.24	14.81
Probability > *F*	0.0000	0.0000

Notes: ***, **, and * show 1 percent, 5 percent, and 10 percent levels of significance, respectively. The underlying regression does not show significant heteroscedasticity

Source: Authors' calculations

the quadratic term with a positive sign, and both are highly significant (at 1 percent level). That is, the relationship between exporter standards and exports is a U-shaped curve, which is opposite to that in the case of grapes. A plausible explanation of this phenomenon is as follows: Up to a certain level of standards, the pass-through of the cost of complying with the standards of shelled groundnuts to its price weighs over the benefits that higher quality is expected to bring, thereby lowering exports. Beyond a certain level of standards, high quality possibly begins to have a dominant influence on demand, and consequently exports begin to rise. The turning point, however, turns out to be very large at about 49 times CODEX levels.

The data on standards reveal that very few countries have such high levels of aflatoxin standards, and hence practically most countries feel only the negative effects of the standards on exports. The other variables came out significant with expected signs, showing the relevance of the model.

A similar analysis was conducted for the export figures from the year 2003 to test whether the situation had changed since the year 1995.

Qualitatively, the results for 2003 are on similar lines as in 1995 with regard to all variables (Table 9.4).[24] *The clear message from analysis for 1995 and 2003 is that it is the exporter standard, at the world level that actually*

Table 9.4 Regression results for a cross section of 2003 at the world level

Independent variables	*Model A*	*Model B*
Importer standards	0.0650	–
	(0.80)	
Exporter standards	−0.3252***	−0.5027***
	(−3.87)	(−3.21)
Importer standards squared	–	–
Exporter standards squared	–	0.0177
		(1.27)
Exporter GDP	0.4147***	0.4070***
	(6.81)	(6.71)
Importer GDP	0.2431***	0.2340***
	(3.90)	(4.91)
Exporter GDP per capita	−0.4886***	−0.4497***
	(−4.77)	(−4.23)
Importer GDP per capita	−0.0959	–
	(0.83)	
Exporter production	0.0015	0.0013
	(1.21)	(1.05)
Importer production	0.0010	0.0010
	(1.03)	(1.19)
Distance	−0.2677**	−0.3427***
	(−2.33)	(−3.01)
Constant	1.8157	1.9687
	(1.04)	(1.16)
F-value	15.90	18.27
Probability > *F*	0.0000	0.0000
Adjusted R^2	0.1921	0.1949
Number of observations	565	572

Notes: ***, **, and * show 1 percent, 5 percent, and 10 percent levels of significance, respectively. The underlying regression does not show significant heteroscedasticity

Source: Authors' calculations

matters for shelled groundnuts, and most countries face an adverse situation in complying with higher standards. Importer standards do not matter.

9.6.2 India-Level Analysis

Panel data on aflatoxin standards was collected for a period of 9 years across 24 major trading partners for India's groundnut exports.[25] Hence, analysis can be done in a panel data framework. An important advantage is that both importer and exporter variables (GDP and GDP per capita) can be incorporated into the analysis.[26]

In the panel data framework, the commonly used specifications are the fixed effects and/or random effects models. A fundamental assumption in these specifications is that the cross-sectional units are uncorrelated. However, correlations can be expected in a cross-country trade study like this. A framework that allows for covariance between the cross-sectional units is the covariance structures model (Greene 2002). Because this model is estimated using the feasible generalized least squares techniques, they are easily extended to allow for the presence of heteroscedasticity and autocorrelation in the residual term [see (Greene 2002) for further details).

The final reported model is a covariance structure model corrected for heteroscedasticity (auto-correlation not present). High collinearity between India's GDP and GDP per capita is another econometric issue that crops up during estimation. To address this, the GDP variable is dropped from the regression.[27]

Table 9.5 reports the estimation results for this specification.[28] The results show that the importer standards variable is highly significant with a negative sign, meaning that the standards of the importing country have an adverse effect on Indian exports. That is, in the case of Indian exports of groundnuts, importer standards do indeed act as trade barriers. *This result proves the hypothesis that high importer standards do restrict Indian exports of shelled groundnuts in the margin.* All the regular variables of the gravity model are significant with the expected signs.

Finally, we discuss briefly the results from our GTAP model exercise. We employ the coefficient estimate in the table below to capture the general impact of standards on exports of vegetables and fruits from India. Overall, India may gain about 8 million US$ in welfare due to the increase in exports by about 60 million US$. We expect such gains to be higher with an estimation of costs of standards using today's data, since over the years, the standards have become much more stringent than in the early 2000s.

Table 9.5 Regression results for panel analysis at the Indian level

Variables	*Model A*
Importer standards	−.017695***
	(−2.40)
Importer GDP	.436481***
	(8.76)
Importer GDP per capita	−.772911***
	(−6.08)
India production	.8629019**
	(2.56)
India GDP per capita	−2.407631***
	(−3.12)
Distance	−.9275723***
	(−3.32)
Constant	30.15782***
	(5.36)
Log-likelihood	−834.6003
Wald $chi^2(6)$	122.96
Prob > chi^2	0.0000
Number of observations	216 (24 countries × 9 years)

Notes: ***, **, and * show 1 percent, 5 percent, and 10 percent levels of significance, respectively. The result shown in the above table has been corrected for heteroscedasticity, after the regression was tested for it and it showed a significant heteroscedasticity

Source: Authors' calculations

9.7 Conclusions and Policy Suggestions

This chapter studied the impact of food safety measures that are part of sanitary and phytosanitary measures (SPSM) on trade flows. Findings for individual commodities, fresh grapes, and shelled groundnuts reflect that at the world level, importer standards bear no significant impact on exports. Rather, it is the exporter standards that matter. However, in an India-specific analysis, importer standards did turn out to be significant. but the direction of the relationship varied with the commodities.

An implication of this is that generalizations across commodities are not valid and that the analysis has to be carried out at the commodity-level. In the case of fresh grapes, results show an inverted U-shaped relationship of exports with exporter standards at a world level and again an inverted U-shaped relationship with importer standards at an India level. In the case of shelled groundnuts, the relationship is clearer with a U-shaped relationship with exporter standards and a negative relationship with importer standards.

The policy implications of these findings are as follows:

For fresh grapes, developing countries such as India need to increase their standards well beyond the CODEX level to capitalize on the benefits of higher standards. But beyond a particular level, the negative impact of standards begins to show. The inflection point is where the competitive advantage that compliance with high standards offer is outweighed by reduced price competitiveness due to increased costs of compliance. This point comes at about 20 times the CODEX level. For groundnuts, however, higher standards are shown to restrict exports despite all the positive effects that the implementation of standards can have on exports. This strengthens the case of developing countries like India for raising their concerns on the trade restrictive effects of standards pertaining to this commodity.

A few broad results also emerge from the above commodity-specific findings. First, the relationship between standards and trade flows is indeed nonlinear in several cases. And second, the gravity trade model in general holds up well for explaining trade flows at the commodity level, and the incorporation of commodity output levels in the trading countries improves its performance.

Our CGE analysis suggests that India stands to gain a lot (at least 60 million $US in terms of increased exports of vegetables and fruits, if not more) if the implicit trade restrictiveness of SPS standards is addressed by negotiations and by going through the dispute settlement mechanism of the WTO, arguing against unfair imposition of such standards in cases where they are not justifiable.

Notes

1. SPSM are designed to protect human and animal life or health (sanitary) and plant life or health (phytosanitary).
2. http://www.wto.org/english/news_e/archive_e/sps_arc_e.htm
3. http://www.wto.org/english/tratop_e/sps_e/sps_e.htm – See the disputes search segment.
4. Details can be seen on the WTO website http://www.wto.org/English/Tratop_E/dispu_e/dispu_status_e.htm#134 as dispute number DS58.
5. India raised its concerns, arguing that an alert raised by one country would result in the loss of exports to other EU countries also, as well as several consequent consignment checks which can also be trade restrictive. For details, please see www.indiainthewto.wordpress.com/category/sps-issues/
6. Sustained administrative and structural reforms pertaining to the fishery supply chain were carried out to meet the stringent food safety norms set

by the EU. This resulted in Kenyan exporters not only reinstating their access in EU markets (after the 1997 restrictions) but also being better able to compete in other markets such as Australia, Japan, and the United States (Henson and Mitullah 2004).

7. The gravity trade model is based on the basic gravity model that comes from Newton's universal law of gravitation, which states that the gravitational force between two bodies is directly proportional to the masses of the bodies and inversely proportional to the distance between them.
8. For more on the theoretical foundations of the gravity model, see (Anderson 1979) and (Bergstrand 1989).
9. This may be justified because agricultural output, being typically fraught with several uncertainties, may not be export-led (as may be the case with manufacturing goods). Also, actual exports (especially from developing countries) would be constrained by output levels even if the export demand was much higher. Hence, we choose to regress exports on output, and interpret output as a determinant of the supply capacity of the exporting country.
10. O_i captures the output in exporting country; the higher the output, the higher can it export and hence β_7 is expected to have a positive coefficient. O_j stands for output in the importing country. Here, it is vice versa. The higher the output, the lower will the country *j* import from country *i*. So, the coefficient β_8 is expected to be negative.
11. Fresh grapes accounted for 28 percent (averaged over 1995–1996 to 2003–2004. Source: APEDA, 2003–2004) of the fresh fruits category, which is arguably the most SPS-sensitive category among Indian agricultural and allied exports. This figure rose to 39 percent (averaged over 2004–2005 to 2006–2007. Source: APEDA, 2008–2009). The fact that fresh grapes have a high export potential has been acknowledged by the Agricultural and Processed Foods Export Development Authority (APEDA 2006).
12. Shelled groundnuts accounted for 20 percent (averaged over 1995–1996 to 2003–2004. Source: APEDA, 2003–2004) of the "Others including processed food" category of Indian agricultural and allied exports, which by itself is an important and highly SPS-sensitive category (RBI 2006). This figure has risen to 22 percent (averaged over 2004–2005 to 2006–2007. Source: APEDA, 2008–2009).
13. Tables of calculated stringency codes for different countries can be referred to in the M.Phil. thesis by M. Pratima entitled "Assessment of Impact of Food-Safety Measures on Trade: With Emphasis on India" submitted to Indira Gandhi Institute of Development Research, Mumbai, on September 2007.
14. The standard for grapes was decided after discussions with specialists like the Director and Senior Scientist in the National Research Centre for Grapes, Pune, and the Director, APEDA, New Delhi. In India, more than 45 pesticides are used in grapes cultivation (NRC Referral Report on recommended pesticides for grapes). This is in light of the fact that grapes are a tropical fruit

requiring substantial quantities of pesticides which are applied directly over fruits and vines, hence raising the chances of residues on them.

15. The data have been collected as a six-digit ITC (HS) classification. The codes for the chosen commodities are as follows: Grapes, fresh (080610), and groundnuts, not roasted/otherwise cooked, shelled (120220).
16. However, the source does not provide information about the changes in the standards; due to this limitation of standards data, the standards (downloaded in March 2006) have been assumed to pertain to the year 2004, the latest year for which the trade data was available, and only cross-sectional analysis for 2004 was conducted.
17. Though data on MRL is available for 98 pesticides on the website, there are only 33 pesticides for which CODEX standards are also available, and hence only these are finally considered for construction of the stringency code.
18. Values for aflatoxin B1 are found to be roughly half of the values specified for all aflatoxins (i.e., B1, B2, G1, and G2); thereby, for countries where a separate limit of aflatoxin B1 is not specified, simply the total value is halved. For CODEX, the limit for Aflatoxin B1 is taken to be 7.5 ppb (half of the total limit of 15 ppb).
19. At the world level (a) separate cross-sectional regressions are estimated for these two years, and (b) fixed-effects and random-effects models were estimated by pooling the data for these two years. The latter set of regression, however, did not yield any meaningful results. Only results of the former are reported.
20. The threshold level worked out by equating the first derivative of ln Υ with respect to the exporter standard to zero, keeping all other factors constant, comes out to be approximately 20.1. The high value of the turning point may be due to the presence of EU countries in the sample, which export a major chunk of grapes despite maintaining incidentally the highest level of standards.
21. Exporter GDP per capita turns out to be highly significant, with a negative sign. A higher GDP per capita indicates higher purchasing power of the population; as a result, the domestic consumption of high quality fresh grapes goes up, and hence exports fall. The exporter production is highly significant, with the expected positive sign, which can be interpreted as meaning that the higher is the supply of the commodity, the higher are the exports. The importer production does not turn out to be significant; however, it has a negative sign, which is in line with the logic.
22. Models A and B are variants of Eqs. (9.2) and (9.3), respectively adjusted to be representative of a single exporter country, that is, India.
23. In 2004, 38 percent of Indian exports were to the EU, thus clearly supporting the regression results.
24. It must be noted here that the results of years 1995 and 2003 are strictly not comparable because the number of exporters and importers differ between these two years.

25. The countries are United Kingdom, United Arab Emirates, the Netherlands, Belgium, Luxembourg, Saudi Arabia, Kuwait, Germany, Sri Lanka, France, United States, Malaysia, Mauritius, Canada, Spain, South Africa, Poland, Turkey, Egypt, Japan, Nepal, Singapore, Indonesia, the Russian Federation, and Ukraine.
26. While importing standards are introduced, Indian (exporter) standards cannot be introduced because they do not fulfil the statistical requirement of variability over time.
27. The explicit use of output of the commodity in the exporting country as an explanatory variable makes up for the loss of the GDP variable.
28. The corresponding model B with a quadratic term of importer standards did not yield meaningful results and hence is not reported.

References

Anderson, J. E. (1979). A theoretical foundation for the gravity equation. *The American Economic Review, 69*(1), 106–116.

APEDA. (2006). APEDA website. Retrieved March 2006, from www.apeda.com

Bergstrand, J. (1989). The generalised gravity equation, monopolistic competition, and the factor proportion theory in international trade. *Review of Economics and Statistics, 71*(1), 143–153.

Greene, W. H. (2002). *Econometric analysis.* Englewood Cliffs: Prentice Hall.

Greenway, D. (1987). The new theories of intra-industry trade. *Bulletin of Economic Research, 39*(2), 95–120.

Henson, S., & Mitullah, W. (2004). *Kenyan exports of Nile perch – Impact of food safety standards on export oriented supply chain.* Policy research working paper, World Bank.

Hertel, T. W. (Ed.). (1997). *Global trade analysis: Modeling and applications.* New York: Cambridge University Press.

Iacovone, L. (2003). *Analysis and impact of sanitary and phyto-sanitary measures.* Centre for International Development at Harvard University. India in the WTO (2008, May) Retrieved from http://www.indiainthewto.wordpress.com/category/sps-issues

Jensen, M. F. (2002). *Reviewing the SPS agreement: A developing country perspective.* CDR working paper. Sub-serieson globalisation and economic restructuring in Africa, Copenhagen.

Link, A. (1983). Market structure and voluntary product standards. *Applied Economics, 15*, 393–401.

Moenius, J. (1999). *Information vs product adaptation: The role of standards in trade.* Chicago, USA: North Western University, Kellogg Graduate School of Management.

Narayanan, G. B., Aguiar, A., & McDougall, R. (Eds.) (2015). *Global trade, assistance, and production: The GTAP 9 data base*. West Lafayette: Center for Global Trade Analysis, Purdue University.

Otsuki, T., Wilson, J. S., & Sewadeh, M. (2001). *A race to the top – A case study of food safety standards an African exports*. Policy research working paper no. 2563, World Bank.

Rahman, M. (2003). *A panel data analysis of Bangladesh's trade: The gravity model approach*. A PhD thesis, University of Sydney, Sydney.

RBI. (2006). Retrieved March 2006, from www.rbi.org

Swann, P., Temple, P., & Shurmer, M. (1996). Standards and trade performance-the UK experience. *Economic Journal, 106*(438), 1297–1313.

White, H. (1980). A heteroskedasticity-consistent covariance matrix estimator and a direct test for heteroskedasticity. *Econometrica, 48*(4), 817–838.

Wilson, J., & Otsuki, T. (2001). *Global trade and food safety: Winners and losers in a fragmented system*. Social Science Research Network. Retrieved October 26, 2008, from http://papers.ssrn.com/sol3/papers.cfm?abstract_id=632757

WTO. (2008a). Retrieved from www.wto.org/english/news_e/archive_e/sps_arc_e.htm

WTO. (2008b). Retrieved from http://www.wto.org/english/tratop_e/sps_e/sps_e.htm

WTO. (2008c). Retrieved from http://www.wto.org/English/Tratop_E/dispu_e/dispu_status_e.htm#134

CHAPTER 10

Gains from the India–GCC Free Trade Agreement: A General Equilibrium Analysis

Nitin Arora and Pouria Mohajeri

10.1 Introduction

India and the Gulf Cooperation Council (GCC) are partners in various trading arrangements around the world. Until now, India has been party to 37 such trading arrangements, out of which 9 have been proposed but not acted on, 4 have been signed but not enacted, 11 have had negotiations launched, and 13 have been signed and put into effect.

The GCC group is the latecomer in adopting the policies of regional trade agreements. Currently, it is a party to 9 such trading arrangements, of which 1 is proposed but not acted on, 5 have had negotiations launched, 2 are signed but not enacted, and 1 has been signed and put into effect.

Figure 10.1 presents the engagements of both parties with other regions in the world through the policy of regional trade agreements (RTAs) of the World Trade Organization (WTO). The table included in the figure shows the number of trade agreements through which both are linked with other

N. Arora (✉)
Panjab University, Chandigarh, India

P. Mohajeri
ICCR Fellow from Iran, Panjab University, Chandigarh, India

S.K. Mathur et al. (eds.), *Theorizing International Trade*,
https://doi.org/10.1007/978-981-10-1759-9_10

Fig. 10.1 List of free trade partners of India and the GCC (*Source*: The pattern of figures adapted from Arora et al. 2015)

regions of the world. The first column shows the corresponding partner region with which both states/parties are linked through a trade agreement.

It is worth mentioning that any trade agreement between countries passes through four stages before its implementation. An agreement is firstly proposed (PA) by the policymakers of member countries after which the extent of the proposed agreement is linked to via joint study groups. Subsequently, the agreement is officially signed (SO) by the member countries. After they offer approval, negotiations (NL) are held on the items to be included in positive and negative lists as per the trade agreement. Finally, after the successful negotiations and consensus, an agreement is signed and brought into effect (SE).

Table 10.1 and Fig. 10.1 present a statewide number of trade agreements through which both countries are linked with other major regions of the world. They have also signed a free trade agreement with each other. The Framework Agreement on Economic Cooperation between India and the GCC was signed on August 25, 2004. As per the agreement, both parties shall consider ways and means for extending and liberalizing trade relations.

The GCC as a collective entity has tremendous geographical and economic significance for India. The Gulf countries constitutes the "immediate" neighborhood of India separated only by the Arabian Sea. India,

Table 10.1 List of free trade partners of India and the GCC

Region	*India*				*GCC*			
	SE	*NL*	*SO*	*PA*	*SE*	*NL*	*SO*	*PA*
Australia		✓				✓		
Japan	✓					✓		
Korea	✓					✓		
China				✓		✓		
New Zealand		✓				✓		
Malaysia	✓							✓
Singapore	✓				✓			

SE signed and effective, *NL* negotiation level, *SO* officially signed, *PA* proposed agreement

therefore, has a vital stake in the stability, security, and economic well-being of the Gulf nations. As a group, the GCC has increasingly determined the economic, political, and security policies of its member states. The GCC countries are moving ahead rapidly with their economic integration efforts. The GCC has emerged as a major trading partner for India. It has vast potential as India's investment partner for the future. The GCC's substantial oil and gas reserves hold vital importance for India's energy needs. The GCC countries are collectively host to a large Indian expatriate community. In short, the GCC offers tremendous potential for cooperation in trade, investment, energy supply, manpower, and so on.

In this chapter, we study the impact of trade liberalization between India and the GCC using the GTAP model framework. For this purpose, the entire study has been divided into six sections including the present introductory one. Section 2 presents the economic and commercial relations between India and GCC countries. In Sect. 3, simulation scenarios and data aggregations have been defined. In Sect. 4, implications of tariff reforms in the GTAP model have been discussed in brief. Section 4 presents the simulation results of the GTAP model, and the final section concludes the study.

10.2 Economic and Commercial Relations of India and the GCC

10.2.1 Trade Profile

India enjoys longstanding ties with GCC states. It has increased imports of oil and gas from the GCC. Its trade and investment opportunities have been growing. There is a presence of approximately 6.5 million Indian workers in the region. All these factors are of vital interest to India. India's economic linkages with the GCC have increased steadily, especially due to growth in oil imports. These linkages continue to make steady progress to date. During 2013–2014, India's exports to the GCC were US$ 48,221 billion. The bilateral two-way trade during the period was US$ 147,615 billion, and it has been growing at a steady pace. India's trade with the GCC states during the years 2010–2011, 2011–2012, 2012–2013 and 2013–2014 are given in Table 10.2. Further, Table 10.3 shows the trend of India–GCC trade over the past five years. This table shows that India's trade balance with the GCC is highly negative, to the tune of US$ 51,172.69 million in the year 2013–2014.

In terms of total trade figures, the GCC is the largest trading partner of India and also has a share of 19.31% in total trade with India. The major items of Indian exports and imports to the GCC are the main commodities of Indian exports to the GCC including commodities with HS code 27 (mineral fuels; mineral oils and products of their distillation; bituminous substances; mineral waxes), commodities of HS code 71 (natural or cultured pearls, precious or semiprecious stones, premetals clad with premetal and articles thereof; imitation jewelry; coins), and products of HS code 10 (cereals); Similarly, products in categories 27 and 71 have a major share in Indian imports from PGC.

10.2.2 Tariff Profile of India and GCC

The tariff profile of a region provides the level of protection of that region over the traded products. A country's level of protection is determined by its own tariffs and nontariff barriers imposed on imports from partner countries. It is calculated by evaluating the annual average tariff rate over all the products. A higher level of protection from member countries is associated with significant trade creation and trade diversion effects.

Table 10.4 illustrates various indicators of the level of protection from all partner countries in the world. It shows that India's level of protection relative to the GCC is much higher. If the level of trade between the member countries is very high, then the gains associated with the policy of regional trade agreements are highly dependent upon the level of protection of the member countries. A higher level of initial protection or barriers (i.e., initial tariff rate and nontariff barriers) would lead to larger gains afterwards.

Table 10.2 India's trade with GCC

Countries	*2010–2011*			*2011–2012*			*2012–2013*			*2013–2014*		
	Imports	*Exports*	*Total*	*Imports*	*Exports*	*Total*	*Imports*	*Exports*	*Total*	*Imports*	*Exports*	*Total*
UAE	32,753	33,822	66,575	36,756	35,926	72,682	39,138	36,317	75,455	29,020	30,520	59,540
Saudi Arabia	20,385	4684	25,069	31,818	5683	37,501	31,818	9786	43,784	33,998	12,218	46,216
Kuwait	10,314	1856	12,170	16,440	1181	17,621	16,588	1061	17,649	17,154	1061	18,215
Qatar	6820	375	7195	12,916	808	13,724	15,693	687	16,380	15,708	969	16,677
Oman	4002	1086	5088	3346	1322	4668	2010	2599	4609	2951	2812	5763
Bahrain	641	652	1293	906	440	1346	665	603	1268	563	639	1202
GCC	74,915	42,477	117,392	102,182	45,360	147,542	108,092	51,053	159,145	99,394	48,221	147,615

Source: Export–Import Databank, Ministry of Commerce and Industry, India

Table 10.3 India's balance of trade with the GCC US$ Million

Year	*Exports (X)*	*Imports (M)*	*Total trade (X + M)*	*India's total trade*	*Trade balance (X − M)*
2009–2010	30,479.97 (17.05)	53,497.43 (18.55)	83,977.40 (17.98)	467,124.31	−23017.46
2010–2011	42,476.50 (17.00)	74,915.27 (20.26)	117,391.77 (18.95)	619,584.68	−32,438.77
2011–2012	45,360.29 (14.83)	102,181.93 (20.88)	147,542.22 (18.55)	795,283.41	−56,821.
2012–2013	51,053.65 (17.00)	108,092.06 (22.03)	159,145.71 (20.12)	791,137.23	−57,038.41
2013–2014	48,221.20 (15.34)	99,393.89 (22.61)	147,615.09 (19.31)	764,605.09	−51,172.69

Note: Figures in parentheses are the percentage of India's total exports, imports, and total trade, respectively
Source: Export–Import Databank, Ministry of Commerce and Industry, India

10.2.3 Comparative Advantage Statistics for India and the GCC

Vast differences in comparative advantage over products are beneficial for member countries to be in a trade agreement. The present study calculates bilateral Revealed Comparative Advantage (RCA) productwide to show the comparative advantage of both the countries (see Table 10.5). It may be noticed that India enjoys the highest comparative advantage in processed rice followed by plant-based fibers. However, the GCC's highest comparative advantage is observed in oil products, where the observed difference between the Indian comparative advantage index and that of the GCC is very high. The value of the comparative advantage index for India in oil production is zero and that of the GCC is 94.17.

Further, the second highest RCA value for GCC partners is observed for petroleum and coal products, with a value of 5.85. The third most important product in the GCC's trade basket is gas with an RCA value of 2.06. From Table 10.5, it is evident that for the GCC, a few products have an RCA above unity, while India has a number of products with values above unity in the same index. Thus, India has a huge potential to enhance trade relations with the GCC and the partner can offer oil, petroleum, coal products, and gas to purchase the products for which India enjoys a relative comparative advantage. In the same way, both partners may explore the gains of international trade.

Table 10.4 Indicators of level of protection

India					
Indicator/year	*2009*	*2010*	*2011*	*2012*	*2013*
AVE MFN applied tariff (%) (Simple average at HS-6 digit subheadings)	12.9	13	12.6	13.7	13.5
Non-AV MFN applied duties (%) (Share of HS-6 digit subheadings)	5.2	5.2	5.0	4.9	4.9
Maximum duty (%) (Ad valorem duty)	246	170	315	150	150
Duty-free tariff lines (%) (Share of duty-free HS-6 digit subheadings)	2.8	2.8	3.5	3.0	2.9
Duty > 15 (%) (Share of HS-6 digit subheadings)	17.1	16.6	16.5	19.6	19.0
Number of MFN applied tariff lines (Country-specific)	11,360	11,359	11,377	11,477	11,471
GCC(average)					
AVE MFN applied tariff (%) (Simple average at HS-6 digit subheadings)	5.1	5.0	5.0	4.8	4.7
Non-AV MFN applied duties (%) (Share of HS-6 digit subheadings)	0.8	0.8	1.0	1.25	1.4
Maximum duty (%) (Ad valorem duty)	195	186	170	200	200
Duty-free tariff lines (%) (Share of duty-free HS-6 digit subheadings)	8.9	8.9	9.2	10.3	10.3
Duty > 15 (%) (Share of HS-6 digit subheadings)	0.5	0.5	0.4	0.3	0.2
Number of MFN applied tariff lines (Country-specific)	7104	7103	7117	7041	7288

Notes: AVE Ad valorem equivalent, *MFN* most-favored nation, *Non-AV* non ad valorem
Source: World Tariff Profiles, 2010–2014

10.2.4 Trade Intensity Index for India and the GCC

Further, calculation of the trade intensity index in Table 10.6 is used to measure the country's export competitiveness in a particular market. This helps to shed light on the issue of the extent of domestic substitution in production by partner countries. The index explains the role of any country/region in another country's trade. The comparison of Table 10.6 with Table 10.5 produces interesting evidence; it may be inferred from comparison of the two that the TII is high for the products in which the nation gain's comparative advantage, and vice versa. For food products, the trade

Table 10.5 RCA index value for the year 2013

		Index value				*Index value*	
GTAP code	*Description*	*India*	*GCC*	*GTAP code*	*Description*	*India*	*GCC*
01	Paddy rice	2.15	0.02	23	Processed rice	17.21	0.00
02	Wheat	1.25	0.00	24	Sugar	1.56	0.21
03	Cereal grains n.e.c.	1.48	0.00	25	Food products	1.18	1.42
04	Vegetables, fruit, nuts	1.00	0.05	26	Beverages, tobacco products	0.24	0.01
05	Oil seeds	0.77	0.00	27	Textiles	2.76	0.08
06	Sugar cane, sugar beet	0.00	–	28	Wearing apparel	2.16	0.00
07	Plant-based fibers	13.07	0.00	29	Leather products	1.31	0.01
08	Crops n.e.c.	2.20	0.03	30	Wood products	0.20	0.02
09	Cattle, sheep, goats, horses	0.04	0.00	31	Paper products, publishing	0.28	0.11
10	Animal products	0.21	0.51	32	Petroleum, coal products	3.24	5.85
11	Raw milk	–	–	33	Chemical, rubber, plastic products	0.97	1.14
12	Wool, silk-worm cocoons	0.00	0.00	34	Mineral products n.e.c.	0.77	0.01
13	Forestry	0.61	0.01	35	Ferrous metals	1.32	0.28
14	Fishing	1.40	0.12	36	Metals n.e.c.	0.73	0.13
15	Coal	0.07	0.00	37	Metal products	1.01	0.05
16	Oil	0.00	94.17	38	Motor vehicles and parts	0.42	0.06
17	Gas	0.01	2.06	39	Transport equipment n.e.c.	1.17	0.00
18	Minerals n.e.c.	0.99	0.12	40	Electronic equipment	0.17	0.00
19	Meat: cattle, sheep, goat, horse	3.86	0.00	41	Machinery, equipment n.e.c.	0.36	0.03
20	Meat products n.e.c.	0.06	0.09	42	Manufacturers n.e.c.	6.00	0.01
21	Vegetable oils and fats	1.70	0.13	43	Electricity	0.00	–
22	Dairy products	0.37	0.27	44	Gas manufacture, distribution	0.03	–

Source: Author's calculations

Table 10.6 Trade intensity index for India and the GCC for the other's market access in the year 2013

		Index value				*Index value*	
GTAP code	*Description*	*India*	*GCC*	*GTAP code*	*Description*	*India*	*GCC*
01	Paddy rice	46.65	–	23	Processed rice	7.12	–
02	Wheat	57,974.74	–	24	Sugar	4.17	–
03	Cereal grains n.e.c.	1.87	–	25	Food products	5.76	0.00
04	Vegetables, fruit, nuts	11.64	1.07	26	Beverage, tobacco products	24.33	0.33
05	Oil seeds	3.00	–	27	Textiles	3.75	0.16
06	Sugar cane, sugar beet	–	–	28	Wearing apparel	5.76	0.01
07	Plant-based fibers	1.47	–	29	Leather products	3.34	17.29
08	Crops n.e.c.	4.16	0.02	30	Wood products	3.75	0.51
09	Cattle, sheep, goats, horses	0.02	–	31	Paper products, publishing	10.97	5.38
10	Animal products	11.43	0.12	32	Petroleum, coal products	15.37	0.02
11	Raw milk	–	–	33	Chemical, rubber, plastic products	6.91	1.95
12	Wool, silk-worm cocoons	8.25	84,255.14	34	Mineral products n.e.c.	5.06	20.56
13	Forestry	17.52	0.02	35	Ferrous metals	4.45	1.44
14	Fishing	65.22	0.00	36	Metals n.e.c.	9.02	12.28
15	Coal	32.94	–	37	Metal products	11.84	0.45
16	Oil	–	4092.18	38	Motor vehicles and parts	2.05	0.21
17	Gas	–	1272.85	39	Transport equipment n.e.c.	6.23	–
18	Minerals n.e.c.	4.75	2.32	40	Electronic equipment	11.27	0.02
19	Meat: cattle, sheep, goat, horse	11.47	2.52	41	Machinery, equipment n.e.c.	6.79	0.46

(*continued*)

Table 10.6 (continued)

		Index value				Index value	
GTAP code	*Description*	*India*	*GCC*	*GTAP code*	*Description*	*India*	*GCC*
20	Meat products n.e.c.	2.30	–	42	Manufacturers n. e.c.	4.37	0.53
21	Vegetable oils and fats	2.47	0.14	43	Electricity	–	–
22	Dairy products	14.08	0.04	44	Gas manufacture, distribution	–	–

Note: Trade intensity index has been calculated for each market
Source: Author's calculations

intensity of India is very high, while for oil and gas products, the trade intensity of the GCC is high enough.

10.3 Construction of Simulation Scenarios and Data Aggregations

10.3.1 Simulation Scenarios

Table 10.7 provides data on the tariff reduction for the GCC and India in the two models taken for consideration. In model I, both the regions have to levy the same tariff rate on all the sectors. India charges more in all sectors so it needs to cut more on the tariffs to bring the duty to a level equal to the GCC region's duty. The proposed reduction for both regions is reported in the table under the column for model I. In model II, both regions need to cut the tariff duties to a zero level. Again, it is observed that India reduces more compared to the GCC. From Table 10.7, it is observed that India charges more tariffs in the sector of processed foods by 58.67% and in sector HS-10 it charges less duty by 2.3%.

10.3.2 Data Aggregations

In both of the above models, 19 regions—namely, India, the GCC, China, Japan, the Republic of Korea, New Zealand, Malaysia, Singapore, Australia, the Rest of Oceana, the Rest of East Asia, the Rest of Southeast Asia, the

Table 10.7 Reduction in tariff values by India and the GCC

Commodity	*Level duty Model I*		*Zero duty Model II*	
	GCC	*India*	*GCC*	*India*
HS-27	0	−6.5015	−4.1612	−10.6627
HS-71	0	−11.9444	−3.0577	−15.0021
HS-10	0	−2.3114	−0.0051	−2.3165
HS-85	0	−10.9196	−0.2897	−11.2093
HS-84	0	−10.0171	−4.8115	−14.8286
HS-63	0	−10.1097	−4.9998	−15.1095
HS-62	0	−9.8517	−5.0000	−14.8517
Grains	0	−26.8952	−2.5362	−29.4314
Meat and live stock	0	−2.7372	−3.6266	−6.3588
Extraction	0	−4.7698	−4.9523	−9.7221
Processed food	0	−45.6701	−13.0256	−58.6957
Light manufacture	0	−9.4320	−4.5189	−13.9509
Heavy manufacture	0	−10.1700	−4.6997	−14.8697
Utility and consumption	0	0	0	0
Other services	0	0	0	0

Source: Author's calculations

Rest of South Asia, North America, Latin America, European Union-25, the Middle East and North Africa, Sub-Saharan Africa, and the Rest of World—have been taken into consideration in details furnished in Table 10.8. These regions include all the countries of the world to see the impact of the FTA between India and the GCC countries.

In addition, 15 commodity groups have also been created to portray the impact of the FTA on commodity trading. The groups in these models cover all goods and services used in the GTAP-8 model. However, these 15 groups—namely, HS-27, HS-71, HS-10, HS-85, HS-84, HS-63, HS-62, Grains Crops, Meat and livestock, Extraction, Processed food, Light Manufacture, Heavy Manufacture, Utility and Consumption Goods, and Other Services—are categorized on the basis of their share in India's trade with the GCC countries. In Table 10.9, the commodity groups with the prefix HS have been created for those commodities that have the highest shares in India–GCC trade.

Table 10.8 Region's aggregations

S.N.	*Region*	*Description (countries)*	*S.N.*	*Region*	*Description*
1.	India	India	11.	New Zealand	New Zealand
2.	China	China	12.	Australia	Australia
3.	Japan	Japan	13.	Malaysia	Malaysia
4.	Korea, Rep. of	Korea, Rep. of	14.	Singapore	Singapore
5.	GCC	United Arab Emirates, Saudi Arabia, Qatar, Kuwait, Oman, Bahrain	15.	North America	Canada, United States, Mexico, Rest of North America
6.	Rest of East Asia	Hong Kong, Taiwan, Mongolia, Rest of East Asia	16.	Middle East and North Africa	Rest of Western Asia, Egypt, Morocco, Tunisia, Rest of North Africa
7.	Rest of Southeast Asia	Cambodia, Indonesia, Laos PDR, the Philippines, Thailand, Rest of Southeast Asia	17.	Rest of South Asia	Bangladesh, Nepal, Pakistan, Sri Lanka, Rest of South Asia
8.	Sub-Saharan Africa	Benin, Burkina Faso, Cameroon, Cote d'Ivoire, Ghana, Guinea, Nigeria, Senegal, Togo, Rest of Western Africa, Central Africa, South Central Africa, Ethiopia, Kenya, Madagascar, Malawi, Mauritius, Mozambique, Rwanda, Tanzania, Uganda, Zambia, Zimbabwe, Rest of Eastern Africa, Botswana, Namibia, South Africa, Rest of South African Customs	18.	European Union	Austria, Belgium, Bulgaria, Cyprus, Czech Republic, Denmark, Estonia, Finland, France, Germany, Greece, Hungary, Ireland, Italy, Latvia, Lithuania, Luxembourg, Malta, Netherlands, Poland, Portugal, Romania, Slovakia, Slovenia, Spain, Sweden, United Kingdom

(*continued*)

Table 10.8 (continued)

S.N.	*Region*	*Description (countries)*	*S.N.*	*Region*	*Description*
9.	Latin America	Argentine, Bolivia, Brazil, Chile, Colombia, Ecuador, Paraguay, Peru, Uruguay, Venezuela, Rest of South America, Costa Rica, Guatemala, Honduras, Nicaragua, Panama, El Salvador, Rest of Central America, Caribbean	19.	Rest of World	Iran, Switzerland, Norway, Albania, Bulgaria, Belarus, Croatia, Russian Federation, Ukraine, Rest of Eastern Europe, Rest of Europe, Kazakhstan, Kyrgyzstan, Rest of Former Soviet Union, Armenia, Azerbaijan, Georgia, Israel, Turkey, Rest of the World
10.	Rest of Oceana	Rest of Oceana			

Notes: SSA Sub-Saharan Africa, *EU* European Union countries, *EFTA* European free trade association
Source: Authors' elaboration from GTAP-8 database

10.4 Implications of Tariff Reforms

10.4.1 Trade Effects

With the formation of a free trade agreement, prices of imported goods from countries in the free trade area will decrease due to the reduction in tariffs on the imports. This will permit countries entering into an FTA to shift from expensive imports from the outside world to purchase cheaper imports from within the circle of member nations, thereby resulting in trade creation among them. Thus, a change in trade policy (e.g., tariff liberalization) affects not only the price index/level of the composite goods, but also the relative prices of other goods/products. Any trade policy shock will also have an effect on the entire trade flow (i.e., Imports from different countries).

Trade diversion results when shifting imports from a country selling at a high price to a country with a comparative advantage in the traded commodity (in this case commodity *g*) to a country that is less efficient in producing the goods in question. This shift takes place due to the formation of a trade bloc. Trade diversion in our example is neutral because an increase in imports from the partner countries is balanced by reduction in the imports from all the other countries. The net effect is a reallocation of the market share among the exporting countries with the overall imported

Table 10.9 Sector description of the GTAP

S.N.	*Name of group*	*Group description*
1.	HS-27	Coal (15); oil (16); gas (17); minerals n.e.c. (18); petroleum and coal products (32); chemical, rubber, plastic products (33)
2.	HS-71	Fishing (14), metals n.e.c. (36), manufactures n.e.c. (42)
3.	HS-10	Wheat (2), cereals and grains n.e.c., (3), processed rice (23)
4.	HS-85	Transport equipment n.e.c. (39)
5.	HS-84	Metal products (37), motor vehicles and parts (38), machinery and equipment n.e.c. (41)
6.	HS-63	Textiles (27)
7.	HS-62	Wearing apparel (28)
8.	Grains	Paddy rice (1); vegetables. fruits, nuts (4); oil seeds (5); sugar cane, sugar beet (6); plant-based fiber; (7), crops n.e.c. (8)
9.	Meat and livestock	Cattle, sheep, goats, horses (9); animal products n.e.c. (10); raw milk (11); wool, silkworm cocoons (12); meat: cattle, sheep, goat, horse (19); meat products n.e.c. (20)
10.	Extraction	Forestry (13)
11.	Processed food	Vegetable oils and fats (21), dairy products (22), sugar (24), food products n.e.c. (25), beverages and tobacco products (26)
12.	Light manufacture	Leather products (29), wood products (30), paper products and publishing (31)
13.	Heavy manufacture	Mineral products n.e.c. (34), ferrous metals (35), electronic equipment (40)
14.	Utility and consumer	Electricity (43), gas manufacture-distribution (44)
15.	Other services	Water (45), construction (46), trade (47), transport n.e.c. (48), sea transport (49), air transport (50), communication (51), financial services n.e.c. (52), insurance (53), business services n.e.c. (54), recreation and other services (55), PubAdmin/defense/health/education (56), dwellings (57)

Notes: SSA Sub-Saharan Africa, *EU 25* European Union with 25 countries, *EFTA* European free trade association
Source: Authors' elaboration from GTAP-8 database

quantity not changing. As per the main concepts of trade creation and trade diversion given by Viner, the above concepts are very difficult to test because calculation of the costs of production of various tradable commodities in different countries is complex. Also, Viner's analysis is in the nature of a partial equilibrium, which does not explain how the welfare can be calculated in the case of a multigood trading world.

In most studies, the concepts of trade creation and trade diversion are generally used in the sense of an increase in trade from a member country and a shift of trade from a nonmember to a member country. In view of the foregoing, instead of using the terms "trade creation" and "trade diversion," we use the terms trade "generation" and "shifting" which can be calculated in the GTAP model by using the following equations:

$$VIWS(i,r,s) = pcif(i,r,s) * qxs(i,r,s) \quad (10.1)$$

$$VXWD(i,r,s) = pfob(i,r,s) * qxs(i,r,s) \quad (10.2)$$

$$qxs\ (i,r,s) = qim(i,s) - \sigma_M(i) \times [pms(i,r,s) - pim(i,s)] \quad (10.3)$$

where *VIWS (i, r, s)* is the value of imports of *i* from *r* to *s* valued *CIF* tradable only; *VXWD (i, r, s)* are the exports of *i* from *r* to *s* valued *FOB* (tradable only); *PCIF* is the *CIF* world price of commodity *i* supplied from *r* to *s*; *PFOB* is the *FOB* world price of a commodity supplied from *r* to *s*; *QXS* is the quantity of exports of product *i* from *r* to *s*. The variables in lowercase letters are the percentage counterparts of the original level variables as defined above. To calculate the changes in imports and exports in a post-simulation environment, one can simply subtract the new value of imports from the existing value of imports in the base data. Similarly, changes in the values of exports can be calculated.

10.4.2 Welfare Effect

In the GTAP model, measurement of economic welfare depends on a household's own consumption expenditure, government consumption expenditure (government spending on public goods and services), and the net national savings that will benefit future consumption. Any distortion in the model has an effect on these variables and thus affects the economic welfare of a region. Estimation of the GTAP model provides the regional equivalent variation (EV) measure in monetary terms, which represents the welfare effect in this model.

From a household point of view, the GTAP model measures the cost to the household of the same bundle of goods, before and after a given policy shock. In other words, it is the difference between the expenditure required to obtain the new level of utility at initial prices and the initial expenditure. The regional household utility level depends on the per capita household consumption, per capita government expenditure, and per capita savings.

Any change in this aggregate utility level provides the welfare effect of this model.

In other words, welfare change in the GTAP model is measured by a change in the aggregate utility, due to any distortion, specified over per capita private household consumption, per capita government expenditure, and per capita savings. The calculation of EV provides the value of the same percentage change in the level of utility in terms of money value. Let us consider two policy options, the existing one with prices p^0 and income m^0 and a policy shock with price p^1 and income m^1; then the equivalent variation can be expressed as:

$$EV = \mu(p^0; p^1, m^1) - \mu(p^0; p^0, m^0) = \mu(p^0; p^1, m^1) - m^0 \tag{10.4}$$

where $\mu(q; p, m)$, called the money metric indirect utility function, measures how much income the consumer would need at price q to be as well off as he or she would by facing price p and having income m. McDougall (2001) obtained the EV associated with a perturbation to the GTAP model (see Chap. 8 for details on GTAP methodology and welfare effect).

10.4.3 Terms of Trade Effect

Terms of trade in a region are defined as the ratio of the price index received for tradable goods produced in region r (PSW) compared to the price index paid for tradable goods used in the same region (PDW). This measure in the GTAP model includes the sales of net investments to the global bank and purchases of savings from the global bank. Equation (10.5) shows the percentage change in terms of trade (tot) as the difference between percentage change in PSW and PDW.

$$tot(r) = psw(r) - pdw(r) \tag{10.5}$$

Further, the trade balance of any region is defined as the difference between exports and imports. The variable defined in Eq. (10.6) is the change in the trade balance, which represents changes in the current accounts of each region:

$$DTBAL(r) = \left[\frac{VXWREG(r)}{100}\right] * vxwreg(r) - \left[\frac{VIWREG(r)}{100}\right] * viwreg\ (r) \qquad (10.6)$$

where *VXWREG* is the value of exports from region *r* evaluated at *fob* prices and *VIWREG* is the value of imports in region *r* evaluated at *CIF* prices; *vxwreg* and *viwreg* are the percentage changes in the actual variables.

10.5 GTAP Simulation Results

In this section, the results of changes in imports and exports, welfare, and terms of trade have been compared for both models. By looking at EV for India in Table 10.10, in FTA with the GCC, the value of EV is found to be negative under the framework of both the level duty and zero duty models. However, although India's EV in model II is negative, the loss in model II is less than expected under model I. However, for the GCC, a positive EV has been observed under both models. A positive EV reflects the welfare gain while the negative value indicates a welfare loss. We may conclude that Indian welfare will deteriorate while the GCC countries' welfare will improve because of the India–GCC trade agreement. The model II of zero duty must be preferred, under which the loss of India is less and the gain of welfare for the GCC countries is higher.

Further, to analyze the causes of expected loss and gains to India and the GCC countries, the components of EV have been reported in Table 10.10. Among three components, namely, allocative efficiency gains, terms of trade gains (current account), and investment saving (capital account) gains, the latter two components are negative for India under model I. However, under model II, terms of trade become unfavorable to India while favorable to the GCC countries after the agreement becomes effective.

The product market efficiency will improve while the factor market efficiency will remain stagnant for India. For the GCC countries, the product market efficiency will improve while the factor market allocative efficiency will deteriorate little bit. An improvement in the allocative efficiency in the product market will signify that the products will be available in both countries at cheaper rates while the factor prices will increase a little bit in the GCC countries which will adversely affect the allocative efficiency of these countries in the factor market.

Table 10.10 Comparison of India FTA with PGC and GCC

Region	*India in FTA with GCC*		*GCC in FTA with India*	
	Model I	*Model II*	*Model I*	*Model II*
Panel A: welfare gain				
Equivalent variation	−656.63	−413.54	2430.2	4036.85
Panel B: sources of welfare gain				
(a) Allocative efficiency	180.4	145.02	169.32	178.56
(a1) Product market	180.4	145.02	168.88	174.67
(a2) Factor market	0	0	−0.44	−3.89
(b) Terms of trade	−811.02	−698.11	3133.63	5155.41
(c) Investment-saving	−24.17	148.27	−872.13	−12.96.2

Source: Author's calculations

In sum, the major cause of welfare loss to India under the India–GCC agreement seems to be unfavorable/deteriorated terms of trade. To analyze the causes of deterioration in terms of trade, we need to analyze the impact of said trade agreement on India–GCC imports and exports; unfavorable terms of trade may be noticed either because of lower exports or higher imports. In both models, India tends to import more from the GCC after the trade agreement is in effect. Table 10.11 provides this change: the value of Indian imports will rise on entering into the FTA with the GCC, as per both models, and also in all sectors.

In model II, India's total imports will increase more than in model I. The expected increase of imports for India from the GCC in model I is US$ 4577.89 million (i.e., US$ 235,426.53 million – US$ 230,848.11 million), while in model II it is US$ 9988.41 million (i.e., US$ 240,836.52 million – US$ 230,848.11 million). However, for the GCC countries, the expected increase in imports is US$ 1365.81 million under model I in comparison to US$ 3718.66 million in model II. The highlight products in the Indian import bill from the GCC group include HS-27 and Other Services. By looking at the distribution of all products, the condition of India's FTA with the GCC following model II seems better as compared to model I.

From Table 10.12, it can be observed that Indian exports under the FTA with the GCC will reach US$ 226,114.94 million under model I, while the same figure will be US$ 231,188.58 million under model II when tariffs are reduced to zero. Thus, in reducing duty to a zero level, the increase in Indian exports to the GCC will be higher to a level of US$ 5073.64 million.

Table 10.11 Changes in the value of imports of India and the GCC after the FTA is in effect

Regions	*India*			*GCC*		
Commodity	*Pre-shock*	*Model I*	*Model II*	*Pre-shock*	*Model I*	*Model II*
HS27	56,991.53	60,453.25	63,530.5	437,282.03	438,647.84	441,000.69
HS71	25,600.79	26,322.07	27,792.92	14,178.88	18,876.75	20,559.98
HS10	2723.32	2734.64	2707.91	191.23	186.89	185.07
HS85	1985.95	2003.36	1974.2	3261.6	3317.57	3243.86
HS84	20,198.22	20,541.71	21,211.23	9982.28	9744.98	9645.04
HS63	14,885.94	14,916.72	14,973.9	1345.98	1327.3	1328.24
HS62	9058.74	9061.28	9182.92	688.32	661.09	649.32
Grains	6124.32	6116.03	6084.79	611.19	612.22	608.27
Meat and live stock	1357.54	1352.26	1426.44	457.86	448.19	441.49
Extraction	191.8	190.5	189.2	14.75	14.76	14.78
Processed food	7303.83	7308.51	7639.24	3963.73	4151.99	4296.77
Light manufacture	5102.8	5104.05	5100.88	2109.59	2149.62	2187.62
Heavy manufacture	13,267.46	13,505.25	14,083.84	9122.7	9229.33	9380.55
Utility and consumption	32.89	33.11	32.78	407.48	396.16	389.37
Other services	66,022.99	65,783.81	64,905.76	38,575.51	37,835.97	37,458.5
Total	230,848.11	235,426.53	240,836.52	522,193.13	527,600.67	531,389.57

Source: Author's calculations

Table 10.12 Changes in the value of imports of India and the GCC after an FTA is in effect

Regions	*India*			*GCC*		
Commodity	*Pre-shock*	*Model I*	*Model II*	*Pre-shock*	*Model I*	*Model II*
HS-27	53,590.02	56,818.82	59,688.5	417,942.28	419,340.72	421,657.03
HS-71	25,353.87	26,068.58	27,534.48	13,968.65	18,655.43	20,337.09
HS-10	2367.53	2377.05	2354.66	165.67	162.03	160.5
HS-85	1877.81	1893.98	1866.08	3071.01	3120.11	3050.63
HS-84	19,304.26	19,630.01	20,266.8	9527.37	9303.17	9209.05
HS-63	13,952.04	13,980.56	14,035.54	1263.62	1246.62	1247.79
HS-62	8596.66	8599.07	8715.57	656.74	630.99	619.87
Grains	5531.01	5523.42	5492.75	515.93	517.58	514.57
Meat and live stock	1275.53	1270.65	1340.34	427.77	418.87	412.68
Extraction	178.98	177.79	176.66	13.27	13.29	13.3
Processed food	6735.18	6739.45	7045.27	3601.9	3770.73	3899.76
Light manufacture	4779.35	4780.42	4776.6	1904.33	1940.86	1975.42
Heavy manufacture	12,222.2	12,438.21	12,956.78	8484.51	8587.94	8733.31
Utility and consumption	32.89	33.11	32.78	407.48	396.16	389.37
Other services	66,022.99	65,783.81	64,905.76	38,575.51	37,835.97	37,458.5
Total	221,820.33	226,114.94	231,188.58	500,526.03	505,940.48	509,678.89

Source: Author's calculations

Consequently, model II is a better choice for Indian planners to gain from an India–GCC free trade agreement.

Further, if the gains in imports and exports are compared, the Indian imports will increase at higher rate (US$ 9988.41 million) than its exports (US$ 9368.25 million) and, therefore, will adversely affect the terms of trade. In the case of the GCC countries, a gain in exports (US$ 9152.86 million) is higher than the gain in imports (US$ 3718.66 million), thus the terms of trade will be positively affected for the GCC nations. Therefore, it may be inferred that the unfavorable terms of trade between India and the GCC nations after the trade agreement is in effect will be noticed because of the higher growth of Indian imports than the growth rate of Indian exports to the GCC nations. Consequently, the welfare loss will occur to India. The converse argument is valid for the GCC nations to whom the welfare gain will be noticed because of more favorable terms of trade with India.

10.6 Concluding Remarks

The aim of this study was to work out the possible gains from an India–GCC free trade agreement that has been signed by these two regions but is still not in effect. Some trade indices such as RCA and TII in the GCC trade with India have been provided to substantiate the argument in favor of present study. The composition of commodities in the GCC trade with India have been constructed to highlight important products. The degree of protection in India–GCC trade has been discussed in terms of tariff rates levied by both sides in all sectors.

After studying the GCC trade and tariff profile with India, two models have been simulated. Firstly, the countries are assumed to impose equal duties, so that there will be zero variation in duties among the partner countries. Secondly, the partner countries are assumed to reduce the duties up to a zero level, that is, a free trade area will be established among partner nations.

From comparison of the two models, it appears that model II (i.e., the zero duty model) is the better option under which an Indian loss is minimum and a gain by the GCC group of countries is higher. Indian trade will surely be enhanced by the agreement, but Indian imports are expected to increase at a higher rate than its exports. Thus, the agreement will adversely affect Indian terms of trade with the GCC countries. The adverse effect on terms of trade will be reflected in welfare changes that appear to be negative for India.

However, affiliates of the GCC group are found to be the beneficiaries of the FTA under evaluation. The exports of these countries are found to be increasing at a higher rate than their imports. Thus, the terms of trade effect will be positive and favorable to the GCC countries. The favorable terms of trade effect has been reflected in the positive welfare gain to these nations. Thus, it may be inferred that zero duty trade agreement is better for partner countries of the India–GCC trade agreement. The expected gains to the GCC countries are high while the gains to India are only in terms of allocative efficiency in the product market. The share of India will increase marginally in world trade but the adverse impact on its welfare, deterioration in its current account, and so on, are the grey areas of the India–GCC free trade agreement. Indian policy planners are advised to work out suitable policy packages so that the growth of exports under such an agreement may surpass the growth of imports and so that a favorable effect of such an agreement on current accounts may be generated.

References

Arora, R., Singh, S., & Mathur, S. K. (2015). Assessment of the proposed India-China Free Trade Agreement: A general equilibrium approach. *Journal of Centrum Cathedra, 8*(2), 81–108. https://doi.org/10.1108/JCC-08-02-2015-B002

McDougall, R. (2001). *A new regional household demand system for GTAP. Revised in 2003.* GTAP technical paper no. 20, Purdue University.

CHAPTER 11

Lebanon's Accession to the WTO: An *Ex Ante* Macroeconomic Impact Assessment

Ghada Tabbah

The international trade is an essential component of an integrated effort to end poverty, ensure food security and promote economic growth
Ban Ki-Moon, 2014

11.1 Introduction

As the quote highlighted, the Secretary-General of the United Nations, Ban Ki-moon, opened the 2014 WTO public forum joining traditional affirmations of the Bretton Woods Institutions. According to these institutions, openness and trade liberalization are considered to have played a major role in the remarkable expansion of industrial countries since the end of World War II and in the economic performance of countries that have taken off in recent decades. These policies are vital elements in any strategy for development and economic growth.

This development strategy is based on the liberal model of economic policy called the "Washington Consensus" by Williamson (1990). This model sets among its recommendations the liberalization of trade and the adoption of an

G. Tabbah
Lebanese University, Beirut, Lebanon

S.K. Mathur et al. (eds.), *Theorizing International Trade*,
https://doi.org/10.1007/978-981-10-1759-9_11

extrovert growth strategy. Although this consensus was reconsidered (Stiglitz 1998) and was sometimes considered a failure (Rodrik 2001, 2006), its requirements that formed the basis of the structural adjustment programs of the 1980s continue to supply some of the content of programs against poverty in the 2000s.

The international rapid growth of trade is not a new phenomenon, but the terms of opening the economies have evolved (Cling 2006). Recently, we observe an increased trend towards further trade liberalization, which seems to be the result of a combination of unilateral, regional and multilateral liberalization. At the multilateral level, the trade liberalization has been especially strengthened by the creation of the World Trade Organization (WTO), heir to the GATT (General Agreement on Tariffs and Trade) created after the World War II. The WTO succeeded it in 1995 to mainly better support the movement of liberalization of the global market. Indeed, "the World Trade Organization (WTO) is the only international organization dealing with the global rules of trade between nations. Its main function is to ensure that trade flows as smoothly, predictably and freely as possible."

As of November 2015, the organization is composed of 162 members and 22 observers, and includes all the global economics powers with the accession of the Russian Federation in 2012. Despite criticism addressed to the ministerial conference held in Bali in July 2014, and despite the turmoil caused by the impasse in trade negotiations of the current Doha Round and the growing number of regional and bilateral trade agreements concluded outside the sphere of the WTO, there are few candidates willing to leave their place in the queue. Lebanon is not an exception.

Qualified once for Switzerland of the Middle East, Lebanon was considered before the civil war of the 1970s as a dynamic regional center, linking the East and the West. Lebanon is indeed one of the first signatories of the GATT in 1947 and had contributed significantly in the development and shaping of the GATT rules. Lebanon had to retreat in 1951 for political reasons (Dagher 2005).

Since 1990, at the end of the civil war that lasted fifteen years, Lebanon has tried to find again its commercial role. Trade liberalization and economic openness have been the two main pillars of the agenda of the Lebanese governments that have succeeded since 1990. Since 1999, Lebanon has submitted its application for membership in the WTO, and to this day, that is to say, after sixteen years of negotiations, the country is not admitted yet. The reasons are imperfectly known. They can be classified in three categories: political, technical and legislative.

On another level, Lebanon's accession to the WTO reflects currently a major concern domestically that opposes the supporters and opponents of this process. For supporters, Lebanon is ready to face the liberalization shock; it has already relaxed its trade policy and the adherence shall promote a better access to export markets, reduce costs of imported inputs and encourage foreign direct investment. In front of these arguments, we can find those of the opponents reflecting the concerns of producers, especially the farmers, unable to face foreign competition, and are likely to exit the market before taking advantage of the probable export opportunities that such membership could offer.

This same debate taking place between the Lebanese supporters and opponents regarding the effects of further trade liberalization on growth and welfare in Lebanon is the subject of a debate, far from being concluded, among economists at the global level. It resulted in a developed economic literature, seeking to establish a link between trade and growth, and more recently between trade and poverty. This controversy among economists on the links between trade, growth and poverty is far from being settled, each part having its own theoretical and empirical arguments to advance and to defend.

The objective of this study is to identify the channels through which will pass the effects of WTO accession on the Lebanese economy, making use of a recursive dynamic Computable General Equilibrium Model (CGE Model). Taking into account the structure of the economy in general and the various interrelationships between economic agents, this model turns out to be the most appropriate tool to evaluate the potential impacts of trade liberalization policies at the macro level (Mage-Bertomeu 2006). This model has the advantage of presenting an overall view of the economy and the shock transmission channels on microeconomic agents while taking into account macroeconomic constraints within which they operate. The general equilibrium model is recursive dynamic; this implies that the economic interactions between agents and their behaviors are based on adaptive expectations. It is solved one period at a time, separating the within-period component from the between-period component (Thurlow 2008).

However, the difficulty of empirical modeling of the impact of the WTO on Lebanon is threefold: firstly, we do not really know the offer made by Lebanon to the WTO and we must therefore formulate necessarily approximate assumptions on commitments made and their impact, given that the price to pay to join the WTO is increasing and that any assumption made here will be outdated quickly if negotiations fail; secondly, there is the problem of the lack of statistical data in Lebanon. Finally, an intrinsic difficulty in macroeconomic modeling is that it assumes a stable macro-economic structure (however, joining the WTO can precisely cause a structural shock, such as the emergence of new productive sectors nonexistent in Lebanon so far).

This chapter is structured as follows: Sect. 11.2 reviews briefly the existing literature addressing the effects of trade liberalization/accession to the WTO on economic growth. Section 11.3 describes briefly the socio-economic context in Lebanon and the main challenges related to the WTO. Section 11.4 deals with the specification of database. Section 11.5 describes the methodology adopted and the different scenarios considered. Section 11.6 presents the results and analyzes the simulations. Section 11.7 concludes.

11.2 Literature Review

What link is there between trade openness and economic growth? Between the accession of a country to the WTO and its well-being? Answering these questions is a delicate task, due to the fact that the theory of international trade led to conflicting results in this area and that the economic tools, econometrics and statistics at our disposal encounter many limitations (lack of data, selection bias, etc.). At the empirical level, to test the nature of the link between trade, growth and poverty, econometric studies have multiplied. A number of empirical studies show indeed a positive correlation between trade openness and economic growth. Thus, Michaely (1977) found a positive correlation between export growth and GDP growth, taking as sample developing countries. Feder (1983) undertook the same exercise for the semi-industrialized countries, and found the same positive relationship. Syrquin and Chenery (1989) demonstrated that the trade liberalization adds 0.2–1.4 percentage points to the growth rate. Balassa (1985), in his study of the developing countries, has shown that the most open countries have on average the highest growth rates. The same observation was made in the study of Edwards (1991) and the report of the World Bank (1987).

A landmark study was conducted in 1995 by Sachs and Warner to test the trade liberalization policies' impact on growth. For this purpose, they proceeded to the classification of countries between "closed" and "open" and compared the respective growth of both groups. Their conclusion is that open economies have recorded an annual average growth rate of 4.5% in the 1970s and 1980s, while the number of closed economies barely reached 0.7%. According to them, not only do open countries grow faster than closed countries, but also poor open economies grow faster than rich open economies. The authors identify a conditional convergence: developing countries can catch up with rich countries under the condition that they are open and integrated into the global economy. For their part, the two economists from the World Bank, Dollar and Kray (2001) in their study, "growth is good for the poor," also detect a significant positive effect of trade on growth and argue that this "leads to proportionate increases in incomes."

However, Rodriguez and Rodrik (2001) attacked those "pro-trade" findings. They especially criticized the methods used to measure the opening, which lead economists to overestimate the value of free trade regimes for developing countries. In their view, the focus on trade policy generates expectations unlikely to materialize. Bhagwati and Srinivasan (2002), for their part, consider that the regression analysis is not an appropriate method to understand the complexity of the trade-growth relationship; most studies has problems of measuring the opening and isolating the impacts of trade liberalization on growth.

As for the direct impact of the WTO on economic growth, more or less recent studies have been conducted to estimate these effects. The study of Rose (2004) is the first to estimate the impact of the WTO on trade. This study comes to the following conclusion, described as "interesting mystery": there is no empirical evidence that the WTO has promoted international trade. The study, using a large database and relevant quantitative analysis, questioned the impact of the WTO as a multilateral institution promoting international trade. The author titled his study, "*Do We Really Know that the WTO Increases Trade?*" claiming that he has doubts about the fact that the WTO has really promoted international trade.

These remarks have led many economists to empirically test the findings of Rose and the impacts of WTO accession on growth and trade. In a critical analysis of Rose's affirmations, and in an article commenting on the study, Tomz et al. (2007) argue that the solution of the mystery revealed by Rose is in the specification of the countries participating in the WTO. The authors emphasize the institutional detail and identify all the countries participating in the WTO. They reuse the same data and methods of Rose, and conclude that the WTO significantly increases the trade of formal members and non-member country participants in comparison with non-member countries not subject to the agreement.

Rose replied to the critical analysis of Tomz et al. in a paper published in 2007 entitled: "*Do We Really Know that the WTO Increases Trade? Reply*". He accords with the three authors of the specifications to be used. However, in his demonstrations, he not only shows that the affirmations of Tomz et al. and those of Subramanian and Wei (2006) subsequently were wrong, but he still insists that the GATT, and later the WTO, has only small effects on trade. He concluded by asking how participation in the WTO can have significant effects on trade if it does not change trade policies.

The impact of accession to the WTO has attracted the interest of other researchers, including Gowa and Kim (2005), who focus their analysis on the role of "primary supplier," which has the rights of the initial negotiator in terms of tariff concessions. Using 2004 data, the two authors conclude that the WTO accession will have a positive and significant impact on trade only established between the most industrialized countries (the Great Britain, the United States, Canada, France and Germany).

Balding (2010), for his part, was interested in bilateral trade flows between countries. He concluded confirming the results of Subramanian and Wei that the impact of the WTO on trade flows is asymmetrical depending on the country and its initial level of economic development.

In conclusion, we note that these findings remain controversial, highlighting the highly variable nature of the effects of increased trade openness on economic growth of countries, which largely depends on the starting conditions of countries and their structural features.

11.3 The Lebanese Economy: Socio-economic Context

Qualified once for Switzerland of the Middle East, Lebanon was in the 1960s and early 1970s, a dynamic regional center, linking the east to the west. Its history and its demographic, geographic, religious and cultural characteristics made Lebanon a unique country in the Middle East. Historically, many civilizations had occupied the country and the Lebanese state was only created in 1920, under the name of Grand Lebanon under the French mandate (Shehadi and Mills 1988).

However, this model of democracy and economic development presented by the country after independence in the 1950s and 1960s disappeared with the civil war, which took place from 1975 to 1990. Although the causes of this war and its conduct were not justified and not clear, it resulted in structural imbalances on many levels, which are accumulating and increasingly felt: a public debt-to-GDP ratio among the highest in the world according to the IMF's 2014 report, and whose sustainability is questioned, a low coverage of imports by exports, a chronic trade deficit denoting structural weaknesses in the agricultural and industrial sectors in the country where the services sector represents more than 70% of GDP.

On the commercial side, and in an attempt to revive the "golden age" of the pre-war period, the country has tried to find its commercial role linking the Arab countries to the European ones (Corm 2012). To this end, Lebanon signed the Association Agreement with the countries of the European Union (EuroMed agreement), and it is engaged in a process of tariff dismantling with the Arab countries, as part of the Greater Arab Free Trade Area (GAFTA). On the multilateral level, Lebanon is actively pursuing its accession to the WTO. Since 1999, Lebanon has submitted its application for membership in the WTO. The Lebanese Republic's Working Party was established on 14 April 1999. The Memorandum on the Foreign Trade Regime was circulated in June 2001. The seventh meeting of the Working Party was held in October 2009, and to this date (2017) Lebanon is still not part of the organization.

The issue of Lebanon's accession to the WTO remains an intrigue at several levels: the accession process in Lebanon remains one of the longest (the second after Algeria) even though Lebanon is one of the twenty-three founding members of the GATT. Internally, this process is postponed because of the social and political priorities that continue to weigh (the most recent IMF Report on Lebanon (2014) does not mention the issue of accession to the WTO). Empirically, to our knowledge, no quantitative study has assessed yet the effects of Lebanon's accession to the WTO. The originality of our study therefore emerges.

11.4 Specification of Database

This section sets out the framework of the Social Accounting Matrix (SAM), used for the calibration of the model to the Lebanese economy. "A social accounting matrix is simply defined as a single entry accounting system whereby each macroeconomic account is represented by a column for outgoings and a row for incomings" (Round 1981). Thus, SAM is a matrix representation of transactions between all institutional groups in a socio-economic system. It is a disaggregated framework representing the generation of income by activities of production and the reallocation of income between the economic agents (Round 2003).

In a country where statistics data are almost non-existent, and where quantitative economic studies are very rare, the use of an already existing social accounting matrix was almost impossible for several reasons. Indeed, the social accounting matrices used in quantitative studies applied in Lebanon are either very aggregated or using 1997 data. Thus, a key challenge in this study was to elaborate a SAM based on national data and its disaggregation subsequently to extend the scope of analysis. The SAM that was used is calibrated to the year 2010. It was disintegrated thereafter to include seven industrial subsectors, instead of one, according to those existing in the accounting national accounts: (1) Food products, (2) Textiles, (3) Non-metallic minerals, (4) Metals, machinery, (5) Wood, rubber and chemistry, (6) Furniture, and (7) Other branches.

The SAM is composed of forty-two aggregated accounts. It first distinguishes the sectors and the commodities produced to better visualize the assumption of the International Food Policy Research Institute (IFPRI) Model that the same commodity can be produced by several activities and one activity can produce many commodities.

The trade data are collected in the account, "rest of the world." One characteristic of the dynamic model of IFPRI is that it allows a regional disaggregation of international trade. For this purpose, the data of foreign trade of Lebanon have been classified into seven geographical areas, rather than including a single account "rest of the world". This specification allows us to account for the heterogeneity of foreign trade by region and to better examine regional substitution phenomena and the evolution of import prices following trade liberalization policies (Punt 2004). There are first the two major trading partners—the countries of the European Union (EU 28) and the Arab country members of the GAFTA. Also considered are trade relations with EFTA (Iceland, Liechtenstein, Norway and Switzerland) with other major trading partners, namely the NAFTA group (the United States, Canada and Mexico), China and Turkey.

Information on trade flows with these countries/groups of countries are collected from the MacMap database (Market Access Map), developed jointly by the International Trade Centre ITC (UNCTAD-WTO, Geneva) and the CEPII, which refers to the French *Centre d'Etudes Prospectives et d'Informations Internationales.*

The calculation of the model parameters is based on the SAM and several assumptions. The growth rate of the population is estimated at 1.3% per year, according to projections made by the International Monetary Fund (IMF 2013). The estimation of these elasticities is not available for Lebanon. This led us to review the literature of CGE models and the empirical studies applied to other developing economies.

11.5 Methodology

In this section, we quantify the macroeconomic effects of Lebanon's accession to the WTO. Specifically, we will assess whether the macro impacts of such a shock are positive or negative, and will try to identify the winners and losers. To this end, economists generally use computable general equilibrium models, which seem to be the most rigorous quantitative methods to evaluate the impact of economic shocks/reforms in the economy as a whole. Taking into account the different interactions between economic agents, these models turn out to be the most appropriate tools to evaluate the potential impacts of trade liberalization policies at the macro level. The CGE Models are a set of linear and non-linear equations describing the behavior interactions between the agents based on optimizing behavior ensuring that the macroeconomic constraints are satisfied (Thurlow and Seventer 2002). They can describe the way in which different sectors of the economy, prices, wages, and trade with the rest of the world, etc. would be affected.

Our general equilibrium model is recursive dynamic, visualizing the economic interactions between agents and their behaviors based on adaptive expectations. It is solved one period at a time, separating the within-period component from the between-period component. Also, our model is calibrated on the SAM of 2010, newly built and disaggregated to better assess the sectorial impacts of WTO accession. Several shocks, inspired by the existing literature and Lebanese context, are simulated to better understand and analyze the effects of further trade liberalization in Lebanon on different macroeconomic variables.

This study includes several "value added," which constitute the originality and contribution of our study:

- First, the impact of trade reforms on the Lebanese economy has been little studied so far in Lebanon, and most of the studies simply describe events and historical facts by introducing a qualitative analysis related this question, not making use of any model or quantitative study.
- This study aims to evaluate the effects of trade opening by using a computable general equilibrium model. It therefore can be added to the small number of studies in Lebanon using such models.
- The general equilibrium model used is recursive dynamic, developed by Thurlow in 2008 for application to South Africa.

- The simulated scenarios constitute a projection and simulation of the evolution of the Lebanese economy over the studied period, under the various shocks and reforms arising from the accession to the WTO.

11.5.1 The Scenarios Description

Several scenarios are presented in order to analyze the effects of Lebanon's accession to the WTO. They are modeled through an exogenous adjustment of model parameters to assess the effects of tariff elimination and increased competition in local markets exerted by the induced increase in imports, the increased productivity and technological efficiency induced by trade and the improvement of the investment climate. Note that WTO membership would also strengthen export opportunities as Lebanese products could access any market of a Member State benefiting from the same conditions as those granted to all member countries (as the principle of non-discrimination advocated by the organization). But this effect has not been taken into account directly in our simulations, because it would have claimed to develop assumptions about global growth supplement addressed to Lebanon, which is a heavy exercise conducted only by very few studies (Cling et al. 2009). The simulations carried out in the model are inspired by the existing literature, regional agreements already signed with trading partners and the Lebanese context. Five scenarios are studied:

- The baseline scenario reproduces the trends of the Lebanese economy in the absence of shock.
- Scenario 1 studies the effects of immediate and full tariff reduction. It has the advantage to generate a direct and cumulative effect of tariff elimination.
- Scenario 2 associates tariff reform with the effects of improving the investment climate in Lebanon.
- Scenario 3 examines the combined effects of tariff reform and an increase in total factor productivity related to trade liberalization.
- Scenario 4 combines the first three scenarios.

11.5.2 And the Services?

Because of the increasing role of services in world trade, economists have become more interested in this field. For a long time, services were considered as non-tradable internationally. However, as shown by Lautier (2013), the opportunities of the tertiary sector in international trade seem to be underestimated. Indeed, it is expected that this sector will represent half of the world trade by 2020, as is currently recording the fastest expansion.

However, for services, the current framework of the WTO is insufficiently structured for services liberalization. It is the internal regulation, rather than border measures, that significantly affects trade in services. Thus, liberalization of trade in services requires a country to adapt its own regulations. Furthermore, measuring the actual level of protection in services, theoretically or empirically, is a difficult task. The first difficulty concerns the intangible nature of services (the barriers against trade in services are different from those imposed on trade in goods). Having said that, instead of referring to a single tariff list, as is the case in the goods sector, policymakers must implement an information-building strategy and study all the regulations for each sector (Hoekman and Mavroidis 2002). This process is long and does not allow for clear quantification of the level of barriers in place in each sector.

Given these elements (few liberalization commitments in services at this stage, the difficulties to take them into account quantitatively, etc.), the impact of Lebanon's accession to the WTO will only concern in our study its effects on goods. Those on services may be the subject of further research.

11.6 The Model Results

This section presents the results of two exercises carried out with the CGE Model. The first exercise is a projection, which is the "counterfactual scenario" (also called "base" in the tables). It shows the future trend of the Lebanese economy, in the absence of Lebanon's accession to the WTO (in the absence of an exogenous shock). The second exercise is to simulate the four scenarios described earlier. The scenarios results have been reported to those of the reference path (the counterfactual or baseline scenario). They concern the impact on prices and the exchange rate, on GDP and different macroeconomic variables and on the flow of trade. Also, the study will analyze the dynamic trajectories of macroeconomic variables during the simulated period from 2010 to 2020, and the evolution of the Lebanese sectors under the four scenarios.

Table 11.1 Regional average customs in %

	EU	*GAFTA*	*EFTA*	*ALENA*	*China*	*Turkey*	*ROW*	*Average*
Agriculture	24.0	0.0	24.0	24.0	24.0	24.0	24.0	19.2
Livestock	53.1	0.0	33.1	33.1	33.1	33.1	53.1	45.2
Energy and water	2.8	0.0	2.8	2.8	2.8	2.8	2.8	2.4
Agro-food products	17.0	0.0	17.0	17.0	17.0	17.0	17.0	13.5
Textiles	8.0	0.0	8.0	8.0	1.0	8.0	8.0	5.3
Non-metallic minerals	13.9	0.0	13.9	13.9	13.9	13.9	13.9	6.9
Metals, machinery	4.3	0.0	4.3	4.3	0.0	4.3	4.3	3.1
Wood, rubber and chemistry	2.3	0.0	2.3	2.3	2.3	2.3	2.3	2.1
Furniture	3.7	0.0	3.7	3.7	3.7	3.7	3.7	3.5
Other branches	7.6	0.0	7.6	7.6	3.2	7.6	7.6	6.4

Source: Market Access Map (2013)

11.6.1 Changes in Tariffs and Impacts on Prices

Before analyzing the effects of shocks on prices, note that the tariff structure of Lebanon is extracted from databases prepared jointly by the ITC, the CEPII and the Customs Administration in Lebanon and collected in 2013 for the 2007 (it was the most recent data at the time). Table 11.1 shows the tariffs applied in 2007 with the major trading partners.

From the table, we see that the most protected sectors are livestock (45.2% on average), agriculture (19.2%) and agri-food products (13.5%). This is consistent with the global trend to protect the agricultural sector, assumed as a fragile sector, and which remains one of the most sensitive issues in the international negotiations.

Industrial sectors are subject to lower rates than those of the agricultural sector, especially in the case of industrial goods used as inputs in the production, such as wood, rubber and chemicals (2.1%), energy and water (2.4%) and metals and machinery (3.1%).

Changes in import and intermediate goods prices are presented in the following table. The four scenarios assume a complete dismantling of tariffs; the direct effect is to lower import prices of all tradable goods (see Table 11.2). Increased trade liberalization in Lebanon will eventually generate a removal of customs duties on imports, which will directly lower import prices and will involve a decline in domestic demand addressed to domestic goods for those imported. Therefore, we observed lower prices in concerned sectors.

This drop in import prices affects in the other hand the prices of imported intermediate goods, used as inputs in the production of certain

Table 11.2 Cumulative price variation (deviation from baseline scenario, in %)

		Scénario 1	*Scénario 2*	*Scénario 3*	*Scénario 4*
Imports	Agriculture	−5.2	−1.8	−12.1	−9.4
	Elevage	−5.2	−1.8	−12.1	−9.4
	Energie et eaux	−9.1	−5.8	−15.7	−13.1
	Production Agro-alimentaires	−12.0	−8.8	−18.4	−15.9
	Textiles	−6.6	−3.2	−13.4	−10.7
	Minéraux non-métalliques	−5.5	−2.1	−12.4	−9.7
	Métaux, Machines et appareils	−6.7	−3.3	−13.5	−10.8
	Bois, caoutchouc et chimie	−2.7	−6.4	−4.8	−1.9
	Meubles	−22.5	−19.7	−28.2	−25.9
	Autres branches	−1.5	−5.2	−5.9	−3.0
Intermediate products	Agriculture	5.2	8.6	−16.0	−13.7
	Livestock	3.2	4.7	−7.9	−7.1
	Energy and water	−3.4	−0.3	−15.1	−12.8
	Agro-food products	3.8	5.9	−7.0	−5.5
	Textiles	3.2	6.0	−14.6	−12.7
	Non-metallic minerals	−8.0	−1.5	−15.6	−10.8
	Metals, machinery	0.1	3.7	−17.1	−14.5
	Wood, rubber and chemistry	2.1	5.6	−12.8	−10.2
	Furniture	−0.2	3.4	−12.0	−9.3
	Other branches	2.2	6.1	−14.8	−12.0
	Construction	−6.4	−1.1	−12.1	−8.2
	Transport and communications	−7.4	−6.0	−8.5	−7.1
	Merchant service	−3.2	−2.0	−5.6	−4.5
	Trade	0.8	0.8	0.2	0.3
	Administration	3.7	2.5	4.9	4.0

Source: CGE Model results

commodities, allowing a reduce production costs in these areas and lead to improved competitiveness. The increase in exports that follows will cause an increase in production in sectors oriented towards exports and rising prices for their products.

These effects are combined within each sector and the predominant final effect depends on the characteristics of each sector, on the initial tariff rates and on the share of imports in domestic consumption. Compared to the baseline scenario, we note that the most protected products, subject to the higher tariffs, namely, agriculture, livestock and food products, are those that record the most significant reduction in import prices. It can also be observed from the table a reduction in the agricultural and industrial goods imported prices, which implies a lower average inputs cost, leading to a decline in the average production price of industrial goods. The latter will be more important for tradable industrial goods, such as metallic minerals and furniture. The combination of lower production and imported prices results in lower prices for the composite commodity. Prices of goods composites are formed by combining the prices of imported goods with the prices of domestic goods produced locally. These price changes are more important when taking into account improvements in total factor productivity in simulated scenarios 3 and 4.

11.6.2 The Evolution of Macroeconomic Variables and the Exchange Rate

Counterfactual Scenario

This scenario is represented in the column "base" in the tables. It is observed that imports increase in an average of 3.8% per year over the study period, while exports increase at an average rate of 6.5% per year. This seems consistent with the recent evolution of foreign trade in Lebanon, where exports are growing at a slightly faster pace than imports. If this trend continues, there would be a decrease in the chronic external deficit.

The projected growth of the productive sectors resulted in an annual increase of 4.3% of GDP. Thus, the growth rates in the domestic production and consumption are nearly equivalent. Private consumption expenditure increased at an annual average rate of 3.8%, while the population is growing at an annual rate of 1.3%, implying an increase in the consumption per capita.

The First Scenario: Tariff Dismantling

Table 11.3 shows the evolution of the Lebanese economy after a total dismantling of tariffs (scenario 1). The model has the originality to show what could happen with each regional group or country separately, in addition to the effects of a multilateral agreement in a column called "Multi".

Table 11.3 Scenario 1: Annual growth rates in % (in volume)

S1	*Structure in % baseline*	*FTAEU*		*FTAALENAFTACHINA FTATURKEY MULTI*			
GDPMP	100.0	4.3	3.9	4.0	4.2	4.1	4.4
PRVCON	77.3	3.8	5.1	4.2	3.8	4.2	4.0
FIXINV	31.7	3.0	3.0	3.0	3.0	3.0	3.0
GOVCON	13.3	3.7	3.7	3.6	3.7	3.7	3.6
EXPORTS	23.1	6.5	6.0	6.3	6.5	6.2	7.1
IMPORTS	−45.4	3.7	6.3	4.8	3.8	4.7	4.2

Source: CGE Model

The direct effect of the elimination of tariffs results in the reduction of import prices, leading to higher growth of imports compared to the baseline scenario. The average import growth over the period studied is 4.2% per year. Since these imports meet 80% of the Lebanese domestic consumption, reducing import prices also enables households to increase their consumption in almost the same proportions.

This growth in imports does not alter the balance of the current account. The current account balance is equilibrated by an adjustment of the exchange rate. The latter depreciates by 1.1% per year (Table 11.4), stimulating exports, which are increasing at an average annual rate of 7.2%. This depreciation is slightly greater than that which can occur in the absence of shock. The explanation for stimulating exports is the fact that the decline in import prices implies a reduction in average prices for imported inputs, reducing the cost of local production. Thus, the domestic production becomes more competitive and able to compete on export markets.

It turns out that the application of the most favored nation clause following Lebanon's accession to the WTO promotes trade, boosting both increased imports and exports in comparison with the baseline scenario, with the fact that the increase in exports exceeds the increase in imports. This relatively significant increase in exports can be explained by the depreciation of the exchange rate on one hand and falling inputs prices on the other.

This effect, coupled with an increase in private and public consumption leads to an increase in domestic production. The latter, considered at the market price, is experiencing an annual average growth of 4.4% per year, which is higher than that prevailing in the baseline scenario.

Table 11.4 Annual change in exchange rate in % (a positive sign of the exchange rate variation indicates depreciation)

	S0	*S1*	*S2*	*S3*	*S4*
Exports	6.5	7.1	7.6	12.1	12.2
Imports	3.7	4.2	4.5	7.6	7.7
Exchange rate	0.4	1.1	1.6	0.4	0.7

Source: CGE Model

Another account affected by the tariff reduction is the account of public savings. The public savings flexibility constraint being adopted, tariff elimination generates lower revenue and a worsening of the public deficit. However, trade liberalization stimulating the economy could generate additional tax revenue, which limits the widening of public savings.

One should note that a removal of tariffs with each partner took apart, causes a slowing of the rate of growth of Lebanon's GDP compared to the baseline scenario, and will only lead to improved results if it concerns all trading partners. Indeed, as shown in the simulation results, it is only in the case of multilateral liberalization, called "Multi," that Lebanon will experience an improvement in its economic growth. However, this improvement is not significant (4.4% per year in the scenario compared with 4.3% per year in the baseline). This can be explained mainly by the weakness of current customs duties in Lebanon.

The Second Scenario: Tariff Dismantling and Improvement in the Climate Investment

This scenario is obtained by combining the tariff reform with an increase in the investment rate. The latter is always exogenous, according to the neoclassical closure of our model. The growth of the volume of investment, however, is set at a higher level (6% per year instead of 3% per year) (Table 11.5).

An increased investment leads to increased overall production and income. This effect, combined with tariff reform reducing the cost of imported intermediate goods results in an annual increase in the overall production of 4.8%, higher than that which takes place in the isolated case of tariff reform envisaged in the previous scenario. The effects on the current account are almost the same as that of the first scenario; the increase in exports outweighed the increase in imports. However, the increase in

Table 11.5 Scenario 2: Annual growth rates in % (in volume)

S2	*Structure in % baseline*	*FTAEU*		*FTAALENAFTACHINA FTATURKEY MULTI*			
GDPMP	100.0	4.7	4.4	4.5	4.6	4.5	4.8
PRVCON	77.3	3.0	4.5	3.5	3.1	3.5	3.2
FIXINV	31.7	6.0	6.0	6.0	6.0	6.0	6.0
GOVCON	13.3	3.7	3.9	3.7	3.7	3.7	3.6
EXPORTS	23.1	6.9	6.2	6.6	6.9	6.5	7.6
IMPORTS	−45.4	4.0	6.5	5.0	4.1	4.9	4.5

Source: CGE Model

exports is more pronounced than in the case of a tariff reduction (scenario 1). Improving the investment climate improves productive performance; the result is a higher export growth.

The Third Scenario: Tariff Dismantling and an Increase in the TFP

A striking difference in the magnitude of the evolution of economic indicators can be observed in the third scenario. This third scenario assumes in addition to the tariff reform of the first scenario an increase in total factor productivity, resulting in a better allocation of resources. The results put in evidence the potential dynamic gains following trade liberalization (Table 11.6).

The average annual increase in GDP is much higher than that estimated in the baseline scenario; it exceeds 7% per year regardless of the studied regional liberalization, and it is the highest in the context of multilateral liberalization (7.7% per year). With improved total factor productivity, which results in increased quality of Lebanese production, local products that quality standards required in export markets can compete with foreign products not only in the domestic markets, but also in the overseas markets. Thus, the most important change can be observed with the exports, which record an increase of 12.1% per year compared to an increase of 6.5% per year in the baseline scenario, of 7.1% per year in scenario 1 and 7.8% in scenario 2.

The Fourth Scenario: Tariff Dismantling, Improvement in the Climate Investment and an Increase in the TFP

Scenario 4 combines the increase in total factor productivity with the tariff reform and the improvement of the investment climate. The results are positive, significant and suggest positive effects on Lebanon's accession to

Table 11.6 Scenario 3: Annual growth rates in % (in volume)

S3	*Structure in % baseline*	*FTAEU*		*FTAALENAFTACHINA MULTI*		*FTATURKEY*	
GDPMP	100.0	4.3	7.2	7.4	7.5	7.4	7.6
PRVCON	77.3	3.8	8.6	7.9	7.7	7.9	7.9
FIXINV	31.7	3.0	3.0	3.0	3.0	3.0	3.0
GOVCON	13.3	3.7	6.1	6.0	6.1	6.0	6.0
EXPORTS	23.1	6.5	11.6	11.6	11.5	11.5	12.1
IMPORTS	−45.4	3.7	9.3	8.0	7.3	7.9	7.6

Source: CGE Model

the WTO. The GDP will experience an exceptional growth rate of 8% per year, roughly double that of the reference scenario, and we will observe an annual increase in private consumption of 7.3% per year, which implies an improvement in the well-being of the Lebanese population (Table 11.7).

11.6.3 Dynamic Trajectories of the Economy

To visualize the dynamic effects of trade liberalization, we present the trajectories of evolution of the main economic variables, namely imports, exports and GDP, to observe the adjustment of the Lebanese economy between 2010 and 2020.

Evolution of Imports
Greater trade openness creates a faster increase in imports, regardless of the scenario considered. However, the evolution of imports is more important when we take into account the dynamic improvement in total factor productivity. Scenario 4, combining the first three shocks, records the largest increase. The explanation lies in the opening of the market, resulting in increased imports of consumer goods and foreign intermediaries. These come to meet the needs of a growing domestic production not only turned to the domestic market, but also to the exports (Fig. 11.1).

Evolution of the Exports
Figure 11.2 traces the evolution of exports in the reference scenario and the four simulated scenarios. Isolated tariff reform or combined with an improved investment climate appears to induce a decline in the export

Table 11.7 Scenario 4: Annual growth rates in % (in volume)

S4	*Structure in % baseline*	*FTAEU*		*FT AALENAFT ACHINA FTATURKEY MULTI*			
GDPMP	100.0	4.7	7.6	7.7	7.8	7.7	8.0
PRVCON	77.3	3.0	8.1	7.4	7.1	7.4	7.3
FIXINV	31.7	6.0	6.0	6.0	6.0	6.0	6.0
GOVCON	13.3	3.7	6.3	6.2	6.3	6.2	6.1
EXPORTS	23.1	6.9	11.6	11.7	11.7	11.6	12.2
IMPORTS	−45.4	4.0	9.4	8.1	7.4	8.0	7.7

Source: CGE Model

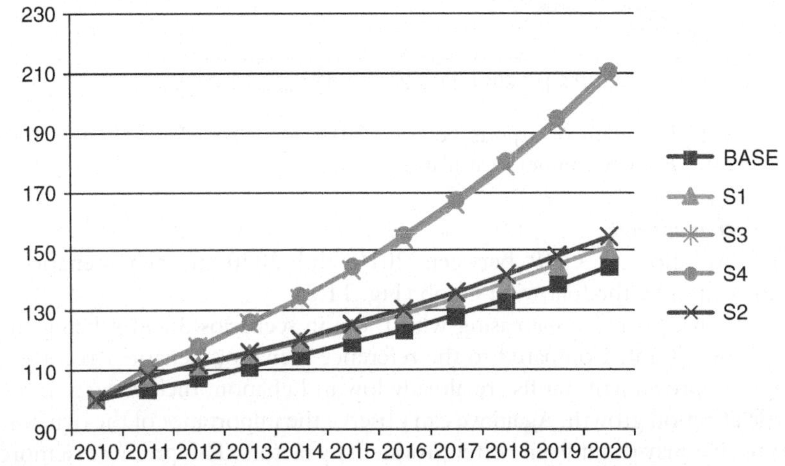

Fig. 11.1 Evolution of imports between 2010 and 2020 (Base 2010 = 100) (*Source*: CGE Model, author's calculations)

expansion rate in comparison with the counterfactual scenario. The change is much more marked and favorable when we take into account the improvement of factor productivity in scenario 3 and scenario 4. It strengthens the Lebanese productive base and the opportunity to benefit from new export opportunities.

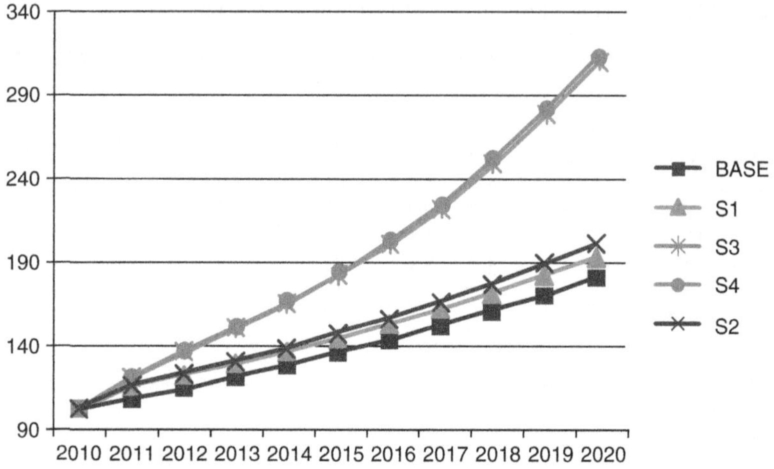

Fig. 11.2 Evolution of exports between 2010 and 2020 (Base 2010 = 100) (*Source*: CGE Model, author's calculations)

Evolution of GDP
The evolution of GDP between 2010 and 2020 in each scenario is represented by the following graph (Fig. 11.3).

The five paths are increasing with those in scenarios 3 and 4 being the most significant. Compared to the reference scenario, scenario 1 records a slight improvement; tariffs are already low in Lebanon, their reduction has little effect on growth. Again we can observe the importance of the dynamic gains that may result from better productivity factors. This promotes a more sustained economic growth.

11.6.4 *The Sectorial Impacts*

Table 11.8 shows the cumulative evolution of sectorial output in real terms and its deviation from the reference or baseline scenario in the four scenarios studied:

Although the sectorial effects are small, it remains that the examination of real GDP by sector shows that all sectors are experiencing an increase in their level of activity. This is the service sector, which already ranks first in the Lebanese economy, which recorded the highest increase (scenario 4), especially for transport and communications and trade. The industrial sector

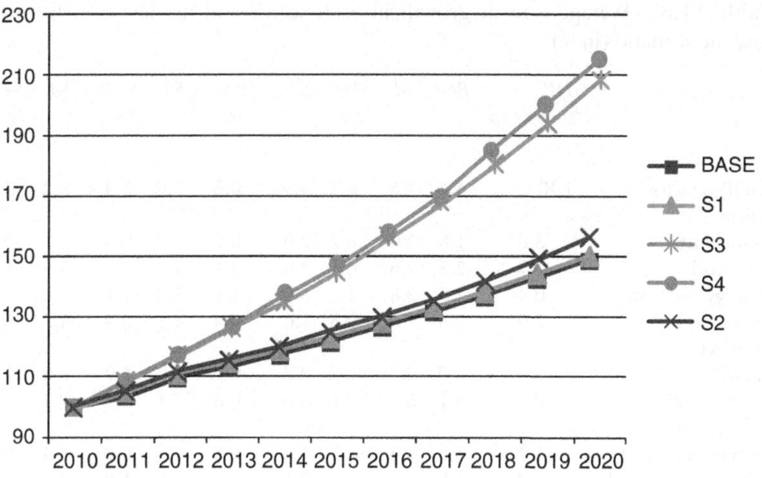

Fig. 11.3 Evolution of GDP between 2010 and 2020 (Base 2010 = 100) (*Source*: CGE Model, author's calculations)

knows in turn significant growth, particularly for food products and furniture.

The effects of the tariff reform simulated in the first scenario cause a small increase in agricultural growth rate compared to the baseline scenario, a more favorable growth in the industrial sector, and a small reduction in service sector growth. This observation reflects the fact that although the tariffs are already low, they are more pronounced in the agricultural sector. Their removal induced a resources reallocation from the most protected sector to the least protected sector, that is to say, towards the industrial sector, which knows the most marked expansion. The combination of an improved investment climate with tariff reform (scenario 2) mainly causes an improvement in the construction sector growth rate due to its strong reliance on investment. The result is a strengthening of the real annual growth rate of GDP in comparison with the baseline scenario. This is the third scenario, which assumes an increase in total factor productivity that records the highest growth gains. With the exception of construction, all sectors experienced an increase in production in comparison with the two other scenarios. The growth of the primary sector is less marked given its structural weakness. Both industrial and service sectors seem to be the more advantaged, recording exceptional growth rates. The resulting sectorial

Table 11.8 Average rate of growth in each sector and its deviation from the baseline scenario (in %)

	GDP structure in %	*Base*	*S1*	*S1 – base*	*S2*	*S2 – base*	*S3*	*S3 – base*	*S4*	*S4 – base*
GDP at factor prices	**100**	**4.4**	**4.5**	**0.1**	**4.9**	**0.5**	**7.9**	**3.4**	**8.2**	**3.7**
Agriculture	3.8	1.8	2.0	0.2	2.0	0.2	2.7	0.9	2.7	0.9
Livestock	1.1	2.5	2.6	0.1	2.6	0.1	3.5	1.0	3.5	1.0
Energy and water	0.4	2.7	3.8	1.1	3.8	1.1	3.8	1.1	3.8	1.1
Agro-food products	2.0	0.8	1.6	0.8	1.6	0.8	4.2	3.4	4.3	3.5
Textiles	0.8	3.0	3.7	0.7	3.7	0.7	6.0	2.9	6.0	2.9
Non-metallic minerals	0.9	5.1	5.7	0.6	5.6	0.5	7.4	2.2	7.4	2.2
Metals, machinery	1.1	3.6	4.4	0.8	4.4	0.8	4.4	0.8	4.4	0.8
Wood, rubber and chemistry	1.2	1.8	2.1	0.3	2.1	0.3	3.6	1.8	3.6	1.8
Furniture	0.4	7.1	8.9	1.7	8.7	1.5	10.2	2.9	10.0	2.7
Other branches	0.5	8.6	9.0	0.4	9.0	0.4	10.3	1.5	10.2	1.5
Construction	14.8	3.0	3.0	0.0	6.0	2.9	3.0	0.0	6.0	2.9
Transport and communications	5.3	9.4	9.9	0.4	10.0	0.5	13.7	4.0	13.8	4.0
Merchant service	32.5	4.4	4.4	0.0	4.4	0.0	7.6	3.0	7.5	3.0
Trade	26.0	4.7	4.7	0.0	4.7	0.0	10.7	5.8	10.7	5.7
Administration	*93*	*3.7*	*3.6*	*−0.1*	*3.6*	*−0.1*	*6.0*	*2.2*	*6.1*	*2.3*

Source: CGE Model, and author calculations

growth stimulated by the increase in factor productivity is a significant increase in GDP (7.9% per year), much higher than that of the first scenarios. Combined together in scenario 4, the sectors experienced similar average annual growth rate as the scenario 3, with no significant differences, registering an average annual increase of 8.1% of GDP over the considered period.

11.7 Conclusion

The simulation conducted using the computable general equilibrium model recursive dynamic was used to assess the medium- and long-term effects of further trade liberalization in Lebanon. Arguably, our results confirm that open trade promotes economic performance of a country. Whether through a simple tariff reform, or through the restructuring of the legal system in the form of an improved investment climate, or through the accumulation of dynamic gains from improved total factor productivity, it seems that Lebanon's accession to the WTO can be beneficial to the country. The tariff removal, causing export competitiveness boost causes a depreciation of the exchange rate thus stimulating exports. The effects on GDP and other macroeconomic variables are accentuated when combining the elimination of tariffs with increased investment (the construction sector will be the first recipient), or with an improvement in factor productivity.

To be admitted to this organization appears to achieve positive and more favorable results than remaining marginalized and outside the sphere of international trade. If the magnitude of effects and the nature of some of them depend on the envisaged macroeconomic adjustment process, we observe, however, many similarities between the results of the four simulations. The most important challenge concerns the capacity to enhance the productivity of factors, the latter stimulating the most significant results. The analysis of sectorial impacts identified that the agricultural sector remains the least favored because of its structural weakness and its initial high level of protection. The industrial sector recorded significant growth rate especially when we take into account the improved technological efficiency of products strengthening the Lebanese productive base. The examination of the impact on the services sector confirms the essential role played by this sector since the Lebanese economy seems to benefit most from such process, observation concluded from the analysis of its favorable evolution whatever the scenario considered. Nevertheless, we have to note that our quantitative analysis cannot answer alone the scale of the challenges facing Lebanon during its multilateral integration. These challenges are huge and increasingly complex with the socio-political and economic context within which Lebanon currently operates. Also, is it appropriate to note that our work provides only a provisional answer to the question of Lebanon's accession to the WTO and should not be considered as a prediction instrument, especially considering that the details of negotiations for membership are kept secret and are still ongoing. It is only a starting point for further analysis and can be completed later by richer work, overcoming the shortcomings of quantitative models and benefiting from more completed and updated macroeconomic and microeconomic data when they become available.

References

Balassa, B. (1985). Exports, policy choices, and economic growth in developing countries after the 1973 oil shock. *Journal of Development Economics, 18*, 23–35.

Balding, C. (2010). Joining the World Trade Organization: What is the impact? *Review of International Economics, 18*(1), 193–206.

Bhagwati, J., & Srinivasan, T. (2002). Trade and poverty in poor countries. *The American Economic Review, 92*(2), 180–183.

Cling, J. P. (2006). Commerce, croissance, pauvreté et inégalités dans les PED: une revue de littérature. Développement Institutions et Analyses de Long terme, DIAL. Document de travail DT 2006–07.

Cling, J. P., Razafindrakoto, M., & Roubaud, F. (2009). Vietnam's WTO accession and export-led growth. *International Economics, 118*, 5–12.

Corm, G. (2012). *Le Liban contemporain: Histoire et Société.* Paris: La découverte.

Dagher, A. (2005). *Quelle politique industrielle pour le Liban? Une approche différente du rôle de l'Etat dans l'économie.* Beirut, Lebanon: LCPS.

Dollar, D., & Kray, A. (2001). *Growth is good for the poor.* Policy research working paper no. 2587, World Bank.

Edwards, S. (1991). *Trade orientation, distortions and growth in developing countries.* NBER working paper no. 3716, National Bureau of Economic Research.

Feder, G. (1983). On exports and economic growth. *Journal of Development Economics, 12*(1–2), 59–73.

Gowa, J., & Kim, S. Y. (2005). An exclusive country club: The effects of the GATT on trade, 1950–94. *World Politics, 57*(4), 453–478.

Hoekman, B., & Mavroidis, P. (2002). *Economic development, competition policy, and the World Trade Organization.* Policy research working paper no. 2917, World Bank.

IMF. (2013). *World economic outlook.* IMF Database. https://www.imf.org/external/pubs/ft/weo/2013/02/weodata/index.aspx

IMF. (2014). *Lebanon.* IMF country report no. 14/237, International Monetary Fund.

Lautier, M. (2013). Le développement des échanges internationaux de services de santé: Perspectives des exportations en Afrique du Nord. *ADBF.* Note Economique, African Development Bank Group.

Mage-Bertomeu, S. (2006). Les modèles d'équilibre général appliqué à la politique commerciale: développements récents. *Revue d'économiepolitique, 116*, 357–381.

Michaely, M. (1977). Exports and growth. *Journal of Development Economics, 4*, 49–53.

Punt, C. (2004). *The organisation of trade data for inclusion in social accounting matrix.* Technical paper series no. 2, Provide Project.

Rodriguez, F., & Rodrik, D. (2001). Trade policy and economic growth: A Skeptic's guide to the cross-national evidence. In B. Bernanke & K. Rogoff (Eds.), *NBER macroeconomics annual 2000.* Cambridge: MIT Press.

Rodrik, D. (2001). Trading in illusions. *Foreign Policy, 123*, 54–62.

Rodrik, D. (2006). Goodbye Washington consensus, hello Washington confusion? A review of the world banks economic growth in the 1990s: Learning from a decade of reform. *Journal of Economic Literature, 44*(4), 973–987.

Rose, A. (2004). Do we really know that the WTO increases trade? *The American Economic Review, 94*(1), 98–114.

Round, J. (1981, March). *Income distribution within a social accounting matrix: A review of some experience in Malaysia and other LDCs.* Discussion paper no. 3, Development Economics Research Centre, University of Warwick.

Round, J. (2003). Constructing SAMs for development policy analysis: Lessons learned and challenges ahead. *Economic Systems Research, 15*(2), 161–183.

Shehadi, N., & Mills, D. H. (1988). *Lebanon: A history of conflict.* Lebanon: The Center for Lebanese Studies.

Stiglitz, J. (1998). *Towards a new paradigm for development: Strategies, policies, and processes.* Geneva: Prebisch Lecture at UNCTAD.

Subramanian, A., & Wei, S.-J. (2006). The WTO promotes trade, strongly but unevenly. *Journal of International Economics, 72*(1), 151–175.

Syrquin, M. & Chenery, H. B. (1989). *Patterns of development, 1950 to 1983.* World Bank discussion paper no. 41.

Thurlow, J. (2008). *A recursive dynamic CGE model and microsimulation poverty module for South Africa.* Washington, D.C.: International Food Policy Research Institute.

Thurlow, J., & Seventer, V. D. (2002). *A standard computable general equilibrium model for South Africa.* Trade and macroeconomics discussion paper no. 100, International Food Policy Research Institute, Washington, DC.

Tomz, M., Goldtsein, R., & Rivers, D. (2007). Do we really know that the WTO increases trade? Comment. *The American Economic Review, 97*(5), 2005–2018.

Williamson, J. (1990). *Latin American adjustment: How much has happened?* Washington, DC: Institute for International Economics.

World Bank. (1987). *Rapport sur le développement dans le monde 1987.* Washington, DC: Oxford University Press pour la Banque Mondiale.

CHAPTER 12

Goods Trade Liberalization Under Canada-India FTA and Its Impact: Partial and General Equilibrium Analysis

Somesh K. Mathur, Rahul Arora, and Mayank Tripathi

12.1 Introduction

The negotiations for Canada-India FTA started in November 2010 and since then nine rounds of negotiations have been completed. The latest round of negotiation focused on the Canada-India CEPA, which includes both good and services trade. Progress has been made in all agreed areas of the negotiations, including market access of goods, rule of origin, trade facilitation, origin procedures, technical barriers to trade, sanitary and phytosanitary measures, institutional provisions, and trade in service, including temporary entry for business persons, telecommunications and financial services. Both of the countries eagerly want to conclude this FTA. A joint study suggests that the CEPA could increase bilateral trade by 50 percent and boost the gross domestic product of each country by $ 6 billion. The

S.K. Mathur (✉)
Indian Institute of Technology Kanpur, Kanpur, India

R. Arora
Consumer Unity & Trust Society (CUTS) International, Jaipur, India

M. Tripathi
Academic Associate, Indian Institute of Management-Ahmedabad, Ahmedabad, India

S.K. Mathur et al. (eds.), *Theorizing International Trade*,
https://doi.org/10.1007/978-981-10-1759-9_12

recent meeting of the prime ministers of India and Canada is one step forward towards better and enhanced trade relations.

The business environment is changing in India. International agencies including the World Bank and International Monetary Fund (IMF) rated India as a fastest growing economy. Canada has the raw material and India is promoting its manufacturing sector and infrastructure sector. So there is huge opportunity for bilateral trade between India and Canada. The trade data reveals that infrastructure has always been a priority in India, followed by goods and services, automotive, healthcare and ICT. Canada has been recognized for its expertise in architectural and engineering services and plans to invest in the infrastructure segment, which can surely contribute towards India's economic growth and will increase the pace of growth in the construction front. India's auto sector is also growing rapidly—going from 1.5 million automobiles exported in 2009–2010 to more than 3 million in 2013–2014. The spur in the growth of the automobile sector absolutely matches with expertise in vehicle assembly line of Canada, which has been a greatest beneficiary of Indo-Canada trade in the recent past. India is a major potential market for Canadian agriculture and agro-food products. Currently, India has food tariff policies and non-tariff barriers, which limit trade and growth of Canadian agriculture and its agro-food sector. A successful trade agreement with India would allow Canadian farmers to more fully benefit from a growing large market and Indian consumers to benefit from high-quality and lower-priced Canadian products.

The service sector is the other area where Canada has untapped opportunity. India is a services-based economy, and its growing middle class is rapidly expanding its demand for high-value services, such as insurance and telecommunications. Not only is India a massive market, it is moving toward more openness to international firms. Moreover, Indian demand and areas of openness align with Canadian expertise. Services have been Canada's fastest-growing export sector in the past decade.

In investment terms, India is a small part of Canada's destination for foreign direct investment (FDI), registering less than 1 percent of Canada's total FDI outflow. In 2005, Canadian FDI in India made it to the 46th position, only contributing to 0.04 percent of total Canadian FDI abroad. A decade later things have improved and the position has significantly jumped. The trends depict that during April 2000–2014 (up to September 2014) the cumulative FDI flows into India were Rs. 1,132,170.60 crores (US$ 232.27 billion). Out of this, FDI inflows from Canada (which ranks 26th) are Rs. 2,436.73 crores (US$ 0.51 billion), which represents 0.22 percent of the cumulative inflows received. Canada showed interest in investing its pension funds in India. There are several opportunities for Canadian investors in India, such as developing 100 smart cities, 100,000 megawatts of solar power, and 60,000 megawatts of wind power by 2022, providing vocational training to 400 million people, building general industrial corridors, coal gasification, underground mining of coal, hydrocarbon sector and high-speed trains. Recently Canada agreed to supply 3000 metric tonnes of uranium to energy-hungry India under a $ 254 million five-year deal to power Indian reactors.

12.1.1 *Objectives of the Study*

On the basis of preceding complementarities, one can intuitively say that it will be a win-win situation for both of these countries if they tie in a broad trade agreement. The present study is an attempt to verify this intuition with the help of ex-ante evaluation of agreement FTA between Canada and India. The main objective of the study is to evaluate the impact of the proposed Canada-India FTA on member and non-member countries. The study is expected to provide new reflections and updated figures on the potential economic benefits of a Canada-India FTA on South Asian countries, TPP member countries, EU25 members, Canada and India. The study works out the economic and welfare effects of trade liberalization using the partial (SMART) and general equilibrium (GTAP) approaches. The study has also evaluated the trade profiles of both of the countries and found out their specialized products along with markets at various levels of disaggregation using UN Commodity Trade Statistics data in World Integrated Trade Solutions (WITS) using various trade indices. It is expected that the study would form a guideline for negotiators in detailing the proposed Canada-India FTA. To pursue the whole task, the study has been divided into six sections including the present introductory one. Section 12.2 presents the trade profile of both of the countries with the help of calculating various trade indicators. Sections 12.3 and 12.4 consist of empirical analysis pertaining to the partial and general equilibrium analyses. Section 12.5 explains in detail the other contentious issues related to the integration between both of the countries. It also highlights the limitations of the present study and suggests scope for future research. The final Sect. 12.6 concludes the whole study with some suggested policy implications.

Table 12.1 Bilateral product trade Canada–India

In million Canadian dollar		
Year	*Exports*	*Imports*
2011	2628.71	2533.83
2012	2360.67	2856.54
2013	2800.46	2976.49
2014	3224.62	3181.22
2015	4316.75	3944.79

Source: www.canadainternational.gc.ca/—Foreign Affairs, Trade and Development Ministry, Canada

12.2 Trade Profile of India and Canada

Trade between India and Canada has been increasing and holds huge opportunities for the future. Between 2011 and 2015, compound annual growth rate (CAGR) was 14 percent for Canadian exports to India and 12 percent for Indian exports to Canada (see Table 12.1).

In 2015, exports from India to Canada were highest in textiles (C$ 743 million) followed by chemical products (C$ 615 million), mechanical and electrical products (C$ 476 million), base metal production (C$ 366 million), vegetable products (C$ 312 million), mineral products (C$ 289 million) and precious metals/stones (C$ 266 million). Exports from Canada to India were highest in vegetable products (C$ 1.5 billion) followed by precious metals/stones (C$ 558 million), mineral products (C$ 532 million), chemical products (C$ 442 million), paper products (C$ 439 million) and mechanical and electrical products (C$ 290 million).

12.2.1 Calculation of Specialized Products

The study follows the method suggested by Balassa (1965) for the purpose of calculation of Revealed Comparative Advantage (RCA) Index.[1] In the available literature, this method has been widely used to see the comparative advantage of economies. This index has been calculated product-wise to check the comparative advantageous products of both of the countries. The study calculated RCA index for both countries at the HS 2-digit, 4-digit and 6-digit levels of product classification and looked for the product in case the value of RCA was greater than one. For RCA calculation, we considered start year 2013 and end year 2014 with India and Canada as reporter countries and the world as a partner region. We see the comparative advantage at end year for each product.

In case of India, at HS 2-digit, there are 40 products in which India had RCA > 1 in 2013. Out of these, in product code 13 (Lac, Gums, Resins and Other Vegetable Saps and Ext), India has the largest comparative advantage, but the compound annual growth rate is negative. The compound annual growth rate is highest in product code 88 (Aircraft, Spacecraft and Parts). India's specialized products are vegetables, food production, chemicals, plastics, hide skins, textile clothing, footwear, stone glass and metals (see Appendix Table 12.18 for 40 specialized products of India). At HS 4-digit, India has comparative advantage in 345 products. The highest comparative advantage is in product code 0501 (Human hair, un-worked, whether or not washed) but comes with negative compound annual growth rate. The compound annual growth rate is highest in product code 9705 (Collections and collectors' pieces of zoological). Finally, at HS 6-digit level, there are total 1387 products in which India has comparative advantage.[2]

In the case of Canada, at HS 2-digit, there are 29 such products for which the value of RCA is greater than one. The highest comparative advantage is in product code 75 (Nickel and Articles) with positive compound annual growth rate. The compound annual growth rate is highest in product code 01 (Live Animals). Canada's Specialized Products are vegetables, animals, food production, minerals, woods and metals, among others (see Appendix Table 12.19 for all the 29 products). At HS 4-digit level of classification, Canada has comparative advantage in 235 products. The highest comparative advantage is in product code 4705 (Wood pulp obtained by a combination of mechanical) but negative compound annual growth rate. The compound annual growth rate is highest in product code 2604 (Nickel ores and Concentrates). Further, at HS 6-digit level, Canada has comparative advantage in 820 products. Table 12.2 summarizes the analysis by working out RCA for various aggregated product groups for India and Canada in 2014.

12.2.2 *Calculation of Trade Intensity and Complementarity*[3]

Trade Intensity

Trade intensity indicates whether a reporter exports more, as a percentage, to a partner than the world does on average. It is measured as country *i*'s

Table 12.2 RCA for various aggregated product groups for India and Canada in 2014

Product code	*India RCA*	*Canada RCA*
01–05_Animal	3.67	0.52
06–15_Vegetable	2.76	7.07
16–24_FoodProd	0.74	0.12
25–26_Minerals	0.78	2.65
27–27_Fuels	0	0.46
28–38_Chemicals	1.88	1.21
39–40_PlastiRub	0.8	0.2
41–43_HidesSkin	4.09	0.01
44–49_Wood	0.29	4.04
50–63_TextCloth	11.74	0.33
64–67_Footwear	2.98	0.06
68–71_StoneGlas	2.59	0.46
72–83_Metals	1.71	0.57
84–85_MachElec	0.46	0.32
86–89_Transport	0.11	1.19
90–99_Miscellan	0.28	0.34

Source: Authors' calculation in WITS

export to country *j* relative to its total exports divided by the world's exports to country *j* relative to the world's total exports. This index is calculated at HS 6-digit level of product classification. In the calculation of Trade Intensity Index (TII), India merchandise reaching Canada, we considered reporter as India, partner as Canada and took years as 2013 and 2014. In the case of India, the value of the Index is 27.49 for 2013 and 27.08 for 2014. It seems that there is decline in trade intensity index in year 2014 in comparison with year 2013. In the case of Canada, the resulting index is 30.89 for 2012, 37.09 for 2013 and 35.82 for 2014. It seems that first index increased for year 2012–2013 then decreased for year 2013–2014. From the results, we can conclude that the value of TII of Canada is greater than India for both years 2013 and 2014. Table 12.3 summarizes the results by working out TII for various aggregated products for year 2014. The relative low scores for each country show potential of trade between India and Canada. The higher relative value of TII than its partner shows its potential for exports to the trading partner.

Trade Complementarity Index

To measure the degree of matching between export patterns of one partner with the import patterns of the other, Trade Complementarity Index (TCI)

Table 12.3 Trade Intensity Index (TII) for various aggregated product codes in 2014

Product code	*India TII*	*Canada TII*
01–05_Animal	74.1	17.13
06–15_Vegetable	42.84	122.39
16–24_FoodProd	32.05	10.74
25–26_Minerals	23.11	110.12
27–27_Fuels	0.07	7.82
28–38_Chemicals	42.65	61.64
39–40_PlastiRub	39.62	7.14
41–43_HidesSkin	54.11	2.17
44–49_Wood	30.32	94.75
50–63_TextCloth	70.12	56.45
64–67_Footwear	51.27	5.77
68–71_StoneGlas	21.07	15.86
72–83_Metals	55.23	15.75
84–85_MachElec	29.83	30.49
86–89_Transport	2.96	19.97
90–99_Miscellan	27.14	26.76

Source: Authors' calculation in WITS

has been utilized. High value of this index indicates that two countries would stand to gain from increased trade, and may be particularly useful in evaluating prospective bilateral or regional trade agreements. The calculation is done at the HS 6-digit level of product classification. In the case of India, we considered reporter as India and partner as Canada for the years 2013 and 2014. The resulting index is 54.81 for 2013 and 55.25 for 2014. It shows increase in TII in year 2014 than year 2013. For Canada, we considered reporter as Canada, partner as India for the years 2012, 2013 and 2014. The index value is 30.89 for 2012, 37.09 for 2013 and 35.82 for 2014. Like its TII, Canada's TCI also first increased for year 2012–2013 then decreased for year 2013–2014. Overall, the TCI of India is greater than Canada for both the years 2013 and 2014. Hence, we can conclude that India may be more benefitted by exporting more to Canada after the conclusion of the free trade agreement.

12.3 SMART Analysis: A Partial Equilibrium Approach

SMART tool in WITS can be used to anticipate the likely economic effects of various trade policy alternatives. It allows us to investigate the impact of preferential trade reforms at home or abroad on various variables such as trade flows (imports and exports volumes, trade creation and trade diversion), tariff revenue, economic welfare and world prices.[4] While simulating different scenarios, it assumes that products from different countries are imperfect substitutes by automatically setting import demand elasticity to 1.5. On the other hand, it assumes infinite export elasticity, that is, export supplies are perfectly elastic, which implies that world prices of each variety of products are given. Specialized products of India and Canada worked out using RCA index used for simulations using SMART model under different tariff-reduction scenarios. This tool is included in the WITS software developed by the World Bank to produce aggregate statistics and to simulate the impact of tariff changes on country-wide variables.

12.3.1 Empirical Results

The study carried out two-sided simulations that account for the reciprocity in tariff liberalization. Two types of scenarios have been defined for simulation purposes: In the first category, full liberalization has been assumed on all products and in the second, full liberalization has been assumed on specialized products of the exporting country. Here, the term full liberalization means that the complete elimination of import tariffs, that is, the new rate of import tariffs becomes zero. For the simulations, data for the year 2013 has been utilized. The results given in Table 12.4 show that India gains more than Canada in terms of welfare effect, consumer surplus and total trade effects (sum of trade creation and trade diversion effect) when the Canadian products (all or specialized ones) enter India after adopting the policy of free trade by India. The magnitude of the changes for this reciprocal liberalization is given below.

Further, the study has worked out the trade diversion effect under all simulation scenarios and the results have been reported in Table 12.5. The broad results indicate that when India liberalizes its trade with Canada (makes zero tariffs for products coming from Canada), countries that would see substantial trade diversion (shift of trade from non-member to member countries) would be Australia, Russia and the United States, among others. On the other hand, when Canada liberalizes its trade with India, most of the trade diversion would happen in China and small Asian economies such as Bangladesh and Pakistan, among others. The table shows the magnitude of the trade diversion impact.

Table 12.4 Impact of full reciprocal trade liberalization of India and Canada under the proposed free trade agreement using SMART

In 1000 USD

Simulation scenario	*Imports before tariff reduction*	*Welfare effect*	*Total trade effect*	*Trade creation*	*Trade diversion*	*Price effect*
Canadian total products enter India after India reduces tariff rates to zero (97 in number and at 2-digit level of disaggregation)	452,213,663	74,169	682,115	417,514	264,602	0
Canadian specialized products enter India after India reduces tariff rates to zero (29 in number and at 2-digit level disaggregation)	310,728,920	47,900	276,655	188,277	88,378	0
Indian total products enter Canada after Canada reduces tariff rates to zero (97 in number and at 2-digit level disaggregation)	453,342,391	9411	229,070	113,341	115,729	0
Indian specialized products enter Canada after Canada reduces tariff rates to zero (40 in number in number and at 2-digit level disaggregation)	144,218,579	8426	188,616	91,993	96,622	0

Source: Authors' calculations in WITS using SMART. Price effect is zero as we assume the importing country to be a small economy that cannot have an impact on world prices (terms of trade)

12.4 GTAP Analysis: A General Equilibrium Approach[5]

The Global Trade Analysis Project (GTAP) model is a static multi-region general equilibrium model that divides the whole economy into various agents' dependent upon each other. It is static in nature in the sense that it provides a comparison of the state of the economy before and after changing the value of shock variable and its impact on economy-wide variables. The framework of this model is provided under the GTAP, which was started in 1992 to facilitate the researchers working in the area of quantitative analysis

Table 12.5 Trade diversion for selected partners under different complete reciprocal liberalization scenarios

(In 1000 US dollars)							
Simulation scenario	**Australia**	**Russia**	**US**	**China**		**Germany**	
Canadian total products enter India after India reduces tariff rates to zero (97 in number and at 2-digit level disaggregation)	−29,126	−40,675	−52,941	−12,021		−10,323	
Simulation scenario	**Australia**	**Russia**	**US**	**China**		**France**	
Canadian specialized products enter India after India reduces tariff rates to zero (29 in number and at 2-digit level disaggregation)	−22,069	−21,525	-34,778	−702		-3024	
Simulation scenario	**Cambodia**	**Pakistan**	**US**	**China**	**Turkey**	**Bangladesh**	**Macao**
Indian total products enter Canada after Canada reduces tariff rates to zero (97 in number and at 2-digit level disaggregation)	−3859	−4114	−18,226	−48,234	−2023	−11,031	−2956
Simulation scenario	**Cambodia**	**Pakistan**	**US**	**China**	**Vietnam**	**Bangladesh**	**Macao**
Indian specialized products enter Canada after Canada reduces tariff rates to zero (40 in number in number and at 2-digit level disaggregation)	−3860	−4072	−7655	−43,851	−3534	−11,012	−2286

Source: Authors' calculations in WITS using SMART

of international trade. Under this project, a fully documented database, the GTAP database, is also provided, which gives economy-wide data of all 140 defined regions of the world. The analysis of trade liberalization and its impact on economy-wide variables among countries are the main research application of this project. It also provides the software, a tool to implement the GTAP model using data from the GTAP database.

The present study has used the GTAP database version 9 provided by Purdue University in Indiana, US. It is the most suited available database used for the purpose of general equilibrium analysis that provides data for three reference years: 2004, 2007 and 2011. The whole database is the reflection of world economy and consists of data on all-important macro-economic variables such as output, employment, wages, prices and welfare. For the analysis purpose, all 140 GTAP regions of the world have been aggregated into seven regions (see Table 12.6). Similarly, the total 57 GTAP sectors have been aggregated into 10 new sectors (see Table 12.7). The trade flows across these commodities are distinguished by their origin and are based on agents such as intermediate demand, final demand by private households, government and investment.

For the analysis purpose, two main scenarios have been defined. The first scenario assumes the elimination of import tariffs by India on all products coming from Canada and the second scenario assumes the complete elimination of import tariffs by Canada on all products coming from India. The results have been reported in Tables 12.8, 12.9, 12.10, 12.11, 12.12, 12.13, 12.14, 12.15, 12.16 and 12.17.

Table 12.8 shows the GTAP simulation results in terms of changes in value of GDP, changes in trade balance and in terms of welfare change for all regions considered in this study under the assumption that all Canadian products (GTAP Aggregated Products) entering India at zero rate of import tariffs.

Table 12.6 Regional aggregation

S.N.	*Aggregated region*
1.	India
2.	Canada
3.	China
4.	TPP[a]
5.	EU
6.	South Asia[b]
7.	Rest of the world

Notes: [a]Excludes Canada; [b]Excluding India

Source: Authors' elaboration from GTAP-9 database

Table 12.7 GTAP product classification

Aggregated product	*GTAP sector*
Grains and crops	Paddy rice
	Wheat
	Cereal grains nec (other grains)
	Vegetables, fruit, nuts
	Oil seeds
	Sugar cane, sugar beet (cane and beet)
	Plant-based fibers
	Crops nec (other crops)
	Processed rice
Livestock and meat products	Bovine cattle, sheep and goats, horses
	Animal products nec (other animal products)
	Raw milk
	Wool, silk-worm cocoons
	Bovine meat products (cattle meat)
	Meat products nec (other meat)
Extraction	Forestry
	Fishing
	Coal
	Oil
	Gas
	Minerals nec (other mining)
Processed food	Vegetable oils and fats
	Dairy products (milk)
	Sugar
	Food products nec (other food)
	Beverages and tobacco products
Textiles	Textiles
	Wearing apparel
Light manufacturing	Leather products
	Wood products (lumber)
	Paper products, publishing (paper and paper products)
	Metal products (fabricated metal products)
	Motor vehicles and parts
	Transport equipment nec (other transport equipment)
	Manufactures nec
Heavy manufacturing	Petroleum, coal products
	Chemical, rubber, plastic products
	Mineral products nec (non-metallic minerals)
	Ferrous metals (iron and steel)
	Metals nec (non-ferrous metals)
	Electronic equipment
	Machinery and equipment nec

(*continued*)

Table 12.7 (continued)

Aggregated product	*GTAP sector*
Utility and construction	Electricity
	Gas manufacture, distribution (gas distribution)
	Water
	Construction
Transport and communication	Trade
	Transport nec (other transport)
	Water transport
	Air transport
	Communication
Other services	Financial services nec (other financial intermediation)
	Insurance (insurance)
	Business services nec (other business services)
	Recreational and other services
	Public administration, defense, education, health (other services (government))
	Dwellings

Source: Authors' elaboration from GTAP-9 database

Table 12.8 clearly indicates that Canada, India and the European Union would gain in terms of welfare while TPP, South Asia, China and ROW would lose due to negative welfare effect. India's welfare is USD 353 million while that of Canada is approximately USD 298 million. We have also observed positive percentage change in value of GDP for Canada while having negative change in value of GDP for India and South Asia. Canada and India would see the negative trade balance while TPP, South Asia, EU25, China and ROW gains in terms of changes in trade balance due to Canadian products entering India. The negative trade balance may be having negative impact on change in value of GDP in India.

Table 12.9 shows the results of welfare decomposition among various regional groups due to Canadian products entering India without any import tariff. India would see an improvement in allocative efficiency, decline in terms of trade and decline in investment and savings summing to positive total change in welfare in terms of equivalent variation. On the other hand, Canada would see a negative allocative efficiency, positive terms of trade, negative investment and savings summing up to positive total welfare. In the comparative static model, we keep population, technology

Table 12.8 Impact on welfare, changes in trade balance and changes in value of GDP
Scenario: Indian liberalization with all Canadian products entering India

Region	*Vgdp (% change)*	*Changes in trade balance (Million USD)*	*Welfare in terms of EV (Million USD)*
Canada	0.09	−138.05	298.20
India	−0.07	−132.27	352.19
TPP	0	144.22	−112.69
South Asia	−0.03	5.71	−8.85
EU25	0	81.33	6.72
China	0	7.60	−40.69
ROW	0	31.46	−7.24

Source: GTAP simulation results

Table 12.9 Welfare decomposition (Million USD) when all products from Canada enters India

Region	*Allocative efficiency (a)*	*Terms of trade (b)*	*Investment-savings (c)*	*Total welfare (a + b + c)*
Canada	−26.2	329	−4.33	298
India	505	−129	−24.00	352
TPP	2.33	−124	9.19	−113
South Asia	−1.03	−385	−3.97	−8.85
EU25	2.13	2.64	1.99	6.76
China	−4.15	−9.00	6.02	−7.23
ROW	9.12	−65.6	15.9	−40.6
Total	488	−.095	0.736	488

Source: GTAP simulation results

and endowments fixed, so the only way to increase welfare is to reduce excess burden arising from existing distortions. Changes in allocative efficiency are directly related to tax or tax changes interacting with equilibrium quantities changes. Thus, policy simulations result in changes in real income due to change in endowments net of depreciation (usually comes zero in a comparative static model), tax on output of any good, tax on use of endowment and intermediate input of any industry, tax on private household consumption and government consumption, export-import taxes,

Table 12.10 Impact on welfare, trade balance and changes in value of GDP Scenario: Canadian liberalization with all Indian products entering Canada

Region	*Vgdp (percentage change)*	*Changes in trade balance in million US dollar*	*Welfare in terms of EV (in million US dollars millions)*
Canada	−01	−21.66	22.06
India	0.06	−39.78	146.49
TPP	0	37.20	−34.54
South Asia	−0.01	6.93	−9.04
EU25	0	113.45	−24.09
China	0	−7.86	−24.74
ROW	0	11.76	−22.77

Source: GTAP simulations

changes in regional terms of trade and change in relative price of savings and investment (Huff and Hertel 2000).

This would improve welfare gain, as it would increase the level of taxed activity by relocating commodity and endowment from low-value use to high-value use. Goods that yield trade tax would be beneficial for economy. If the export prices post-liberalization rise more than import prices that would contribute positively to the society even though investment doesn't contribute in regional utility as saving does, but it does generate current income.

Table 12.10 shows the impact on welfare on different regions when all products from India enter Canada under complete liberalization. The results reveal that India and Canada would gain from increase in welfare to the tune of USD 146 million while Canada would gain in welfare to the tune of USD 22 million. Negative welfare figure for the other regions shows the loss in welfare under the assumed policy change between Canada and India. Canada and India have negative change in trade balance while TPP, South Asia, EU and ROW have positive change in trade balance. India sees an increase in change in value of GDP in percentage (0.06 percentage points), Canada sees a marginal decline in GDP. The reason we see a larger positive change in welfare for India under both the scenarios of complete liberalization is that India's average tariff rates are greater than Canadian average tariff rates (see Appendices 12.20 and 12.21 for the product-wise tariff rates).

Table 12.11 Welfare decomposition of total welfare (Million USD) in different regions when all products from India enters Canada

Region	*Allocative efficiency (a)*	*Terms of trade (b)*	*Investment-savings (c)*	*Total welfare (EV) (a + b + c)*
Canada	37.6	−15.4	−124	22.1
India	31.3	95.8	19.4	146
TPP	−2.32	−21.3	−10.9	−34.5
South Asia	−0.919	−6.22	−1.90	−9.04
EU25	−6.27	−13.6	−4.23	−24.1
China	−158	−24.7	−1.53	−24.7
ROW	−4.40	−14.6	−3.77	−22.8
Total	53.4	0	0	53.4

Source: GTAP simulation results

Table 12.11 decomposes total welfare into allocative efficiency, terms of trade and investment saving effects resulting from complete liberalization undertaken by Canada on all products coming into Canada from India. The results show an increase in allocative efficiency in both Canada and India. Terms of trade in Canada are negative while they are positive for India. Investment saving is positive for India, but negative for Canada. Total welfare is negative for TPP, EU, ROW and China because of negative allocative efficiency, terms of trade and investment savings.

Table 12.12 shows the changes in product-wise trade balance for complete liberalization undertaken by Canada for products coming from India. Canada shows negative change in trade balance in sectors of processed food, mining and extraction, and textiles and apparel while India, through its exports, would see an increase in trade balance in these same three sectors, with larger improvement in trade balance of textiles and apparel. India would see negative change in trade balance (exports minus imports) in sectors like light and heavy manufacturing, transport and communications, utility and construction and other services. India would also see a negative change in trade balance in the sectors of grains and crops and livestock and meat products.

Table 12.13 shows changes in product-wise trade balances in different regions when India does complete liberalization of products coming into India from Canada. Canada shows massive increase in trade balance of grains and crops, while India shows a negative change in this sector. All sectors in India except grains and crops, light manufacturing and mining

Table 12.12 Changes in trade balance (DTBAL) product wise (Million USD) under all products coming into Canada from India

Sector	*Canada*	*India*	*TPP*	*South Asia*	*EU25*	*China*	*ROW*
Grains and crops	1.89	−23.67	4.53	3.39	2.48	6.24	6.35
Livestock and meat products	0.91	−5.51	1.14	0.22	.03	2	1.40
Mining and extraction	−4.58	10.10	−1.23	−.61	3.26	−6.45	.24
Processed food	−8	7.03	−4.13	1.84	−1.86	2.08	2.40
Textile and wearing apparel	−57.27	343.89	−95.54	−11.33	−20.69	−114	−46.34
Light manufacturing	19.29	−49.38	4.37	2.46	−6.02	20.09	.69
Heavy manufacturing	16.98	−178.80	71.02	6.07	−3.59	69.7	17.89
Utility and construction	.60	−3.59	1.55	0.30	−.05	0.67	0.52
Transport and communication	2.58	−36.69	16.08	1.66	7.52	5.89	6.09
Other services	5.94	−103.15	39.40	2.93	32.36	0.6	16.33

Source: GTAP simulation results

Table 12.13 Changes in trade balance (DTBAL) product wise (Million USD) under all products coming into India from Canada

Sector	*Canada*	*India*	*TPP*	*South Asia*	*EU25*	*China*	*ROW*
Grains and crops	570.94	−353.20	−22	−29.54	−9.53	−4.93	−192.77
Livestock and meat products	−95.76	24.93	44.13	0.44	3.22	5.38	19.55
Mining and extraction	−17.30	−36.12	−1.48	0.69	2.07	−.32	−11.14
Processed food	−59.26	64.85	−2.05	1.15	−7.27	1.83	1.32
Textile and wearing apparel	−24.82	139.76	−24.08	19.81	−47.68	−45.94	−21.10
Light manufacturing	−198.96	−32.30	110.39	2.57	19.60	40.70	43.69
Heavy manufacturing	−76.53	21.58	−35.58	3.70	8.38	−2.39	68.78
Utility and construction	−11.27	1.16	1.88	0.16	1.17	0.22	6.66
Transport and communication	−72.18	23.67	32.07	2.63	66.01	10.27	70.13
Other services	−152.91	13.41	40.94	4.09	45.35	2.79	46.34

Source: GTAP simulation results

Table 12.14 Sectoral changes in India when all Canadian products (GTAP classification) enters India

Sector	*Sectoral output before simulation shock of reducing tariffs to zero (Million USD)*	*Sectoral output after simulation shock of reducing tariffs to zero (Million USD)*	*Change in sectoral output*	*Percentage change*
Grains and crops	206,070.58	205,478.03	−592.528	−0.29
Meat and livestock products	76,313.79	76,375.86	62.07	.08
Mining and extraction	62,849.53	62,856.65	7.12	0.01
Processed food	113,105.61	113,282.32	176.71	0.16
Textiles and wearing apparel	7,479,281	75,018.27	225.45	0.30
Light manufacturing	181,356.78	181,362.28	5.50	0.00
Heavy manufacturing	463,867.34	463,995.66	128.31	0.03
Utility and construction	325,610.22	3,255,673.31	63.09	0.02
Transport and communication	448,832.31	449,051.31	219	0.05
Other services	402,960.94	403,055.04	94.13	0.02
CGDS	424,268.44	424,413.34	144.91	0.03

Source: GTAP simulation results

and extraction show increase in trade balance due to Canadian products coming into India. Canada, on the other hand, shows all negative increase in trade balance in all sectors except grains and crops.

Table 12.14 shows sectoral changes in industry in India due to Canadian products entering India. Again, we observe that grains and crops is the only sector that gets impacted negatively in India in comparison with all products (including the capital goods sector, CGDS, which shows positive change). If India is to think of full liberalization under the Canada-India FTA, it needs to protect its agriculture sector or think of liberalization of all sectors except the agricultural sector at the beginning. Special safeguard mechanisms, as discussed in the recent Nairobi Ministerial meeting of the WTO,

Table 12.15 Sectoral changes in Canada when all Indian products enters Canada

Sector	*Sectoral output before simulation shock of reducing tariffs to zero (Million USD)*	*Sectoral output after simulation shock of reducing tariffs to zero (Million USD)*	*Change in sectoral output*	*Percentage change*
Grains and crops	18,426.29	18,428.17	1.88	0.01
Meat and live-stock products	40,403.91	40,404.77	0.85	0.00
Mining and extraction	132,567	132,570	3	0.00
Processed food	74,243.65	74,238.6	−5.19	−0.01
Textiles and wearing apparel	13,056.42	12,995.01	−61.41	−0.47
Light manufacturing	274,853.94	274,893	39.06	0.01
Heavy manufacturing	324,251.78	324,285.25	33.97	0.01
Utility and construction	254,030.50	254,043.70	12.20	0.00
Transport and communication	439,715.16	439,716.34	1.69	0.00
Other services	976,620.19	976,612.69	−7.50	0.00
CGDS	329,495.75	329,513.94	18.19	0.01

Source: GTAP simulation results

need to be implemented to protect India's agricultural sector, which gives major employment to the Indian work force.

Table 12.15 shows sectoral changes in Canada due to Canada's full liberalization for products coming into Canada from India. Processed food, textile and apparel and other services show negative changes in their outputs, while all other sectors would gain (including CGDS).

12.4.1 Partial Liberalization Using the GTAP Model

In case of partial liberalization, if India thinks of exporting only one of the specialized products to Canada, namely, textile and apparel, then India and Canada would gain in terms of welfare while all other regions would see negative welfare (see Table 12.16).

Table 12.16 Welfare effect (Million USD) when Indian textiles and apparels enters Canada

Region	*EV*
Canada	24.79
India	113.57
TPP	−22.12
South Asia	−8.65
EU25	−18.93
China	−23.88
ROW	−21.01

Source: GTAP simulation results

Table 12.17 Welfare effect (Million USD) when Canadian heavy manufacturing enters India

Region	*EV*
Canada	91.89
India	−3.39
TPP	−32.29
South Asia	−.30
EU25	−12.42
China	−7.82
ROW	−7.69

Source: GTAP simulation results

In case of another partial liberalization scenario, if Canada thinks of exporting only one of the specialized products to India, namely, heavy manufacturing, then India and Canada would gain in terms of welfare (Canada would see a larger gain than India) while all other regions would see negative welfare (see Table 12.17).

The preceding analysis indicates that it would be beneficial for both India and Canada to align with each other under the Canada-India FTA, at least in terms of welfare change. Also, other regions would see an improvement in trade balance due to full liberalization under the proposed FTA.

12.5 Other Contentious Issues and Limitations of the Study

There are also many other issues on which both countries can work together to enhance the level of integration between the two countries. To encourage more Canadian investment in India, it will be important to conclude the

Foreign Investment Promotion and Protection Agreement (FIPA).The FIPA will create a framework under which investors from both sides will derive greater certainty. It will contribute to increased two-way investment and in particular boost Canadian investment into India's priorities in infrastructure, manufacturing, and smart cities under the Make in India campaign. The Indian government put the brakes on any foreign investment agreements that included an investor-state arbitration mechanism in 2013 (investor can sue the state). This agreement is designed to protect investors by defining their legally binding rights and obligations. Canada has differences with India regarding the Investor-State Dispute Settlement (ISDS) mechanism clause in the proposed FIPA. . India wants investors to exhaust the domestic remedies before approaching international tribunals. But Canada is worried about judicial delays in India. Both countries are also in the phase of resolving issues like taxation and expropriation. The other unsolved issues in the FTA include clauses proposed by Canada, namely 'MFN-forward' and 'ratchet'. India is not in favor of these clauses. So due to these key issues, the tenth round of negotiation could not be held in Canada.

Also, the released text of the TPP agreement also raises many issues related to the inclusion of new and advanced WTO provisions into the upcoming trade deals in the world. These provisions affect trade more than the tariff barriers. These provisions are related to: IPR (market exclusivity and ever-greening of patents), commercial operations of state-owned enterprises, net neutrality, investment and services regulations, environmental regulations like commitments on illegal fishing, wildlife trafficking, illegal logging, illegal fisheries subsidies, minimum wage hours of work, freedom of association, the right to collective bargaining and occupational safety and health, and investment state dispute settlement, among others. In light of these provisions, the study recommends reworking the benefits and costs associated with Canada-India FTA. Trade facilitation and climate change and sustainable development goals are other possible areas that may be discussed under the proposed Canada-India FTA.

12.5.1 Limitations

When two countries come forward to negotiate the terms of their free trade agreement, both countries do not open their markets instantly. While negotiating any trade, members suggest their list of products to start the trade liberalization considering various scenarios. The main limitation of this study is the application of the static general equilibrium model where dynamic aspects, such as savings and investments, are excluded from the assumptions and capital stock is taken constant, mainly focusing on intersectoral allocation of resources, for the assessment of India's position in proposed trade agreement with data from 2011. The results can be further improved by using the dynamic GTAP model. Apart from obtaining results on variables that we are already familiar with for the GTAP model, it also includes changes in foreign and domestic wealth and growth rates in capital. It can answer important policy questions such as: long-run impact of change in policy variables on member countries and the time required to achieve that stage wherein each member country will eliminate all the tariffs in the other member country's exports, among others. We can further incorporate features of imperfect competition and scale economies.

12.6 Concluding Remarks

The present study uses partial and general equilibrium tools to assess and simulate the impact of complete liberalization of '*All*' and '*Specialized products*' (products whose RCA > 1) entering India and Canada. Under the simulation analysis, this study has worked out the economic and welfare effects of trade liberalization using the partial (SMART) and general equilibrium (GTAP) approaches. The simulation results from SMART analysis and static GTAP analysis indicate that India would invariably gain more (than Canada) in terms of welfare change and consumer surplus when '*All*' or '*Specialized*' products of Canada enter India in comparison with the scenario when Indian '*Specialized*' and '*All*' products enter Canada. Product-wise results show that only the grains and crops sector (at GTAP classification) are affected negatively (in terms of sectoral changes in outputs) when all products enter India from Canada. The gains are largest for the textiles and wearing apparel sector. All other products, except textile and wearing apparel, processed food and other services in Canada, have positive changes in sectoral output when all Indian products enter Canada. In addition, TPP member countries, South Asian countries, members of EU25, China and all other countries aggregated under the rest of the world region gain in terms of changes in trade balance under both the scenarios. Only India and Canada under both the scenarios would see a negative change in overall trade balance. This negative trade balance in India probably results in negative change in value of GDP in India under complete liberalization. The negative overall trade balance in India is qualified with Indians having positive change in trade balance for sectors: textile and wearing apparel; processed food; and extraction and mining industries while Canada would have positive changes in trade balance in only the grains and crops sector. There is substantial trade diversion for the United States, Russia and Australia, among others, when India liberalizes its trade with Canada.

In case Canada liberalizes its trade with India, China would see a substantial trade diversion, along with many small Asian economies, Bangladesh, Pakistan and Turkey, among others. Trade intensity and trade complementarity indices further indicate the strong trade ties between India and Canada. The study indicates that the gains in having a Canada-India FTA (in terms of welfare change, consumer surplus and sectoral changes post-liberalization phase) may outweigh the losses in terms of decline in trade balance for both India and Canada and decline in percentage change in value of GDP in India and Canada. The regional groups like TPP, EU25, South Asia and China gain in terms of positive trade balances but lose in terms of welfare changes. However, as soon as one brings in discussion on WTO plus issues in trade talks, namely, issues in IPR (market exclusivity and ever-greening of patents), commercial operations of state-owned enterprises, net neutrality, investment and services regulations, environmental regulations like commitments on illegal fishing, wildlife trafficking, illegal logging, illegal fisheries subsidies, minimum wage hours of work, freedom of association, the right to collective bargaining and occupational safety and health, investment state dispute settlement, among other areas as like what are discussed in the TPP, one needs to rework the benefits and costs associated with the Canada-India FTA.

Appendix

Table 12.18 40 India's specialized products (with their HS product codes) in 2013 at 2 digit level of disaggregation

Product code with product description HS 2 digit level (RCA > 1)
02 Meat and edible meat offal
03 Fish and crustaceans, molluscs and other aquatic i
09 Coffee, tea, maté and spices
10 Cereals
12 Oil seeds and oleaginous fruits; miscellaneous gra
13 Lac; gums, resins and other vegetable saps and ext
14 Vegetable plaiting materials; vegetable products n
17 Sugars and sugar confectionery
23 Residues and waste from the food industries; prepa
24 Tobacco and manufactured tobacco substitutes
25 Salt; sulphur; earths and stone; plastering materi
27 Mineral fuels, mineral oils and products of their
29 Organic chemicals
30 Pharmaceutical products
32 Tanning or dyeing extracts; tannins and their deri
36 Explosives; pyrotechnic products; matches; pyropho
41 Raw hides and skins (other than furskins) and leat
42 Articles of leather; saddlery and harness; travel
50 Silk
52 Cotton
53 Other vegetable textile fibres; paper yarn and wov
54 Man-made filaments; strip and the like of man-made
55 Man-made staple fibres
57 Carpets and other textile floor coverings
58 Special woven fabrics; tufted textile fabrics; lac
61 Articles of apparel and clothing accessories, knit
62 Articles of apparel and clothing accessories, not
63 Other made-up textile articles; sets; worn clothin
64 Footwear, gaiters and the like; parts of such arti
67 Prepared feathers and down and articles made of fe
68 Articles of stone, plaster, cement, asbestos, mica
71 Natural or cultured pearls, precious or semi-preci
72 Iron and steel
73 Articles of iron or steel
74 Copper and articles thereof
75 Nickel and articles thereof
78 Lead and articles thereof
79 Zinc and articles thereof
88 Aircraft, spacecraft, and parts thereof
89 Ships, boats and floating structures

Source: Authors' calculation in WITS

Table 12.19 29 Canada's specialized products (with their HS product codes) in 2014 at 2 digit level of disaggregation

Product code with product description HS 2 digit level (RCA > 1)
01 Live animals
02 Meat and edible meat offal
03 Fish and crustaceans, molluscs and other aquatic i
07 Edible vegetables and certain roots and tubers
10 Cereals
11 Products of the milling industry; malt; starches;
12 Oil seeds and oleaginous fruits; miscellaneous gra
15 Animal or vegetable fats and oils and their cleava
18 Cocoa and cocoa preparations
19 Preparations of cereals, flour, starch or milk; pa
23 Residues and waste from the food industries; prepa
25 Salt; sulphur; earths and stone; plastering materi
26 Ores, slag and ash
27 Mineral fuels, mineral oils and products of their
28 Inorganic chemicals; organic or inorganic compound
31 Fertilisers
36 Explosives; pyrotechnic products; matches; pyropho
43 Furskins and artificial fur; manufactures thereof
44 Wood and articles of wood; wood charcoal
47 Pulp of wood or of other fibrous cellulosic materi
48 Paper and paperboard; articles of paper pulp, of p
71 Natural or cultured pearls, precious or semi-preci
75 Nickel and articles thereof
76 Aluminium and articles thereof
78 Lead and articles thereof
79 Zinc and articles thereof
81 Other base metals; cermets; articles thereof
87 Vehicles other than railway or tramway rolling sto
88 Aircraft, spacecraft, and parts thereof

Source: Authors' calculation in WITS

Table 12.20 Tariff rates of India on Canada's exports reported in WITS

Reporter name	*Product code*	*Duty type*	*Simple tariff line average*	*Product name*
India	3	AHS	30	Fish and crustaceans, molluscs and other aquatic i
India	3	BND	150	Fish and crustaceans, molluscs and other aquatic i
India	3	MFN	30	Fish and crustaceans, molluscs and other aquatic i
India	9	AHS	38.24	Coffee, tea, maté and spices
India	9	BND	111.67	Coffee, tea, maté and spices
India	9	MFN	38.24	Coffee, tea, maté and spices
India	12	AHS	18.19	Oil seeds and oleaginous fruits; miscellaneous gra
India	12	BND	110	Oil seeds and oleaginous fruits; miscellaneous gra
India	12	MFN	18.19	Oil seeds and oleaginous fruits; miscellaneous gra
India	13	AHS	15	Lac; gums, resins and other vegetable saps and ext
India	13	BND	116.67	Lac; gums, resins and other vegetable saps and ext
India	13	MFN	15	Lac; gums, resins and other vegetable saps and ext
India	17	AHS	36.25	Sugars and sugar confectionery
India	17	BND	133.33	Sugars and sugar confectionery
India	17	MFN	36.25	Sugars and sugar confectionery
India	23	AHS	19.29	Residues and waste from the food industries; prepa
India	23	BND	108.33	Residues and waste from the food industries; prepa
India	23	MFN	19.29	Residues and waste from the food industries; prepa
India	25	AHS	5.81	Salt; sulphur; earths and stone; plastering materi
India	25	BND	38	Salt; sulphur; earths and stone; plastering materi
India	25	MFN	5.81	Salt; sulphur; earths and stone; plastering materi
India	27	AHS	5.49	Mineral fuels, mineral oils and products of their
India	27	BND	25	Mineral fuels, mineral oils and products of their

(*continued*)

Table 12.20 (continued)

Reporter name	*Product code*	*Duty type*	*Simple tariff line average*	*Product name*
India	27	MFN	5.49	Mineral fuels, mineral oils and products of their
India	27	AHS	5.49	Mineral fuels, mineral oils and products of their
India	27	BND	25	Mineral fuels, mineral oils and products of their
India	27	MFN	5.49	Mineral fuels, mineral oils and products of their
India	29	AHS	7.41	Organic chemicals
India	29	BND	42.23	Organic chemicals
India	29	MFN	7.41	Organic chemicals
India	30	AHS	9.84	Pharmaceutical products
India	30	BND	39.25	Pharmaceutical products
India	30	MFN	9.84	Pharmaceutical products
India	32	AHS	8.23	Tanning or dyeing extracts; tannins and their deri
India	32	BND	40	Tanning or dyeing extracts; tannins and their deri
India	32	MFN	8.23	Tanning or dyeing extracts; tannins and their deri
India	36	AHS	10	Explosives; pyrotechnic products; matches; pyropho
India	36	BND	40	Explosives; pyrotechnic products; matches; pyropho
India	36	MFN	10	Explosives; pyrotechnic products; matches; pyropho
India	41	AHS	4	Raw hides and skins (other than furskins) and leat
India	41	BND	25	Raw hides and skins (other than furskins) and leat
India	41	MFN	4	Raw hides and skins (other than furskins) and leat
India	42	AHS	10	Articles of leather; saddlery and harness; travel
India	42	BND		Articles of leather; saddlery and harness; travel
India	42	MFN	10	Articles of leather; saddlery and harness; travel
India	50	AHS	10	Silk
India	50	BND		Silk
India	50	MFN	10	Silk

(continued)

Table 12.20 (continued)

Reporter name	*Product code*	*Duty type*	*Simple tariff line average*	*Product name*
India	52	AHS	12.84	Cotton
India	52	BND	25	Cotton
India	52	MFN	12.84	Cotton
India	53	AHS	10	Other vegetable textile fibres; paper yarn and wov
India	53	BND	40	Other vegetable textile fibres; paper yarn and wov
India	53	MFN	10	Other vegetable textile fibres; paper yarn and wov
India	54	AHS	19.94	Man-made filaments; strip and the like of man-made
India	54	BND	21.25	Man-made filaments; strip and the like of man-made
India	54	MFN	19.94	Man-made filaments; strip and the like of man-made
India	55	AHS	11.58	Man-made staple fibres
India	55	BND	22.5	Man-made staple fibres
India	55	MFN	11.58	Man-made staple fibres
India	57	AHS	11.02	Carpets and other textile floor coverings
India	57	BND		Carpets and other textile floor coverings
India	57	MFN	11.02	Carpets and other textile floor coverings
India	58	AHS	11.05	Special woven fabrics; tufted textile fabrics; lac
India	58	BND	31.67	Special woven fabrics; tufted textile fabrics; lac
India	58	MFN	11.05	Special woven fabrics; tufted textile fabrics; lac
India	57	AHS	11.02	Carpets and other textile floor coverings
India	57	BND		Carpets and other textile floor coverings
India	57	MFN	11.02	Carpets and other textile floor coverings
India	58	AHS	11.05	Special woven fabrics; tufted textile fabrics; lac
India	58	BND	31.67	Special woven fabrics; tufted textile fabrics; lac

(*continued*)

Table 12.20 (continued)

Reporter name	*Product code*	*Duty type*	*Simple tariff line average*	*Product name*
India	58	MFN	11.05	Special woven fabrics; tufted textile fabrics; lac
India	61	AHS	16.24	Articles of apparel and clothing accessories, knit
India	61	BND	38.5	Articles of apparel and clothing accessories, knit
India	61	MFN	16.24	Articles of apparel and clothing accessories, knit
India	62	AHS	24.43	Articles of apparel and clothing accessories, not
India	62	BND	46.43	Articles of apparel and clothing accessories, not
India	62	MFN	24.43	Articles of apparel and clothing accessories, not
India	63	AHS	8.71	Other made-up textile articles; sets; worn clothin
India	63	BND	35	Other made-up textile articles; sets; worn clothin
India	63	MFN	8.71	Other made-up textile articles; sets; worn clothin
India	64	AHS	10	Footwear, gaiters and the like; Parts of such arti
India	64	BND		Footwear, gaiters and the like; parts of such arti
India	64	MFN	10	Footwear, gaiters and the like; parts of such arti
India	67	AHS	10	Prepared feathers and down and articles made of fe
India	67	BND		Prepared feathers and down and articles made of fe
India	67	MFN	10	Prepared feathers and down and articles made of fe
India	68	AHS	10	Articles of stone, plaster, cement, asbestos, mica
India	68	BND	40	Articles of stone, plaster, cement, asbestos, mica
India	68	MFN	10	Articles of stone, plaster, cement, asbestos, mica
India	67	AHS	10	Prepared feathers and down and articles made of fe

(*continued*)

Table 12.20 (continued)

Reporter name	*Product code*	*Duty type*	*Simple tariff line average*	*Product name*
India	67	BND		Prepared feathers and down and articles made of fe
India	67	MFN	10	Prepared feathers and down and articles made of fe
India	68	AHS	10	Articles of stone, plaster, cement, asbestos, mica
India	68	BND	40	Articles of stone, plaster, cement, asbestos, mica
India	68	MFN	10	Articles of stone, plaster, cement, asbestos, mica
India	71	AHS	10	Natural or cultured pearls, precious or semi-preci
India	71	BND	40	Natural or cultured pearls, precious or semi-preci
India	71	MFN	10	Natural or cultured pearls, precious or semi-preci
India	72	AHS	5.62	Iron and steel
India	72	BND	40	Iron and steel
India	72	MFN	5.62	Iron and steel
India	73	AHS	10	Articles of iron or steel
India	73	BND	40	Articles of iron or steel
India	73	MFN	10	Articles of iron or steel
India	74	AHS	7.03	Copper and articles thereof
India	74	BND		Copper and articles thereof
India	74	MFN	7.03	Copper and articles thereof
India	75	AHS	2.5	Nickel and articles thereof
India	75	BND	38.33	Nickel and articles thereof
India	75	MFN	2.5	Nickel and articles thereof
India	78	AHS	5	Lead and articles thereof
India	78	BND		Lead and articles thereof
India	78	MFN	5	Lead and articles thereof
India	79	AHS	5	Zinc and articles thereof
India	79	BND		Zinc and articles thereof
India	79	MFN	5	Zinc and articles thereof
India	88	AHS	7.77	Aircraft, spacecraft, and parts thereof
India	88	BND	23.82	Aircraft, spacecraft, and parts thereof
India	88	MFN	7.77	Aircraft, spacecraft, and parts thereof
India	89	AHS	21.25	Ships, boats and floating structures
India	89	BND	40	Ships, boats and floating structures
India	89	MFN	21.25	Ships, boats and floating structures

Source: Authors' calculation in WITS

Table 12.21 Tariff rates of Canada on India's exports reported in WITS

Reporter name	*Product code*	*Duty type*	*Simple tariff line average*	*Product name*
Canada	01	AHS	0.00	Live animals
Canada	01	BND	0.00	Live animals
Canada	01	MFN	0.00	Live animals
Canada	02	PRF	1.89	Meat and edible meat offal
Canada	03	AHS	0.23	Fish and crustaceans, molluscs and other aquatic i
Canada	03	BND	1.05	Fish and crustaceans, molluscs and other aquatic i
Canada	03	MFN	0.23	Fish and crustaceans, molluscs and other aquatic i
Canada	07	AHS	3.66	Edible vegetables and certain roots and tubers
Canada	07	BND	4.61	Edible vegetables and certain roots and tubers
Canada	07	MFN	4.12	Edible vegetables and certain roots and tubers
Canada	10	AHS	0.00	Cereals
Canada	10	BND	0.16	Cereals
Canada	10	MFN	0.00	Cereals
Canada	11	AHS	8.80	Products of the milling industry; malt; starches
Canada	11	BND	9.24	Products of the milling industry; malt; starches
Canada	11	MFN	9.78	Products of the milling industry; malt; starches
Canada	12	AHS	0.29	Oil seeds and oleaginous fruits; miscellaneous gra
Canada	12	BND	1.69	Oil seeds and oleaginous fruits; miscellaneous gra
Canada	12	MFN	1.03	Oil seeds and oleaginous fruits; miscellaneous gra
Canada	15	AHS	8.66	Animal or vegetable fats and oils and their cleava
Canada	15	BND	11.17	Animal or vegetable fats and oils and their cleava
Canada	15	MFN	10.32	Animal or vegetable fats and oils and their cleava
Canada	18	AHS	46.67	Cocoa and cocoa preparations
Canada	18	BND	47.88	Cocoa and cocoa preparations
Canada	18	MFN	47.50	Cocoa and cocoa preparations

(*continued*)

Table 12.21 (continued)

Reporter name	*Product code*	*Duty type*	*Simple tariff line average*	*Product name*
Canada	19	AHS	14.94	Preparations of cereals, flour, starch or milk; pa
Canada	19	BND	17.52	Preparations of cereals, flour, starch or milk; pa
Canada	19	MFN	15.64	Preparations of cereals, flour, starch or milk; pa
Canada	23	AHS	12.75	Residues and waste from the food industries; prepa
Canada	23	BND	14.58	Residues and waste from the food industries; prepa
Canada	23	MFN	13.01	Residues and waste from the food industries; prepa
Canada	25	AHS	0.00	Salt; sulphur; earths and stone; plastering materi
Canada	25	BND	2.26	Salt; sulphur; earths and stone; plastering materi
Canada	25	MFN	0.07	Salt; sulphur; earths and stone; plastering materi
Canada	26	AHS	0.00	Ores, slag and ash
Canada	26	BND	0.00	Ores, slag and ash
Canada	26	MFN	0.00	Ores, slag and ash
Canada	27	AHS	0.00	Mineral fuels, mineral oils and products of their
Canada	27	BND	5.81	Mineral fuels, mineral oils and products of their
Canada	27	MFN	1.81	Mineral fuels, mineral oils and products of their
Canada	28	AHS	0.03	Inorganic chemicals; organic or inorganic compound
Canada	28	BND	3.62	Inorganic chemicals; organic or inorganic compound
Canada	28	MFN	0.06	Inorganic chemicals; organic or inorganic compound
Canada	31	AHS	0.00	Fertilisers
Canada	31	BND	0.54	Fertilisers
Canada	31	MFN	0.00	Fertilisers
Canada	36	AHS	3.00	Explosives; pyrotechnic products; matches; pyropho
Canada	36	BND	6.50	Explosives; pyrotechnic products; matches; pyropho

(*continued*)

Table 12.21 (continued)

Reporter name	*Product code*	*Duty type*	*Simple tariff line average*	*Product name*
Canada	36	MFN	6.50	Explosives; pyrotechnic products; matches; pyropho
Canada	43	AHS	4.63	Furskins and artificial fur; manufactures thereof
Canada	43	BND	6.67	Furskins and artificial fur; manufactures thereof
Canada	43	MFN	6.94	Furskins and artificial fur; manufactures thereof
Canada	43	AHS	4.63	Furskins and artificial fur; manufactures thereof
Canada	43	BND	6.67	Furskins and artificial fur; manufactures thereof
Canada	43	MFN	6.94	Furskins and artificial fur; manufactures thereof
Canada	44	AHS	0.83	Wood and articles of wood; wood charcoal
Canada	44	BND	4.07	Wood and articles of wood; wood charcoal
Canada	44	MFN	2.39	Wood and articles of wood; wood charcoal
Canada	47	AHS	0.00	Pulp of wood or of other fibrous cellu-losic materi
Canada	47	BND	0.00	Pulp of wood or of other fibrous cellu-losic materi
Canada	47	MFN	0.00	Pulp of wood or of other fibrous cellu-losic materi
Canada	48	AHS	0.00	Paper and paperboard; articles of paper pulp, of p
Canada	48	BND	0.00	Paper and paperboard; articles of paper pulp, of p
Canada	48	MFN	0.00	Paper and paperboard; articles of paper pulp, of p
Canada	71	AHS	1.34	Natural or cultured pearls, precious or semi-preci
Canada	71	BND	3.86	Natural or cultured pearls, precious or semi-preci
Canada	71	MFN	2.48	Natural or cultured pearls, precious or semi-preci
Canada	71	AHS	1.34	Natural or cultured pearls, precious or semi-preci

(*continued*)

Table 12.21 (continued)

Reporter name	*Product code*	*Duty type*	*Simple tariff line average*	*Product name*
Canada	71	BND	3.86	Natural or cultured pearls, precious or semi-preci
Canada	71	MFN	2.48	Natural or cultured pearls, precious or semi-preci
Canada	75	AHS	0.00	Nickel and articles thereof
Canada	75	BND	1.78	Nickel and articles thereof
Canada	75	MFN	0.33	Nickel and articles thereof
Canada	76	AHS	1.12	Aluminium and articles thereof
Canada	76	BND	4.40	Aluminium and articles thereof
Canada	76	MFN	1.79	Aluminium and articles thereof
Canada	78	AHS	0.00	Lead and articles thereof
Canada	78	BND	2.67	Lead and articles thereof
Canada	78	MFN	0.00	Lead and articles thereof
Canada	79	AHS	0.50	Zinc and articles thereof
Canada	79	BND	2.00	Zinc and articles thereof
Canada	79	MFN	1.00	Zinc and articles thereof
Canada	81	AHS	0.00	Other base metals; cermets; articles thereof
Canada	81	BND	2.38	Other base metals; cermets; articles thereof
Canada	81	MFN	0.00	Other base metals; cermets; articles thereof
Canada	87	AHS	2.65	Vehicles other than railway or tramway rolling sto
Canada	87	BND	4.57	Vehicles other than railway or tramway rolling sto
Canada	87	MFN	3.02	Vehicles other than railway or tramway rolling sto
Canada	88	AHS	0.00	Aircraft, spacecraft, and parts thereof
Canada	88	BND	3.09	Aircraft, spacecraft, and parts thereof
Canada	88	MFN	1.38	Aircraft, spacecraft, and parts thereof

Source: Authors' calculation in WITS

Notes

1. See Mikic and Gilbert (2007) for the formulas of trade indicators.
2. Due to space restrictions, the results of RCA at HS 4-digit and 6-digit level have not been reported. One can easily calculate these results by using 'Trade Outcome Indicators' utility in WITS.
3. See Mikic and Gilbert (2007) for the formulas of trade indicators.
4. See Jammes and Olarreaga (2005) for detail on SMART model and its derivation.
5. See Brockmeier (1996/2001), Hertel (1997), Arora and Mathur (2015), Arora et al. (2015) for details on GTAP model and implications of change in trade policy.

References

Arora, R., & Mathur, S. K. (2015). Welfare implications of India's trade liberalization within Asia: A general equilibrium assessment under conjecture of free trade area. *Trade and Development Review, 8*(2), 69–95.

Arora, R., Singh, S., & Mathur, S. K. (2015). Assessment of the proposed India-China Free Trade Agreement: A general equilibrium approach. *Journal of Centrum Cathedra, 8*(2), 81–108. https://doi.org/10.1108/JCC-08-02-2015-B002

Balassa, B. (1965). Trade liberalization and revealed comparative advantage. *Manchester School of Economic and Social Studies,* 33, 99–123.

Brockmeier, M. (1996/2001). *A graphical exposition of the GTAP model.* GTAP technical paper no. 3-1-2001. Center for Global Trade Analysis, Purdue University.

Hertel, T. W. (Ed.). (1997). *Global trade analysis: Modeling and applications.* New York: Cambridge University Press.

Huff, K., & Hertel, T. (2000). *Decomposing welfare changes in the GTAP model.* GTAP technical paper no. 5, Center for Global Trade Analysis, Purdue University.

Jammes, O., & Olarreaga, M. (2005). *Explaining smart and GSIM,* The World Bank. Retrieved from http://citeseerx.ist.psu.edu/viewdoc/download?doi=10.1.1.547.8636&rep=rep1&type=pdf

Mikic, M., & Gilbert, J. (2007). *Trade statistics in policymaking—A handbook of commonly used trade indices and indicators.* Bangkok: United Nations.

PART III

Other Related Topics

CHAPTER 13

Estimating the Impact of Technical Barriers to Trade: The Case of Perfumes and Toilet Waters in Ecuador

Gonzalo E. Sánchez and Patricia A. Vargas

13.1 Introduction

Countries actively use policies that limit international trade. Understanding the opportuneness of these policies from a theoretical point of view has attracted the attention of policy makers and academics for decades. See for instance (Mill 1848; Bhagwati 1965; Brander and Krugman 1983; Krugman 1986; Anderson and Neary 2005). The need to quantify the effects of specific barriers to trade has also brought about the development of empirical methods in this field. In that context, the main objective of this chapter is to contribute to the understanding of the effects of barriers to trade using a novel empirical method.

The measures that countries might impose to limit international trade are categorized as tariff or non-tariff barriers. Non-tariff barriers (NTBs) imply restrictions that have the form of prohibitions or specific market

G.E. Sánchez
Facultad de Ciencias Sociales y Humanísticas, Campus Gustavo Galindo, Escuela Superior Politécnica del Litoral, ESPOL, Guayaquil, Ecuador

P.A. Vargas
Dirección de Docencia, Pontificia Universidad Católica del Ecuador, PUCE, Quito, Ecuador

S.K. Mathur et al. (eds.), *Theorizing International Trade*,
https://doi.org/10.1007/978-981-10-1759-9_13

requirements that limit or make the importation or exportation of a product more expensive. "NTBs include all policy-related trade costs incurred from production to final consumer, with the exclusion of tariffs" (United Nations Conference on Trade and Development 2013). NTBs are broadly categorized as technical barriers: sanitary and phytosanitary (SPS), certification procedures and pre-shipment inspections, among others; and non-technical measures.

The World Trade Organization (WTO) has specific agreements for NTBs. WTO agreements allow countries to achieve legitimate objectives in the use of these kinds of barriers. For instance, the "Technical Barriers to Trade (TBT) Agreement aims to ensure that technical regulations, standards, and conformity assessment procedures are non-discriminatory and do not create unnecessary obstacles to trade" (GATT Secretariat 1994).

TBTs refer to regulations, standards, testing and certification procedures imposed with non-trade objectives that seek to protect human, animal or plant life or health, and so on. Despite their objectives, TBTs may have substantial impacts on international trade. This chapter attempts to identify the effects on import flows of the two TBTs adopted by Ecuador in November 2013: Resolution 116 and Resolution RTE 093. In particular, we study the impact on the Ecuadorian imports of perfumes and toilet waters (HS 330300). We selected these products because of their relative importance among those affected by Resolution 116, and because we were able to obtain trade flows under the same codification for other countries.[1]

The literature has developed empirical methods to estimate effects of international trade policies. They include general and partial equilibrium models, applications of Industrial Organization, gravity model of trade, comparative case studies, time series analysis and panel data models, among others.[2]

In this chapter, we use a comparative case study to consistently estimate the causal effect of a specific TBT. In particular, we use an application of the synthetic control method proposed in Abadie and Gardeazabal (2003) and Abadie et al. (2010). This method uses convex combinations of potential control units to construct a counterfactual for the unit under study.

The main advantage that this method offers over traditional time series options is that it does not require that the policy under study does not coincide with other unobserved shocks, or that is exogeneous. The method instead uses a data-driven approach to construct an appropriate control, the "synthetic control," which by construction was not affected by the policy under study, but by assumption was impacted by those other shocks. We combine the results of this method with a difference-in-difference estimation to obtain the causal effect. Therefore, the identifying assumption is that in the absence of the policy change, the treatment unit would have had the same tendency as the synthetic control. Hence, we use a standard parallel trends assumption, and do not need to impose any structural assumption.

To our knowledge, this is the first study that uses synthetic control to estimate the causal effect of a particular barrier to trade. In that sense, the contribution of this chapter is mainly methodological. The results indicate that the TBTs under study produced a statistically significant reduction in imports of around 61%, which is equivalent to 147.32 dollars per thousand people per month. We compare this estimate to a simpler before-and-after calculation and find that they are very similar. This comparison is evidence that the policy shock is not confounded with other relevant but unobserved shocks, or that it is exogenous. This implies that the method utilized in this chapter can be used as a robustness check for time series estimations, and as an indirect test for exogeneity of policy shocks.

Importantly, if the shock under study occurred simultaneously with other relevant shocks, then the synthetic control method might be the best reduced form option to estimate the causal effect of interest. We believe that the estimation method utilized in this chapter has also the potential to be used to evaluate the impact of particular trade policies on outcome variables such as taxes collected, investment flows and job creation, among many others. This chapter is organized as follows. Section 13.2 makes a brief review of the technical barriers to trade reforms in Ecuador in 2013, Sect. 13.3 describes the data and methodology used, Sect. 13.4 presents the results and Sect. 13.5 concludes.

13.2 The 2013 Technical Barriers to Trade Reforms in Ecuador

In Ecuador, the Foreign Trade Committee (Consejo de Comercio Exterior – COMEX in Spanish) is the highest authority that regulates international trade. The Organic Code of Production, Trade and Investment (Código Orgánico de Comercio e Inversiones – COPCI in Spanish) states that, among other functions, COMEX issues rules about records, authorizations, licenses, and import and export procedures, except customs formalities. This is important because COMEX issues the rules about which products have to demonstrate conformity with Ecuadorian technical regulations, but is the Ecuadorian Institute for Standardization (Instituto Ecuatoriano de Normalización, INEN in Spanish) that is in charge of the technical standards and their implementation.

In November 2013, COMEX issued Resolution 116, affecting 293 Nandina System 10-digit codes (Resolución 116 2013). This regulation requires certificates of recognition for certain products in order to demonstrate compliance with Ecuadorians' technical regulations. According to COMEX, the application of the measure was justified under the arrangements in the Ecuadorian Political Constitution, and the WTO TBT Agreement that allowed the establishment of rules that guarantee the quality of the products sold in the country. However, this justification was not satisfactory to some members of the WTO who "raised concerns that Resolution 116 and the various technical regulations may be intended to address Ecuador's trade balance rather than address legitimate health or safety concerns." (United States Trade Representative 2015).

Resolution 116 was subject of analysis within a WTO TBT Committee. Specifically, it was matter of concern six times for 11 members. The principal concerns were about the lack of early notification of the measure, the duplication of requirements in the case of some products such as food and cosmetics and lack of accredited test laboratories and accredited certification bodies. (World Trade Organization – Committee on Technical Barriers to Trade 2016a).

13.3 Data and Methodology

Data on imports were obtained from Trade Map, International Trade Centre, www.intracen.org/marketanalysis. For the analysis that follows, the treatment period is November 2013, the pre-treatment period ranges from December 2012 to October 2013, and the post-treatment period goes from December 2013 to October 2014. Therefore, each period of analysis has 11 months. We do this to include the same months within a year in each period. Table 13.1 shows the products that experienced the biggest reduction among the 293 codes affected by Resolution 116. The code with the biggest absolute reduction was "Generating sets, diesel/semi-diesel engines, of an output exceeding 375 KVA" (USD 102 million CIF), whereas the biggest reduction in percentage terms was "Hot rolled bar/rod, irregular coils, nes" (−98%).

We decided not to consider products belonging to the groups 85 (Electrical and electronic equipment) and 72 (Iron and Steel), since the

Table 13.1 Products with the biggest import reductions after Resolution 116

In millions of dollars (C.I.F.)

Code	*Code description (HS 6-digits)*	*Pre-treatment* (A)	*Post-treatment* (B)	*Difference* (B-A)	*Percentage change* (%)	*Coefficient of variation (pre-treatment)*
8502131000	Generating sets, diesel/semi-diesel engines, of an output exceeding 375 KVA	133.6	31.4	102.2	−77	1.01
8544609000	Electric conductors, for a voltage exceeding 1000 V, nes	68.2	11.3	56.9	−83	0.47
7213990000	Hot rolled bar/rod, irregular coils, nes	33.3	0.6	32.7	−98	1.11
8502209000	Generating sets with spark-ignition internal combustion piston engines	36.7	9.9	26.8	−73	2.48
8544491000	Electric conductors, for a voltage not exceeding 80 V, nes, of copper	72.4	47.1	25.3	−35	0.26
3303000000	Perfumes and toilet waters	39.0	15.1	23.8	−61	0.24
8544499000	Electric conductors, for a voltage not exceeding 80 V, nes	27.8	8.3	19.4	−70	0.68
9503009900	Tricycles, scooters, pedal cars and similar wheeled toys; dolls	29.4	13.0	16.3	−56	0.48
3305900000	Hair preparations, nes	38.8	25.8	13.0	−34	0.22
3305100000	Hair shampoos	46.2	33.8	12.4	−27	0.21

Source: Trade Map

Notes: The pre-treatment periods goes from December 2012 to October 2013; the post-treatment period ranges from December 2013 to October 2014. The descriptions of the product codes correspond to HS 6-digits to avoid unnecessary long names

Ecuadorian government invested heavily in construction, electric and transport infrastructure in the years surrounding our period of study. These investment decisions were also very volatile. For instance, the public investment in natural resources (including hydroelectric generators), communications, urban development and housing were USD 2769 million in 2012, USD 4068 in 2013, and USD 3668 in 2014.(Secretariat of Planning and Development – SENPLADES). Changes in imports of products belonging to these codes might be explained by public investment decisions and not by the application of Resolution 116. The relatively high coefficient of variation of the monthly imports for the pre-treatment period is suggestive evidence that products under these codes were responding to factors exogenous to the Ecuadorian commercial policy.

Taking into account the aforementioned restriction, and considering Table 13.1, were are left with products belonging to the code 33 (Essential oils, perfumes, cosmetics, toiletries). In particular, we selected the code 3303000000 (Perfumes and toilet waters) for analysis since it had the biggest absolute and relative reductions (See Table 13.1).The selection of 3303000000 has the additional advantage of being the only product included in the HS 6-digit code 330300. This means that we can compare the Ecuadorian imports of this product to the imports of other countries. This is especially important considering the estimation methodology we propose later.

It is important to mention that in November 2013 another regulation affecting the imports of perfumes and toilet waters was issued (Resolución 13392 – RTE 093 2013). This regulation, which applies to cosmetic products (including perfumes and toilet waters), specifies that importers have to demonstrate conformity with Ecuadorian quality standards. This technical regulation establishes requirements for cosmetic products to protect the life, safety and health of people and the environment and avoid practices that may misinform the users. This standard includes requirements on labeling, safety, microbiological quality and procedures for conformity assessment. RTE 093 is applied in conjunction with Resolution 116, which demands the submission of recognition certificate (INEN-1) as a supporting document with the customs declaration. Therefore, the estimations that follow include the combined effect of both technical regulations.

In order to estimate the causal effect of a shock such as the implementation of a barrier to trade, one may want to use a time series approach. To do this, the researcher has to assume that the estimations are not confounded by events happening around the implementation of the policy, in particular, economic shocks at the national or international level that are not observed by the researcher. Notice that a before-and-after estimation that assumes stationarity, and is the simplest time series estimation, was already calculated in Table 13.1 for certain products.

Given this potential threat, an option is to focus attention on a particular group of products (treated group), and find a suitable "counterfactual" for it. Once the counterfactual is estimated, the causal effect can be obtained by its difference with the treated group, or by using a difference-in-difference method, depending on the assumptions the researcher is willing to accept. We have already discussed the selection of the Ecuadorian imports of perfumes and toilet waters for analysis. The next step is to select a proper counterfactual.

In the context of this study, one alternative is to select, within the Ecuadorian imports, products not affected by the policy under analysis. This option has the potential benefit of reducing the bias caused by shocks affecting all the economy. However, it is likely that the cross-elasticities are non-zero. Meaning that the potential control units are likely influenced indirectly by the trade policy.

Another option is to consider imports of the same treated products by another country as potential counterfactuals. By using this approach, we have to assume that the changes in Ecuadorian imports of perfumes and toilet waters do not affect international prices. This is most likely the case given the small participation of Ecuador in this market. Between 2009 and 2012, the Ecuadorian imports of perfumes and toilet waters represented on average 0.15% of the world imports.

The next question is which country or countries to use. One might be tempted to select a country or group of countries that are similar to Ecuador considering certain relevant variables. Instead of doing this arbitrarily, the alternative we take is to use a data-driven method to perform the selection. In particular, we use the method proposed in (Abadie and Gardeazabal 2003) and (Abadie et al. 2010). This method uses convex combinations of potential control units (donors) to construct a counterfactual for the unit under study.

Consider $J + 1$ countries and T periods. The treated country is Ecuador and we call it J, the remaining countries are called the "donor countries." The treatment starts at period T_0 and continues until the last period of analysis. The treatment in our case is the implementation of resolutions 116 and RTE 093 in November 2013. The outcome of interest for the treated unit (imports of perfumes and toilet waters in thousands of dollars

C.I.F. per 1000 people) is denoted Υ_A and the matrix containing the outcome for the donor units is denoted Υ_B.[3]

The synthetic control method chooses weights for each donor country to solve the following minimization problem:

$$\widehat{W} = \text{argmin}_W (X_A - X_B W)' S (X_A - X_B W) \tag{13.1}$$

Where X_A is the vector of pre-intervention variables used as predictors of Υ_A, $X_B W$ is a weighted average of the same pre-treatments variables, but corresponding to the donor countries. W is a (J × 1) vector of non-negative weights that add up to one. S is a positive (k × k) semidefinite matrix used to allow different weights to the predictor variables. Once $\widehat{W}$ has been estimated, the counterfactual, or synthetic control for period t is calculated as $\widehat{\Upsilon_{At}} = \widehat{W}' \Upsilon_{Bt}$. We will call this estimate the "synthetic Ecuador." For the estimation of the causal effects, we use a difference-in-difference approach, which uses the synthetic Ecuador as control. Therefore, the identifying assumption is the usual common trends one. In words, in the absence of resolutions 116 and RTE 093, Ecuador would have had the same trend as the synthetic Ecuador.

The estimations were obtained using the Stata code provided in (Abadie et al. 2011). We utilized the default option for the S matrix, which uses a regression-based approach to minimize the mean squared error for the pre-intervention period. The fully nested method produced the same estimates, so we decided not to report them. For the results that follow, we used the pre-treatment values of the outcome variables as predictors. In an additional specification, used as robustness check, we included pre-treatment values of the annual Real GDP and the monthly Real Exchange Rate as additional predictors.[4]

The group of donor countries from which we obtained the weights to estimate the synthetic control belong to the World Bank classifications: lower-middle-income economies, and upper-middle-income economies.[5] Hence, we excluded from analysis low-income and high-income economies. We do this to avoid comparing Ecuador to countries with dissimilar economies. We also exclude from analysis countries with no imports of perfumes and toilet waters in more than four months in the pre-treatment period. We therefore have 46 countries for analysis, 45 donors and Ecuador. Another option would have been to use only countries in Latin America and the Caribbean region. However, there are only 24 countries in this group with information available for analysis, so we decided to use them to perform a robustness exercise. If a country imposed barriers to commerce for perfumes and toilet waters in the period under analysis, then it must be excluded because these barriers can be consider treatments similar to the regulations imposed by Ecuador. We carefully explored this possibility and discarded it. In the period ranging from 2012 to 2015, the only country that faced trade concerns specific to perfumes and toilet waters (HS 330300), raised by WTO members, was Ecuador (World Trade Organization 2016b).

To our knowledge, this is the first study that uses synthetic control to estimate the causal effect of a particular barrier to trade. Nonetheless, this method has been used to study the effect of economic liberalization (Billmeier and Nannicini 2013); anti-immigration policy (Bohn et al. 2014; Sanchez 2017); comparative politics (Abadie et al. 2015) and in many other topics.

To perform inference analysis, we follow (Abadie et al. 2010). Specifically, we use a permutation approach in which we repeat the estimation outlined before, but for each of the donor countries. For each repetition we exclude Ecuador as a potential donor. This exercise provides the distribution of "placebo" estimates. Then we compare the estimated effects for Ecuador within this distribution. This is equivalent to compare the estimated effect to that of a country chosen at random. By doing this, we can study the null hypothesis of non-negative effect. In other words, the hypothesis that resolution 116 and RTE 093 did not reduce the Ecuadorian imports of perfumes and toilet waters. In particular, if the estimated effect takes an atypically large negative value, then there is evidence against the null hypothesis. To obtain one-sided p-values, we rank the estimated treatment effects from the smallest (most negative) to the largest, then the position of Ecuador over the total number of countries gives the p-value.[6]

13.4 Results

Table 13.2 presents the weights that were selected to construct the synthetic control applied to the Ecuadorian imports of perfumes and toilet waters. The presence of Colombia, with a contribution to the synthetic Ecuador of more than 15.7%, is not a surprise, given the similarities of the two Andean countries. In contrast, the presence of Thailand, which was given a weight of nearly 30%, and the Republic of Congo with a weight close to 29%, is somehow surprising. Nevertheless, and as pointed out in the previous section, the method does not rely on – any priors and only uses

Table 13.2 Weights for the construction of the synthetic control

Country	*Weight*
Thailand	0.295
Republic of Congo	0.289
Colombia	0.157
Malaysia	0.105
Paraguay	0.093
Tunisia	0.042
Fiji	0.012
Dominican Republic	0.006

historical information to construct the synthetic control. Therefore, despite the differences between Ecuador and the selected donors, what is relevant is the capacity of them to reproduce the pre-treatment trajectory of the former. Notice that we are using a difference-in-difference approach to calculate the treatment effect. Hence, the assumption we need is that in the absence of the treatment, Ecuador and its synthetic counterpart had the same trends. The other countries that received positive weights were Malaysia (10.5%), Paraguay (9.3%), Tunisia (4.2%), Fiji (1.2%) and Dominican Republic (0.6%).

Figure 13.1 plots the results. The synthetic Ecuador tracks very closely the trajectory of Ecuador before November 2013. In contrast, starting in December 2013, the two series diverge, and stay separated until the last period analyzed. Notice that the figure also suggests that the shock seems to have changed the level, but not the tendency of series.

This graphic evidence suggests that there is a negative treatment effect. Table 13.3 presents the difference-in-difference estimates obtained from the synthetic control results. The average difference between Ecuador and its synthetic counterpart before treatment is −1.12, whereas the post-treatment average difference is −148.4. This brings about a difference-in-difference estimate of the average treatment effect of −147.32 dollars per thousand people per month. Notice that this estimate corresponds to the average over 11 months. A back-of-the-envelope calculation brings about a reduction in imports of around USD 24.6 million, or 63%.[7]

Notice that the simple before-and-after calculation in Table 13.1 produced an estimated reduction of approximately 61%. In other words, if our estimations are correctly specified, then the before-and-after approach has a small positive bias. However, we cannot rule out the possibility that the two estimates are equal to each other. Moreover, these results suggest that the policy under study was indeed exogenous and did not coincide with other

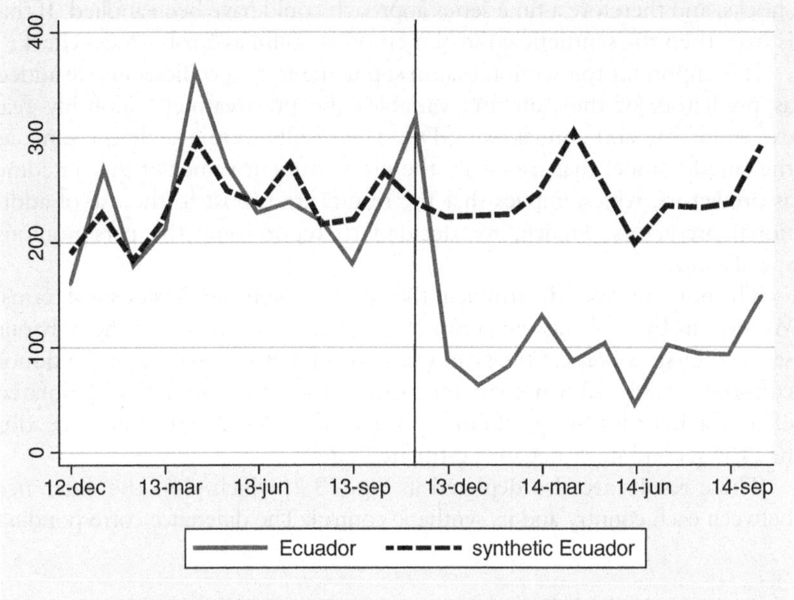

Fig. 13.1 Synthetic control method. Imports of perfumes and toilet waters (C.I.F. dollars per 1000 people)

Table 13.3 Synthetic control estimates

In C.I.F. dollars per thousand people		
Donor countries	*Middle-income economies (1)*	*Latin America and the Caribbean (2)*
Pre-treatment average difference	−1.12	−3.68
Post-treatment average difference	−148.44	−181.74
Difference-in-difference	−147.32	−178.06
Percent change	−63.1%	−76.3%
Implied -one-sided p-value	0.043	0.125

Source: Authors' calculations

Notes: Middle-income economies include the countries in the lower-middle-income, and upper-middle-income groups according to the World Bank. See the text for details shocks, and therefore a time series approach could have been applied. If this is true, then the synthetic control method is useful as a robustness check.

It is important to mention that in supplementary specifications we added as predictors of the outcome variables the pre-treatment monthly real exchange rate and annual real GDP. The results were exactly the same as the simple model that uses only the pre-treatment values of the outcome as predictors, which implies that the results are robust to the use of additional predictors. Hence, we decided to report only the parsimonious specification.

The next step is to determine if the effect is significant in statistical terms. We do this by applying the permutation method described in the previous section. First, we repeat the synthetic control method to each of the donor countries. Table 13.3 present the corresponding p-values. The estimated effect for Ecuador brings about a p-value of 0.043 (2/46), since Ecuador had the second most negative estimated effect.

These results are also depicted in Fig. 13.2, which plots the difference between each country and its synthetic control. The difference corresponding

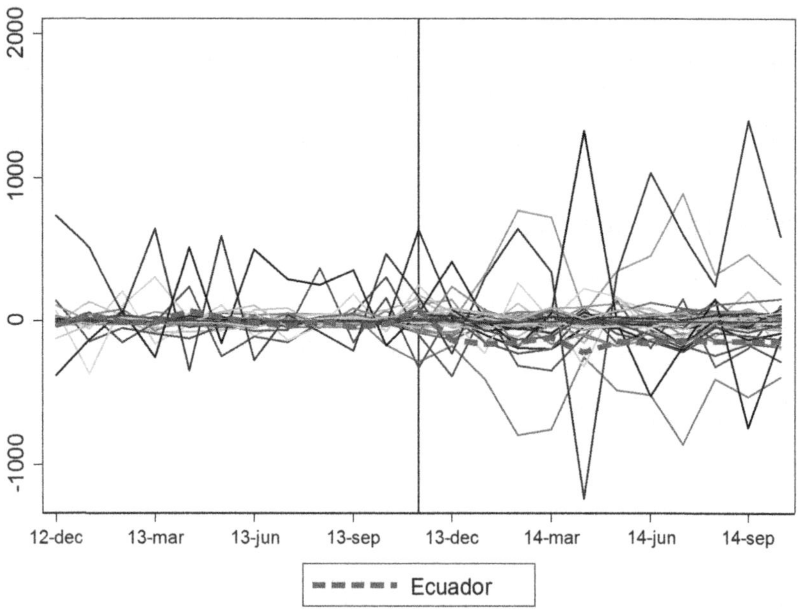

Fig. 13.2 Permutation exercise (all donors). Imports of perfumes and toilet waters (C.I.F. dollars per 1000 people)

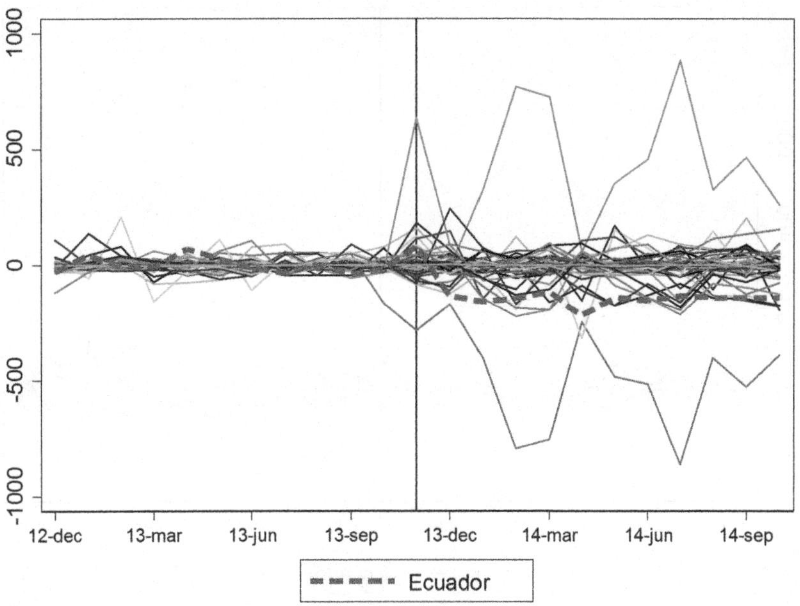

Fig. 13.3 Permutation exercise (excludes countries with MSE 20 times greater than Ecuador). Imports of perfumes and toilet waters (C.I.F. dollars per 1000 people)

to Ecuador seems to be among the most negative; however, it also seems to be significantly smaller than some of the most volatile series. Notice that for most countries, the difference in the pre-treatment period is small and comparable to the corresponding to Ecuador. However, for some the fit is very poor. In order to get a better graphic sense of the relative position of Ecuador, and following Abadie et al. (2010), we do not consider countries with pre-treatment mean squared error 20 times larger than that of Ecuador. Figure 13.3 plots the results. It is easier to see that Ecuador is among the countries with most negative differences. Finally, Fig. 13.4 plots the results excluding countries with pre-treatment mean squared error twice as large of that of Ecuador. This figure makes it more evident Ecuador has an atypically larger negative effect. It is important to point out that the p-values reported in Table 13.3 were obtained without excluding any country.

As a robustness check, we repeat the synthetic control estimations, but considering countries in the Latin America and the Caribbean Region.

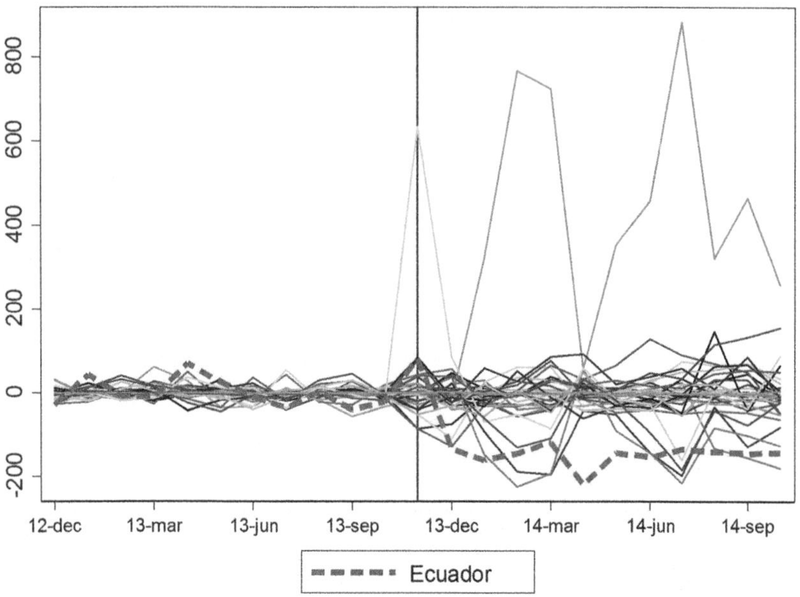

Fig. 13.4 Permutation exercise (excludes countries with MSE 2 times greater than Ecuador). Imports of perfumes and toilet waters (C.I.F. dollars per 1000 people)

Results are reported in Table 13.3, column 2. The difference-in-difference estimate is −178 dollars per thousand people per month, which implies an effect of −76%. By using the inference method outlined before, we find a p-value of 0.125. Hence, the estimates in the second column are larger but imprecisely estimated. Taking this into account, we consider column 1 our preferred specification.

13.5 Concluding Remarks

Technical barriers to trade are frequently used by most countries. In that sense, it is important to quantify their effects. A better understanding of these effects can be very useful for policy designers and to academics interested in studying trade policy empirically. This chapter contributes to the literature by applying a method that allows the estimation of the causal effect of a particular technical barrier to trade on import flows.

In particular, this chapter studies the impact of technical barriers to trade imposed by the Ecuadorian government in 2013, which require certificates of recognition and conformity with Ecuadorian quality standards. We focus attention on the products belonging to the HS code corresponding to perfumes and toilet waters in Ecuador (330300). In order to get an unbiased estimate, we use a difference-in-difference approach combined with a synthetic control method, which builds a suitable control by combining information from units not affected by the policy change.

The results indicate that these restrictions produced a statistically significant reduction in imports of around 63%, which is equivalent to 147.32 dollars per thousand people per month. Interestingly, this estimate is very similar to a before-and-after calculation. This might be evidence that the policy shock we study did not happen simultaneously with other relevant but unobserved (by the researcher) shocks, or that it is exogenous. The exogeneity, together with the seemingly stationarity of the series, imply that a before-and-after comparison provides a good estimate of the treatment effect.

In this sense, the main contribution of this chapter is methodological. The synthetic control method has potential to be used as a robustness check for more traditional specifications, and as an indirect test for exogeneity of policy shocks. Moreover, if the policy under study coincides with other observed changes at the national or international level, and hence is confounded with them, then the synthetic control method might be the best reduced form option to estimate the causal effect of interest.

Finally, the estimation method utilized in this chapter has also the potential to be used to evaluate the impact of particular trade policies on outcome variables different than trade flows, such as taxes collected, investment flows and job creation, among others. We believe that more work needs to be done to explore this possibility.

Notes

1. See Sect. 13.2 for details.
2. For a detailed review of empirical methods applied to quantify the impact of TBT trade, see (Maskus and Wilson 2001).
3. We analyze monthly series of imports by country. In order to obtain a comparable metric among countries, we calculate the imports of perfumes

and toilet waters in thousands of dollars C.I.F. per 1000 people. We use the population corresponding to 2011 (World Bank 2016). The use of other years as denominator did not change our results.
4. We obtained the Real GDP from the World Development Indicators (World Bank 2016) and the Real Exchange Rate from (Darvas 2012).
5. See World Bank: http://data.worldbank.org/about/country-and-lending-groups
6. Notice that the p-value is bounded from below to $1/46 = 0.022$
7. We use a population of 15.17 million to get these calculations.

References

Abadie, A., & Gardeazabal, J. (2003). The economic costs of conflict: A case study of the Basque country. *The American Economic Review, 93*(1), 113–132.
Abadie, A., Diamond, A., & Hainmueller, J. (2010). Synthetic control methods for comparative case studies: Estimating the effect of California's tobacco control program. *Journal of the American Statistical Association, 105*(490), 493–505.
Abadie, A., Diamond, A., & Hainmueller, J. (2011). *SYNTH: Stata module to implement synthetic control methods for comparative case studies.* Statistical Software Components S457334, Boston College Department of Economics, revised 28 January 2014.
Abadie, A., Diamond, A., & Hainmueller, J. (2015). Comparative politics and the synthetic control method. *American Journal of Political Science, 59*(2), 495–510.
Anderson, J., & Neary, J. (2005). *Measuring the restrictiveness of international trade policy.* Cambridge, MA: MIT Press.
Bhagwati, J. N. (1965). On the equivalence of tariff and quotas. In R. E. Baldwin (Ed.), *Trade growth and balance of payment.* Amsterdam: North Holland.
Billmeier, A., & Nannicini, T. (2013). Assessing economic liberalization episodes: A synthetic control approach. *Review of Economics and Statistics, 95*(3), 983–1001.
Bohn, S., Lofstrom, M., & Raphael, S. (2014). Did the 2007 legal Arizona workers act reduce the state's unauthorized immigrant population? *Review of Economics and Statistics, 9*(2), 258–269.
Brander, J. A., & Krugman, P. R. (1983). A reciprocal dumping model of international trade. *Journal of International Economics, 15*, 313–321.
Darvas, Z. (2012). *Real effective exchange rates for 178 countries: A new database.* Working paper. Department of Mathematical Economics and Economic Analysis, Corvinus University of Budapest, Budapest. Retrieved from http://unipub.lib.uni-corvinus.hu/612/
GATT Secretariat. (1994). *The results of the Uruguay Round of multilateral negotiations: The legal texts.* Geneva: GATT.

Krugman, P. (1986). *Strategic trade policy and the new international economics.* Cambridge, MA: MIT Press.

Maskus, K., & Wilson, J. (Eds.). (2001). *Quantifying the impact of technical barriers to trade: Can it be done?* Ann Arbor: University of Michigan Press.

Mill, J. S. (1848). *Principles of political economy.* London: John W. Parker.

Resolución 116. (2013). Consejo de Comercio Exterior del Ecuador. Published in Registro Oficial 140, Quito.

Resolución 13392 – RTE 093. (2013). Subsecretaría de Calidad del Ecuador. Published in Registro Oficial 121, Quito.

Sánchez, G. E. (2017). The short-term response of the Hispanic noncitizen population to anti-illegal immigration legislation: The case of Arizona SB 1070. *Journal of Economics, Finance and Administrative Science, 22*(42), 25–36.

UNCTAD. (2013). *Non-tariff measures to trade: Economic and policy issues for developing countries.* New York/Geneva: United Nations.

United States Trade Representative. (2015). *2015 National Trade Estimate Report on Foreign Trade Barriers (NTE).* Office of the United States Trade Representative, Washington, DC. Retrieved from https://ustr.gov/sites/default/files/NTE%20Final%20Printed_0.pdf

World Bank. (2016). *World development indicators 2016.* Washington, DC. Retrieved from http://data.worldbank.org/products/wdi

World Trade Organization. (2016a). *Committee on technical barriers to trade.* 21st annual review of the implementation and operation of the TBT agreement, Geneva.

World Trade Organization. (2016b). *Integrated analysis and retrieval of notified non-tariff measures.* Retrieved from http://i-tip.wto.org/goods/Default.aspx

CHAPTER 14

Does Trade Openness Increase Wage Elasticity of Labour Demand in Indian Manufacturing Industries?

Simontini Das, Ajitava Raychaudhuri, and Saikat Sinha Roy

14.1 Introduction

International trade in emerging market economies including India has registered significant increases in recent periods, accompanied by notable changes in structure. Along with trade in finished goods, these emerging market economies have emerged as traders of a wide range of intermediate goods, parts and accessories, and services. Such emerging patterns of trade in these economies have been facilitated by cross-border investments by developed countries and related restructuring of production. Accompanying wide-ranging changes in trade policies since the mid-1980s and in a more comprehensive manner from 1991 onwards, India like many other emerging market economies emerged as a trading nation.[1] India's share stands at 1.4 per cent in world merchandise trade in 2010, increasing substantially from a low of 0.4 per cent in 1985. The share is even higher at about 1.8 per cent in 2010 when commercial services trade is also taken into account. Further, exports of goods and services account for nearly 30 per cent of GDP in India. In specific, export growth was higher at

S. Das (✉) • A. Raychaudhuri • S.S. Roy
Department of Economics, Jadavpur University, Kolkata, India

S.K. Mathur et al. (eds.), *Theorizing International Trade*,
https://doi.org/10.1007/978-981-10-1759-9_14

19.59 per cent during post reforms, accompanied by wide-ranging changes in commodity composition of merchandise exports. The shift in comparative advantage towards a wide range of manufactures, both intermediate and final goods, during trade liberalisation has a strong influence on the organised manufacturing labour market. This chapter investigates into the impact of international trade on wage elasticities of labour demand in Indian organised manufacturing industries.

Wage elasticity of derived labour demand is an important channel through which trade liberalisation affects the factor markets. The common belief is that trade liberalisation makes the derived labour demand curve more elastic. Bruno et al. (2005), Greenaway et al. (1999), Goldar (2008), Haouas and Yagoubi (2004), Hasan et al. (2007), Jean (2001), Jayanthakumaran (2004), Krishna and Mitra (1998), Krishna et al. (2001), Rodrik (1997), and Slaughter (2001) worked on the impact of trade liberalisation on wage elasticity.

In 1997, Rodrik first provided the basic theory behind the relation between trade liberalisation and wage elasticity. Trade liberalisation had two effects on the labour demand. Import liberalisation made available the imported raw materials, intermediate inputs, machineries and so on that would substitute domestic labour in the production process. Therefore the derived domestic labour demand became more elastic. This effect of trade liberalisation was known as substitution effect. Another effect was scale effect. On account of an increase in trade, much more varieties of consumer product would be available in the international as well as in the domestic market. Therefore the price elasticity of consumer good would increase and this, in turn, would reduce the price-marginal cost mark-up ratio. As a result, derived input demand (here labour) became more elastic. He showed that substitution effect as well as scale effect increased the own price elasticity of labour.

Krishna and Mitra (1998) used the firm-level panel data of various industries to check the impact of trade liberalisation, taking place in India, on the competitiveness and productivity growth of the firm. He introduced a new technique of estimation by allowing changing returns to scale after trade liberalisation. Estimated result showed that trade liberalisation reduced the price marginal cost mark-up ratio significantly at firm level. They also concluded that there was a marginal growth in productivity after trade liberalisation.

Similar to Krishna and Mitra (1998), Greenaway et al. (1999) conducted a similar study in the United Kingdom by using panel data of 167 manufacturing industries to estimate the impact of trade liberalisation on the derived labour demand through the induced productivity changes. They estimated the dynamic labour demand function. They found that growth in trade, in terms of an increase in export volume and import volume, increased the wage elasticity of derived labour demand. The most notable finding was that, here, productivity growth was induced by the increased export volume, which made the derived labour demand more elastic.

Following Greenaway et al. (1999), Jean (2001) examined the impact of trade liberalisation on the derived labour demand, through the change in productivity. But the approach, adopted by Jean, was different from Greenaway et al. Jean constructed a simple theoretical model, following the Armington Hypothesis, to show that increase in export intensity due to trade liberalisation reduced the price-marginal cost mark-up ratio of the domestic firm and therefore increased the wage elasticity of derived labour demand. Apart from theoretical model, Jean also provided an empirical support of the theoretical findings by using industry data of France.

The most notable observation was that Greenaway et al. (1999) and Jean (2001) were the only two economists who had analysed the impact of export promotion on the derived labour demand. All other works in this field adopted different import-related measures as the indicator of trade liberalisation. Krishna et al. (2001) show the impact of trade liberalisation on the wage elasticity of the derived labour demand by using plant-level data of Turkey. But they did not find any statistically significant empirical relation between these two. Slaughter (2001) re-examines the wage elasticity hypothesis for four digit manufacturing industries of the United States over the time period 1960–1990. The analysis was done for production as well as for non-production workers. The estimation of dynamic labour demand function showed that trade liberalisation increased the wage elasticity for the productive workers in five out of eight industries. But for non-production workers, trade liberalisation had no such effect for all eight industries.

Haouas and Yagoubi (2004) tested the same hypothesis by using the manufacturing industry data for the years 1971–1996. They failed to find any statistically significant impact of trade liberalisation on the own price elasticity of derived labour demand. Haouas et al. said that strict labour market regulation dampened the impact of trade liberalisation on the labour demand. At the same time, Jayanthakumaran (2004), using data on Australian manufacturing industry for the period 1989–2000, estimated the relation among trade reforms, employment and intra-industry trade.

He found that trade reforms increased employment opportunities in the manufacturing industries and also increased the intra industry trade. In 2005, Bruno, Falzoni and Helg used an unbalanced panel data for thirty-one Italian manufacturing sectors. They employed least square dummy variable (LSDV) estimation method and general methods of moment (GMM) to estimate dynamic labour demand equation. But their finding rejected the relationship between trade liberalisation and wage elasticity of labour demand.

None of the aforementioned studies (except Krishna and Mitra (1998)) worked on Indian manufacturing sector to test the hypothesis of Rodrik. Hasan et al. (2007), and Goldar (2008) made the first attempt to estimate econometrically the impact of trade liberalisation on the elasticity of labour demand. Hasan et al. (2007) first did a systematic study for Indian manufacturing industries to check Rodrik's hypothesis for eighteen two-digit organised manufacturing industries across fifteen states of India over the time period 1980–1997. Employing GMM method to estimate dynamic labour demand, the estimated results showed that a reduction in tariff rate (measure of trade liberalisation) increased the wage elasticity of labour demand. The inter-state analysis revealed that the impact of trade liberalisation was relatively stronger in the states with relatively flexible labour regulation. In fact, the wage elasticity was also much higher in those states.

Goldar (2008) made another attempt to check the hypothesis related to the impact of trade liberalisation on the labour demand elasticity for India over the time period 1980–1981 to 1997–1998. Here he considered reduction in tariff and non-tariff barriers as the measures of trade liberalisation. Estimated results showed that trade liberalisation made labour demand more elastic for Indian industries.[2] He also calculated the trend of wage elasticity for 1973–1974 to 2003–2004. The contradicting observation was that estimated elasticity was higher in pre-reform period relative to post-reform period. But it was also found that after trade reform in 1991, the fall in elasticity was arrested.

Rodrik's hypothesis, as we see, cannot be established for all countries, however, it is generally accepted for India. The previous studies ignored the impact of export on wage elasticity of derived labour demand, and considered import liberalisation as the sole measure of trade liberalisation. Another drawback is that labour demand function is estimated only for the production workers in both the studies related to India. This chapter intends to include import as well as exports measures. Here, a more comprehensive measure of trade liberalisation, trade openness index,[3] is considered for analysis. We want to estimate the impact of trade openness on the wage elasticity of Indian organised manufacturing sector for both production and non-production workers.[4]

The following section explains the theoretical model and the estimable equations, Sect. 14.3 briefs on the methods and the dataset used to study. Section 14.4 presents the empirical results at aggregate and dis-aggregate level. The last section summarises the major findings.

14.2 Trade Openness and Wage Elasticity: Underlying Theory

Trade liberalisation increases elasticity of labour demand in manufacturing industries through two channels. First, international trade increases the imports of intermediate inputs, capital goods, semi-finished products and unassembled products (outsourcing), which can possibly substitute labour in the production process. As a result, own price elasticity of labour demand in manufacturing industries increases. This is known as substitution effect. Second, following Hicks–Marshallian theory, own price elasticity of factor input demand increases with price elasticity of final products. This is known as scale effect. While import liberalisation leads substitution effect to work, export promotion and import liberalisation generate the scale effect. The present study concentrates on both the substitution effect and on the scale effect, as it consider the trade openness index (ratio of export and import to the value added) as a trade liberalisation index. Larger trade openness indicates greater interactions in international market. Increasing interactions with the global economy lead to an increase in price elasticity of traded commodities, which in turn leads to an increase in own price elasticity of labour demand.

14.2.1 Labour Demand Under Monopolistic Competition[5]

In a monopolistic competitive market, a firm faces a downward-sloping market-demand curve given by,

$$P = \theta P^* Q^{-1/e} \tag{14.1}$$

where P and Q are the price and quantity of the product, P^* = average price level of the industry and e = constant product price elasticity faced by the representative firm. It is also assumed that there is no strategic interaction among the firms in the market. The production function of the firm is given by,

$$Q = k^{\alpha} l^{\beta} \tag{14.2}$$

where k = capital used in the production process, and l = labour demand of the firm. The objective of the representative firm is to maximise profit (π) subject to given factor prices, user cost of capital R and wage rate of labour W. The profit optimisation of the representative firm is given by,

$$\underset{k,l}{\text{Max}}\ \pi = PQ - Rk - Wl \tag{14.3}$$

With fixity of capital, there will be only one profit-maximising condition with respect to $\tilde{l}$. The profit-maximising conditions in capital constrained situation give derived labour demand function for the industry as,

$$\begin{aligned}\text{Log}(\tilde{L}) = B &- [1/\{1-(1-1/e)\beta\}]\text{Log}(W/P^*) \\ &- [\{(1-1/e)\alpha\}/\{1-(1-1/e)\beta\}]\text{Log}(K)\end{aligned} \tag{14.4}$$

where $B = \text{Log}(nb)$, and b is the constant in the derived labour demand function for an individual firm in a capital constrained situation. In a capital constrained situation, the absolute value of real wage elasticity of labour demand is given as,

$$\left|\tilde{\delta}_w\right| = \left|\frac{\partial \text{Log}\tilde{L}}{\partial \text{Log}(W/p^*)}\right| = \left\{\frac{1}{1-(1-1/e)\beta}\right\} \tag{14.5}$$

Differentiating both sides with respect to e, we get

$$\frac{\partial\left|\tilde{\delta}_w\right|}{\partial e} = \frac{\beta}{e^2\{1-(1-1/e)\beta\}^2} > 0 \tag{14.6}$$

The profit-maximising conditions, in unconstrained situation, give the derived labour demand function for individual firm as,

$$l = a(W/P^*)^{-[\{1-(1-1/e)\}/\{1-(1-1/e)(\alpha+\chi)\}]}$$
$$(R/P^*)^{-[\{(1-1/e)\alpha\}/\{1-(1-1/e)(\alpha+\beta)\}]} \tag{14.7}$$

If there are n numbers of identical firms in the industry, then the aggregate labour demand for the industry is given by,

$$L = nl = na(W/P^*)^{-[\{1-(1-1/e)\}/\{1-(1-1/e)(\alpha+\beta)\}]}$$
$$(R/P^*)^{-[\{(1-1/e)\alpha\}/\{1-(1-1/e)(\alpha+\beta)\}]} \tag{14.8}$$

In logarithmic form, the industry's derived labour demand can be given as,

$$\mathrm{Log}(L) = A - [\{1-(1-1/e)\}/\{1-(1-1/e)(\alpha+\beta)\}]\mathrm{Log}(W/P^*)$$
$$-[\{(1-1/e)\alpha\}/\{1-(1-1/e)(\alpha+\beta)\}]\mathrm{Log}(R/P^*) \tag{14.9}$$

where $A = \mathrm{Log}(na)$

Equation (14.9) shows the unconstrained derived labour demand for a monopolistic competitive industry.

The absolute real wage elasticity of the derived labour demand is given by,

$$|\delta_w| = \left|\frac{\partial \mathrm{Log}L}{\partial \mathrm{Log}(W/p^*)}\right| = \left\{\frac{1-(1-1/e)\alpha}{1-(1-1/e)(\alpha+\beta)}\right\} \tag{14.10}$$

Differentiating both sides with respect to e, we get

$$\frac{\partial|\delta_w|}{\partial e} = \frac{\beta}{e^2\{1-(1-1/e)(\alpha+\beta)\}^2} > 0 \tag{14.11}$$

Equation (14.11) shows that absolute value of real wage elasticity of labour demand increases with absolute value of product price elasticity.

Equations (14.6) and (14.11) show that, in an imperfectly competitive market, the absolute value of real wage elasticity of labour demand is an increasing function of absolute product price elasticity.[6] This result is irrespective of whether the industry is capital constrained or not.

14.2.2 Dynamic Labour Demand Function

Equations (14.4) and (14.9) are the potential derived labour demand functions of the industry. However, on account of labour market rigidity, actual labour demand is different from potential labour demand. In capital unconstrained situation, let us assume that Log$L$ is the potential labour demand and LogL_A is the actual labour demand in capital unconstrained situation. The actual labour demand (LogL_{At}) is the weighted average of current potential labour demand (LogL_t) and actual labour demand in previous year (Log$L_{At\text{-}1}$). Therefore actual labour demand can be written as,

$$\mathrm{Log}L_{At} = \lambda(\mathrm{Log}L_{At-1}) + (1-\lambda)(\mathrm{Log}L_t); 0 < \lambda < 1 \tag{14.12}$$

where λ represents labour market rigidity, with smaller values of λ indicating greater labour market flexibility. Substituting Eq. (14.4) in Eq. (14.12), the capital constrained actual labour demand function for the industry can be obtained as,

$$\begin{aligned}\mathrm{Log}\tilde{L}_{At} &= (1-\lambda)A + \lambda\left(\mathrm{Log}\tilde{L}_{At-1}\right) - (1-\lambda)\left[{}^{1}/_{\{1-(1-1/e)\beta\}}\right]\mathrm{Log}\left({}^{W}/_{P^*}\right)\\ &+(1-\lambda)\left[{}^{\{(1-1/e)\alpha\}}/_{\{1-(1-1/e)\beta\}}\right]\mathrm{Log}(K)\end{aligned} \tag{14.13}$$

Similarly in the unconstrained case, the actual labour demand function for the industry is given by,

$$\begin{aligned}\mathrm{Log}L_{At} &= (1-\lambda)A + \lambda(\mathrm{Log}L_{At-1}) - (1-\lambda)\left[\frac{\{1-(1-1/e)\alpha\}}{\{1-(1-1/e)(\alpha+\beta)\}}\right]\\ &\times \mathrm{Log}\left({}^{W}/_{P^*}\right) - (1-\lambda)\left[\frac{\{(1-1/e)\alpha\}}{\{1-(1-1/e)(\alpha+\beta)\}}\right]\mathrm{Log}\left({}^{R}/_{P^*}\right)\end{aligned} \tag{14.14}$$

From Eqs. (14.13) and (14.14), real wage elasticity can be derived. The real wage elasticities, in capital constrained and unconstrained cases, are given by,

$$\left|\tilde{\delta}_W\right| = (1-\lambda)\left\{\frac{1}{1-(1-1/e)\beta}\right\} \tag{14.15}$$

And

$$|\delta_w| = (1-\lambda)\left\{\frac{1-(1-1/e)\alpha}{1-(1-1/e)(\alpha+\beta)}\right\} \tag{14.16}$$

Equations (14.15) and (14.16) show the absolute real wage elasticity of labour demand is a positive function of the absolute product price elasticity.

On the whole, it can be observed that if product price elasticity increases due to increase in trade openness, the real wage elasticity of the labour demand for the industry will increase in unconstrained as well as in capital constrained situations. The effect of trade openness on wage elasticity is estimated for both production labour and non-production labour. Production workers are mainly engaged in direct manufacturing process, while the non-production workers are engaged in supervision, management and administrative work.

14.2.3 *The Estimable Models*

It is often argued the trade openness increases the number of varieties and hence results in higher price elasticity of demand for final goods, which in turn reduces the mark-up ratio. The variations in mark-up results in more elastic derived labour demand. Such an effect of trade liberalisation influences the capital constrained and unconstrained labour demand. The capital constrained and unconstrained labour demand functions are estimated to measure the effect of trade openness on wage elasticity.

The *capital constrained* labour demand function is,

$$\begin{aligned}\text{Log}\tilde{L}_{it} = {} & a_1 + g_0\text{Log}\tilde{L}_{it-1} + g_1\text{Log}w_{it} + g_2\text{Log}K_{it} + g_3 to_{it}\text{Log}w_{it} \\ & + \varepsilon_{1it}\end{aligned} \tag{14.17}$$

Where, L_{it} = employment level of *i*th industry in *t*th time period

w_{it} = real wage rate in *i*th industry in *t*th time period

K_{it} = fixed capital in *i*th industry in *t*th time period

to_{it}= trade openness index of *i*th industry in *t*th time period

= (Export + Import)/value of output

ε_{1it} = disturbance term

The coefficient of the interaction term ($to_{it}\text{Log}w_{it}$) shows the effect of trade openness index on wage elasticity of derived labour demand in capital constrained situation. Partial derivation of Eq. (14.17) gives $\tilde{\delta}$, the wage elasticity of labour demand in capital constrained situation.[7]

$$\widetilde{\delta} = \left(\frac{\left({}^{\partial \bar{L}_{it}} / {}_{\bar{L}_{it}} \right)}{\left({}^{\partial w_{it}} / {}_{w_{it}} \right)} \right) = g_1 + g_3 to_{it} \tag{14.18}$$

Differentiating both sides with respect to to_{it} we get,

$$\left({}^{d\widetilde{\delta}} / {}_{dto_{it}} \right) = g_3 < 0 \tag{14.19}$$

g_3 shows the effect of trade openness index on real wage elasticity of labour demand. Negative g_3 implies that trade openness increases the real wage elasticity of labour demand, given negative wage elasticity $((g_1 + g_3 to_{it}) < 0)$. In a capital constrained situation, wage elasticity of labour demand in manufacturing industries thus increases with trade openness.

The ***unconstrained*** labour demand function can be expressed as,

$$\begin{aligned} \text{Log}L_{it} = a_2 + f_0 \text{Log}L_{it-1} + f_1 \text{Log}w_{it} + f_2 \text{Log}r_{it} + f_3 to_{it} \text{Log}w_{it} \\ + \varepsilon_{2it} \end{aligned} \tag{14.20}$$

Where, r_{it} = real user cost of capital in ith industry in tth time period.

$\varepsilon_{2\text{it}}$ = disturbance term.

Similar to the capital constrained case, the impact of trade openness on wage elasticity of labour demand in an unconstrained situation can be written as,

$$\left({}^{d\delta} / {}_{dto_{it}} \right) = f_3 < 0 \tag{14.21}$$

f_3 shows the impact of trade openness on real wage elasticity of labour demand in an unconstrained situation. $f_3 < 0$ implies that, given negative wage elasticity of labour demand, wage elasticity of labour demand of manufacturing industries increases with trade openness in an unconstrained situation.

Equations (14.17) and (14.20) estimate the impact of trade openness on aggregate wage elasticity of labour demand in capital constrained and unconstrained situations, respectively. On account of differences in industry-specific characteristics, trade effect varies from industry to industry. In order to capture the industry specific effect, slope dummy for each industry is introduced in the static labour demand function.[8] At industry-specific level, similar to aggregate manufacturing, a rise in trade openness following trade liberalisation can impact on labour demand via wage elasticity in capital constrained and unconstrained situations. The capital constrained static labour demand equation, after introducing slope dummy variable to capture industry specific effect, is given by,

$$\begin{aligned}\mathrm{Log}\tilde{L}_{it} &= a_3 + g_1\mathrm{Log}w_{it} + g_2\mathrm{Log}K_{it} + g_3 to_{it}\mathrm{Log}w_{it} + g_{31}(D_1)to_{1t}\mathrm{Log}w_{1t} \\ &+ g_{32}(D_2)to_{2t}\mathrm{Log}w_{2t} + \ldots\ldots\ldots + g_{315}(D_{15})to_{15t}\mathrm{Log}w_{15t} + \varepsilon_{3it}\end{aligned} \tag{14.22}$$

where K_{it} = real value of capital used in ith industry in t time period.
ε_{3it} = disturbance term

$$D_i = \begin{cases} 1 \text{ for } & i^{th}\text{industry}, i = 1, 2, \ldots, n \\ 0 \text{ for } & \text{other industry} \end{cases}$$

The wage elasticity of labour demand for ith industry in capital constrained situation, with $D_i = 1$ for ith industry, is given by,

$$\tilde{\delta}_i = \left(\frac{\left({}^{\partial \tilde{L}_{it}}/_{\tilde{L}_{it}} \right)}{\left({}^{\partial w_{it}}/_{w_{it}} \right)} \right) = g_1 + g_3 to_{it} + g_{3i} to_{it}; \; i = 1, 2, \ldots, n; \tag{14.23}$$

Differentiating Eq. (14.23) with respect to to_{it} we get,

$$\left({}^{d\tilde{\delta}_i}/_{dto_{it}} \right) = g_3 + g_{3i} \tag{14.24}$$

Equation (14.24) shows the total effect of trade openness on the wage elasticity of labour demand for ith industry. In Eq. (14.24), while g_3 is the common effect, g_{3i} is the industry specific effect.

In order to avoid the problem of multicollinearity, one dummy variable out of n is dropped. For instance, if g_{3j} is dropped, then,

$$\tilde{\delta}_j = g_1 + g_3 to_{jt}; \text{for } j\text{th industry} \tag{14.25}$$

Differentiating $\tilde{\delta} j$ with respect to $to_{jt,}$ we get,

$$\left(\tilde{d\delta_j}/_{dto_{jt}}\right) = g_3; \text{for } j\text{th industry} \qquad (14.26)$$

Otherwise, Eq. (14.24) is valid for i^{th} industry where $i \neq j$.

The industry-specific effect g_{3i}, estimated by subtracting $\left(\tilde{d\delta_j}/_{dto_{jt}}\right)$ from $\left(\tilde{d\delta_i}/_{dto_{it}}\right)$, shows the difference between the effect of trade openness index on wage elasticity of labour demand in *i*th industry and *j*th industry.

The industry specific effect can be captured in unconstrained static labour demand equation by introducing slope dummy variable. This reformulated equation is given by,

$$\begin{aligned} \text{Log}L_{it} = a_4 + f_1\text{Log}w_{it} + f_2\text{Log}r_{it} + f_3 to_{it}\text{Log}w_{it} + f_{31}(D_1)to_{1t}\text{Log}w_{1t} \\ + f_{32}(D_2)to_{2t}\text{Log}w_{2t} + \cdots + f_{315}(D_{15})to_{15t}\text{Log}w_{15t} + \varepsilon_{4it} \end{aligned} \qquad (14.27)$$

where ε_{4it} = disturbance term.

In this case, the wage elasticity of labour demand in *i*th industry, with $D_i = 1$ for *i*th industry, is given by,

$$\text{or,} \quad \delta_i = \left(\frac{\left(\partial L_{it}/_{L_{it}}\right)}{\left(\partial w_{it}/_{w_{it}}\right)}\right) = f_1 + f_3 to_{it} + f_{3i} to_{it} \;; i = 1, 2, \ldots, n \qquad (14.28)$$

Differentiating both sides of Eq. (14.28) with respect to to_{it} we get,

$$\left(d\delta_i/_{dto_{it}}\right) = f_3 + f_{3i} \qquad (14.29)$$

Equation (14.29) shows the total effect of trade openness index on the wage elasticity of labour demand for *i*th industry. In Eq. (14.29), while f_3 is the common effect, f_{3i} is the industry specific effect.

In order to avoid the problem of multicollinearity, one dummy variable out of *n* is dropped. For instance, if f_{3j} is dropped, then,

$$\delta_j = f_1 + f_3 to_{jt}; \text{for } j\text{th industry} \qquad (14.30)$$

Differentiating δ_{uj} with respect to to_{jt} we get,

$$\left({}^{d\delta_j}/{}_{dto_{jt}}\right) = f_3; \text{for } j\text{th industry} \tag{14.31}$$

Otherwise, Eq. (14.30) is valid for ith industry where $i \neq j$.

The industry-specific effect f_{3i}, estimated by subtracting $\left({}^{d\delta_j}/{}_{dto_{jt}}\right)$ from $\left({}^{d\delta_i}/{}_{dto_{it}}\right)$, shows the difference between the effect of trade openness index on wage elasticity of labour demand in ith industry and jth industry.

14.3 Estimation Method and Data Description

This section delineates the methodology and the data used for the analysis of impact of merchandise trade on wage elasticity of labour demand in Indian manufacturing industries.

14.3.1 Dynamic Panel Data Method

For estimation of dynamic labour demand function, the lagged dependent variable ($\text{Log}L_{it\text{-}1}$) is included in the set of explanatory variables. This term is correlated with the disturbance terms. As a result, Least Square Dummy Variable (LSDV) method and Feasible Generalised Least Square (FGLS) methods are inappropriate to estimate the model. Dynamic panel data model, in this case, is estimated using Generalised Method of Moments (GMM). GMM IV estimation of Arellano and Bond (1991) will be applied to obtain unbiased, consistent estimators. To avoid cross-section fixed effect, first differences of the variables in Eqs. (14.17) and (14.20) are used for the purpose of estimation. A two-stage iteration method is used to get Arellano and Bond two-step estimators. In this type of estimation, Sargan test of over-identifying restriction is done, where J-statistic is the Sargan statistic. For estimating labour demand function in case of specific industries, slope dummy is introduced in the static labour demand functions. As first difference transformation of the original model is used in the GMM method of estimation, it cannot be used in this case of estimating industry-specific effect. Instead, the estimation of the static labour demand function for individual industries is done using OLS method.

14.3.2 Data Description

Industry specific data is taken from the Annual Survey of Industry (ASI) during the time period 1991–2010. The data on product-specific exports and imports of India at the 2-digit HS (Harmonised System) classification are obtained from World Integrated Trade solution (WITS) and India Trade Statistics. For production, fifteen industries at 3-digit National Industrial Classification (NIC) 2008 are considered here for analysis. Production data are obtained from Central Statistical Organisation, Annual Survey of Industries, factory sector, summary results database. In the Appendix, the classification concordance between NIC1987, NIC1998, NIC2004, NIC2008 and Harmonised System (HS) classification is given. The definition of each variable used in the econometric analysis is as follows.

Production workers: This is the number of workers employed;

Non-production workers: This is defined as the difference between total number of workers engaged and the number of production workers;

Real wage rate of production workers: This is defined as nominal wage rate deflated by the industry specific wholesale price index (WPI). Nominal wage rate is arrived at by dividing total wages paid to workers by the number of productive workers employed;

Real wage to the non-production workers: total income to the non-production workers is obtained by subtracting wage to the workers from the total emolument. Nominal wage rate to the non-production workers is obtained by dividing this with total number of non-production workers. Nominal wage rate is deflated by the industry-specific WPI to get real wage rate;

Real value of capital: Real value of capital is arrived at by deflating monetary value of fixed capital by industry-specific WPI;

Real value of output: This is arrived at by deflating nominal value of output by industry-specific WPI to obtain real value of output;

Real user cost of capital: It is obtained by deflating nominal user cost of capital by industry specific WPI. Nominal user cost of capital is arrived at by multiplying WPI of machinery, transport equipment and construction with the sum of average prime lending rate and the rate of depreciation. Following Hasan et al. (2007), the rate of depreciation is considered at 10 per cent;

Exports: Exports in current value, as given in WITS and India Trade Statistics, in US $ terms, are converted in the domestic currency by multiplying with nominal exchange rate (Re/$);

Imports: Imports in current value, as given in WITS and India Trade Statistics, in US $ terms, are converted in the domestic currency by multiplying with nominal exchange rate (Re/$);

14.4 The Empirical Analysis

Empirical analysis has two parts. The first part describes the impact of trade openness index on wage elasticity for production workers and non-production workers at aggregate level, while the second one elucidates the impacts of trade openness on labour demand elasticities at the industry-specific level.

14.4.1 Aggregate Level Analysis

Table 14.1 depicts the econometric estimation on the impact of trade openness on aggregate wage elasticity of labour demand. The Sargan test results for both unconstrained and capital constrained cases, as presented in Table 14.1, show the validity of over-identifying restriction for both production and non-production workers. The models, estimated here, are thus over-identified. The AR (2) test shows that there is no serial correlation of order 2 in the errors. The estimates both in the capital constrained and unconstrained cases show that trade openness has the expected positive and statistically significant impact on wage elasticity of both production and non-production labour demand measured by the interaction term to_{it}. Logw_{it}. This implies that an increase in trade openness increases the absolute value of wage elasticity of demand for both production as well as non-production workers. Hasan et al. (2007) and Goldar (2008) also find that wage elasticity for production workers rises with trade liberalisation. Both of these are silent about the non-production workers.

In the presence of significant impact on wage elasticity of labour demand, the factor price elasticity of production labour demand in both capital constrained as well as unconstrained cases is negative and significant at 1 per cent level, while the corresponding coefficients for non-production labour demand are also significant at 10 and 1 per cent, respectively. Real user cost of capital has significant positive impact on demand for both production as well as non-production workers in the unconstrained

Table 14.1 Impact of trade openness index on the wage elasticity of labour demand of Indian manufacturing industries

Capital constrained case				
Regressors	*Production workers*		*Non-production workers*	
	Coefficient	*Probability*	*Coefficient*	*Probability*
$\text{Log}L_{it\text{-}1}$	0.1830278***	0.002	0.081578	0.228
$\text{Log}L_{it\text{-}2}$	0.3622779***	0.005	0.0383503	0.668
$\text{Log}w_{it}$	−0.3182365***	0.001	−0.2241104*	0.052
$\text{Log}K_{it}$	0.254943***	0.000	0.25816***	0.001
$to_{it}\text{Log}w_{it}$	−0.0064996*	0.083	−0.0074496***	0.002
Sargan test	chi2(32) = 13.05 Prob> chi2 = 0.9988		chi2(32) = 12.68 Prob> chi2 = 0.9991	
Arellano-Bond (2) test	$z = -0.21$ Pr > $z = 0.8363$		$z = -0.63$ Pr > $z = 0.5278$	
Unconstrained case				
Regressors	Production workers		Non-production workers	
	Coefficient	Probability	Coefficient	Probability
$\text{Log}L_{it\text{-}1}$	0.2365563***	0.001	0.0929413	0.381
$\text{Log}L_{it\text{-}2}$	0.5894861***	0.000	0.1220255*	0.090
$\text{Log}w_{it}$	−0.3099767***	0.000	−0.6035593***	0.000
$\text{Log}r_{it}$	0.0962317***	0.000	0.0774339***	0.000
$to_{it}\text{Log}w_{it}$	−0.0109605***	0.000	−0.0141519***	0.000
Sargan test	chi2(12) = 14.10 Prob > chi2 = 0.2946		chi2(12) = 12.62 Prob > chi2 = 0.3970	
Arellano-Bond (2) test	$z = -1.42$ Pr > $z = 0.1547$		$z = -0.96$ Pr > $z = 0.3358$	

Source: Authors' calculations

Notes: Dependent variable is $\text{Log}L_{it}$; *** indicates significance at 1 per cent level, ** indicates significance at 5 per cent level, * indicates significance at 10 per cent level situation, implying that both types of workers are substitute to capital. In the capital constrained case, capital stock is found to have a significant positive impact on labour demand. This shows that a binding capital constraint, as is often the case in economies like India, lowers labour demand implying complementarity between the two factors. The results also show persistence in production labour demand.

The preceding results on positive impact of trade openness on the absolute value of wage elasticity of labour demand in aggregate manufacturing are thus similar irrespective of whether in a short-run capital-constrained situation or a long-run unconstrained situation. Hence it can be said that the trade openness makes the labour demand for both types of workers more elastic in the short run as well as in the long run.

14.4.2 Industry-Specific Analysis

The industry-specific results vary widely. It is evident from Table 14.2 that in the grain mill products, starch, starch products industry; the wood, cork, straw and plaiting materials industry; the basic precious and non-ferrous metals industry; the television and other electronic product industry; and the optical instruments and photographic equipment industry, the trade openness index increases the absolute wage elasticity of demand for production workers in the short run as well as in the long run. For non-production workers, impact of trade openness on wage elasticity of demand is negative across a larger number of industries both in capital constrained and unconstrained situations. Trade openness index makes labour demand for non-production workers more elastic in the grain mill products, starch, starch products industry; the tobacco industry; the footwear industry; the basic precious and non-ferrous metals industry: the television and other electronic product industry; and the optical instruments and photographic equipment industry in the short run as well as in the long run. In the wood, cork, straw and plaiting materials industry, trade impact coefficient for non-production workers is positive in short run, while being negative in the long-run unconstrained situation. The opposite trend is observed in the glass and glass product industry. It implies that trade liberalisation increases absolute wage elasticity for non-production workers in the wood, cork, straw and plaiting materials industry in the long run and in the glass and glass product industry in the short run.

It can also be said that the observed negative impact is more evident for non-production workers than production workers across a larger

Table 14.2 Effect of trade openness Index on wage elasticity of labour demand for production and non-production workers: *Capital constrained and unconstrained situations*

Industry	*Production workers*		*Non-production workers*	
	Capital constrained	*Unconstrained*	*Capital constrained*	*Unconstrained*
Grain mill product, starch, starch products, etc.	**−2.971732**	**−3.904755**	**−0.9868486**	**−2.314221**
Tobacco product	0.7726182	0.7150277	**−0.0169199**	**−0.1225238**
Footwear	0.0456604	0.0425166	**−0.0146801**	**−0.0040653**
Wood, cork, straw and plaiting materials	**−0.0095837**	**−0.0031774**	0.001209	**−0.0063866**
Rubber product	0.0638155	0.08239	0.0087338	0.0396002
Glass and glass product	0.0320543	0.0985971	**−0.0552418**	0.0309953
Non-metallic mineral product	0.4450454	0.7956472	0.0131094	0.7899968
Iron and steel	0.0819144	0.1519329	0.3649113	0.1130105
Basic precious and non-ferrous metals	**−0.0569751**	**−0.0318821**	**−0.1088464**	**−0.0665069**
Television and other electronic product	**−.0310096**	**−0.0313205**	**−0.0116578**	**−0.0119408**
Optical instruments and photographic equipment	**−0.0200924**	**−0.0174605**	**−0.0100156**	**−0.0062063**
Transport equipment	0.0423204	0.0341187	0.0265812	0.0191365
Manufactures of furniture	0.0593618	0.0542184	0.0511395	0.0496878
Textiles, etc.	0.1994151	0.2293977	0.0668012	0.1081108
Basic chemical and other chemical product	0.0204064	0.0616097	0.1403534	0.1982578

Source: Authors' calculations

cross-section of industries. Labour demand becomes more elastic with the increase in trade openness in the grain mill products, starch, starch products industry, the basic precious and non-ferrous metals industry, the television and other electronic product industry and the optical instruments and photographic equipment industry for both types of workers in the short run as well as in the long run.

14.5 Conclusion

The empirical analyses show that trade openness increases absolute value of wage elasticity of labour demand for production and non-production workers in aggregate manufacturing in a short-run capital-constrained situation as well as in a long-run unconstrained situation. The industry-specific results depicts that, during post-reforms, the estimated magnitude of wage elasticity increases on account of trade across a large number of manufacturing industries for non-production workers than production workers. Hence it can be concluded that trade liberalisation makes non-production labour demand more elastic across a larger number of industries. In the grain mill products, starch, starch products industry, the basic precious and non-ferrous metals industry, the television and other electronic product industry and the optical instruments and photographic equipment industry, labour demand for both types of workers becomes more elastic with the increase in trade openness in the short run as well as in the long run. However, there are some exceptions. In the wood, cork, straw and plaiting materials industry, wage elasticity for non-production workers increases in the long run, but in the glass and glass product industry, wage elasticity for non-production workers increases in the short run.

The findings of this chapter are robust as they conform to earlier findings in the literature. The results existing in the literature are qualified in this chapter in the sense that trade openness increases wage elasticity for production and non-production labours of aggregate manufacturing industry in India. The results, however, vary across industries.

Appendix

Table 14.3 Classification concordance between HS-1998, NIC 1987, NIC 1998, NIC 2004 and NIC2008

Description	*HS-1996*	*NIC 1987*	*NIC 1998 3-digit*	*NIC 2004 3-digit*	*NIC 2004 4-digit*	*NIC 2008 4-digit*	*Computational note*
Manufacture of grain mill products, starches and starch products, and prepared animal feeds	11	204 + 217 + 218	153	153	1531 1532 1533	1061 1062 1080	
Manufacture of tobacco products [tobacco related products are also included while preliminary processing of tobacco leaves is classified in class 0111]	24	225 + 226 + 227 + 228 + 229	160	160	1600	1200	
Manufacture of footwear.	64	291 + 311	192	192	1920	1520	
Manufacture of products of wood, cork, straw and plaiting materials	44 + 45	271 + 272 + 273 + 274 + 275 + 279	202	202	2021 2022 2023(p) 2023(p)	1621 1622 1623 3319 (1/13th)	1721(p) + 1723(p) + 2023(p) +2029(p) + 2519(p) + 2520 (p) + 2610(p) + 2699(p) + 3311(p)

							+ 3312(p) + 3330 (p) + 3692(p) + 3694(p) = 3319
					2029(p)	1629 (1/2)	2029(p) + 3699(p) = 1629
					2029	3319 (1/13th)	1721(p) + 1723(p) + 2023(p) + 2029 (p) + 2519(p) + 2520(p) + 2610(p) + 2699(p) + 3311 (p) + 3312(p) + 3330(p) + 3692(p) + 3694(p) = 3319
Manufacture of rubber products	40	310+312	251	251	2511	2211	
					2519(p)	2219	
					2519(p)	3319 (1/13th)	1721(p) + 1723(p) + 2023(p) + 2029 (p) + 2519(p) + 2520(p) + 2610 (p) + 2699(p) + 3311(p) + 3312(p) + 3330(p) + 3692 (p) + 3694(p) = 3319
Manufacture of glass and glass products	70	321	261	261	2610(p)	2310	
					2610(p)	3319 (1/13th)	1721(p) + 1723(p) + 2023(p) + 2029 (p) + 2519(p) + 2520(p) + 2610(p) + 2699(p) + 3311 (p) + 3312(p) + 3330(p) + 3692(p) + 3694(p) = 3319

(continued)

Table 14.3 (continued)

Description	*HS-1996*	*NIC 1987*	*NIC 1998 3-digit*	*NIC 2004 3-digit*	*NIC 2004 4-digit*	*NIC 2008 4-digit*	*Computational note*
Manufacture of non-metallic mineral products n.e.c.	65 + 68 + 69	320 + 322 +323 + 324 + 325 + 326 + 327 + 329	269	269	2691(p) + 2693	2392	
					2691(p)	2393	
					2692	2391	
					2694	2394	
					2695	2395	
					2696	2396	
					2699	2399	
Manufacture of Basic Iron & Steel	72 + 73	330 +331 + 332	271	271	2711 + 2712 + 2713 + 2714 + 2715 + 2716 + 2717 + 2718 + 2719	2410	
Manufacture of basic precious and non-ferrous metals	74 + 75 + 76 + 78 + 79	333 + 334 + 335 + 336 + 338 + 339	272	272	2720	2420	
Manufacture of television and radio receivers, sound or video recording or reproducing apparatus, and associated goods	85	366	323	323	3230(p)	2640	
					3230(p)	9521(1/2)	3230(p) + 5260(p) = 9521
Manufacture of optical instruments and photographic equipment	37	381	332	332	3320(p)	2670(1/2)	3320(p) + 3312(p) = 2670
					3320(p)	3250(1/2)	3311(p) + 3320(p) = 3250
					3320(p)	3313 (1/5th)	3220(p) + 3311(p) + 3312(p) + 3313 (p) + 3320(p) = 3313

Manufacture of transport equipment n.e.c.	87	375 + 376 + 378 + 379	359	359	3591	3091	
					3592	3092	
					3599(p)	3099	
					3599(p)	3316(1/6th)	3511(p) + 3512(p) + 3520(p) + 3530 (p) + 3599(p) + 6303(p) = 3315
Manufacture of furniture	94	276 + 277 + 342	361		3610	3100	
Manufacture of basic chemicals + Manufacture of other chemical products	28 + 29 + 30 + 31 + 33 + 34+36	300 + 301 + 302 + 303 + 304 + 305 + 208 + 307 + 309	241 + 242	241 + 242	2411	2011 (1/3rd)	2330(p) + 2411 + 2429(p) = 2011
					2412	2012	
					2413	2013	
					2421	2021	
					2422	2022	
					2424	2023	
					2429(p)	2029	
					2429(p)	2680	
					2429(p)	2011 (1/3rd)	2330(p) + 2411 + 2429(p) = 2011
					2423	2100	
Textile Industry	50 + 51 + 52 + 57 + 60 + 61 + 62	[231 + 232 + 233 + 234 + 235 + 236 + 240 + 241 + 242 + 243 + 244 + 245 + 246 + 247 + 248 + 250 + 251 + 252 + 253 + 254 + 255 + 256 + 257 + 258 + 259] + [261 + 262 +	171 + 172 + 173	171 + 172 + 173	1711(p) + 1713(p)	1311	
					1711(p) + 1713(p)	1312	
					1712 + 1714	1313	
					1721(p) + 1722(p) +1725(p)	1392	
					1722(p) + 1725(p)	1393	
					1723(p)	1394	
					1724 + 1729	1399	

(*continued*)

Table 14.3 (continued)

Description	*HS-1996*	*NIC 1987*	*NIC 1998 3-digit*	*NIC 2004 3-digit*	*NIC 2004 4-digit*	*NIC 2008 4-digit*	*Computational note*
		263 + 264 + 267 + 268 + 269] + [260]			1721(p)	3319 (1/13th)	1721(p) + 1723(p) + 2023(p) + 2029 (p) + 2519(p) + 2520(p) + 2610(p) + 2699(p) + 3311 (p) + 3312(p) + 3330(p) + 3692(p) + 3694(p) = 3319
					1723(p)	3319 (1/13th)	1721(p) + 1723(p) + 2023(p) + 2029 (p) + 2519(p) + 2520(p) + 2610(p) + 2699(p) + 3311 (p) + 3312(p) + 3330(p) + 3692(p) + 3694(p) = 3319
					1730(p)	1391	
					1730(p)	1430	

Note: (p) denotes parts; + denotes aggregation of classes
Source: Authors' calculation based on various concordance tables of National Industrial Classifications

Notes

1. The debate on whether trade reforms in India have led to higher growth in trade is far from conclusive. A view can however be put forth that trade reforms at best relaxed the hitherto constraints operating in the external sector thereby creating conditions for better trade performance.
2. However, Goldar's analysis is aggregative in nature. He does not undertake any industry-level study. It is not expected that the wage elasticity is going to be affected in the same way across the industries as the labour market, production technology, and so on vary across the sectors. Hence, in this chapter we intend to estimate the impact of trade liberalisation on wage elasticity across fifteen important industries.
3. Trade openness index is a more exposed measure of liberalisation in a sense that it is actual share of traded output (export +import) of total produced output. However, some researchers argued that it is an endogenous variable and hence there would be some econometric problems during estimation. In this chapter, we use GMM to estimate the dynamic labour demand, where the problem of endogenous variable can be solved.
4. Production workers imply the workers are directly involved in the production process. Besides production workers, there is another type of worker consisting of managerial staffs, supervisors, cleaning staffs, and so on who are not directly involved in the production process. These types of workers are known as non-production workers. However, this classification of workers is not skills based. As ASI does not provide any information about the education level of workers or employees we cannot classify them as skilled or unskilled workers.
5. A similar approach is used in, among others, Haouas and Yagoubi (2004) and Hasan et al. (2007).
6. Hasan et al. (2007), however, show that, even in a perfectly competitive market, the absolute nominal wage elasticity of labour demand is also positively related with the absolute product price elasticity both in the unconstrained as well as capital constrained situations.
7. Wage elasticity is assumed to be a linear function of trade openness index (to_{it}).
8. The GMM method cannot be used to estimate industry-specific effect, since it considers the first difference of the original model. The estimation of static labour demand function is done using the OLS method.

References

Arellano, M., & Bond, S. (1991). Some tests of specification for panel data: Monte Carlo evidence and an application to employment equations. *Review of Economic Studies, 58*(2), 277–297.

Bruno, G. S. F., Falzoni, A. M., & Helg, R. (2005). *Estimating a dynamic labour demand equation using small, unbalanced panels: An application to Italian manufacturing sectors.* Università Bocconi, Milano; Università degli Studi di Bergamo; LIUC – Università Carlo Cattaneo.

Goldar, B. (2008). *Trade liberalization and labour demand elasticity in Indian manufacturing.* Delhi: Institute of Economic Growth.

Greenaway, D., Hine, R. C., & Wright, P. (1999). An empirical assessment of the impact of trade on employment in the United Kingdom. *European Journal of Political Economy, 5*(2), 485–500.

Haouas, I., & Yagoubi, M. (2004). *Trade liberalization and labour-demand elasticities: Empirical evidence from Tunisia.* IZA discussion paper no. 1084, Institute for the Study of Labour, Bonn.

Hasan, R., Mitra, D., & Ramaswamy, K. V. (2007). Trade reforms, labour regulations and labour-demand elasticities: Empirical evidence from India. *Review of Economics and Statistics, 89*(3), 466–481.

Jayanthakumaran, K. (2004). *An empirical assessment of the impact of inter-industry trade on employment: Australia 1989/90–2000/01.* Working paper no. 04-11, Department of Economics, University of Wollongong, Wollongong.

Jean, S. (2001). The effect of international trade on labour demand elasticities: Inter-sectoral matters. *Review of International Economics, 8*(3), 504–516.

Krishna, P., & Mitra, D. (1998). Trade liberalization, market discipline and productivity growth: New evidence from India. *Journal of Development Economics, 56*(2), 447–462.

Krishna, P., Mitra, D., & Chinoy, S. (2001). Trade liberalization and labour-demand elasticities: Evidence from Turkey. *Journal of International Economics, 55*(2), 391–409.

Rodrik, D. (1997). *Has globalization gone too far?* Washington, DC: Institute for International Economics.

Slaughter, M. J. (2001). International trade and labour-demand elasticities. *Journal of International Economics, 54*(1), 27–56.

CHAPTER 15

An Analysis of Dynamic Spillover in India's Forex Derivatives Markets

Wasim Ahmad, Shirin Rais, and Ritesh Kumar Mishra

15.1 Introduction

The continuous depreciation of Indian currency has sparked an intense interest in examining not only the degree of financial market integration along with the flow of foreign capital in the country, but also investigating the potential role of domestic currency trading platforms in the process of informational spillover. In the continuation of its aggressive economic liberalization measures, India set-up its own currency derivatives exchange on 29 August 2008 with the introduction of currency futures in US dollar paired with Indian rupee (USD/INR). The main objective was set out to minimize the currency risk in the event of awkward exchange rate fluctuation and to increase the international outreach of Indian rupee. Since then, the currency derivatives trading has been expanded by introducing futures trading in three more currency pairs viz. Euro (EURO/INR), British Pound (GBP/INR) and Japanese Yen (JPY/INR). At present, there are

W. Ahmad (✉)
Department of Economic Sciences, Indian Institute of Technology Kanpur, Kanpur, India

S. Rais
Department of Economics, Aligarh Muslim University, Aligarh, India

R.K. Mishra
Guru Gobind Singh Indraprastha University, Delhi, India

S.K. Mathur et al. (eds.), *Theorizing International Trade*,
https://doi.org/10.1007/978-981-10-1759-9_15

four major trading platforms i.e. Bombay Stock Exchange (BSE), Multi-Commodity Exchange-Stock Exchange (MCX-SX), National Stock Exchange (NSE) and United Stock Exchange (USE). Analyzing the trading figures, as on April 2013, India's forex trading platform accounted for about 0.5% of global foreign exchange market turnover, which is higher compared to 0.1% in 1998 (see BIS 2013). The market size is about 31 billion US dollars, which is low compared to 38 billion US dollars in 2007. This reveals the fact that India's forex market is indeed under pressure. More interestingly, the USD/INR pair has about 0.9% (50 billion US dollars) share in all the currencies paired with US dollar, which is lower than most of the emerging markets except Brazil. Analyzing the trading figure domestically, as of December 2013, NSE had the traded value of 30,107 million dollars followed by MCX-SX (14,181 million dollars) and USE (3077 million dollars) (see SEBI 2013 for details).[1] Since September 2010, when the currency derivatives trading was started even on USE, the trading figures still suggest that NSE is the largest player with the trading share of more than 52% followed by MCX-SX (39%) and USE only (9%).[2] The exchange rate trend indicates that since November 2011, the Rupee has continuously depreciated against US dollar and subsequently the other major currencies traded on India's currency derivatives platforms.[3] The consistent decline in the value of the Indian rupee has been one of the leading cause of concerns for not only policy makers, but also for hedgers who are involved in import/export of commodity. The possible reason for this decline appears to be the large outflow of capital from debt market that further led to the increase in bond yield and consequently a sharp depreciation of major emerging markets currencies in May 2013 (see Miyajima and Shim 2014). Considering the enormous implication of foreign exchange market upheavals on the economy, an insufficient number of studies have tried to study the phenomenon of currency market interdependence in the light of directional information spillover especially at the time when the rupee is passing through a difficult phase of decline. The objective of this study is twofold. First, to examine the level and direction of return and volatility spillover in India's two currency derivatives trading platforms to shed some light on the interdependence between futures and spot and between futures markets interactions. Second, we then explore whether the interactions between futures and spot and between futures series are inter-currency or intra-currency in nature. This is mainly because it has a lot of policy implications from cross-market hedging and speculation. To state it more intuitively, this chapter aims to provide answers to questions such as: First, what is the level and direction of information transmission in India's foreign exchange market? As this will address the issue of market efficiency in the currency market. Second, is the direction of informational spillover inter-currency or intra-currency? Third, has currency futures market started playing an important role in information transmission process? Fourth, which trading platform is dominant or satellite with respect to returns and volatility-based informational spillover? The answers to these questions are expected to provide important direction in undertaking policy measures and also for traders and investors concerned. As studies have noted, one of the salient features of the currency derivatives market is to provide a hedging platform for the exporters and traders in the event of strong currency market upheavals. Particularly, in the case of India, the research mentioned above questions appear to be relevant as for a quite long time, the introduction of forex derivatives has been one of the hotly debated topics among academics, researchers, traders, and regulators with regards to its constructive role in price discovery and the volatility spillover process in India. This is mainly because of the predatory pricing and market-dominant strategies adopted by large players in the currency derivatives markets (see MCX-SX 2014). The examination of informational spillover also plays a significant role in the formulation of a trading strategy for investors and traders and containing the risk of currency market speculation for policy makers. In the context of India's currency derivatives market, this is the first study that examines the directional spillover in returns and volatility of two prominent trading exchanges viz., National Stock Exchange (NSE) and Multi-Commodity Stock Exchange (MCX-SX). The study considers the four prominent exchange rates viz., United States Dollar (USD/INR), Euro (EURO/INR), British Pound (GBP/INR) and Japanese Yen (JPY/INR). This study is based on the daily data for the sample period of 01 February 2010 to 25 November 2014.

Focusing on the research concerning spillover analysis in case of derivatives markets, a close appraisal of existing literature reveals that two issues that have been widely investigated are price discovery and volatility spillovers between futures and spot and between futures prices of various commodities ranging from agriculture to currencies (see Harvey and Huang 1991; Abhyankar 1995; Lin et al. 1994; Tse 1999; Fung et al. 2001; Hong 2001; Han and Ozocak 2002; Roope and Zurbruegg 2002; Xu and Fung 2005; Hua and Chen 2007; Inagaki 2007; Karmakar 2009; Mahalik et al. 2010; McMillan and Speight 2010; Antonakakis 2012). Regarding volatility spillover, according to Chan et al. (1991) volatility spillover helps in investigating the process through which volatility in one market affects that of another market. In the words of Hong (2001), the identification of volatility spillover across assets or markets is important because it helps describing how one large shock increases the volatility not only in its asset or market but also in other assets or markets as well. Hence, there is general agreement that volatility spillovers correspond to information transmission between different assets or markets (Tse 1999; Gagnon and Karolyi 2006; Rittler 2012). Further, the examination of shock spillover across currency markets has grave implications for the formulation of currency trading strategies, currency risk diversification and exchange rate management policies usually formulated by the central bank. As mentioned, the examination of the currency derivatives market volatility in India is important because it is inextricably linked with trade policy of the country and liberalization measures undertaken in the recent past. As the experiences of many economies clearly suggest that due to globalization related free flow of capital and continuous innovation in the financial system, many economies have observed abnormal behaviour in their exchange rates. A volatile foreign exchange market not only affects the price and returns volatility of other assets in the system, but also it disturbs the trade flow and balance of payment of countries (See Claessens et al. 2001).The study of magnitude and direction of spillover between currencies and markets in which they are traded, that is, spot and futures, are important for the reason that it enables a researcher to gauge the level of informational efficiencies between markets. Volatility spillover between currencies and markets lead to the characterization of whether a particular market is dominant or satellite, where fluctuation in the value of one currency causes substantial changes in the relative prices of other currencies and assets in response to the first shock originated in a different market. This further leads to increased volatility following the cause and effect process found in the feedback systems. Sometimes these spillover effects are too large to ignore and for a country like India that is already struggling with the unfavourable balance of payment position and exchange rate volatility complicates the issue further. Diebold and Yilmaz (2009, 2012) define spillover regarding the share of the forecast error variance decomposition (FEVD) in a market that is caused by shocks mainly originated from other markets. The rate of flow of information between assets and markets has often been linked to volatility. It is argued that in case of the clustered flow of information, asset prices or returns may display volatility even if the market's reaction and correction mechanism is perfect and instantaneous. And an absence of spillover provides support to the proposition that the main factors responsible for changes in volatility are asset or market-specific fundamentals. And if this is the case, then a large shock will only disturb the volatility of a particular related asset or market. But in the presence of spillover effect, one large shock originated in a market will disturb volatilities in other assets and markets as well (see Hong 2001). Therefore, an explicit knowledge of volatility spillover across assets and markets is crucial in understanding the mechanism through which information and shocks are transmitted or spilled over to other markets and sectors of the economy.

15.2 Review of Literature

A large number of studies have examined the process of information transmission covering equity and commodities markets (see Engle et al. 1990; Harvey and Huang 1991; Lin et al. 1994; Tse 1999; Fung et al. 2001; Hong 2001; Han and Ozocak 2002; Roope and Zurbruegg 2002; Xu and Fung 2005; Hua and Chen 2007; Inagaki 2007; Karmakar 2009; Mahalik et al. 2010; Kumar 2011; Antonakakis 2012; Sehgal et al. 2015). The main thrust of most of these studies has been on examining spillover phenomenon on either well-developed markets or the equity component of financial market linkages. Although the research issue of informational spillover in case of currency derivatives market is not a new phenomenon, there is an insufficient number of studies that have examined the shock spillover by exploring the different dimensions in case of emerging markets like India. Fung and Patterson (1999) study the dynamic relationship in terms of return volatilities, volume and market depth for five currency futures markets viz., Canadian dollar, German mark, Japanese yen, Pound sterling and Swiss franc for the period 1977–1994. Using VAR methodology, the study concludes that there is a substantial evidence of reversal effects from trading volume and market depth and volatilities have predictive power on volume but not in the market depth. Asimakopoulos et al. (2000) investigate return spillovers across currency futures markets and detect some support for nonlinear causality, although they argue that the causality disappears when the series are controlled for common ARCH effects. Chan and Lien (2006) examine the impact of the introduction of options on the underlying asset's price formation by taking the futures and spot prices of Deutsche mark, British pound, Swiss franc, Japanese yen and Canadian dollar for the period 1982–1988. The study also examines the impact before and after the introduction of option in currency markets. Using the measure of linear dependence, the study concludes that there is significant and instantaneous feedback between futures and spot markets post introduction of options. Regarding volatility spillovers, in recent work, Nikkinen et al. (2006) analyze the linkages between the markets using implied volatilities from currency option prices, focusing on European currencies, and detect significant influence from the euro to the pound and Swiss franc. Inagaki (2007) examines volatility spillover between the euro and the British pound and show unidirectional causality from the euro to the pound. Elyasiani et al. (2007) examine the information transmission and spillover in currency markets using generalized variance decomposition analysis for the period 1985–2005. Considering the case of the British pound, Deutsche mark, Swiss franc and Japanese yen, the study supports the hypothesis of interdependency against the segregation model with a greater degree of shock spillover varying across countries. They further report that internal forces are more dominant for British pound and Japanese yen, whereas Deutsche mark and Swiss franc are vulnerable to external shocks. Kitamura (2010) examines the intra-day interdependence and volatility spillover among the euro, the pound and the Swiss franc markets for the period 2008–2009. Using varying-correlation (VC) model of multivariate generalized autoregressive conditional heteroskedasticity (MV-GARCH), the study concludes that return volatility in the euro spills over to the pound and Swiss franc. Bubak et al. (2011) in their study find out the volatility transmission in emerging European markets by taking the intra-day data of Central European currencies and EUR/USD foreign exchange. Their study uses the spillover index method developed by Diebold and Yilmaz (2009, 2012). Based on the empirical results, the study concludes that there is intra-regional volatility spillover among emerging foreign exchange rates. Finally, the study reports that volatility spillovers tend to increase in periods characterized by market uncertainty. Antonakakis (2012) investigates the exchange rate co-movements and volatility spillovers by taking the case of before and after the introduction of the euro. The study uses four major internationally traded currencies, namely the euro, the British pound, the Japanese yen and the Swiss franc against the US dollar. Using directional spillover measure suggested by Diebold and Yilmaz (2012) and Dynamic Conditional Correlation (Engle 2002; henceforth DCC), the study finds high bi-directional spillover rather than unidirectional spillover. Tamakoshi and Hamori (2014) study the cross-currency transmissions between the US dollar and euro LIBOR-OIS spreads by using the causality-in-variance and causality-in-mean tests of Hong (2001) for the period 2005–2011. Considering the case during the global financial crisis period, the study finds a bi-directional causal relationship between the two spreads. Particularly during Eurozone crisis (2009), the study finds no significant causality-in-mean and causality-in-variance between the spreads. Ciner (2011) examines the information transmission across futures markets by taking the case of euro, yen, British pound and Swiss franc currency futures markets for the period 1999–2009. Based on the empirical findings, the study reports significant international informational linkages.

As far as the examination of volatility spillovers in foreign exchange market is concerned, the published evidence on Indian economy is very scarce. Some relevant studies in this strand are Behera (2011), Kumar (2011, 2014), Sharma (2011), Patnaik (2013), and Sehgal et al. (2015). Behera (2011) examined the onshore and offshore markets of Indian rupee for volatility and shock spillover. The study found the evidence of mean spillover impact of onshore spot on non-deliverable forward (NDF), but the inverse was not true. Sharma (2011) examined the relationship between currency futures and exchange rate volatility in India. Using Granger causality, the study exhibited bilateral causality between the volatility in the spot exchange rate and trading activity in the currency futures market. It may be noted that though these two studies have strong policy implications for the Indian currency market, the objectives of these studies were different from the present work as this study not only provides the evidence of price discovery and volatility spillovers in spot and futures markets, but also examines the cross market informational linkages with the use of recent data. Sharma (2011) examines the return and volatility spillover among US dollar, euro and British pound using Diebold and Yilmaz (2009). The study finds that there is a significant contemporaneous relationship among the three exchange rate returns and volatility spillover indices. The empirical results of spillover suggest that the euro exchange rate contributes to pound rates, in terms of both return and volatility spillovers. US dollar exchange rates are largely unaffected by innovations in other exchange rates. Patnaik (2013) applies dynamic conditional correlation on spot series of four exchange rates. The study reports high volatility in individual spot series, while cross-volatility spillovers are very limited. In line with the previous study, Kumar (2014) applies the multivariate GARCH model on the nominal exchange rate of four currency pairs. The study finds substantial inter-currency volatility spillover between currency pairs and reports high volatility during the financial crisis period. Sehgal et al. (2015) investigate the price discovery and volatility spillover in India's foreign exchange market by examining the futures and spot prices of four currencies viz.

USD/INR, EUR/INR, GBP/INR and JPY/INR for the period 2010–2012. Using a different set of methodology, including the Diebold and Yilmaz (2009, 2012) spillover index measure, the study suggests that the volatility spillovers are stronger from futures to spot in the short run while the inverse is the case in the long run. Based on the empirical results, the study suggests that in India's foreign exchange market, it is the futures price that assimilates new market information more quickly in its price than spot, while, the inverse is found in the long run.

It is apparent from the preceding studies that there are not many studies that have examined the spillover in an emerging market setting. In case of India, this is the first study that examines the currency market spillover by considering four important traded currencies on NSE and MCX-SX platforms. Unlike the study of Kumar (2011, 2014) and Sehgal et al. (2015), the present study attempts to examine not only return and volatility spillover between futures and spot market of currencies, but also attempts to confirm whether the spillover is inter-currency or intra-currency only. The study of Sehgal et al. (2015) is closest to our study. Further, the study updates the literature by covering recent data that captures the important phases of recent and persistent depreciations of Indian currency.

The present study is organized as follows. In Sect. 15.3, we elaborate the methodology of directional spillover and dynamic conditional correlation. Section 15.4 explains the data and formula of calculating range based volatility. Section 15.5 discusses empirical results, followed by Sect. 15.6, which deals with conclusion and policy implications of this study.

15.3 Methodology

15.3.1 Directional Spillover and Spillover Index

In this section, we discuss the directional spillover measure proposed by Diebold and Yilmaz (2009, 2012) in brief. The study models currency market return and volatility as N market vector autoregression (VAR). According to Diebold and Yilmaz (2012, also as DY) a spillover index is calculated using forecast error variance decomposition under VARframework. The forecast error variance decomposition shows the portion of the variance to variable i that is the result of innovations (shocks) to variable j represented as a percentage. We apply generalized VAR framework of Koop et al. (1996) and Pesaran and Shin (1998) to compute the variance decompositions, which is insensitive to the order of variables. It further helps in calculating the net spillover between variables. The model is specified as follows: Let volatility of futures and spot series of sample currencies is modeled as a vector autoregressive process. A VAR (p) model of N variables (in generalized form) can be written as

$$x_t = \sum_{t=1}^{n} \psi_i x_{t-i} + \varepsilon_t \tag{15.1}$$

where ε error vector which is i.i.d and Σ is the variance-covariance matrix. The moving average representation of VAR (p) model can be written as $x_t = \sum_{t=1}^{\infty} A_i \varepsilon_{t-i}$, where the $N \times N$ coefficient matrices observe the recursion $A_i = \psi_1 A_{i-1} + \psi_2 A_{i-2} + \ldots\ldots\ldots\ldots + \psi_p A_{i-p}$ with A_0 an $N \times N$ matrix and A_i=0 for $i < 0$. The variance decompositions further allow the fraction of the H-step-ahead residual variance in forecasting y_i to shocks to x_j, $\forall j \neq i$, for each i to be measured. Under Koop et al. (1996) and Pesaran and Shin (1998) frameworks, the formula to calculate the H-step-ahead generalized forecast error decompositions is given by

$$\theta_{ij}(H) = \frac{\sigma_{ii}^{-1} \sum_{h=0}^{H-1} \left(e_i' h_h \sum e_j\right)^2}{\sum_{h=0}^{H-1} \left(e_i' h_h \sum e_j\right)} \tag{15.2}$$

Where σ_{ii} is the i element on the principle diagonal of Σ. Since each row of $\theta_{ij}(H)$ does not sum to one, therefore, we normalize each element of the matrix by the summing the row as $\widetilde{\theta}_{ij}(H) = \frac{\theta_{ij}(H)}{\sum_{j=1}^{N} (\theta_{ij}(H))}$ so that decomposition including shocks in each market sums to 1, i.e., $\sum_{j=1}^{N} (\theta_{ij}(H)) = 1$ and total decomposition over all markets sums to N i.e., $\sum_{j=1}^{N} (\theta_{ij}(H)) = N$ Following Diebold and Yilmaz (2012), the total spillover index is calculated as

$$S(H) = \frac{\sum_{\substack{j=1 \\ i \neq j}}^{N} \widetilde{\theta}_{ij}(H)}{N} \times 100 \tag{15.3}$$

In this study, we measure the directional spillover between futures and spot of sample currencies. It is the sum of the proportions of the forecast error variance of i series due to shocks to $j \forall\ i \neq j$. The directional spillover from futures to spot is calculated as

$$S_{i^o}(H) = \frac{\sum_{\substack{j=1 \\ i \neq j}}^{N} \widetilde{\theta}_{ij}(H)}{\sum_{j=1}^{N} \widetilde{\theta}_{ij}(H)} \times 100 \tag{15.4}$$

It is noteworthy that directional spillover measures are not ordering sensitive. In similar vein, directional spillover received from spot to futures is obtained as

$$S_{^o i}(H) = \frac{\sum_{\substack{j=1 \\ i \neq j}}^{N} \widetilde{\theta}_{ij}(H)}{\sum_{j=1}^{N} \widetilde{\theta}_{ij}(H)} \times 100 \tag{15.5}$$

Lastly, we calculate the net spillovers from futures to spot in the cases of all sample currencies by offsetting the (15.4) and (15.5) as

$$S_i(H) = S_{i^o}(H) - S_{^o i}(H) \tag{15.6}$$

The net spillover shows whether the futures market is a net transmitter or net receiver in a system of volatility spillovers (see Awartani and Maghyereh 2013).

15.3.2 Dynamic Conditional Correlation Analysis

To further distill the directional spillover analysis, this study moves a step ahead to estimate the dynamic conditional correlation model of multivariate generalized autoregressive conditional heteroskedasticity (henceforth, DCC). The Engle (2002) dynamic conditional correlation (DCC) model is estimated in two steps. In the first step, GARCH parameters are estimated followed by correlations in the second step

$$H_t = D_t R_t D_t \tag{15.7}$$

In Eq. (15.7), H_t is the $n \times n$ conditional covariance matrix, R_t is the conditional correlation matrix and D_t is a diagonal matrix with time-varying standard deviations on the diagonal.

$$D_t = \text{diag}\left(h_{11_t}{}^{1/2} \ldots . h_{33_t}{}^{1/2}\right)$$

$$R_t = \text{diag}\left(q_{11_t}{}^{-1/2} \ldots \ldots q_{33_t}{}^{-1/2}\right) Q_t \text{diag}\left(q_{11_t}{}^{-1/2} \ldots \ldots q_{33_t}{}^{-1/2}\right)$$

Where Q_t is a symmetric positive definite matrix:

$$Q_t = (1 - \theta_1 - \theta_2)\bar{Q} + \theta_1 \varepsilon_{t-1} \varepsilon'_{t-1} + \theta_2 Q_{t-1} \tag{15.8}$$

$\bar{Q}$ is the $n \times n$ unconditional correlation matrix of the standardized residuals ε_{it}. The parameters θ_1 and θ_2 are non-negative with a sum of less than unity. Under the DCC specification, the time-varying correlations are defined as:

$$\rho_{ij,t} = \frac{q_{ij,t}}{\sqrt{q_{ii,t} q_{jj,t}}} \tag{15.9}$$

The MGARCH models estimated by Quasi-Maximum Likelihood Estimation (QMLE) using the Broyden-Fletcher-Goldfarb-Shanno (BFGS) algorithm. T-statistics are calculated using a robust estimate of the covariance matrix.

15.4 Data

The sample data of the daily futures prices of four currencies viz., USD/INR (US Dollar/INR), EURO/INR (Euro/INR), GBP/INR (British Pound/INR) and JPY/INR (Japanese Yen/INR) are retrieved from the two Indian stock exchanges, MCX-SX and NSE (www.mcx-sxindia.com, www.nseindia.com). The spot prices are collected from Reserve Bank of India (RBI). All closing prices of futures series from both platforms are taken to the nearest contract to maturity. The sample period of the study is from 1 February 2010 to 25 November 2014 (894 observations). While estimating the model, we have converted the sample series in logarithmic returns. To calculate the volatility, we have calculated the range-based volatility by using the following formula suggested by Garman and Klass (1980).

$$\begin{aligned}\sigma_{it}^2 = {} & 0.511(H_{it} - L_t)^2 \\ & - 0.019[(C_{it} - O_{it})(H_{it} + L_{it} - 2O_{it}) - 2(H_{it} - O_{it})(L_{it} - O_{it})] \\ & - 0.383(C_{it} - O_{it})^2\end{aligned}$$

where H, L, O and C are the open, high, low and close, respectively. Since, there is no high, open and low in case of spot prices, we have calculated 20 days moving variance from return series for estimation purpose.

15.5 Empirical Results

The study provides time-series plots of spot prices of sample currencies (see Fig. 15.1), also a variety of summary statistics in Table 15.1. The plots shown in Fig. 15.1 show the depreciating trend of Indian currency post-2012 and continuing till 2014. The biggest jump seems to be during 2012 and towards middle and end of 2013, indicating that during these periods foreign exchange market has passed through high phases of volatility. Seeing the Table 15.1 (panel A) of summary statistics, it appears that the daily mean returns of all the sample currencies are positive with the highest return found in case of GBPMCX (0.028%) followed by USDNSE (0.024%), SUSD (0.024%), GBPNSE (0.023%) and SGBP (0.022%). The lowest daily mean return is observed in case of SJPY (0.0004%). The standard deviation as a measure of volatility is highest for SJPY and JPYMCX (0.008) and lowest in cases of USDMCX and USDNSE (0.005). Analyzing range-based volatility (see Table 15.1, panel B), it appears that all the sample currencies exhibit negative average daily return volatility. The maximum return volatility is observed in spot market of all four currencies ranging between 0.008% (SJPY) to 0.003% (SUSD). However, it is noteworthy that the least volatile futures currency market are JPY and most volatility futures contracts are EURO, GBP and USD. The calculated statistics of skewness and kurtosis along with Jarque–Bera statistics support the non-normality characteristics of sample currencies. All returns and volatility series of sample currencies exhibit volatility clustering and persistence as reported by the significant values of Ljung-Box (Q) and ARCH statistics. Hence, an application of volatility based empirical models appears to be the appropriate case.

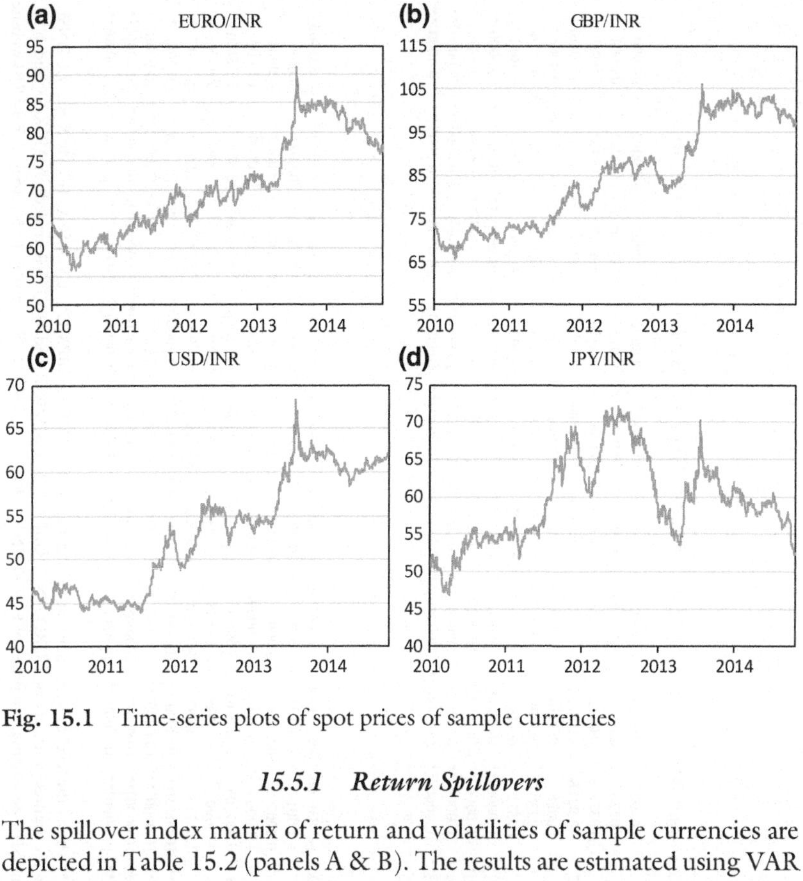

Fig. 15.1 Time-series plots of spot prices of sample currencies

15.5.1 Return Spillovers

The spillover index matrix of return and volatilities of sample currencies are depicted in Table 15.2 (panels A & B). The results are estimated using VAR model of order 2 and generalized variance decompositions of 10 days ahead of forecast errors.[4] The (i, j) entry in each panel is the estimated contribution to the forecast error variance of market i coming from innovations to market j. To All indicates the directional spillovers from one market to all other sample markets. From All shows the directional spillovers from all markets to a particular market. The total spillover index as in Eq. (15.7) is reported in the lower right corner of each panel. Panel A shows the static return spillover matrix. Following results from Table 15.2 (Panel A), the total spillover index indicates average contribution (77.4%) of unexpected changes to returns in the dependent variables (futures and spot prices of four sample currencies) in the 10-steps-ahead FEVD of all variables in the

Table 15.1 Descriptive statistics

Panel A

Summary statistics of return series

	EURMCX	EURNSE	GBPMCX	GBPNSE	USDMCX	USDNSE	JPYMCX	JPYNSE	SEURO	SGBP	SUSD	SJPY
Mean	0.0002	0.0001	0.0003	0.0002	0.0002	0.0002	0.0000	0.0000	0.0002	0.0002	0.0002	0.0000
Mean (%)	0.0184	0.0128	0.0285	0.0238	0.0195	0.0246	0.0022	0.0019	0.0156	0.0226	0.0241	0.0004
Max	0.0256	0.0356	0.0344	0.0333	0.0342	0.0326	0.0385	0.0384	0.0415	0.0368	0.0402	0.0481
Min.	−0.0212	−0.0263	−0.0362	−0.0218	−0.0231	−0.0228	−0.0431	−0.0384	−0.0237	−0.0278	−0.0268	−0.0453
Std. Dev.	0.0058	0.0060	0.0060	0.0058	0.0056	0.0056	0.0086	0.0084	0.0065	0.0062	0.0059	0.0086
Skewness	0.2116	0.2914	0.1810	0.2239	0.3390	0.3192	0.1060	0.1333	0.3243	0.1643	0.3265	−0.0160
Kurtosis	4.5890	5.2429	6.7115	4.9572	6.4457	6.3072	6.0737	5.3434	5.4925	5.1397	6.9466	5.3014
Jarque-Bera	[0.0000]**	[0.0000]**	[0.0000]**	[0.0000]**	[0.0000]**	[0.0000]**	[0.0000]**	[0.0000]**	[0.0000]**	[0.0000]**	[0.0000]**	[0.0000]**
Q(10)	[0.0000]**	[0.0002]**	[0.0020]**	[0.0006]**	[0.0079]**	[0.0032]**	[0.4511]	[0.1813]	[0.0976]	[0.0293]**	[0.0066]**	[0.3335]
$Q^2(10)$	[0.0000]**	[0.0000]**	[0.0000]**	[0.0000]**	[0.0000]**	[0.0000]**	[0.0170]**	[0.0000]**	[0.0000]**	[0.0000]**	[0.0000]**	[0.0000]**
ARCH(10)	[0.0000]**	[0.0000]**	[0.0000]**	[0.0000]**	[0.0000]**	[0.0000]**	[0.0181]**	[0.0000]**	[0.0000]**	[0.0000]**	[0.0000]**	[0.0000]**

Panel B

Summary statistics of volatilities

	EURMCX	EURNSE	GBPMCX	GBPNSE	USDMCX	USDNSE	JPYMCX	JPYNSE	SEURO	SGBP	SUSD	SJPY
Mean	−7.51E-06	−8.06E-06	−8.74E-06	−7.85E-06	−8.45E-06	−1.00E-05	−1.65E-05	−1.36E-05	4.16E-05	3.89E-05	3.45E-05	7.53E-05
Mean (%)	−0.001	−0.001	−0.001	−0.001	−0.001	−0.001	−0.002	−0.001	0.004	0.004	0.003	0.008
Max.	0.0003	0.0003	0.0002	0.0002	0.0003	0.0001	0.0003	0.0004	0.0003	0.0002	0.0003	0.0004
Min.	−0.0006	−0.0008	−0.0009	−0.0008	−0.0011	−0.0009	−0.0012	−0.0010	0.0000	0.0000	0.0000	0.0000
Std. dev.	3.10E-05	4.45E-05	4.21E-05	3.93E-05	5.33E-05	3.69E-05	6.42E-05	6.62E-05	3.30E-05	3.00E-05	3.85E-05	5.73E-05
Skewness	−4.892	−8.653	−9.163	−7.690	−11.946	−13.619	−7.067	−4.522	4.080	3.879	3.883	2.105
Kurtosis	114.170	162.840	160.267	130.768	236.982	301.370	106.025	68.810	24.693	23.087	22.919	8.910
Jarque-Bera	[0.0000]**	[0.0000]**	[0.0000]**	[0.0000]**	[0.0000]**	[0.0000]**	[0.0000]**	[0.0000]**	[0.0000]**	[0.0000]**	[0.0000]**	[0.0000]**
Q(10)	[0.0001]**	[0.0000]**	[0.0000]**	[0.0000]**	[0.0000]**	[0.0000]**	[0.0000]**	[0.0000]**	[0.0000]**	[0.0000]**	[0.0000]**	[0.0000]**
$Q^2(10)$	[0.7379]	[0.0000]**	[0.0002]**	[0.0000]**	[0.9083]	[0.8068]**	[0.0000]**	[0.0000]**	[0.0000]**	[0.0000]**	[0.0000]**	[0.0000]**
ARCH(10)	[0.8006]	[0.0000]**	[0.0006]**	[0.0000]**	[0.0000]**	[0.8308]	[0.0000]**	[0.0000]**	[0.0000]**	[0.0000]**	[0.0000]**	[0.0000]**

Note: Values in parentheses [] are p-values. ** shows the level of significance at 5% and better. EURMCX, GBPMCX, USDMCX, JPYMCX and EURNSE, GBPNSE, USDNSE and JPYNSE represent the futures contracts of EURO/INR, GBP/INR, USD/INR and JPY/INR traded on MCX-SX and NSE, respectively. While, SEURO, SGBP, SUSD and SJPY denote the spot prices of EURO/INR, GBP/INR, USD/INR and JPY/INR retrieved from RBI website

Table 15.2 Returns and volatility spillover results

Panel A: Return spillovers

	EURMCX	*EURNSE*	*GBPMCX*	*GBPNSE*	*USDMCX*	*USDNSE*	*JPYMCX*	*JPYNSE*	*SEURO*	*SGBP*	*SUSD*	*SJPY*	*From all*	*Net spillover*
EURMCX	26.8	19.3	12	9.1	3.8	4.1	4.5	3.2	10.6	4.3	1.2	1.2	73	−2
EURNSE	16.5	23.4	7.3	11.6	5.6	5.6	2.7	4.4	13.2	5.8	2.1	1.8	77	14
GBPNSE	11.2	8.4	24.7	17.7	5.9	6.3	6.1	4.1	3.6	8.3	2.1	1.5	75	3
GBPMCX	7.1	10.6	14.8	21.5	8.2	8.4	3	5.4	4.9	10.5	3.6	2.1	79	24
USDMCX	3	5.2	5	8.4	21.3	20.8	6.2	10	1.5	3.2	11.1	4.3	79	23
USDNSE	3.1	5.1	5.2	8.5	20.6	21.1	6.3	10	1.5	3.2	11.1	4.2	79	24
JPYMCX	4.1	3.2	6.5	4	8.4	8.6	26.9	19.7	0.9	1.6	3.8	12.3	73	−6
JPYNSE	2.3	4.2	3.4	5.8	10.8	10.9	16.2	22.9	1.4	2.5	5.2	14.5	77	14
SEURO	13.3	18.3	5.6	9	5.4	5.4	2.5	4	21.5	9	3.5	2.4	79	−29
SGBP	5.8	8.6	11.1	16.7	7.2	7.2	2.4	4.4	7.8	19	6.1	3.6	81	−22
SUSD	3	4.5	4.3	7.3	16.3	16.4	4.8	7.7	2.8	6.1	19.4	7.4	81	−23
SJPY	1.8	3.4	2.6	4.9	9.3	9.2	12.5	18.2	2.2	4.6	8.9	22.6	77	−22
To all	71	91	78	103	102	103	67	91	50	59	58	55	929	
All	98	114	103	125	123	124	94	114	72	78	78	78		
	Total spillover index = 77.4%													

Panel B: Volatility spillovers

	EURMCX	*EURNSE*	*GBPMCX*	*GBPNSE*	*USDMCX*	*USDNSE*	*JPYMCX*	*JPYNSE*	*SEURO*	*SGBP*	*SUSD*	*SJPY*	*From all*	*Net spillover*
EURMCX	33.1	10.1	7.4	8.6	4.9	9.3	5.5	6.8	3.7	6.7	3.2	0.8	67	−27
EURNSE	6.7	25.6	9.3	10.7	4.8	12.1	7.2	7	4.5	7.5	3.8	0.9	74	2
GBPNSE	3.5	8	22.2	13.3	5.9	13.8	9.7	6	4.9	7.9	3.9	1	78	1
GBPMCX	4.9	8.9	11.9	26.6	5.3	13.8	7.1	6.1	4	6.7	3.7	1	73	21
USDMCX	5.1	7.2	7.3	8.7	32.7	12.9	5.6	5.8	3.6	5.7	4.4	1.1	67	−21
USDNSE	4.9	8.9	9.7	12.1	6.9	22.4	7.7	8.2	4.7	7.9	5.3	1.4	78	30
JPYMCX	2.9	7.1	11.4	9.2	4.7	12.7	25.6	11	4.1	6.5	3.5	1.4	74	−2
JPYNSE	2.9	6.9	5.1	6.1	4.1	10.3	12.3	38.9	3.2	5.3	3.2	1.7	61	8
SEURO	2.4	5	4.4	6.7	2.2	5.1	3.4	4	26.3	23.2	10.5	6.9	74	2
SGBP	2	5.4	5.2	8.7	2.9	6.9	3.9	4.3	16.6	28.1	9.6	6.5	72	36
SUSD	2.3	4.5	4.9	6	2.5	7.6	4.5	5.7	15.2	17.2	20.5	9.1	80	−19
SJPY	1.9	4.2	2.9	4	2.1	3.5	5.2	4.4	11.2	13.1	10.2	37.2	63	−31
To all	40	76	79	94	46	108	72	69	76	108	61	32	861	
All	73	102	101	121	79	130	98	108	102	136	82	69		
	Total spillover index = 71.7%													

VAR system. About currencies, it appears that the futures of USD/INR (USDNSE and USDMCX) and GBP (GBPMCX) are the largest contributors to the FEVD of the other variables in the VAR. These variables contribute to the FEVD of the other variables on average by 103% (USDNSE and GBPMCX) and 102% (USDMCX), while these futures contracts receive from other currencies by 79% (each). Hence, in net terms, USDNSE and GBPMCX contribute 24% points more to the forecasting of other variables than they receive from other sample currencies. The second largest contributor to the FEVD of all other currencies is USDMCX with a net contribution of 23%. EURNSE and JPYNSE are also net transmitters, with the contribution standing at 14%. The smallest net contributor is GBPNSE, with net contributions of 3%. Important to note that all spot series of all four currencies contribute less than they receive from all other currencies. Overall, the findings suggest that the return spillover index divides the sample currencies into two groups based on whether they are net transmitters or net receivers of spillovers. The former comprises futures contracts, while the latter comprises spot series of sample currencies. The observed pattern in return spillovers indicates evidence of strong market interdependence between prices of futures and spot series of sample currencies, wherein the futures contracts of all four currencies are identified as the net transmitters of return spillovers with a particular emphasis on USD/INR, GBP/INR, and EURO/INR. The reason could be because these three currency pairs are highly liquid and traded in the large volume on MCX-SX and NSE. Further, according to recent forex trading figures, as on April 2013, the US dollar dominated the Indian currency trading platforms with a share in total trades with 43.5% followed by euro (16.5%), Japanese yen (11.5%) and British pound (about 6%) (see BIS 2013). In the context of Indian currency derivatives markets, it is apparent that futures market has started playing an important role in not only spillover but also regarding assimilation of new information. More importantly, the nature of information transmission is not only intra-currency but also inter-currency. As can be observed in Table 15.2 (Panel A) that futures of GBP/INR (GBPMCX and GBPNSE) not only explain the FEVD of its spot (SGBP) but also the futures of EURO/INR and USD/INR. Like for example, GBPMCX describes the FEVD of EURNSE and USDMCX and USDNSE by more than 11% and 8%, respectively. The strongest inter-currency spillover is seen between USD/INR and JPY/INR followed by GBP/INR and EURO/INR. These findings are in line with Kumar (2011) and Sehgal et al. (2015) who also report the dominance of

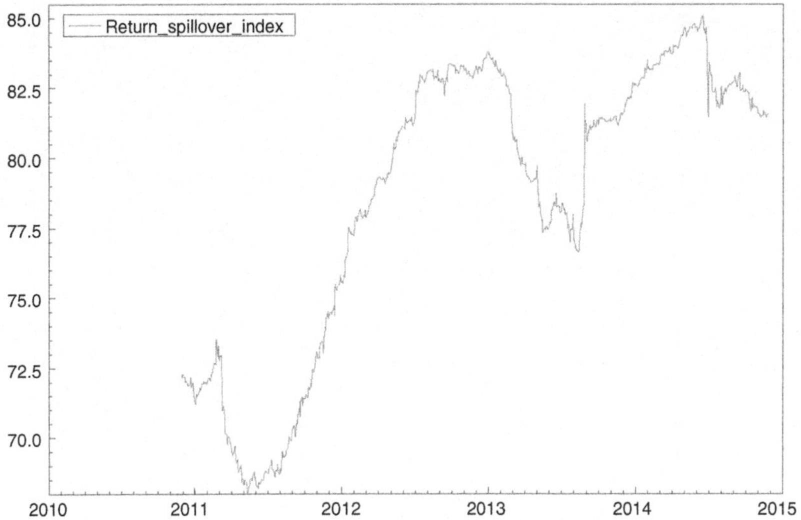

Fig. 15.2 Returns spillovers, 200-day rolling windows

USD/INR and GBP/INR concerning return spillover over other currencies traded on Indian currency derivatives trading platform.

After discussing the static return spillover index which is time-invariant and constant across time, we now examine these results under the dynamic framework. This is mainly because by adding the time-dimension in spillover analysis may help in examining the impacts of various economic and financial fluctuations that have taken place during the sample period. For example, the dynamic return spillover index exhibited Fig. 15.2 suggests that the magnitude as well as direction of return spillovers, can significantly deviate from the average total return spillover index (77.4%) reported in Table 15.2. Indeed, the time-varying return spillover index has varied from 68% in mid-2011 to 85% in mid-2014. Specifically, it has undergone periods of gradual decline (2012–2013), steep decline (mid-2011), and accelerated growth (2012). The identification of these turning points reveals to the fact that the time-varying spillover index can capture the significant events related to the weakening of Indian currency including the visible impact of the announcement of the US Federal Reserve decision to withdraw quantitative easing in May 2013 (see Economic Survey 2014–2015). Consequently, during August 2013, the spillover index graph shows a steep

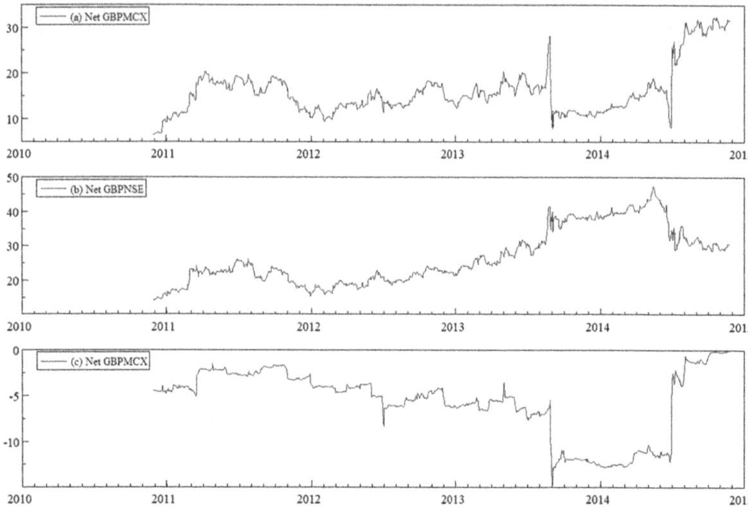

Fig. 15.3 Directional return spillovers of EURO/INR currency traded on MCX-SX and NSE. Directional net return spillovers of EURMCX SEURO and EURNSE. Net spillovers are calculated by subtracting directional 'To' spillovers from directional 'From' spillovers. Positive (negative) values (*above zero line*) indicate that variables are net transmitters (receivers) of spillovers. Net spillovers are estimated using 200-days rolling windows. (**a**) Shows the net spillover from EURMCX to SEURO. (**b**) Shows the net spillover between EURNSE and SEURO and (**c**) Exhibits net spillovers between EURMCX and EURNSE

jump in volatility. Although, Table 15.2 sufficiently sheds light on the level and direction of net volatility spillovers, there are periods in which net return spillovers are above or below average levels. Figs. 15.3, 15.4, 15.5, and 15.6 reports bar charts of dynamic net return spillovers, which also complements the static spillover results reported in Table 15.2. We estimate rolling windows and compute the time-varying net return spillovers. Focusing on net spillovers, we can infer whether one of the variables of interest is either a net transmitter or a net receiver of spillover effects. A variable is considered to be a net transmitter of spillover effects when the bar charts lie within the positive upper part of each figure. The plots of net spillovers are shown in Fig. 15.3, 15.4, 15.5, and 15.6. Though the findings summarized

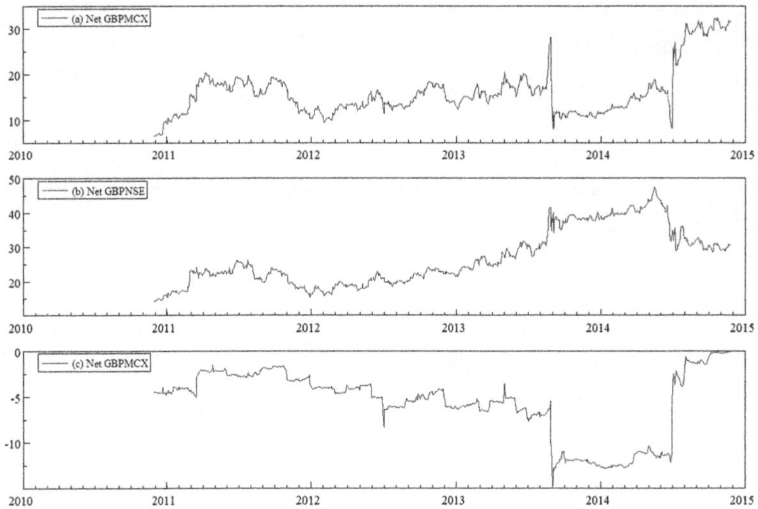

Fig. 15.4 Directional return spillovers of GBP/INR currency traded on MCX-SX and NSE. Directional net return spillovers of GBPMCX SGBP and GBPNSE. (**a**) Shows the net spillover from GBPMCX to SGBP. (**b**) Shows the net spillover between GBPNSE and SGBP and (**c**) Exhibits net spillovers between GBPMCX and GBPNSE

in Table 15.2 (panel A) are generally supported by the dynamic net return spillovers. Spot receives return spillovers from futures throughout the sample period in case of all sample currencies except JPYMCX. In case of between futures returns of MCX-SX and NSE, it is the MCX-SX that receives the return spillovers from NSE in the case of all currencies. It implies that the futures contracts of sample currencies traded on NSE assimilate new information more quickly than MCX-SX. It further means that NSE leads MCX-SX concerning return based information spillover.

15.5.2 Volatility Spillovers

In this section, we analyze the total static spillover index among sample currencies and decompose it by emitters and receivers of spillover. It also measures the extent to which variables under consideration are net volatility receivers or net transmitters. The results reported in Table 15.2 (panel B)

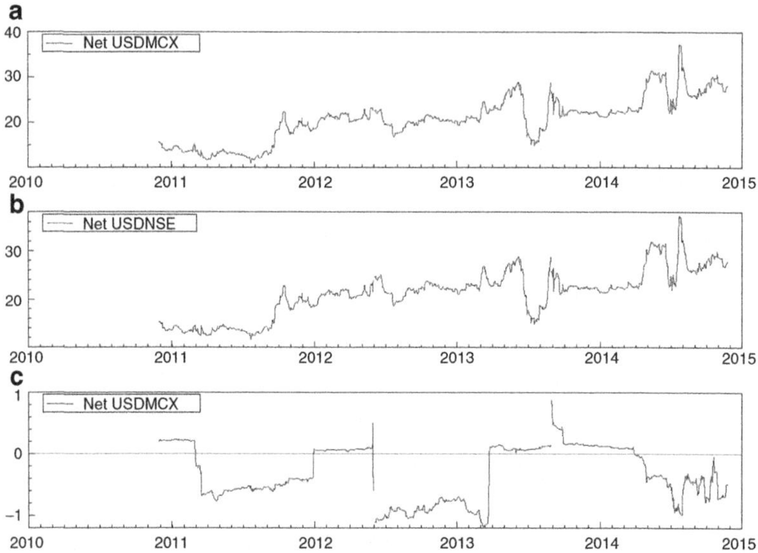

Fig. 15.5 Directional return spillovers of USD/INR currency traded on MCX-SX and NSE. Directional net return spillovers of USDMCX SUSD and USDNSE. Net spillovers are calculated by subtracting directional 'To' spillovers from directional 'From' spillovers. Positive (negative) values (*above zero line*) indicate that variables are net transmitters (receivers) of spillovers. Net spillovers are estimated using 200-days rolling windows. (**a**) Shows the net spillover from USDMCX to SUSD. (**b**) Shows the net spillover between USDNSE and SUSD and (**c**) Exhibits net spillovers between USDMCX and USDNSE

indicate that the average contribution of unexpected shocks to sample currencies in the 10-step-ahead forecast error variance decomposition is of all other variables in the VAR is 71.7%. Within sample currencies, futures of USD/INR and a spot of GBP/INR are identified as the largest average contributors of volatility spillovers to the other variables in the VAR (108%) each, followed by futures of GBP/INR, that is, GBPNSE and GBPMCX by 94% and 79%, respectively. It may be noted that the average contributions of futures contracts traded on MCX-SX are relatively lesser than the futures of NSE. This implies that NSE leads MCX-SX concerning volatility spillover. Regarding net volatility spillovers, a similar pattern as for the directional return spillovers is observed. Within futures contracts, USDNSE and GBPMCX are identified as net transmitters, while, EURMCX and

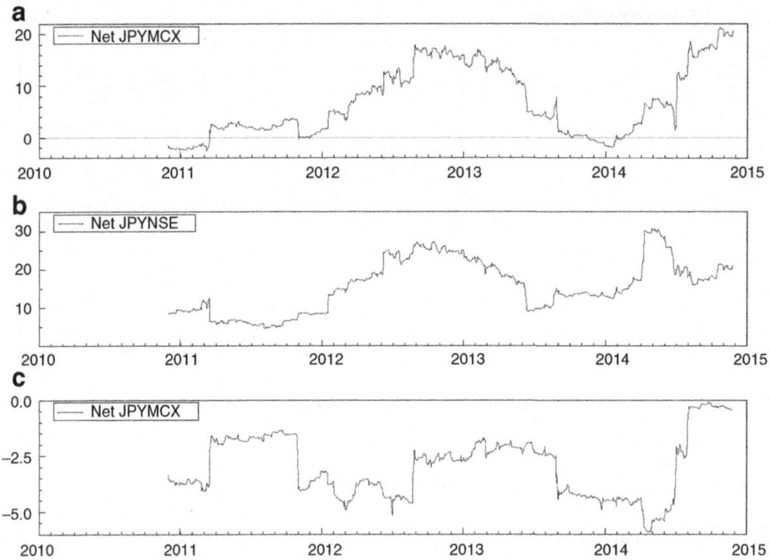

Fig. 15.6 Directional return spillovers of JPY/INR currency traded on MCX-SX and NSE. Directional net return spillovers of JPYMCX SJPY and JPYNSE. Net spillovers are calculated by subtracting directional 'To' spillovers from directional 'From' spillovers. Positive (negative) values (*above zero line*) indicate that variables are net transmitters (receivers) of spillovers. Net spillovers are estimated using 200-days rolling windows. (**a**) Shows the net spillover from JPYMCX to SJPY. (**b**) Shows the net spillover between JPYNSE and SJPY and (**c**) Exhibits net spillovers between JPYMCX and JPYNSE

USDMCX are identified as the net receivers of volatility spillovers. Within spot markets, SGBP is the largest net emitter of volatility spillover followed by SEURO, while SUSD and SJPY are net receivers of volatility spillovers. USD/INR is again the largest net transmitter of volatility spillovers with its net contribution of 30%. The possible explanation of USD/INR could be because of its largest share in total trade as mentioned earlier. The results are broadly in agreement with Kumar (2011, 2014) who also report strong information spillover from USD/INR to other currency pairs. Focusing on the direction of volatility spillovers, it appears that the direction of volatility spillover is not only intra-currency but also inter-currency. Like for example, futures contracts of USD/INR traded on NSE (USDNSE) explains the

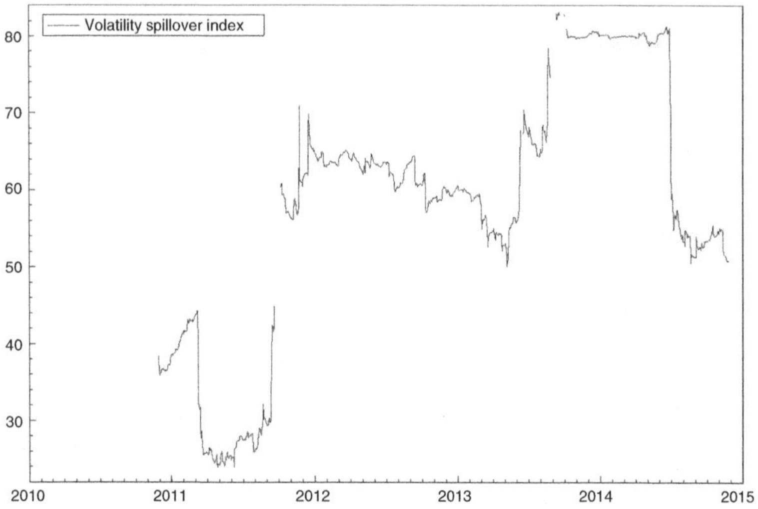

Fig. 15.7 Volatility spillovers, range based estimator (200 days rolling windows)

FEVD of not only its own spot market volatility but also the volatility of other currencies such as EURO/INR and GBP/INR. Seemingly is the case of GBPNSE. These findings receive support from return spillover results as USD/INR and GBP/INR appear to be stronger currencies with respect to intra-currency spillover compared to other currency pairs. The findings are also in agreement with Kumar (2011, 2014) and Sehgal et al. (2015) in case of India's foreign exchange market.

As mentioned, one key drawback of static volatility spillover matrix is that the intensity of interdependence among sample variables are constant over time. Therefore, we now analyze the time-varying total spillover index presented in Fig. 15.7. The salient features of the total volatility spillover are in order. First, the spillover index varies between 25% and 85% and it remained stable during 2011. Second, the spillover index remained stable during 2012 and started to increase during mid-2013, and it experienced as the notable jump from mid-2013 to the beginning of 2014. Hence, dynamic spillover resonates well with the time-varying return spillover. Indeed, the time-variation in the total volatility spillover has endured four phases, (i) steep jump (mid-2011), (ii) relative stability (2012), (iii) accelerated growth (2013–2014) and (iv) steep decline (2014). Although, Table 15.2 (panel B) sheds light on the level and direction of net volatility

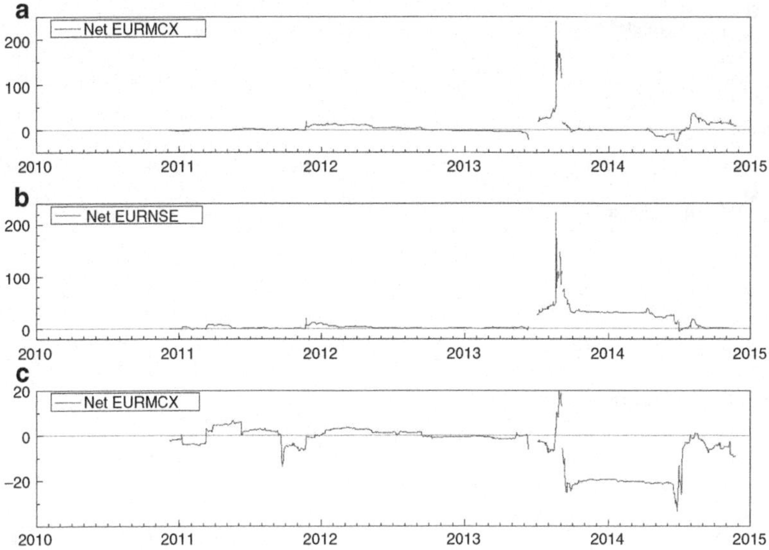

Fig. 15.8 Directional volatility spillovers of EURO/INR currency traded on MCX-SX and NSE. See notes of Fig. 15.3 for details about pair-wise net directional spillovers

spillover, there are periods in which actual dynamic volatility spillovers are above or below the average level. Fig. 15.8, 15.9, 15.10, and 15.11 reports time-varying net volatility spillovers which also extend and complement spillover matrix reported in Table 15.2 (panel B). Although, futures contracts of all sample currencies are net transmitters to their respective spot markets except the case of GBPNSE which appears as the net recipient of net volatility spillovers from the spot market, in certain periods futures contracts also act as the net recipient. Like for example, in case of EURO/INR, EURMCX becomes a net recipient of volatility spillover for some periods in 2014. GBPMCX receives volatility spillovers in mid-2013 and beginning of 2014. It is important to note that almost all the net spillover plots exhibit steep jump in volatility spillover during mid-2013. Like for example, in case of EURO/INR, USD/INR and JPY/INR, net spillover plots show a sudden jump in mid-2013 and afterward. Analyzing the actual exchange rates figures shown in Fig. 15.1, it can be found that during mid-2013, the rupee depreciated sharply in May–August 2013. The possible explanation could be because of the rise in uncertainty due to the

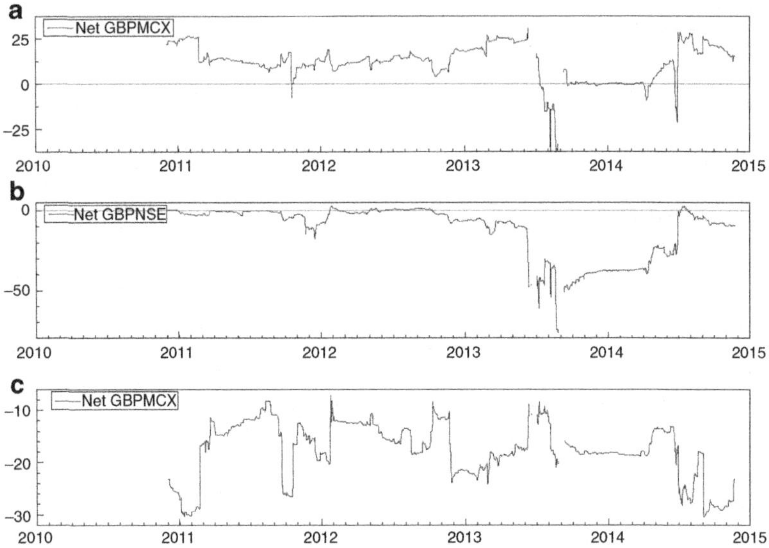

Fig. 15.9 Directional volatility spillovers of GBP/INR currency traded on MCX-SX and NSE. See notes of Fig. 15.4 for details about pair-wise net directional spillovers

US Federal Reserve's decision to withdraw quantitative easing in May 2013 (see World Bank 2013). As reported by Ray (2014), during June 2013 and August 2013, the rupee depreciated against US dollar by 16%. Considering the case of between futures contracts traded on both platforms, it appears that NSE is net transmitter of volatility spillovers to MCX-SX. This further complements the findings of net return spillover. Therefore, it can be concluded that NSE is a dominant trading platform compared to MCX-SX with respect to return and volatility spillovers. This particular finding is in agreement with Sehgal et al. (2015) who also arrive at the same conclusion. There is a surprising result that needs attention that in case of return spillover, the forecast error variance of futures explains the forecast error variance of spot, but in case of volatility spillover it is quite opposite. Like, for example, for volatility spillover, the FEVD of spot explain insufficient amount of the forecast error variance of futures. It suggests that for the futures market, the market makers are not bothered about the impact of new information in spot market. Rather, they are more interested in evaluating the cross-currency spillover. Further, spot market seems to be

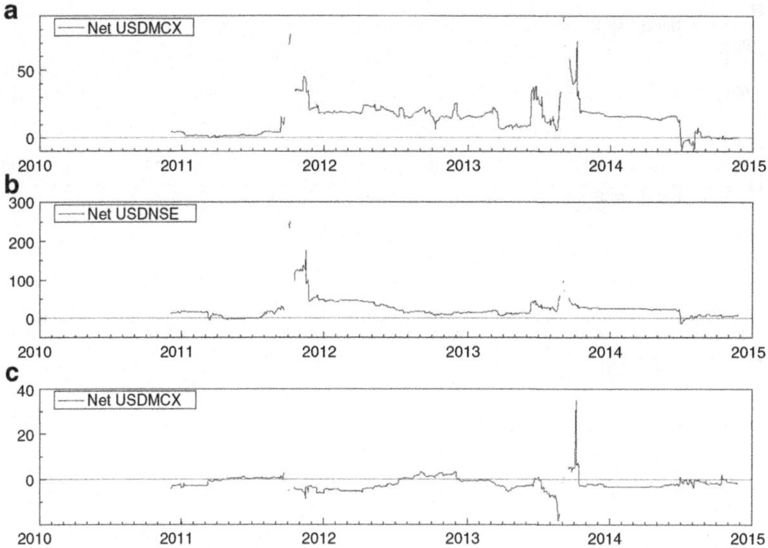

Fig. 15.10 Directional volatility spillovers of USD/INR currency traded on MCX-SX and NSE. See notes of Fig. 14.5 for details about pair-wise net directional spillovers

an independent market as shocks emanating from futures market spot do not appear to impact market volatility. In this regard, Najand et al. (1992) provide two explanations: first, this often happens when a lot of currency traders specialize in one market only. Second, this could be due to lack of sufficient information and expertise, especially traders (exporters and importers), who do not able to assimilate new information in their investment strategy. This appears to be highly appropriate in case of India.

15.5.3 Robustness Checks

In order to check the robustness of DY methodology, we undertake various robustness checks. First, we try to find it out whether the use of alternative H-step-ahead FEVDs and alternative rolling windows affects the estimated results of directional return and volatility spillovers. Specifically, we allow the forecast horizon H to range from 5 to 20 days, while holding constant the rolling windows of 200 days. The results remain qualitatively similar.

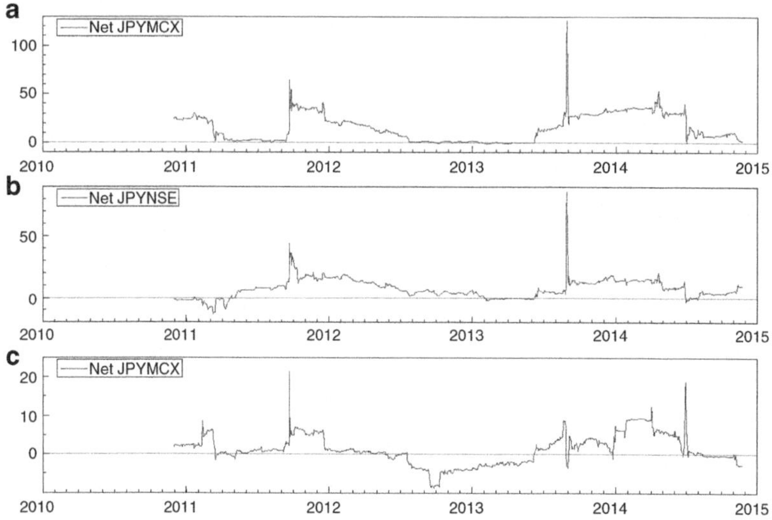

Fig. 15.11 Directional volatility spillovers of JPY/INR currency traded on MCX-SX and NSE. See notes of Fig. 15.6 for details about pair-wise net directional spillovers

Second, we choose alternative rolling windows from 100, 200 and 300 days, while holding the forecast period as 10 days. The reported results in this study obtained based on the rolling window of 200 days are again validated. Lastly, we apply the spillover approach of Diebold and Yilmaz (2009), which is based on the Cholesky decomposition and in which FEVDs are highly sensitive to the ordering of variables in the VAR. In particular, we analyze 200 random permutations (different variables orderings in the VAR) and calculate the corresponding spillover indices for each order.[5] The minimum and maximum values that the return and volatility spillovers receive based on Cholesky factorization are in agreement with those of our main results reported previously.

15.5.4 Dynamic Conditional Correlation Analysis

To re-confirm the directional spillover results, the study employs the dynamic conditional correlation popularly known as the DCC-GARCH model. Table 15.3 (panel A) shows the first step procedure of simple GARCH estimation. The results indicate that all the variance coefficients are significant. The results of the second step shown in panel B indicate that the estimated coefficients θ_1 and $\theta_2$for examined currencies are positive and sum to less than one, implying that dynamic conditional correlations of all currencies are mean reverting for sample currencies. Fig. 15.12 shows the plotted results of dynamic conditional correlations results between futures and spot of sample currencies. It can be found that the magnitude of the correlation is quite high and it is ranging between 0.60 and 0.80, implying that the magnitude of information transmission is in line with the estimated directional spillover results. Fig. 15.12 exhibits the dynamic conditional correlation between futures returns of MCX-SX and NSE. The plots exhibited in (a to d) clearly suggests that conditional correlations between futures are quite high (more than 0.90) can capture the ups and downs caused by external shocks such as Eurozone turmoil and its aftermath. Further, the dynamic conditional correlation clearly captures the recent upheavals in currency markets with regards to fear of outflow of capital owing to the apprehension of the Federal Reserve increasing the interest rate. The magnitude of conditional correlation appears to be very high and USD, in particular, shows strongest co-movement between MCX-SX and NSE than any other currency.

15.6 Conclusion and Discussion

In this chapter, we examine the return and volatility spillovers in India's currency derivatives markets. More precisely, based on daily data of futures and spot series of four exchange rates (EUR/INR, GBP/INR, USD/INR and JPY/INR) over the period from February 2010 to November 2014, we report the following empirical regularities. First, the analysis of static spillover effects in the sample exchange rates shows that USD/INR and GBP/INR are net transmitters of return and volatility spillovers during the sample period. Whereas EURO/INR and JPY/INR are net receivers. These results suggest that the information contents of USD/INR and GBP/INR can help improve forecast accuracy of returns and volatility on EURO/INR and JPY/INR return and volatilities. Second, USD/INR is the largest gross exchange rate transmitter of return and volatility spillovers to the remaining exchange rates in our study. Third, pairwise exchange rates

Table 15.3 DCC estimation results

Panel A: First-step, univariate GARCH estimation results												
	EUROMCX	*EURONSE*	*GBPMCX*	*GBPNSE*	*USDMCX*	*USDNSE*	*JPYMCX*	*JPYNSE*	*SEURO*	*SGBP*	*SUSD*	*SJPY*
1. Return equations												
Constant (μ)	1.6E-04	8.9E-05	2.0E-04	1.8E-04	1.7E-05	8.1E-05	−1.4E-04	−1.2E-04	8.7E-05	1.7E-04	5.0E-05	−2.0E-04
2. Volatility equations												
Constant	3.500	3.221*	2.355	1.509*	0.620*	0.560	4.840*	4.554*	3.970	1.747*	0.973*	2.530
α	0.057**	0.066**	0.051**	0.060**	0.084**	0.080**	0.074**	0.080**	0.094**	0.063**	0.137**	0.099**
β	0.839**	0.841**	0.878**	0.893**	0.897**	0.903**	0.859**	0.854**	0.810**	0.890**	0.836**	0.869**
Panel B: Second-step, correlation equation results												
θ_1			0.0273									
			[0.000]**									
θ_2			0.9457									
			[0.000]**									
Log Likelihood			60471.44									
Q(10)	17.727	12.601	19.961	22.767	27.781	32.085	26.248	16.011	14.924	16.632	23.586	26.749
	[0.191]	[0.280]	[0.089]	[0.071]*	[0.065]*	[0.042]**	[0.157]	[0.200]	[0.220]	[0.190]	[0.351]	[0.160]
Q2(10)	21.010	18.532	7.029	9.615	8.183	5.873	27.579	26.888	6.476	11.466	16.664	3.110
	[0.080]	[0.056]*	[0.564]	[0.474]	[0.640]	[0.825]	[0.060]	[0.082]	[0.773]	[0.322]	[0.082]*	[0.978]

Note: Q (10) and Q^2 (10) are the Ljung-Box statistics for serial correlation. The values in parentheses are p-values. ** and * indicate the level of significance at 1% and better, 5% and above, respectively

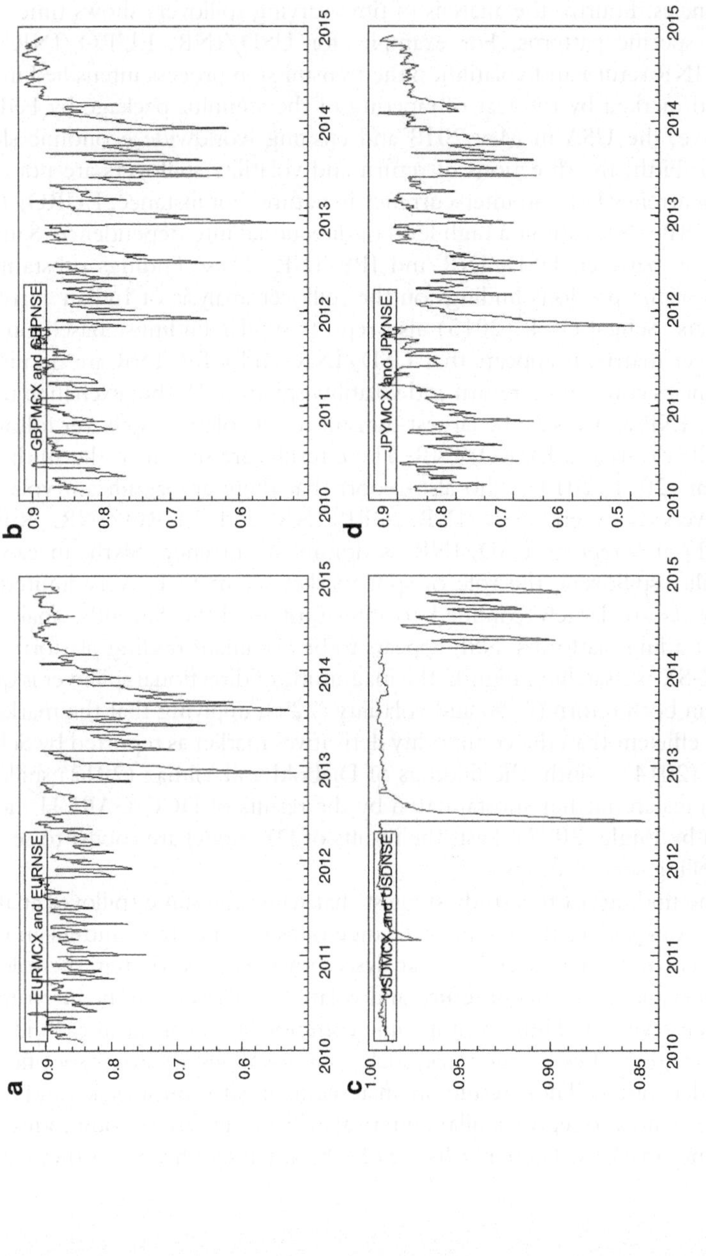

Fig. 15.12 Dynamic conditional correlation results between futures and spot of sample currencies

return and volatility spillovers reveal relatively stronger bilateral interdependencies between futures and spot and between futures contracts of sample currencies. Fourth, the analysis of time-varying spillovers shows time- and event-specific patterns. For example, for USD/INR, EURO/INR and JPY/INR return and volatilities, the transmission process intensified in the period marked by the fear of tapering of the stimulus package by Federal Reserve, the USA in May 2013 and ensuing worldwide economic slowdown. Fifth, the directions of return and volatility spillovers are not only intra-currency but also inter-currency in nature. For instance, EURO/INR and GBP/INR exhibit a high level of directional interdependence. Same is the case between USD/INR and JPY/INR. These findings substantiate some of the previous findings on the spillover analysis of Indian currency markets. Sehgal et al. (2015) also reports similar findings. Based on the spillover matrix, it appears that USD/INR, and GBP/INR are dominant currencies concerning return and volatility spillover. Within exchange rates, USD/INR appears as the largest transmitter of volatility spillover followed by GBP/INR and EURO/INR. These results are similar to the studies of Kumar (2011, 2014), who also report that there are significant volatility spillovers between USD/INR, GBP/INR and EURO/INR. Kumar (2011) also reports USD/INR as dominant currency. Sixth, in case of volatility spillovers, the role of spot market seems to be very limited, as spillovers are largely confined to inter-spot markets. Seventh, analyzing both trading platforms, NSE appears to be dominant trading platform and MCX-SX as a satellite. Eighth, the magnitude of directional spillover is quite high in both return (77%) and volatility (72%), implying that the market is quite efficient than the commodity derivatives market as reported by Sehgal et al. (2014). Ninth, the findings of Diebold and Yilmaz (2012) spillover measures are further substantiated by the results of DCC-GARCH model given by Engle (2002). Last, the results of DY-model are robust to several modelling specifications.

The findings of this study suggest that while the static spillover analysis clearly categorizes the sample exchange rates into net transmitters and net receivers, the dynamic spillover analysis shows periods wherein the roles of emitters and recipients of return and volatility spillovers can be interrupted or even reversed. Thus, even if some commonalities appear in each identified category of exchange rates, such commonalities are event specific and time dependent. These results are in agreement with Antonakakis and Kizys (2015) who also report similar empirical evidence in case of commodity and currency markets. These results are of substantial significance as they can be used to formulate the trading strategies and can also help investors to undertake superior investment decisions. Further, based on findings of this study it can be said that the introduction of futures contracts has yielded the India's foreign exchange market as it has started playing an important role in informational spillover. There is need to focus more on enhancing the knowledge base of not only traders but also small and large investors who can not only understand the dynamics of informational spillover but also benefit it by applying in their hedging strategies. However, future research may take up this issue as an academic exercise. Further studies in this direction may consider inter-currency spillover by using intra-day data across several markets to examine the phenomenon of 'meteor shower' or 'heat wave'.

Notes

1. The figures are converted in terms of dollars by taking the exchange rate of USD as on 28 February 2014.
2. The percentage is calculated by authors of the SEBI Handbook of Statistics by compiling the trading data of MCX-SX, NSE and USE.
3. Considering the standard average exchange rate mark of ₹ 48/USD, the rupee has depreciated by about 30% as on 28 February 2014.
4. VAR order is selected based on the Schwartz Bayesian criterion (SBC).
5. Figures are available with the authors upon request.

References

Abhyankar, H. A. (1995). Trading-round-the clock: Return, volatility and volume spillovers in the Eurodollar futures markets. *Pacific-Basin Finance Journal, 3*, 75–92.

Antonakakis, N. (2012). Exchange return co-movements and volatility spillovers before and after the introduction of euro. *Journal of International Financial Markets, Institutions & Money, 22*, 1091–1109.

Antonakakis, N., & Kizys, R. (2015). Dynamic spillovers between commodity and currency markets. *International Review of Financial Analysis*, 41, 303–319.

Asimakopoulos, I., Ayling, D., & Mahmood, W. M. (2000). Non-linear Granger causality in currency futures returns. *Economics Letters, 68*, 25–30.

Awartani, B., & Maghyereh, I. A. (2013). Dynamic spillovers between oil and stock markets in the Gulf Cooperation Council countries. *Energy Economics, 36*, 28–42.

Behera, K. H. (2011). Onshore and offshore market for Indian rupee: Recent evidence on volatility and shock spillover. *Macroeconomics and Finance in Emerging Market Economies, 4*(1), 43–55.

BIS. (2013). *Triennial central bank survey*. Basel: Bank for International Settlements.

Bubak, V., Kocenda, E., & Zikes, F. (2011). Volatility transmission in emerging European foreign exchange markets. *Journal of Banking & Finance, 35*, 2829–2841.

Chan, L., & Lien, D. (2006). Are options redundant? Further evidence from currency futures markets. *International Review of Financial Analysis, 15*, 179–188.

Chan, K., Chan, K. C., & Karolyi, G. A. (1991). Intraday volatility in the stock index and stock index futures markets. *The Review of Financial Studies, 4*(4), 657–684.

Ciner, C. (2011). Information transmission across currency futures markets: Evidence from frequency domain tests. *International Review of Financial Analysis, 20*, 134–139.

Claessens, S., Dornbusch, R., & Park, C. Y. (2001). Contagion: Why crises spread and how this can be stopped. In S. Claessens & J. K. Forbes (Eds.), *International Financial Contagion* (pp. 19–41). New York: Springer.

Diebold, F. X., & Yilmaz, K. (2009). Measuring financial asset return and volatility spillovers, with application to global equity markets. *Economic Journal, 119*, 158–171.

Diebold, F. X., & Yilmaz, K. (2012). Better to give than to receive: Predictive directional measurement of volatility spillovers. *International Journal of Forecasting, 28*, 57–66.

Economic Survey (2014–2015). State of the economy. New Delhi: Ministry of Finance, Government of India.

Elyasiani, E., Kocagil, E. A., & Mansur, I. (2007). Information transmission and spillover in currency markets: A generalized variance decomposition analysis. *The Quarterly Review of Economics and Finance, 47*, 312–330.

Engle, R. F. (2002). Dynamic conditional correlation: A simple class of multivariate generalized autoregressive conditional heteroskedasticity models. *Journal of Business & Economic Statistics, 20*, 339–350.

Engle, R. F., Ito, T., & Lin, W.-L. (1990). Meteor showers or heat waves? Heteroskedastic intra-daily volatility in the foreign exchange market. *Econometrica, 58*(3), 525–542.

Fung, H. G., & Patterson, G. A. (1999). The dynamic relationship of volatility, volume, and market depth in currency futures markets. *Journal of International Financial Markets, Institutions and Money, 9*, 33–59.

Fung, H. G., Leung, K. W., & Xu, X. (2001). Information role of US futures trading in a global financial market. *Journal of Futures Markets, 21*(11), 1071–1090.

Gagnon, L., & Karolyi, A. G. (2006). Price and volatility transmision across borders. *Financial Markets, Institutions and Instruments, 17*(3), 107–158.

Garman, B. M., & Klass, J. M. (1980). On the estimation of security price volatilities from historical data. *The Journal of Business, 53*(1), 67–78.

Han, L. M., & Ozocak, O. (2002). Risk-return relationships in foreign-currency futures following macroeconomic announcements. *Journal of Futures Markets, 22*(8), 729–764.

Harvey, C. R., & Huang, R. D. (1991). Volatility in the foreign currency futures. *Review of Financial Studies, 4*(3), 543–569.

Hong, Y. (2001). A test for volatility spillover with application to exchange rates. *Journal of Econometrics, 103*(1–2), 183–224.

Hua, R., & Chen, B. (2007). International linkages of the Chinese futures markets. *Applied Financial Economics, 17*(6), 1275–1287.

Inagaki, K. (2007). Testing for volatility spillover between the British pound and the euro. *Research in International Business and Finance, 21*, 161–174.

Karmakar, M. (2009). Price discoveries and volatility spillovers in S&P CNX Nifty future and its underlying index CNX Nifty. *Vikalpa, 34*(2), 41–56.

Kitamura, Y. (2010). Testing for intraday interdependence and volatility spillover among the euro, the pound and the Swiss franc markets. *Research in International Business and Finance, 24*, 158–171.

Koop, G., Pesaran, M. H., & Potter, S. M. (1996). Impulse response analysis in nonlinear multivariate models. *Journal of Econometrics, 74*, 119–147.

Kumar, M. (2011). Return and volatility spillovers: Evidence from Indian exchange rates. *International Journal of Economics and Business Research, 3*(4), 371–387.

Kumar, D. (2014). Correlations, return and volatility spillovers in Indian exchange rates. *Global Business Review, 15*(1), 77–91.

Lin, W. L., Engle, R. F., & Ito, T. (1994). Do bulls and bears move across borders? International transmission of stock returns and volatility. *Review of Financial Studies, 7*(3), 507–537.

Mahalik, K. M., Acharya, D., & Babu, S. M. (2010). *Price discovery and volatility spillovers in futures and spot commodity markets: Some empirical evidence from India*. IGIDR working paper no. PP-062-10.

McMillan, D. G., & Speight, A. E. (2010). Return and volatility spillovers in three euro exchange rates. *Journal of Economics and Business, 62*, 79–93.

MCX-SX. (2014). *Compat uphelds CCI order on "zero pricing" in favour of MCX-SX*. Mumbai: MCX-SX.

Miyajima, K., & Shim, I. (2014, September). Asset managers in emerging market economies. *BIS Quarterly Review*, pp. 19–34.

Najand, M., Rahman, H., & Yung, K. (1992). Inter-currency transmission of volatility in foreign exchange futures. *Journal of Futures Markets, 12*(6), 609–620.

Nikkinen, J., Salhstrom, P., & Vahamaa, S. (2006). Implied volatility linkages among major European currencies. *Journal of International Financial Markets, Institutions and Money, 19*, 289–305.

Patnaik, A. (2013). A study of volatility spillover across select foreign exchange rates in India using dynamic conditional correlations. *Journal of Quantitative Economics, 11*(1&2 (Combined)), 28–47.

Pesaran, M. H., & Shin, Y. (1998). Generalized impulse response analysis in linear multivariate models. *Economics Letters, 58*, 17–29.

Ray, P. (2014, July). The rupee in distress. *ICRA Bulletin, Money and Finance*, 41–62.

Rittler, D. (2012). Price discovery and volatility spillovers in the European Union emissions trading scheme: A high-frequency analysis. *Journal of Banking & Finance, 36*(3), 774–785.

Roope, M., & Zurbruegg, R. (2002). The intraday price discovery process between the Singapore exchange and Taiwan futures exchange. *Journal of Futures Markets, 22*(3), 219–240.

SEBI. (2013). *Handbook of statistics on Indian securities market 2013*. Mumbai: Security and Exchange Board of India (SEBI).

Sehgal, S., Ahmad, W., & Deisting, F. (2014). An empirical examination of the process of information transmission in India's agriculture futures markets. *Journal of Quantitative Economics, 12*(1), 97–126.

Sehgal, S., Ahmad, W., & Deisting, F. (2015). An investigation of price discovery and volatility spillovers in India's foreign exchange market. *Journal of Economic Studies, 42*(2), 261–284.

Sharma, S. (2011). *An empirical analysis of the relationship between currency futures and exchange rate volatility in India*. RBI working paper series no. WPS DEAP, 1/2011.

Tamakoshi, G., & Hamori, S. (2014). On cross-currency transmissions between US dollar and euro LIBOR-OIS spreads. *Research in International Business and Finance, 30*, 83–90.

Tse, Y. (1999). Price discovery and volatility spillovers in the DJIA index and futures markets. *Journal of Futures Markets, 19*(8), 911–930.

World Bank. (2013). *India development update*. Washington, DC: Economic Policy and Poverty Team, The World Bank.

Xu, X. E., & Fung, H. G. (2005). Cross-market linkages between US and Japanese precious metals futures trading. *Journal of International Financial Markets, Institutions and Money, 15*(2), 107–124.

CHAPTER 16

Future Avenues in Trade Policy Research

Somesh K. Mathur, Rahul Arora, and Sarbjit Singh

The empirical research in international trade is growing at a very rapid pace and the present book very lucidly presents some of the existing and future issues in the field of quantitative analysis of international trade. The book has highlighted the recent developments in trade theories and their diverse explanations of gains from trade while explaining the changing pattern of trade over the years. Some common and frontier methodologies related to empirical research in international trade have also been presented in this book. The application part of this book further explains the ways to answer various researchable questions related to the trade policy of any country. The advancements in the empirical methods, particularly in the field of econometrics and general equilibrium analysis, have simplified the quantitative analysis to some extent and it has now become possible because of availability of country-wide disaggregated data over the years. Although, the book has covered many issues, many more issues still require further attention. The dynamic nature of trade policy provides many new areas of research that can be fruitful for any researcher working in this field. This chapter concludes with a discussion of some new areas of research that can be pursued with the help of advanced applications of empirical tools.

S.K. Mathur (✉)
Indian Institute of Technology-Kanpur, Kanpur, India

R. Arora • S. Singh
Consumer Unity & Trust Society (CUTS) International, Jaipur, India

S.K. Mathur et al. (eds.), *Theorizing International Trade*,
https://doi.org/10.1007/978-981-10-1759-9_16

16.1 Future Avenues in Trade Policy Research

Following are some of the main areas of empirical research in international trade that should be necessary to pursue for guiding a diverse set of countries in the world while taking decisions about their trade policies.

- Future role of the World Trade Organization (WTO) as a trade facilitator;
- Evaluation of country-specific trade policy;
- Country-specific sectoral analysis to evaluate the real comparative advantage;
- Impact of trade distortions such as trade subsidies and quotas on trade growth;
- Country-wide impact of signing trade facilitation agreements of the WTO;
- Calculation of trade costs in goods and services at high level of product disaggregation;
- Calculation of Ad Valorem Equivalents (AVEs) of non-tariff barriers;
- Identification of non-tariff barriers used as protection measures;
- Effect of non-tariff barriers on trade growth;
- Evaluation of the impact of emerging 'Mega-Regional' trade agreements in the world;
- Possibilities of multilateral trade talks in the presence of Mega-Regionals in the world;
- Comparative analysis of Intellectual Property Rights (IPRs) between the developed and developing world;
- Economy-wide analysis of change in trade policy using country-specific general equilibrium models;
- Usage of dynamic general equilibrium model in trade policy analysis;
- Identification of Global Value Chains (GVCs) over the world;
- Evaluation of the benefits associated with fragmentation of the production processes;
- Trade and environment;
- Negotiating position of India regarding the General Agreement on Trade in Services (GATS), the Agreement on Trade-Related Aspects of Intellectual Property Rights (TRIPS), trade facilitation, and WTO+ and X issues;
- Trade and wage inequality;
- Trade and poverty;

- Trade liberalization and selection and scale effects;
- Sustainable Development Goals (SDGs) and positions of member states;
- Oligopoly and trade;
- Trade, endogenous growth and innovation;
- Trade and economic geography;
- Determinants of horizontal and vertical FDI and spillovers;
- Spatial modelling;
- Measuring protection at sectoral level;
- Trade and wage employment, estimated rates of nominal protection (NRP), effective rate of protection (ERP), non-tariff barriers; and
- Estimation of the Baldwin and Taglioni gravity model, among other areas.

References

Abadie, A., & Gardeazabal, J. (2003). The economic costs of conflict: A case study of the Basque country. *The American Economic Review, 93*(1), 113–132.

Abadie et al. (2014). Synthetic control methods for comparative case studies of aggregate interventions: Estimating the effect of California's tobacco control programm. *Journal of the American Statistical Association, 105*(490), 493–505. 2010.

Abadie, A., Diamond, A., & Hainmueller, J. (2014). *SYNTH: Stata module to implement synthetic control methods for comparative case studies.*

Abadie, A., Diamond, A., & Hainmueller, J. (2015). Comparative politics and the synthetic control method. *American Journal of Political Science, 59*(2), 495–510.

Abhyankar, H. A. (1995). Trading-round-the clock: Return, volatility and volume spillovers in the Eurodollar futures markets. *Pacific-Basin Finance Journal, 3*, 75–92.

Amiti, M., & Davis, D. R. (2011). Trade, firms, and wages: Theory and evidence. *Review of Economic Studies, 79*, 1–36. [Accepted in 2011].

Amjadi, A., Schuler, P., Kuwahara, H., & Quadros, S. (2011). *User manual, world integrated trade solutions (WITS)*. Washington, DC: World Bank.

Anderson, J. E. (1979). A theoretical foundation for the gravity equation. *The American Economic Review, 69*(1), 106–116.

Anderson, J., & Neary, J. (2005). *Measuring the restrictiveness of international trade policy.* Cambridge, MA: MIT Press.

Anderson, E. J., & Wincoop, V. E. (2003). Gravity with gravitas: A solution to the border puzzle. *The American Economic Review, 93*, 170–192.

Anderson, E. J., & Wincoop, V. E. (2004). Trade costs. *Journal of Economic Literature, 42*(3), 691–751.

S.K. Mathur et al. (eds.), *Theorizing International Trade*,
https://doi.org/10.1007/978-981-10-1759-9

Antonakakis, N. (2012). Exchange return co-movements and volatility spillovers before and after the introduction of euro. *Journal of International Financial Markets, Institutions & Money, 22*, 1091–1109.

Antonakakis, N., & Kizys, R. (2015). Dynamic spillovers between commodity and currency markets. *International Review of Financial Analysis, 41*, 303–319.

Antras, P., & Helpman, E. (2004). Global sourcing. *Journal of Political Economy, 112*(3), 552–580.

Antras, P., & Helpman, E. (2007). *Contractual frictions and global sourcing*. CEPR discussion paper no. 6033. London: CEPR.

APEDA. (2006). APEDA website. Retrieved March 2006, from www.apeda.com

Arellano, M., & Bond, S. (1991). Some tests of specification for panel data: Monte Carlo evidence and an application to employment equations. *Review of Economic Studies, 58*(2), 277–297.

Arellano, M., & Bover, O. (1995). Another look at the instrumental variable estimation of error-components models. *Journal of Econometrics, 68*(1), 29–51.

Arkolakis, C., & Muendler, M. A. (2010/2011). *The extensive margin of exporting products*. NBER working paper no. 16641. Cambridge, MA: National Bureau of Economic Research.

Arora, R., & Mathur, S. K. (2015). Welfare implications of India's trade liberalization within Asia: A general equilibrium assessment under conjecture of free trade area. *Trade and Development Review, 8*(2), 69–95.

Arora, R., Singh, S., & Mathur, S. K. (2015). Assessment of the proposed India-China Free Trade Agreement: A general equilibrium approach. *Journal of Centrum Cathedra, 8*(2), 81–108. https://doi.org/10.1108/JCC-08-02-2015-B002

Arvis, J. F., Ben, Y. D., & Utoktham, S. C. (2013). *Trade costs in the developing world 1995–2010*. Policy research working paper no. 6309, The World Bank.

Asimakopoulos, I., Ayling, D., & Mahmood, W. M. (2000). Non-linear Granger causality in currency futures returns. *Economics Letters, 68*, 25–30.

Awartani, B., & Maghyereh, I. A. (2013). Dynamic spillovers between oil and stock markets in the Gulf Cooperation Council countries. *Energy Economics, 36*, 28–42.

Bagwell, K., & Ramey, G. (1991). Oligopoly limit pricing. *RAND Journal of Economics, 22*(2), 155–170.

Bain, J. S. (1956). *Barriers to competition*. Cambridge: Harvard University Press.

Balassa, B. (1966). Tariff reductions and trade in manufacturers among the industrial countries. *The American Economic Review, 56*(3), 466–473.

Balassa, B. (1985). Exports, policy choices, and economic growth in developing countries after the 1973 oil shock. *Journal of Development Economics, 18*, 23–35.

Balding, C. (2010). Joining the World Trade Organization: What is the impact? *Review of International Economics, 18*(1), 193–206.

Baldwin, R. E., & Flam, H. (1989). Strategic trade policy in the market for the 30–40 seat commuter aircraft. *Weltwirtschaftliches Archive, 125*, 484–500.

Baldwin, R. E., & Krugman, P. R. (1988). Industrial policy and international competition in wide-bodied jet aircraft. In R. Baldwin (Ed.), *Trade policy issues and empirical analysis.* Chicago: University of Chicago Press for the NBER.

Baldwin, R., & Taglioni, D. (2011). *Gravity chains: Estimating bilateral trade flows when parts and components trade is important.* National Bureau of Economic Research working paper series no. 16672, NBER.

Barrett, A., Bergin, A., & Duffy, D. (2006). The labour market characteristics and labour market impacts of immigrants in Ireland. *Economic and Social Review., 37*(1), 1–26.

Behera, K. H. (2011). Onshore and offshore market for Indian rupee: Recent evidence on volatility and shock spillover. *Macroeconomics and Finance in Emerging Market Economies, 4*(1), 43–55.

Ben-zvi, S., & Helpman, E. (1992). Oligopoly in segmented market. In G. Grossman (Ed.), *Imperfect competition and international trade* (pp. 31–54). Cambridge, MA: MIT Press.

Bergstrand, J. (1989). The generalised gravity equation, monopolistic competition, and the factor proportion theory in international trade. *Review of Economics and Statistics, 71*(1), 143–153.

Bernard, A. B., Eaton, J., Jensen, J. B., & Kortum, S. (2003). Plants and productivity in international trade. *The American Economic Review, 93*, 1268–1290.

Bernard, A. B., Jensen, J. B., Redding, S. J., & Schott, P. K. (2007a). Firms in international trade. *Journal of Economic Perspectives, 21*(3), 105–130.

Bernard, A. B., Redding, S. J., & Schott, P. K. (2007b). Comparative advantage and heterogeneous firms. *Review of Economic Studies, 74*(1), 31–66.

Bernhofen, D. M. (1996). Vertical integration and international predation. *Review of International Economics, 4*, 90–98.

Berry, S., & Waldfogel, J. (2003). Product quality and market size. *Journal of Industrial Economics, 51*(1), 1–31.

Bhagwati, J. N. (1965). On the equivalence of tariff and quotas. In R. E. Baldwin (Ed.), *Trade growth and balance of payment.* Amsterdam: North Holland.

Bhagwati, J., & Srinivasan, T. (2002). Trade and poverty in poor countries. *The American Economic Review, 92*(2), 180–183.

Bhattacharya, B. B., & Sakthivel, S. (2003). Economic reforms and jobless growth in India in the 1990s. *Indian Journal of Labour Economics, 46*(4), 845–865.

Billmeier, A., & Nannicini, T. (2013). Assessing economic liberalization episodes: A synthetic control approach. *Review of Economics and Statistics, 95*(3), 983–1001.

BIS. (2013). *Triennial central bank survey.* Basel: Bank for International Settlements.

Blundell, R., & Bond, S. R. (1998). Initial conditions and moment restrictions in dynamic panel data model. *Journal of Econometrics, 87*(1), 115–143.

Bohn, S., Lofstrom, M., & Raphael, S. (2014). Did the 2007 legal Arizona workers act reduce the state's unauthorized immigrant population? *Review of Economics and Statistics, 9*(2), 258–269.

Bonanno, G. (1987). Location choice, product proliferation and entry deterrence. *Review of Economic Studies, 54*, 37–45.

Bouet, A. (2008). *The expected benefits of trade liberalization for world income and development: Opening the "black box" of global trade modeling*. Food policy review no. 8, International Food Policy Research Institute, Washington, DC.

Bowen, H. P., Leamer, E. E., & Sveikauskas, L. (1987). Multi-country, multi-factor tests of the factor abundance theory. *The American Economic Review, 77*(5), 791–809.

Brander, J. A. (1981). Intra-industry trade in identical commodities. *Journal of International Economics, 11*, 1–14.

Brander, J. A., & Krugman, P. R. (1983). A reciprocal dumping model of international trade. *Journal of International Economics, 15*, 313–321.

Brander, J. A., & Spencer, B. J. (1981). Tariff and the extraction of foreign monopoly rents under potential entry. *Canadian Journal of Economics, 14*, 371–389.

Brander, J. A., & Spencer, B. J. (1983). International R&D rivalry and industrial strategy. *Review of Economic Studies, 50*, 707–722.

Brander, J. A., & Spencer, B. J. (1985). Export subsidies and international market share rivalry. *Journal of International Economics, 18*, 83–100.

Brockmeier, M. (1996/2001). *A graphical exposition of the GTAP model*. GTAP technical paper no. 3-1-2001. Center for Global Trade Analysis, Purdue University.

Bruno, G. S. F. (2005). Estimation and inference in dynamic unbalanced panel-data models with a small number of individuals. *The Stata Journal, 5*(4), 473–500.

Bruno, G. S. F., Falzoni, A. M., & Helg, R. (2005). *Estimating a dynamic labour demand equation using small, unbalanced panels: An application to Italian manufacturing sectors*. Università Bocconi, Milano; Università degli Studi di Bergamo; LIUC – Università Carlo Cattaneo.

Bubak, V., Kocenda, E., & Zikes, F. (2011). Volatility transmission in emerging European foreign exchange markets. *Journal of Banking & Finance, 35*, 2829–2841.

Burfisher, M. E. (2011). *Introduction to computable general equilibrium models*. New York: Cambridge University Press.

Cabral, L. M. B., & Thomas, W. R. (2008). Are sunk costs a barrier to entry? *Journal of Economics & Management Strategy, 17*, 97–112.

Carlton, D. W. (2004). Why barriers to entry are barriers to understanding. *The American Economic Review, 94*(2), 466.

Carrere, C. (2006). Revisiting the effects of regional trade agreements on trade flows with proper specification of the gravity model. *European Economic Review, 50*(2), 223–247.

Caves, R. E. (1974). *International trade, international investment and imperfect markets.* Special paper in international economics no. 10, International finance section, Princeton University.

Chacoliades, M. (1978). *The theory of monopolistic competition.* Cambridge, MA: Harvard University Press.

Chamberlin, E. (1933). *The theory of monopolistic competition.* Cambridge MA: Harvard University Press.

Chan, L., & Lien, D. (2006). Are options redundant? Further evidence from currency futures markets. *International Review of Financial Analysis, 15*, 179–188.

Chan, K., Chan, K. C., & Karolyi, G. A. (1991). Intraday volatility in the stock index and stock index futures markets. *The Review of Financial Studies, 4*(4), 657–684.

Chaney, T. (2008). Distorted gravity: The intensive and extensive margins of international trade. *The American Economic Review, 98*(4), 1707–1721.

Chang, W., & Chen, F. Y. (1994). Vertically related markets: Export rivalry between DC and LDC firms. *Review of International Economics, 2*, 131–142.

Chang, W., & Kim, J. C. (1991). Strategic tariff policy in a model of trade in intermediate and final products. In A. Takayama, M. Ohyama, & H. Ohta (Eds.), *Trade policy, international adjustments* (pp. 36–59). New York: Academic Press.

Chen, N., & Novy, D. (2012). On the measurement of trade costs: Direct vs. indirect approaches to quantifying standards and technical regulations. *World Trade Review, 11*(03), 401–414.

Chowdhury, I. R., & Chaudhuri, P. R. (2003). Import protection as export promotion. *Keio Economic Studies, 15*, 17–35.

Ciner, C. (2011). Information transmission across currency futures markets: Evidence from frequency domain tests. *International Review of Financial Analysis, 20*, 134–139.

Claessens, S., Dornbusch, R., & Park, C. Y. (2001). Contagion: Why crises spread and how this can be stopped. In S. Claessens & J. K. Forbes (Eds.), *International Financial Contagion* (pp. 19–41). New York: Springer.

Cling, J. P. (2006). Commerce, croissance, pauvreté et inégalités dans les PED: une revue de littérature. Développement Institutions et Analyses de Long terme, DIAL. Document de travail DT 2006–07.

Cling, J. P., Razafindrakoto, M., & Roubaud, F. (2009). Vietnam's WTO accession and export-led growth. *International Economics, 118*, 5–12.

Corden, W. M. (1974). *Trade policy and economic welfare.* Oxford: Oxford University Press.

Corm, G. (2012). *Le Liban contemporain: Histoire et Société.* Paris: La découverte.

Dagher, A. (2005). *Quelle politique industrielle pour le Liban? Une approche différente du rôle de l'Etat dans l'économie.* Beirut, Lebanon: LCPS.

Das, D. K. (2008). *Trade liberalization, employment, labour productivity, and real wages: A study of the organized manufacturing industries in India in the 1980s and 1990s.* Asia-Pacific working paper series. Geneva: International Labour Organisation.

Das, D. K., & Kalita, G. (2009). *Do labor intensive industries generate employment? Evidence from firm level survey in India.* Working paper no. 237, Indian Council for Research on International Economic Relations, New Delhi.

Davis, D. R., & Weinstein, D. E. (2001). An account of global factor trade. *The American Economic Review, 91*(5), 1423–1453.

De, P. (2006). Trade, infrastructure and transaction costs: The imperatives for Asian economic cooperation. *Journal of Economic Integration, 21*, 708–735.

De, P. (2007). *Impact of trade costs on trade: Empirical evidence from Asian countries.* ARTNeT working paper no. 27. Asia-Pacific Research and Training Network on Trade. Retrieved from http://www.unescap.org/sites/default/files/AWP%20No.%2027.pdf

Deardorff, A. V. (1979). Weak links in the chain of comparative advantage. *Journal of International Economics, 9*, 197–209.

Deardorff, A. V. (1984). Testing trade theories and predicting trade flows. In R. W. Jones & P. B. Kenen (Eds.), *Handbook of international economics* (Vol. I). Amsterdam: North.

Deardorff, A. V. (1985). Comparative advantage and international trade and investment in services. In R. M. Stern (Ed.), *Trade and investment in services: Canada/US perspectives.* Toronto: Ontario Economic Council.

Deardorff, A. V. (2005). *Gains from trade and fragmentation.* Research seminar in international economics discussion paper no. 543. Ann Arbor: University of Michigan.

Diebold, F. X., & Yilmaz, K. (2009). Measuring financial asset return and volatility spillovers, with application to global equity markets. *Economic Journal, 119*, 158–171.

Diebold, F. X., & Yilmaz, K. (2012). Better to give than to receive: Predictive directional measurement of volatility spillovers. *International Journal of Forecasting, 28*, 57–66.

Dimaranan, B., Ianchovichina, E., & Martinr, W. (2007). *China, India, and the future of the world economy: Fierce competition or shared growth?* Policy research working paper no. 4304, The World Bank group.

Dixit, A. K. (1980). The role of investment in entry deterrence. *Economic Journal, 90*, 95–106.

Dixit, A. K. (1984). International trade policy for oligopolistic industries. *Economic Journal, 94*, 1–16.

Dixit, A. K., & Grossman, G. M. (1986). Targeted export promotion with several oligopolistic industries. *Journal of International Economics, 21*, 23–29.

Dixit, A. K., & Kyle, A. S. (1985). The use of protection and subsidies for entry promotion and deterrence. *The American Economic Review, 75*, 139–152.

Dixit, A. K., & Norman, V. (1980). *Theory of international trade.* Cambridge: Cambridge University Press.

Dixit, A. K., & Stiglitz, J. E. (1977). Monopolistic competition and optimum product diversity. *The American Economic Review, 67*, 297–308.

Doing Business Report. (2015). *Going beyond efficiency* (12th ed.), provided by World Bank Group. http://www.doingbusiness.org/reports/global-reports/doing-business-2015

Dollar, D., & Kray, A. (2001). *Growth is good for the poor.* Policy research working paper no. 2587, World Bank.

Duval, Y., & Utoktham, C. (2011a). Intraregional trade costs in Asia: A primer. *Asia-Pacific Development Journal, 18*(2), 1–23.

Duval, Y., & Utoktham, C. (2011b). *Trade costs in the India-Mekong subregion: Identifying policy priorities for trade facilitation.* Staff working paper no. 04/11, Trade and Investment Division.

Duval, Y., Saggu, A., & Utoktham, C. (2015). *Value added trade costs in goods and services.* TID working paper no. 01/15, ESCAP Trade and Investment Division, Bangkok.

Eaton, J., & Grossman, G. M. (1986). Optimal trade and industrial policy under oligopoly. *Quarterly Journal of Economics, 101*(2), 383–406.

Eaton, J., & Kortum, S. (2002). Technology, geography, and trade. *Econometrica, 70*(5), 1741–1779.

Eaton, J., & Panagariya, A. (1979). Gains from trade under variable returns to scale, commodity taxation, tariff and factor market distortions. *Journal of International Economics, 9*, 481–501.

Eckel, C., & Neary, J. P. (2010). Multi-product firms and flexible manufacturing in the global economy. *The Review of Economic Studies., 77*(1), 188–217.

Economic Survey (2014–2015). State of the economy. New Delhi: Ministry of Finance, Government of India.

Edwards, S. (1991). *Trade orientation, distortions and growth in developing countries.* NBER working paper no. 3716, National Bureau of Economic Research.

Ellickson, P. B. (2013). Supermarket as a natural oligopoly. *Economic Inquiry, 51*(2), 1142–1154.

Elyasiani, E., Kocagil, E. A., & Mansur, I. (2007). Information transmission and spillover in currency markets: A generalized variance decomposition analysis. *The Quarterly Review of Economics and Finance, 47*, 312–330.

Engle, R. F. (2002). Dynamic conditional correlation: A simple class of multivariate generalized autoregressive conditional heteroskedasticity models. *Journal of Business & Economic Statistics, 20*, 339–350.

Engle, R. F., Ito, T., & Lin, W.-L. (1990). Meteor showers or heat waves? Heteroskedastic intra-daily volatility in the foreign exchange market. *Econometrica, 58*(3), 525–542.

Feder, G. (1983). On exports and economic growth. *Journal of Development Economics, 12*(1–2), 59–73.

Feenstra, R., & Judd, K. (1982). Tariff technology transfer and welfare. *Journal of Public Economics, 90*, 1142–1165.

Flaherty, M. T. (1980). Dynamic limit pricing, barriers to entry, and rational firms. *Journal of Economic Theory, 23*, 160–182.

Francois J., & Pindyuk O. (2013). *Consolidated data on international trade in services v8.7.* IIDE discussion paper no. 20130101. Retrieved from www.I4ide.org/content/wpaper/dp20130101

Friedman, J. W. (1979). On entry preventing behaviour. In S. J. Brams (Ed.), *Applied game theory* (pp. 236–253). Vienna: Verlag.

Friedman, J. W. (1983). Limit price entry prevention when information is lacking. *Journal of Economic Dynamics and Control, 5*, 187–199.

Fudenberg, D., & Tirole, J. (1983). Capital as a commitment: Strategic investment to deter mobility. *Journal of Economic Theory, 31*, 227–250.

Fung, H. G., & Patterson, G. A. (1999). The dynamic relationship of volatility, volume, and market depth in currency futures markets. *Journal of International Financial Markets, Institutions and Money, 9*, 33–59.

Fung, H. G., Leung, K. W., & Xu, X. (2001). Information role of US futures trading in a global financial market. *Journal of Futures Markets, 21*(11), 1071–1090.

Gagnon, L., & Karolyi, A. G. (2006). Price and volatility transmision across borders. *Financial Markets, Institutions and Instruments, 17*(3), 107–158.

Garman, B. M., & Klass, J. M. (1980). On the estimation of security price volatilities from historical data. *The Journal of Business, 53*(1), 67–78.

Gaskins, D. W. (1971). Dynamic limit pricing: Optimal pricing under threat of entry. *Journal of Economic Theory, 3*, 306–322.

Ghironi, F., & Melitz, M. J. (2005). International trade and macroeconomic dynamics with heterogeneous firms. *Quarterly Journal of Economics, 120*(3), 864–915.

Ghose, A. K. (2000). *Trade liberalization and manufacturing employment.* Employment paper no. 2000/3, International Labour Organization, Geneva.

Ghose, A. K. (2003). *Jobs and income in a globalizing world.* Geneva: International Labour Organization.

Gilbert, R., & Vives, X. (1986). Entry deterrence and free rider problem. *Review of Economic Studies, 53*, 71–83.

Goldar, B. (1989). Determinants of India's export performance in engineering products, 1960–79. *The Developing Economies, 27*(1), 3–18.

Goldar, B. (2000). Employment growth in organised manufacturing in India. *Economic and Political Weekly, 34*(12), 989–991.

Goldar, B. (2002). *Trade liberalization and manufacturing employment: The case of India*. Employment paper no. 2002/34, International Labour Organization, Geneva.

Goldar, B. (2008). *Trade liberalization and labour demand elasticity in Indian manufacturing*. Delhi: Institute of Economic Growth.

Gowa, J., & Kim, S. Y. (2005). An exclusive country club: The effects of the GATT on trade, 1950–94. *World Politics, 57*(4), 453–478.

Greenaway, D., Hine, R. C., & Wright, P. (1999). An empirical assessment of the impact of trade on employment in the United Kingdom. *European Journal of Political Economy, 5*(2), 485–500.

Greene, W. H. (2002). *Econometric analysis*. Englewood Cliffs: Prentice Hall.

Greenway, D. (1987). The new theories of intra-industry trade. *Bulletin of Economic Research, 39*(2), 95–120.

Grossman, G. M. (Ed.). (1992). *Imperfect competition and international trade*. Cambridge, MA: MIT Press.

Grubel, H. G., & Lloyd, P. J. (1975). *The international economy, MIT Press, Intra-industry trade: The theory and measurement of international trade in differentiated products*. London: Macmillan.

Hahn, F. H. (1962). The stability of the Cournot oligopoly solution. *Review of Economic Studies, 32*, 329–331.

Han, L. M., & Ozocak, O. (2002). Risk–return relationships in foreign-currency futures following macroeconomic announcements. *Journal of Futures Markets, 22*(8), 729–764.

Haouas, I., & Yagoubi, M. (2004). *Trade liberalization and labour-demand elasticities: Empirical evidence from Tunisia*. IZA discussion paper no. 1084, Institute for the Study of Labour, Bonn.

Harrington, J. E. (1986). Limit pricing when the potential entrant is uncertain about its cost functions. *Econometrica, 54*, 429–437.

Harrington, J. E. (1987). Oligopolistic entry deterrence under incomplete information. *RAND Journal of Economics, 18*, 211–229.

Harvey, C. R., & Huang, R. D. (1991). Volatility in the foreign currency futures. *Review of Financial Studies, 4*(3), 543–569.

Hasan, R., Mitra, D., & Ramaswamy, K. V. (2007). Trade reforms, labour regulations and labour-demand elasticities: Empirical evidence from India. *Review of Economics and Statistics, 89*(3), 466–481.

Heckscher, E. F., & Ohlin, B. G. (1991). *Heckscher-Ohlin trade theory*. Cambridge, MA: MIT Press.

Helpman, E., & Krugman, P. (1985a). *Market structure and foreign trade: Increasing returns, imperfect competition and the international economy*. Brighton: Wheatsheaf Books.

Helpman, E., & Krugman, P. (1985b). *Market structure and foreign trade: Increasing returns, imperfect competition and the international economy*. Cambridge: MIT Press.

Helpman, E., & Razin, A. (1984). Increasing return, monopolistic competition and factor movements: A welfare analysis. In H. Kierzkowski (Ed.), *Monopolistic competition and international trade*. Oxford: Clarendon Press.

Helpman, E., & Razin, A. (Eds.). (1988). *International trade and trade policies*. Cambridge, MA: MIT Press.

Helpman, E., Melitz, M. J., & Yeaple, S. R. (2004). Exports versus FDI with heterogeneous firms. *The American Economic Review, 94*(1), 300–316.

Helpman, E., Itskhoki, O., & Redding, S. (2011). *Trade and labor market outcomes*. NBER working paper no. 16662, National Bureau of Economic Research.

Henson, S., & Mitullah, W. (2004). *Kenyan exports of Nile perch – Impact of food safety standards on export oriented supply chain*. Policy research working paper, World Bank.

Hertel, T. W. (Ed.). (1997). *Global trade analysis: Modeling and applications*. New York: Cambridge University Press.

Hoekman, B., & Mavroidis, P. (2002). *Economic development, competition policy, and the World Trade Organization*. Policy research working paper no. 2917, World Bank.

Hong, Y. (2001). A test for volatility spillover with application to exchange rates. *Journal of Econometrics, 103*(1–2), 183–224.

Hopenhayn, H. A. (1992). Entry, exit and firm dynamics long-run equilibrium. *Econometrica, 60*, 1127–1150.

Hua, R., & Chen, B. (2007). International linkages of the Chinese futures markets. *Applied Financial Economics, 17*(6), 1275–1287.

Huff, K., & Hertel, T. (2000). *Decomposing welfare changes in the GTAP model*. GTAP technical paper no. 5, Center for Global Trade Analysis, Purdue University.

Iacovone, L. (2003). *Analysis and impact of sanitary and phyto-sanitary measures*. Centre for International Development at Harvard University. India in the WTO (2008, May) Retrieved from http://www.indiainthewto.wordpress.com/category/sps-issues

IMF. (2013). *World economic outlook*. IMF Database. https://www.imf.org/external/pubs/ft/weo/2013/02/weodata/index.aspx

IMF. (2014). *Lebanon*. IMF country report no. 14/237, International Monetary Fund.

Inagaki, K. (2007). Testing for volatility spillover between the British pound and the euro. *Research in International Business and Finance, 21*, 161–174.

Ishikawa, J., & Lee, K.-D. (1997). Backfiring tariffs in vertically related markets. *Journal of International Economics, 42*, 395–423.

Jammes, O., & Olarreaga, M. (2005). *Explaining smart and GSIM*, The World Bank. Retrieved from http://citeseerx.ist.psu.edu/viewdoc/download?doi=10.1.1.547.8636&rep=rep1&type=pdf

Jayanthakumaran, K. (2004). *An empirical assessment of the impact of inter-industry trade on employment: Australia 1989/90–2000/01*. Working paper no. 04-11, Department of Economics, University of Wollongong, Wollongong.

Jean, S. (2001). The effect of international trade on labour demand elasticities: Inter-sectoral matters. *Review of International Economics, 8*(3), 504–516.

Jensen, M. F. (2002). *Reviewing the SPS agreement: A developing country perspective*. CDR working paper. Sub-series on globalisation and economic restructuring in Africa, Copenhagen.

Jones, R. W. (1989). Raw materials, processing activities and protectionism. *Canadian Journal of Economics, 22*, 469–486.

Jones, R. W. (1996). *Vertical markets in international trade*. Working paper no. 432, Rochester Center for Economic Research.

Kamien, M. I., & Schwartz, N. L. (1971). Limit pricing and uncertain entry. *Econometrica, 39*, 441–454.

Karmakar, M. (2009). Price discoveries and volatility spillovers in S&P CNX Nifty future and its underlying index CNX Nifty. *Vikalpa, 34*(2), 41–56.

Kee, H. L., Nicita, A., & Olarreaga, M. (2009). Estimating trade restrictiveness indices. *The Economic Journal., 119*, 172–199.

Kitamura, Y. (2010). Testing for intraday interdependence and volatility spillover among the euro, the pound and the Swiss franc markets. *Research in International Business and Finance, 24*, 158–171.

Klemperer, P. (1987a). Markets with consumer switching costs. *Quarterly Journal of Economics, 102*, 375–394.

Klemperer, P. (1987b). The competitiveness of markets with switching costs. *RAND Journal of Economics, 18*, 139–150.

Klemperer, P. (1995). Competition when consumers have switching costs: An overview with applications to industrial organization, macroeconomics, and international trade. *Review of Economic Studies, 62*, 515–539.

Koop, G., Pesaran, M. H., & Potter, S. M. (1996). Impulse response analysis in nonlinear multivariate models. *Journal of Econometrics, 74*, 119–147.

Krishna, P., & Mitra, D. (1998). Trade liberalization, market discipline and productivity growth: New evidence from India. *Journal of Development Economics, 56*(2), 447–462.

Krishna, P., Mitra, D., & Chinoy, S. (2001). Trade liberalization and labour-demand elasticities: Evidence from Turkey. *Journal of International Economics, 55*(2), 391–409.

Krugman, P. (1970). Scale economies, product differentiation and pattern of trade. *The American economic review., 70*, 952–959.

Krugman, P. (1979). Increasing returns, monopolistic competition, and international trade. *Journal of International Economics, 9*(4), 469–479.
Krugman, P. (1980a). *Differentiated products and multinational trade*. US: Mimeo.
Krugman, P. (1980b). Scale economies, product differentiation, and the pattern of trade. *The American Economic Review, 70*(5), 950–959.
Krugman, P. (1981). Intra-industry specialization and the gains from trade. *Journal of Public economies, 89*, 959–973.
Krugman, P. (1984). Import protection as export promotion: International competition in the presence of oligopoly and economies of scale. In H. Kierzkowski (Ed.), *Monopolistic competition and international trade*. Oxford: Oxford University Press.
Krugman, P. (1986). *Strategic trade policy and the new international economics*. Cambridge, MA: MIT Press.
Krugman, P. (1990). *Rethinking international trade*. Cambridge, MA: MIT Press.
Krugman, P., & Venables, T. (1996). Integration, specialization, and adjustment. *European Economic Review, 40*, 959–968.
Kumar, M. (2011). Return and volatility spillovers: Evidence from Indian exchange rates. *International Journal of Economics and Business Research, 3*(4), 371–387.
Kumar, D. (2014). Correlations, return and volatility spillovers in Indian exchange rates. *Global Business Review, 15*(1), 77–91.
Lall, S. (1999). India's manufactured exports: Comparative structure and prospects. *World Development., 27*(10), 1769–1786.
Lall, S. (2002). *The employment impact of globalisation in developing countries*. QEH working paper series no. 93, Queen Elizabeth House, University of Oxford, Oxford.
Lancaster, K. (1979). *Variety, equity and efficiency*. New York: Columbia University Press.
Lancaster, K. (1980). Intra-industry trade under perfect monopolistic competition. *Journal of International Economics, 10*, 151–175.
Lardy, N. R. (2014). *Markets over Mao: The rise of private business in China*. Washington, DC: Peterson Institute for International Economics.
Lautier, M. (2013). Le développement des échanges internationaux de services de santé: Perspectives des exportations en Afrique du Nord. *ADBF*. Note Economique, African Development Bank Group.
Leamer, E. E. (1980). The Leontief paradox, reconsidered. *The Journal of Political Economy, 88*(3), 495–503.
Leamer, E. E., & Levinsohn, J. (1995). International trade theory: The evidence. In G. M. Grossman & K. Rogoff (Eds.), *Handbook of international economics* (pp. 1339–1396). Amsterdam: Elsevier Science.
Leontief, W. W. (1953). Domestic production and foreign trade: The American capital position re-examined. *Proceedings of the American Philosophical Society,*

97(4), 332–349. Reprinted in Richard, C., & Harry, G. J. (Eds.) (1968). *Readings in international economics*. Homewood: Irwin.

Lin, W. L., Engle, R. F., & Ito, T. (1994). Do bulls and bears move across borders? International transmission of stock returns and volatility. *Review of Financial Studies, 7*(3), 507–537.

Link, A. (1983). Market structure and voluntary product standards. *Applied Economics, 15*, 393–401.

Linnemann, H. (1966). *An econometric study of international trade flows*. Amsterdam: North Holland.

Mage-Bertomeu, S. (2006). Les modèles d'équilibre général appliqué à la politique commerciale: développements récents. *Revue d'économiepolitique, 116*, 357–381.

Mahalik, K. M., Acharya, D., & Babu, S. M. (2010). *Price discovery and volatility spillovers in futures and spot commodity markets: Some empirical evidence from India*. IGIDR working paper no. PP-062-10.

Marinoso, G. B. (2001). Technological incompatibility, endogenous switching costs and lock-in. *Journal of Industrial Economics, 49*, 281–298.

Marjit, S., & Acharyya, R. (2002). *International trade, wage inequality and the developing economy: A general equilibrium approach*. Heidelberg: Physica-Verlag.

Markusen, J. R. (1981). Trade and gains from trade with imperfect competition. *Journal of International Economics, 11*, 531–551.

Markusen, J. R., & Melvin, J. (1981). Trade factor prices and gains from trade with increasing returns to scale. *Canadian Journal of Economics, 14*, 450–469.

Markusen, J. R., & Melvin, J. (1984). *The gains from trade theorem with increasing returns to scale, monopolistic competition and international trade*. New York: Oxford University press.

Mathur, S. K. (2012). *Trade in climate smart and other specialized products of Ecuador*, E-book, bookboon.com, Denmark and UK. http://bookboon.com/en/trade-in-climate-smart-goods-ebook

Matthews, S. A., & Mirman, L. J. (1983). Equilibrium limit pricing: The effects of private information and stochastic demand. *Econometrica, 51*, 981–996.

Mayer, T., Melitz, M. J., & Ottaviano, I. P. (2014). Market size, competition, and the product mix of exporters. *The American Economic Review, 104*(2), 495–536. [Final version of many references since 2010].

Mazumdar, D. (2003). Trends in employment and the employment elasticity in manufacturing, 1971–92: An international comparison. *Cambridge Journal of Economics., 27*(4), 563–582.

McAfee, R. P., Mialon, H. M., & Williams, M. A. (2004). What is a Barrier to entry? *The American Economic Review, 94*(2), 94–127.

McCallum, J. (1995). National borders matter: Canada-U.S. regional trade patterns. *The American Economic Review, 85*(3), 615–623.

McDougall, R. (2001). *A new regional household demand system for GTAP. Revised in 2003*. GTAP technical paper no. 20, Purdue University.

McMillan, D. G., & Speight, A. E. (2010). Return and volatility spillovers in three euro exchange rates. *Journal of Economics and Business, 62*, 79–93.

MCX-SX. (2014). *Compat uphelds CCI order on "zero pricing" in favour of MCX-SX*. Mumbai: MCX-SX.

Melitz, M. J. (2003). The impact of trade on intra-industry reallocations and aggregate industry productivity. *Econometrica, 71*(6), 1695–1725.

Melitz, M. J., & Ottaviano, G. I. (2008). Market size, trade, and productivity. *Review of Economic Studies, 75*, 295–316.

Melitz, M. J., & Redding, S. J. (2012, December). *Heterogeneous firms and trade*. Working paper, NBER.

Melvin, J. R. (1969). Increasing returns to scale as a determinant of trade. *Canadian Journal of Economics, 11*, 389–402.

Michaely, M. (1977). Exports and growth. *Journal of Development Economics, 4*, 49–53.

Mikic, M., & Gilbert, J. (2007). *Trade statistics in policymaking—A handbook of commonly used trade indices and indicators*. Bangkok: United Nations.

Milgrom, P., & Roberts, J. (1982). Equilibrium limit pricing and entry under incomplete information: An equilibrium analysis. *Econometrica, 50*, 443–460.

Mill, J. S. (1848). *Principles of political economy*. London: John W. Parker.

Miroudot, S., Sauvage, J., & Shepherd, B. (2012). Trade costs and productivity in services sectors. *Economics Letters, 114*(1), 36–38.

Miroudot S., Sauvage J., & Shepherd B. (2013). *Measuring the cost of international trade in services*. Developing Trade Consultants, New York. developing-trade.com/wp-content/uploads/2014/11/DTC-Article-Chapter-2013-5.pdf

Miyajima, K., & Shim, I. (2014, September). Asset managers in emerging market economies. *BIS Quarterly Review*, pp. 19–34.

Modigliani, F. (1956). New developments on the oligopoly front. *Journal of Political Economy, 66*, 215–232.

Moenius, J. (1999). *Information vs product adaptation: The role of standards in trade*. North Western University, Kellogg Graduate School of Management.

Moise, E., & Bris, L. F. (2013). *Trade costs-what have we learned*? OECD trade policy paper no. 150. Retrieved from http://www.oecd-ilibrary.org/trade/trade-costs_5k47x2hjfn48-en

Murti, P. (2004). Exit in duopoly under uncertainty. *RAND Journal of Economics, 35*, 111–127.

Nagaraj, R. (2000). Organised manufacturing employment. *Economic and Political Weekly, 35*(38), 3445–3448.

Najand, M., Rahman, H., & Yung, K. (1992). Inter-currency transmission of volatility in foreign exchange futures. *Journal of Futures Markets, 12*(6), 609–620.

Narayanan, G. B., Aguiar, A., & McDougall, R. (Eds.) (2015). *Global trade, assistance, and production: The GTAP 9 data base.* West Lafayette: Center for Global Trade Analysis, Purdue University.

Nikkinen, J., Salhstrom, P., & Vahamaa, S. (2006). Implied volatility linkages among major European currencies. *Journal of International Financial Markets, Institutions and Money, 19*, 289–305.

Nordas, H. K., & Rouzet, D. (2015). *The impact of services trade restrictiveness on trade flows: First estimates.* OECD trade policy papers no. 178, OECD Publishing. Retrieved from https://doi.org/10.1787/5js6ds9b6kjb-en

Novy, D. (2008). *Gravity redux: Measuring international trade costs with panel data*, University of Warwick. Retrieved from http://economics.uwo.ca/conference/thechangingglobal_apr08/novy.pdf

Novy, D. (2013). Gravity redux: Measuring international trade costs with panel data. *Economic Enquiry, 51*(1), 101–121.

Obstfeld, M., & Rogoff, K. (2000). The six major puzzles in international macroeconomics: Is there a common cause? In B. S. Bernanke & K. Rogoff (Eds.), *NBER macroeconomics annual* (pp. 339–390). Cambridge: MIT Press.

Obstfeld, M., & Rogoff, K. (2001). The six major puzzles in international macroeconomics: Is there a common cause? In B. S. Bernanke & K. Rogoff (Eds.), *NBER macroeconomics annual 2000* (Vol. 15, pp. 339–412). Cambridge, MA: MIT Press.

OECD. (2015). *Services trade restrictiveness index.* www.oecd.org/tad/services-trade/country-notes-trade-restrictiveness-index.htm. Accessed 04 Apr 2016.

OECD/WTO. (2015). *Aid for trade at a glance 2015: Reducing trade costs for inclusive, sustainable growth.* Paris: OECD Publishing.

Otsuki, T., Wilson, J. S., & Sewadeh, M. (2001). *A race to the top – A case study of food safety standards an African exports.* Policy research working paper no. 2563, World Bank.

Owen, R. F., & Ulph, D. (2002). Sunk costs, market access, economic integration and welfare. *Review of International Economics, 1093*, 539–555.

Panagariya A. (2006). *India and China: Trade and foreign investment.* http://www.columbia.edu/~ap2231/Policy%20Papers/Stanford%20India%20China%20Revised%20October%202006.pdf

Patnaik, A. (2013). A study of volatility spillover across select foreign exchange rates in India using dynamic conditional correlations. *Journal of Quantitative Economics, 11*(1&2 (Combined)), 28–47.

Pesaran, M. H., & Shin, Y. (1998). Generalized impulse response analysis in linear multivariate models. *Economics Letters, 58*, 17–29.

Plummer, M. G., Cheong, D., & Hamanaka, S. (2011). *Methodology for impact assessment of free trade agreements.* Manila: Asian Development Bank.

Poyhonen, P. (1963a). A tentative model for the volume of trade between countries. *Weltwirtschaftliches Archiv, 90*(1), 93–100.

Poyhonen, P. (1963b). Toward a general theory of the international trade. *Ekonomiska Samfundets Tidskrift, 16*, 69–77.

Pulliainen, K. (1963). A world trade study: An econometric model of the pattern of the commodity flows of international trade in 1948-60. *Ekonomiska Samfundets Tidskrift, 16*, 78–91.

Punt, C. (2004). *The organisation of trade data for inclusion in social accounting matrix*. Technical paper series no. 2, Provide Project.

Pyatt, G. (1971). Profit maximisation and threat of new entry. *Economic Journal, 81*, 242–255.

Rahman, M. (2003). *A panel data analysis of Bangladesh's trade: The gravity model approach*. A PhD thesis, University of Sydney, Sydney.

Ray, P. (2014, July). The rupee in distress. *ICRA Bulletin, Money and Finance*, 41–62.

RBI. (2006). Retrieved March 2006, from www.rbi.org

Ricardo, D. (1817). *On the principles of political economy and taxation*. London: John Murray.

Richard, S. (2004). Sunk costs and antitrust barriers to entry. *The American Economic Review, 94*, 36–78.

Rittler, D. (2012). Price discovery and volatility spillovers in the European Union emissions trading scheme: A high-frequency analysis. *Journal of Banking & Finance, 36*(3), 774–785.

Rodriguez, F., & Rodrik, D. (2001). Trade policy and economic growth: A Skeptic's guide to the cross-national evidence. In B. Bernanke & K. Rogoff (Eds.), *NBER macroeconomics annual 2000*. Cambridge: MIT Press.

Rodrik, D. (1997). *Has globalization gone too far?* Washington, DC: Institute for International Economics.

Rodrik, D. (2001). Trading in illusions. *Foreign Policy, 123*, 54–62.

Rodrik, D. (2006). Goodbye Washington consensus, hello Washington confusion? A review of the world banks economic growth in the 1990s: Learning from a decade of reform. *Journal of Economic Literature, 44*(4), 973–987.

Roope, M., & Zurbruegg, R. (2002). The intraday price discovery process between the Singapore exchange and Taiwan futures exchange. *Journal of Futures Markets, 22*(3), 219–240.

Rose, A. (2004). Do we really know that the WTO increases trade? *The American Economic Review, 94*(1), 98–114.

Rose, A. (2007). Do we really know that the WTO increases trade? Reply. *The American Economic Review, 97*(5), 2019–2025.

Round, J. (1981, March). *Income distribution within a social accounting matrix: A review of some experience in Malaysia and other LDCs*. Discussion paper no. 3, Development Economics Research Centre, University of Warwick.

Round, J. (2003). Constructing SAMs for development policy analysis: Lessons learned and challenges ahead. *Economic Systems Research, 15*(2), 161–183.

Rutkowski, R. (2015). *Service sector reform in China*. Policy brief no. 15-2, Peterson Institute for International Economics, Washington, DC. www.Piie.com/publications/pb/pb15-2.pdf

Rybczynski, T. M. (1955). Factor endowment and relative commodity prices. *Economica, 22*(88), 336–341.

Sachs, J. D., & Warner, A. (1995). *Economic reform and the process of global integration*. Brookings papers on economic activity no. 1-118.

Salop, S. C. (1979). Strategic entry deterrence. *The American Economic Review, 81*, 242–255.

Sanchez, G. E. (2016). *The short-term response of the Hispanic noncitizen population to anti-illegal immigration legislation: The case of Arizona SB 1070*. Working paper.

SEBI. (2013). *Handbook of statistics on Indian securities market 2013*. Mumbai: Security and Exchange Board of India (SEBI).

Sehgal, S., Ahmad, W., & Deisting, F. (2014). An empirical examination of the process of information transmission in India's agriculture futures markets. *Journal of Quantitative Economics, 12*(1), 97–126.

Sehgal, S., Ahmad, W., & Deisting, F. (2015). An investigation of price discovery and volatility spillovers in India's foreign exchange market. *Journal of Economic Studies, 42*(2), 261–284.

Shaked, A., & Sutton, J. (1982). Relaxing price competition through product differentiation. *Review of Economic Studies, 49*, 1–13.

Shaked, A., & Sutton, J. (1983). Natural oligopolies. *Econometrica, 51*, 1469–1484.

Shaked, A., & Sutton, J. (1987). Product differentiation and industrial structure. *Journal of Industrial Economics, 36*, 131–146.

Sharma, S. (2011). *An empirical analysis of the relationship between currency futures and exchange rate volatility in India*. RBI working paper series no. WPS DEAP, 1/2011.

Shehadi, N., & Mills, D. H. (1988). *Lebanon: A history of conflict*. Lebanon: The Center for Lebanese Studies.

Shepherd, B. (2013). *The gravity model of international trade: A user guide*. ARTNeT Books and Research Reports.

Shoven, J. B., & Whalley, J. (1992). *Applying general equilibrium*. Cambridge: Cambridge University Press.

Sinha, R. S. (2005). Post reform export growth in India: An exploratory analysis. In N. Banerjee & S. Marjit (Eds.), *Development, displacement and disparity: India in the last quarter of the 20th century*. Hyderabad: Orient Longman.

Sinha R. S. (2007). *Demand and supply factors in the determination of India's disaggregated manufactured exports: A simultaneous error-correction approach*. Working paper no. 383, Centre for Development Studies, Thiruvananthapuram.

Slaughter, M. J. (2001). International trade and labour-demand elasticities. *Journal of International Economics, 54*(1), 27–56.

Smith, A., & Venebles, A. (1991). Economic integration and market access. *European Economic Review, 35*, 385–395.

Spencer, B., & Jones, R. W. (1991). Vertical foreclosure and international trade policy. *Review of Economic Studies, 58*(1), 153–170.

Spencer, B., & Jones, R. W. (1992). Trade and protection in vertically related markets. *Journal of International Economics, 32*, 31–35.

Starr, R. M. (2011). *General equilibrium theory: An introduction*. Cambridge: Cambridge University Press.

Stiglitz, J. (1998). *Towards a new paradigm for development: Strategies, policies, and processes*. Geneva: Prebisch Lecture at UNCTAD.

Stolper, W. F., & Samuelson, P. A. (1941). Protection and real wages. *The Review of Economic Studies, 9*(1), 58–73.

Subramanian, A., & Wei, S.-J. (2006). The WTO promotes trade, strongly but unevenly. *Journal of International Economics, 72*(1), 151–175.

Sutton, J. (1991). *Sunk costs and market structure*. Cambridge, MA: MIT Press.

Sutton, J. (1998). *Technology and market structure*. Cambridge, MA: MIT Press.

Swann, P., Temple, P., & Shurmer, M. (1996). Standards and trade performance-the UK experience. *Economic Journal, 106*(438), 1297–1313.

Sylos, L. P. (1956). *Oligopolio e Progresso Técnico*. Milano: Giuffré.

Sylos, L. P. (1969). *Oligopoly and technical progress*. Cambridge: Harvard University Press.

Syrquin, M. & Chenery, H. B. (1989). *Patterns of development, 1950 to 1983*. World Bank discussion paper no. 41.

Tamakoshi, G., & Hamori, S. (2014). On cross-currency transmissions between US dollar and euro LIBOR-OIS spreads. *Research in International Business and Finance, 30*, 83–90.

Thurlow, J., & Seventer, V. D. (2002). *A standard computable general equilibrium model for South Africa*. Trade and macroeconomics discussion paper no. 100, International Food Policy Research Institute, Washington, DC.

Thurlow, J., & Seventer, V. D. (2008). *Who benefits from South Africa's bilateral trade agreements?* Working paper series no. 2008-01, Trade and Industrial Policy Strategies.

Tinbergen, J. (1962). *Shaping the world economy: Suggestions for an international economic policy*. Books (Jan Tinbergen). New York: Twentieth Century Fund. Retrieved from http://hdl.handle.net/1765/16826

Tirole, J. (1988). *The theory of industrial organization*. Cambridge, MA: MIT Press.

Tomz, M., Goldtsein, R., & Rivers, D. (2007). Do we really know that the WTO increases trade? Comment. *The American Economic Review, 97*(5), 2005–2018.

Tse, Y. (1999). Price discovery and volatility spillovers in the DJIA index and futures markets. *Journal of Futures Markets, 19*(8), 911–930.

UNCTAD. (2013). *Non-tariff measures to trade: Economic and policy issues for developing countries*. New York/Geneva: United Nations.

Vanek, J. (1968). The factor proportions theory: The N – Factor case. *Kyklos, 21*(4), 749–756.

Venables, A. (1985). Trade and trade policy with imperfect competition: The case of identical products and free-entry. *Journal of International Economics, 19*, 1–19.

Venables, A. (1990a). The economic integration of oligopolistic markets. *European Economic Integration, 34*, 753–769.

Venables, A. (1990b). International capacity choice and the national market games. *Journal of International Economics, 29*, 23–42.

Whinston, M. D. (1990). Tying, foreclosure, and exclusion. *The American Economic Review, 80*, 837–859.

Williamson, J. (1990). *Latin American adjustment: How much has happened?* Washington, DC: Institute for International Economics.

Wilson, J., & Otsuki, T. (2001). *Global trade and food safety: Winners and losers in a fragmented system.* Social Science Research Network. Retrieved October 26, 2008, from http://papers.ssrn.com/sol3/papers.cfm?abstract_id=632757

Wood, A. (1994). *North-south trade, employment and inequality: Changing fortunes in a skill-driven world.* Oxford: Clarendon Press.

World Bank. (1987). *Rapport sur le développement dans le monde 1987.* Washington, DC: Oxford University Press pour la Banque Mondiale.

World Bank. (2013). *India development update.* Washington, DC: Economic Policy and Poverty Team, The World Bank.

World Trade Organization. (2016a). *Committee on technical barriers to trade.* 21st annual review of the implementation and operation of the TBT agreement, Geneva.

World Trade Organization. (2016b). *Integrated analysis and retrieval of notified non-tariff measures.* Retrieved from http://i-tip.wto.org/goods/Default.aspx

World Trade Report. (2008). *Trade in globalising world.* Geneva: WTO.

World Trade Report. (2015). *Speeding up trade: Benefits and challenges of implementing the WTO trade facilitation agreement.* Geneva: World Trade Organization (WTO).

WTO. (2008a). Retrieved from www.wto.org/english/news_e/archive_e/sps_arc_e.htm

WTO. (2008b). Retrieved from http://www.wto.org/english/tratop_e/sps_e/sps_e.htm

WTO. (2008c). Retrieved from http://www.wto.org/English/Tratop_E/dispu_e/dispu_status_e.htm#134

Xu, X. E., & Fung, H. G. (2005). Cross-market linkages between US and Japanese precious metals futures trading. *Journal of International Financial Markets, Institutions and Money, 15*(2), 107–124.

Zaki, C. (2010). *Does trade facilitation matters in bilateral trade?* GTAP resources no. 4537.

Index

A
Abadie, A., 308
Ad valorem equivalents (AVEs), 4, 29, 30, 116
calculation of, 126–131
of non-tariff barriers, calculation, 115–139
Aflatoxins, 205, 207
Aggregate wage elasticity, trade openness on, 339–341
Allocative efficiency effect, 195
Amiti, M., 14
Anderson, E.J., 17, 24, 26, 27, 33n9, 107, 147, 148
Anderson, J. E., 16, 20
Annual Survey of Industry (ASI), 338
Antonakakis, N., 356, 380
Antras, P., 15
APEC, *see* Asia Pacific Economic Cooperation (APEC)
ARCH effects, 355
Arellano, M., 337
Arkolakis, C., 15
Arora, R., 303n5
Arvis, J. F., 145, 146, 153
Asia Pacific Economic Cooperation (APEC) countries, 4
decomposition of, 104
percentage change in, 102
trade cost calculation of, 102
Asimakopoulos, I., 355
Association Agreement, 249
Augmented gravity equation
estimated results of, 124–126
sectorwide estimated results of, 127
AVEs, *see* Ad valorem equivalents (AVEs)

B
Bagwell, K., 76
Baier, S.L., 103
Bain, J.S., 76
Balance of trade, 193
Balassa, B., 12, 246
Balding, C., 248
Baldwin, R.E., 20–24, 46, 47
Ban Ki-moon, 243
Behavioral equations, 188

Note: Page numbers followed by "n" refers to notes.

S.K. Mathur et al. (eds.), *Theorizing International Trade*,
https://doi.org/10.1007/978-981-10-1759-9

Behera, K.H., 357
Bergstrand, J., 103
Bernard, A.B., 14, 15
Berry, S., 73
Bhagwati, J., 247
Bidirectional gravity equation, 148
Bilateral trade, 4, 5, 19, 21, 23–25, 27, 29, 116, 131, 132
  components of, 104
  costs, 106, 156
Bilbiie, F. O., 70
Bombay Stock Exchange (BSE), 352
Bonanno, G., 97n3
Bond, S., 337
Bouet, A., 183
Brander, J.A., 38, 43–45, 49, 79
Bretton Woods Institutions, 243
Breusch Pagan test, 207
British Pound (GBP/INR), 351, 353, 358, 361, 366, 367, 370, 372, 377, 380
Brockmeier, M., 303n5
Bronze medal mistake, 25
Bruno, G.S.F., 326, 328
Burfisher, M.E., 183, 199n19

C

Cabral, Luis M.B., 72
Canada, trade profile of, 272–275
Canada-India FTA, goods trade liberalization under, 269–303
Canada's specialized products, 272–273
Capital constrained labour demand function, 333
Carlton, D.W., 72
Carrere, C., 23
Causal effect of, TBT, 308, 309, 312–315, 320, 321
CEPA, 269
CES function, *see* Constant elasticity of substitution function
CGE model, *see* Computable general equilibrium model
Chacoliades, M., 40
Chamberlinian approach, 41–43
Chan, K.C., 353
Chan, L., 355
Chaney, T., 15, 18, 19
Chaudhuri, R., 49, 63n1
Chen, N., 147
Chenery, H.B., 246
China, 5
  average bilateral trade costs in, 152
  bilateral trade costs of services in, 141–160
  bilateral trade growth accounting in, 155
  economy policies of, 143
Chowdhury, R., 49, 63n1
Ciner, C., 357
Cobb-Douglas (CD) utility function, 189
CODEX standard, 205
COMEX issues, 309, 310
Commodity-based standards, 204
Comparative advantage, 9–11, 14, 17
  definition of, 9
  in technology, 20
  Ricardian theory of, 9
  source of, 10
Compound annual growth rate (CAGR), 272
Computable general equilibrium model (CGE Model), 183, 201–218, 245, 250, 251, 253–264
Constant elasticity of substitution (CES) function, 12, 20, 190
Consumption taxes, 195
Corruption Perceptions Index (CPI), 123
Cost function, 50
Cost-efficient firm, 38

Cournot, 76, 78, 79
  competition, 45, 49
  equilibrium, 38, 50
  framework, 4
Cournot–Nash equilibrium, 80–82, 92
Cournot-type duopolists, 79
Cross-sectional gravity model, 23

D
Data, source of, 123–124
Data aggregations, 230
Data set, 108
Database, 102, 108
Database specification, 249–250
Dataset, 149
Davis, D.R., 14
DCC-GARCH model, 376, 380
Deardorff, A.V., 10, 11, 16
Demand elasticity, 198n11
Descriptive statistics, in trade, 166–168
Deterministic category, 2
Diebold, F.X., 354, 356–359, 376, 380
Dimaranan, B., 142
Direct approach, trade costs, 147
Direct barriers, 25
Directional spillover, 358–360
Direction of trade, 167
Direction of Trade Statistics (DOTS), 102
Dixit, A.K., 41–43, 45, 46, 49, 97n3
Dixit–Stiglitz utility function, 11, 12, 21
Doha Round, 244
Dollar, 247
Domestic firm, 38
Domestic structure, 184, 188
Donor countries, 313–315, 318
DOTS, *see* Direction of Trade Statistics
Duval, Y., 156
DY methodology, robustness of, 375–376
Dynamic conditional correlation (DCC) model, 360, 361, 376, 377
Dynamic labour demand function, 332–333
Dynamic panel data method, 337

E
Eaton, J., 42, 45, 104
Economic reform guidelines, 143
Ecuadorian imports, of perfumes and toilet waters, 307–322
Edwards, S., 246
Elasticity, of substitution, 102
Ellickson, P.B., 73
Elyasiani, E., 356
Empirical methods, 1, 5
  role of, 3
Endogenous sunk costs
  and barriers to entry and exit, 71–72
  vertical markets in international trade, 69–97
Endowment effect, 196–197
Endowment tax, 195
Engle, R.F., 360, 380
Equivalent variation (*EV*), 194
Euro (EURO/INR), 351, 353, 361, 366, 372, 373, 377, 380
European free trade association (EFTA), 250
Ex ante approach, 165–199
Ex Ante macroeconomic impact assessment, 243–265
Export promotion, import protection as, 47–49
Export subsidy, 38
Export tax, 195
Ex post approach, 165

F
Factor–price equalization theorem, 10, 32n4
Falzoni, A.S.M., 328

Feasible Generalised Least Square (FGLS), 337
Feder, G., 246
Final modification, 204
FIPA, *see* Foreign Investment Promotion and Protection Agreement
Firm heterogeneity, 13, 14, 19
First global sector, 187
Flam, H., 47
FOB, *see* Free on board
Forecast error variance decompostion decomposition (FEVD), 354, 363, 366, 372, 374–376
Foreign direct investment (FDI), 14, 15, 270
Foreign entry threat, 82–85
Foreign Investment Promotion and Protection Agreement (FIPA), 288, 289
Framework Agreement on Economic Cooperation, 222
Francois J., 108, 149, 150
Free entry, import protection, 4, 48, 49
  in countries, 59–61
  in country 1, 54–57
  in country 2, 57–59
Free on board (FOB), 102
Free trade agreement (FTA), 5, 269
Free-entry effect, 62
Fresh grapes, 207–210
Friedman, J.W., 96n3
FTA, *see* free trade agreement (FTA)
Fudenberg, D., 97n3
Fung, H.G., 355

G

GAFTA, *see* Greater Arab Free Trade Area
GAMS, *see* General Algebraic Modeling System
GARCH, *see* generalized autoregressive conditional heteroscedasticity
Gardeazabal, J., 308
Garman, B.M., 362
GATS, *see* General Agreement on Trade in Services
GCC, *see* Gulf Cooperation Council
GDP, *see* Gross domestic product (GDP)
GDP per capita, 217n20
GEMPACK, *see* General Equilibrium Modelling Package
General Agreement on Tariffs and Trade (GATT), 244, 248, 249
General Agreement on Trade in Services (GATS), 107
General Algebraic Modeling System (GAMS), 192
General equilibrium model, 185, 245, 251, 264, 277
  application of, 5
General Equilibrium Modelling Package (GEMPACK), 192
General equilibrium tool, assess proposed trade policy, 183–197
Generalised method of moments (GMM), 328, 337
Generalized autoregressive conditional heteroscedasticity (GARCH), 6
Ghironi, F., 70
Gilbert, J., 166, 168, 303n1, 303n3
Gilbert, R., 97n3
Global Bank, 187
Global trade analysis project, 192
Global Trade Analysis Project (GTAP) model, 5, 124, 206, 277–288, 290
  framework of, 184–192
  implementation of, 192
  model framework, 188
  simulation results, 237
GNP per capita, 203
Goldaer, B., 326

Goldar, B., 328, 339
Gold medal mistake, 24
Goods trade liberalization, Canada-India FTA, 269–303
Government consumption expenditure (E_G) system, 199n18
Gowa, J., 248
Gravity analysis, 23–25
Gravity model, 15–30, 103
  and application, 4
Gravity trade model, 203, 216n7
  variable of, 206
Gravity with gravitas model, 148
Greater Arab Free Trade Area (GAFTA), 249, 250
Greenaway, D., 326, 327
Gross domestic product (GDP), 16, 18, 20–24, 109, 193, 206, 248, 256, 262, 264, 281, 283, 291, 325
  effects on, 265
  evolution of, 262
Grossman, G. M., 45
Groundnuts, 207
GTAP model, *see* Global Trade Analysis Project model
Gulf Cooperation Council (GCC), 221–223

H

Hamori, S., 356
A Handbook of Commonly Used Trade Indices and Indicators, 166
Haouas, I., 326, 327
Harrington, J.E., 76, 77, 97n4
Hasan, R., 326, 328, 339
Heckscher–Ohlin (HO) model, 9, 10, 12, 32n1, 42
Helg, R., 328
Helpman, E., 12, 14, 15, 38, 41, 42, 44
Hertel, T.W., 195, 303n5
Heteroscedasticity, 207
Hicks–Marshallian theory, 329
Hong, Y., 354, 356
Hopenhayn, H.A., 70
Horstmann, 46
Huff, K., 195

I

Imperfect competition market, 37, 41
Import protection
  analysis of, 54–61
  as export promotion, 47
Import tax, 195
Inagaki, K., 356
Income convergence, 106
India, 5, 215n5
  average bilateral trade costs in, 152
  average trade costs for, 152
  bilateral trade costs of services in, 141–160
  bilateral trade growth accounting in, 154
  tariff equivalent of, 109, 111
  trade growth accounting for, 112
  trade growth in, 110
  trade profile of, 272
India–GCC free trade agreement, 221–242
  economic and commercial relations of, 223
  GTAP simulation results, 237–241
  implication of tariff reforms, 233–237
  simulation scenarios and data aggregations, 230–233
India-level analysis, exports, 206, 207, 209, 210, 213
India's forex derivatives markets, 351–381
Indirect approach, trade cost, 147–150
Indirect barriers, 25, 26
Industrial organization literature, 76–78
Industrial organization theory, 37

Industry-specific analysis, 341–342
Input taxes, 195
Integrated home incumbent, upward price distortion and, 85
International Food Policy Research Institute (IFPRI) model, 250
International Monetary Fund (IMF), 248–250, 270
International monetary policy, 2
International monetary theory, 2, 3
International trade data, 149–150
International trade policy, 2, 5
International trade theory, 1–3
  developments in, 9–33
Intra-industry trade, 11, 12, 37, 38, 43
Inverse demand functions, 49
Investment–saving effect, 196
IPR, 289, 291
Ishikawa, J., 75, 76, 96n2

J
Jammes, O., 169, 173, 303n4
Japanese Yen (JPY/INR), 351, 353, 358, 361, 366, 373, 377, 380
Jarque–Bera statistics, 362
Jayanthakumaran, K., 326, 327
Jean, S., 326, 327
Jones, R.W., 79

K
Kee, H.L., 121
Kemp, M.C., 40
Kim, S.Y., 248
Kitamura, Y., 356
Kizys, R., 380
Klass, J.M., 362
Koop, G., 358, 359
Kortum, S., 104
Kray, A., 247
Krishna, P., 326–328
Krugman, P.R., 4, 11–13, 18, 19, 22, 41, 42, 44, 46–49, 62
Kumar, D., 357
Kumar, M., 357, 358, 366, 371, 372, 380
Kyle, A.S., 45

L
Lancaster, K., 41, 42
Lardy, N. R., 157
Lautier, M., 252
Least square dummy variable (LSDV), 328, 337
Lebanese economy, 248, 249, 260–264
  evolution of exports, 260–261
  evolution of GDP, 262
  evolution of imports, 260
  tariff dismantling of, 256–260
Lebanese Republic's Working Party, 249
Lebanon accession, 5
  to World Trade Organization (WTO), 243–265
Lee, K.-D., 75, 76, 96n2
Leontief, W.W., 10
Lien, D., 355
Linear equation, 251

M
MacMap database, 250
Macroeconomic variable and exchange rate, 256–260
Mariñoso, G.B., 74, 79, 93
Markusen, J.R., 46
Marshallian external economy approach, 40–41
Mathur, S. K., 168, 303n5
Matthews, S.A., 77
Maximum residue limits (MRLs), 205, 207

Mayer, T., 15
McAfee, R.P., 72
McCallum, J., 23, 24
McDougall, R., 194
Melitz, M.J., 12–15, 20, 70
Melvin, J., 40, 42
Memorandum on the Foreign Trade Regime, 249
Metric tonnes, 206
Michaely, M., 246
Mikic, M., 166, 168, 303n1, 303n3
Milgrom, P., 76, 77
Mirman, L.J., 77
Miroudot, S., 107, 108, 145, 146, 156
Mitra, D., 326, 328
Modern-day trade theories, 1
Modigliani, F., 76
Moenius, J., 202
Money metric indirect utility function, 194
Monopolistic competitive market, 329–331
Most favored nation (MFN), 170
MRLs, *see* Maximum residue limits (MRLs)
Muendler, M.A., 15
Multi-Commodity Exchange-Stock Exchange (MCX-SX), 352, 353, 358, 361, 366, 369, 370, 374, 377, 380
Multilateral resistance (MR), 17, 18, 24, 27, 28
Multilateral trade, 4
Multilateral trade barrier, 104
Multiproduct firms, 14
Multi-region general equilibrium model, 195, 196
Multi-region GTAP model, 187
Multivariate generalized autoregressive conditional heteroskedasticity (MV-GARCH), 356
Murti, P., 72

N

NAFTA, 250
Najand, M., 375
National Industrial Classification (NIC), 338
National Research Centre, 207
National Stock Exchange (NSE), 352, 358, 361, 366, 369–371, 374, 377, 380
Natural logarithms, 206
Negeshi, T., 40
Negishi, T., 42
NETINV, 188
New trade theories, 11–15, 39
Nikkinen, J., 356
Non tariff barriers (NTBs), 29
Non-deliverable forward (NDF), 357
Non-integrated foreign incumbent, 88–91
Non-linear equation, 251
Non-tariff barriers (NTBs), 54, 307, 308
  ad valorem equivalents (AVEs) of, 115–139
Nordås, H. K., 145
Norman, V., 42, 43, 49
Novy, D., 26, 101–103, 146, 147, 149, 156
Novy's methodology, 4, 154
NTBs, *see* Non-tariff barriers

O

Obstfeld, M., 23
OECD services, 141
OECD STRI index, 145
Olarreaga, M., 169, 173, 303n4
Oligopolistic approach, 43–47
Ordinary least square (OLS) method, 23, 337, 349n8
Ottaviano, G.I., 14, 15, 20
Owen, R.F., 70, 75, 76

P

Panagariya A., 40, 42, 142, 143
Panel data framework, 213
Partial equilibrium approach, 275
Partial equilibrium tool, trade policy, 168–182
Partial liberalization, using GTAP model, 287–288
Patnaik, A., 357
Patterson, G.A., 355
Perfect competition market, 37–41, 43
Pesaran, M.H., 358, 359
Pindyuk O., 72, 108, 149, 150
Plummer, M. G., 168
Population effect, 197
Post-entry competition, in downstream market, 82–84
Post-entry profits, 72, 76–78, 83–85
A Practical Guide to Trade Policy Analysis, 166
Price effect, 173–175
Price elasticity, 171
Price reduction, 171
Product market efficiency, 237
Production subsidy, 38
Protection indices, 167

Q

Quantitative research, 1

R

Ramey, G., 76
Rapid Alert System for Food and Feed (RASFF) system, 202
Ray, P., 374
RBI, *see* Reserve Bank of India
RCA, *see* Revealed comparative advantage (RCA)
RCEP, *see* Regional comprehensive economic partnership (RCEP)
RCEP member, 116, 119, 126, 132
Reciprocal dumping model, 12
Regional comprehensive economic partnership (RCEP), 4, 115, 116
Regional household behavior, 189
Regional trade agreements (RTAs), 107, 115
Regression results
  for cross section, 208, 210–212
  for India-level analysis, 214
Reserve Bank of India (RBI), 361
Resolution 093, 308
Resolution 116, 308, 310, 312, 315
Revealed comparative advantage (RCA), 272, 273
Revenue effect, to exporter, 180–181
Ricardian model, 104
  of comparative advantage, 9
Ricardo, D., 9, 17
Roberts, J., 76, 77
Robustness issues, 62
Rodriguez, F., 247
Rodrik, D., 247, 326, 328
Rogoff, K., 23
Rose, A., 247
Ross, 72
Rouzet, D., 145
RTAs, *see* Regional trade agreements (RTAs)
RTE 093, 312–315
RunGTAP software, 192
Russian Federation, 106, 244
Rutkowski, R., 157
Rybczynski theorem, 10, 32n3

S

Sachs, J.D., 246
Salop, S.C., 77
SAM, *see* Social accounting matrix (SAM)
Sanitary and phytosanitary measures (SPSM), 201, 202, 214, 215n1, 308

Sargan test, 337, 339
Schmalensee, R., 72
Sectoral coverage, 166
Sectoral structure, 167
Sehgal, S., 357, 358, 366, 372, 374, 380
Services trade restrictiveness index (STRI), 144
Shaked, A., 69, 70
Sharma, S., 357
Shelled groundnuts, 210–214
Shin, Y., 358, 359
Shoven, J.B., 183
Silver medal mistake, 24
Single market partial equilibrium simulation tool (SMART), 168, 275, 276, 290
  implementation of, 181–182
Six-digit ITC (HS), 217n14
Slaughter, M.J., 326, 327
SMART, *see* Single market partial equilibrium simulation tool (SMART)
Smith, A., 75
Social accounting matrix (SAM), 249–251
Socio-economic context, 248
Spencer, B.J., 38, 45, 49, 79
Spillover index, 358–360, 363–375
SPSM, *see* Sanitary and phytosanitary measures
Srinivasan, T., 247
Standard code, 205–206
Standard data, 207
Static framework, 79–80
Static multi-region general equilibrium model, 184
Statistics, for India and GCC, 226
Stiglitz, J.E., 41
Stochastic category, 2
Stolper–Samuelson theorem, 10, 32n2
Strategic effect, 38
Strategic entry deterrence, 82
Strategic trade theory, 37–40
  literature survey on, 40–47
STRI, *see* Services trade restrictiveness index (STRI)
Stringency code, 205
Subsidy effects, 38
Substitution effect, 326
Substitution elasticity, 198n12
Sutton, J., 69, 70, 72, 73
Swann, P., 202
Sylos, L.P., 76
Syrquin, M., 246

T
Taglioni, D., 20–23
Tamakoshi, G., 356
Tariff equivalents, 102, 108
Tariff profile, of India and GCC, 224–226
Tariff reforms
  effects of, 263
  implications of, 233
Tariff revenue effect, 179
Tarrif equivalent, of India, 109
Tax revenues, 188
Technical barriers to trade (TBT), 5, 202
  reforms in Ecuador, 309–310
  impact of, 307–322
Technological changes effect, 196
TF, *see* trade facilitation
Three-stage gravity model, 107
Tinbergen, J., 15, 16
Tirole, J., 97n3
Tomz, M., 247
TPP, 281, 283, 289, 291
Trade agreements, 221
Trade and economy, 167
Trade balance, 193
Trade barriers, quantification of, 25

Trade complementarity index (TCI), 274–275
Trade costs
diagnostic of, 25
stages of, 25
Trade creation, 171, 172, 235
with Inelastic export supply elasticity, 175–176
Trade data, 206
Trade diversion, 172, 173, 235
with inelastic export supply elasticity, 176–179
Trade effects, 170, 192, 193, 196, 233–236
Trade facilitation (TF), 115, 121, 132
Trade facilitation measures (TFMs), 121, 122, 124, 131
Trade growth, in India, 110
Trade growth accounting, goods and services, 101–113
Trade indices, 166
Trade intensity index (TII), 273–274
for India and GCC, 227
Trade liberalization, 243–247, 251, 253, 254, 264, 279, 289
Trade openness on wage elasticity, 333–337
effect of, 333–337
labour demand, 325–349
Trade outcome indicators, 166
Trade performance, 167
Trade policy, 39
changes in, 183
research, 5, 385–387
Trade profile, 223–224
Trade theorems, 10
Trade theory, 1, 2
developments in, 4, 5, 13
Trade transaction costs (TTCs), 25, 30, 116, 121, 132
Traditional trade theories, 1, 9–11, 39
Trigger strategy equilibrium, 92–93

U
Ulph, D., 70, 75
UN Commodity Trade Statistics data, 271
UN National Accounts statistics, 150
UNations, 166
Unconstrained labour demand function, 334
United States, 106, 110, 113n1, 150, 152
United Stock Exchange (USE), 352
Upward price distortion
entry prevention by, 84–85
integrated home incumbent and, 85–88
non-integrated foreign incumbent, 88
US dollar paired with Indian rupee (USD/INR), 351–353, 358, 361, 366, 370–373, 377, 380
U-shaped curve, 211
U-shaped relationship, 214
Utility function (U), 169

V
Variable construction, 123
Varying-correlation (VC), 356
Vector autoregression (VAR), 355, 358, 359, 363, 366, 370, 376, 381n4
Venables, A., 42, 44, 46, 47, 49, 61, 75
Venables, T., 22
Vertical markets
static model of, 78–82
of international trade, 75–76
Vives, X., 97n3
Volatility spillovers, 369–375

W
Waldfogel, J., 73
Warner, A., 246

Washington Consensus, 243
Welfare effect, 180, 194–197, 235, 236
Whalley, J., 183
Williamson, J., 243
Wincoop, V., 17, 24, 26, 27, 33n9
Wincoop, V. E., 107, 147, 148
WITS, *see* World Integrated Trade Solutions
World Bank, 168, 246, 247, 270
World bilateral trade matrix, 206
World Development Indicators (WDI), 102, 123, 206
World Trade Organization (WTO), 15, 25, 143, 166, 168, 201, 206, 245, 271, 286, 289, 291, 308, 310, 338
    Lebanon's accession to, 243–265
World War II, 243
World–level analysis, 207–209
World-level studies, 210–212
WTO, *see* World Trade Organization (WTO)

Y

Yagoubi, M., 326, 327
Yilmaz, K., 354, 356–359, 376, 380

Z

Zaki, C., 116, 121